Morality, Reason and Truth

MORALITY, REASON AND TRUTH

New Essays on the Foundations of Ethics

Edited by

DAVID COPP

AND

DAVID ZIMMERMAN

ROWMAN & ALLANHELD
PUBLISHERS

ROWMAN & ALLANHELD

Published in the United States of America in 1985
by Rowman & Allanheld, Publishers
(A division of Littlefield, Adams & Company)
81 Adams Drive, Totowa, New Jersey 07512

Library of Congress Cataloging in Publication Data
Main entry under title:

Morality, reason and truth.

    Bibliography: p.
    Includes index.
    1. Ethics—Addresses, essays, lectures. I. Copp,
David. II. Zimmerman, David, 1942-   .
BJ1012.M6356 1984   170   84-13424
ISBN 0-8476-7368-5
ISBN 0-8476-7369-3 (pbk.)

84 85 86 / 10 9 8 7 6 5 4 3 2 1
Printed in the United States of America

Contents

Preface

This is a collection of original, recent, and mainly previously unpublished essays on the foundations of morality. Several of the authors are established figures in the field; others are philosophers who are just beginning to make important contributions. Most of them spoke at a conference on reason in ethics organized by the editors a few years ago, and all of them were asked to be responsive in their papers to the work of the other contributors. The result is an anthology that constitutes a coherent multilayered debate among some thirteen philosophers.

The introduction aims to identify the major themes and to provide a structure for the discussion. The topics and approaches are varied. It is worth stressing that the familiar issues in the semantics of moral discourse, emphasized so much in the work of ethical theorists for the first two-thirds of this century, are not given pride of place here. They are discussed to some degree. But if any one issue is most emphasized, it is the relation between morality and the theory of moral justification on the one hand and the theory of practical reason on the other. And if one approach is emphasized, it is an approach that seeks to explain the place of morality in a scientific view of the world.

We hope that these essays will help to rekindle an interest in meta-ethical issues. These issues are, after all, among the most ancient of philosophical problems, and they are certainly central to philosophy. Moreover, it is obvious that we need to attach value to our pursuits, both professional and nonprofessional, and so we must come to terms with skepticism about value. We think that if anything has value, then so does the pursuit of the nature of value. That pursuit is meta-ethics.

References to the literature are given throughout the book in the form of an author's name and a date. The consolidated list of references at the end of the book contains the needed bibliographical details in each case, following Sen and Williams (1982).

Among our debts of gratitude, most important is to our contributors, who in many cases revised their essays to our specifications and in all cases waited patiently while we assembled the book. We are grateful to Merrily Allanson, Dennis Bevington, Ishtiyaque Haji, Eric Pye, and Kalen Wild for their help with many of the tedious details.

Simon Fraser University
October, 1984

No-one is just willingly but under compulsion, . . . Every man believes that injustice is much more profitable to himself than justice.

> Plato, *The Republic,* 360 c-d, translated by G. M. A. Grube (1974).

Reason is and ought to be the slave of the passions.

It is not contrary to reason to prefer the destruction of the whole world to the scratching of my finger.

> David Hume, *A Treatise of Human Nature,* II, 3, iii. (1968), pp. 415–416.

The ground of obligation . . . must not be sought in the nature of man or in the circumstances in which he is placed, but sought a priori in the concepts of pure reason.

> Immanuel Kant, *Foundations of the Metaphysics of Morals,* Ak 389, translated by Lewis White Beck (1959).

If the inquirer goes on asking "But why *should* I live like that?" then there is no further answer to give him, because we have already, *ex hypothesi,* said everything that could be included in this further answer. We can only ask him to make up his own mind which way he ought to live, for in the end everything rests upon such a decision of principle.

> R. M. Hare, *The Language of Morals* (1952), p. 69.

The theory of justice is a part . . . of the theory of rational choice.

> John Rawls, *A Theory of Justice* (1971), p. 16.

Introduction

David Copp

META-ETHICS

What are we to make of morality? We are thoughtful citizens in a modern pluralistic society, and we want to decide how to live and behave. We have deeply felt moral convictions, most of us, and we want to take morality seriously, but only if there is a rational basis to morality. If there is no reason to believe in any moral principle, and if there is no reason to commit ourselves to following any given moral precepts, then we may very well decide not to govern our lives by morality, and in doing so we may be deciding quite rationally. We may come to regard our moral convictions as simply an impediment to the pursuit of what we desire for ourselves and for those we care about. Our problem is that although we have moral beliefs we have some reason to doubt that they are on a secure footing. For one thing, there is no culturally entrenched rationally appealing process, comparable to scientific method, that we can appeal to for an answer to our plea for an articulated and defended morality, or even for answers to specific moral disputes. Moreover, tradition does not single out a privileged morality. In fact, society can be torn by disputes between parties, all of whom see themselves as rational and as possessing truth. Even now our own society faces disputes over questions of varying degrees of significance, and competing traditions are sources of competing answers. In any event, we want a morality with a rational foundation, whether or not it be traditional. The existence of seemingly fundamental disputes between apparently rational and well-intentioned people and the absence of an appealing decision procedure provide us with some reason to doubt the rational basis of the whole enterprise of morality. What then are we to make of it?

The issue being raised is not about the specific *content* of the true, correct, or ideal morality; it is not about which moral principles to take into account in deciding how to live and how to behave. It is about the rationality of taking into account any distinctly moral principles at all. Content-related questions do of course arise in moral philosophy. But for present purposes they should be put aside, for the issue being raised here is a logically prior issue about the justifiability of *any* view as to the content of the ideal morality. It is about the underpinning or basis of moral principles. Actually, a number of questions are being raised: whether there is a true morality; what in the world could determine the truth or correctness of a morality; how we would recognize or have knowledge of the true morality, if there is one; whether "correctness" is even required in order for there to be a rational basis for taking our own moral views seriously; whether the known or rationally believed truth of a moral code is by itself enough to give us sufficient reason for conforming to it. These questions about morality, and other closely related ones, are addressed in the discipline known as *meta-ethics*. They are the subject of this anthology.

Unfortunately, some of the concepts used to define meta-ethics are themselves problematical. The prime examples are the concepts of *justification* and of *rationality*. We ask such questions as whether there is a "rational basis" for morality, whether a "rational person" would commit himself to morality, whether belief in some moral principles is "rationally justified," whether there is a "sufficient reason" for conforming to morality, whether any moral code can be "justified." To understand these questions we obviously need to understand the notions of justification and rationality. But these are contested concepts in philosophy. There are different accounts, and in fact much of the debate in meta-ethics concerns how we are to understand them. Therefore, for the moment we need to rely on our commonsense understanding of matters. Some ideas seem obviously correct. For instance, a rationally warranted or justified belief must, with some exceptions, be based on sound evidence or cogent reasons. The notion of a rational course of action or a rational policy is more controversial, but a common view is that rationality here is simply a matter of the efficient pursuit of what one *would* aim or desire to achieve overall, given due reflection and full awareness of what one is rational to believe. Another view is that rationality consists in maximizing one's "expected utility," a measure of one's preference for outcomes as weighted by their probability. Finally, a rational person is one whose beliefs and actions are by and large rationally warranted. The relationships among these concepts are discussed in several of the essays in this volume.

This superficial sketch may help to explain the issue that lies at the bottom of meta-ethics. The fundamental idea is that a justification of morality would be a showing that there is a justification or sufficient reason for taking morality seriously, for governing one's life by it. A rational person presumably would not do so unless cogent reasons could be given for accepting some given set of principles as constituting the correct or ideal morality, and unless sufficient reasons could be given for accepting the policy of conformity to that morality. Here, then, is the source of the series of questions that we used to define meta-ethics. At root, the issue is whether morality has a basis that would allow it to be rationally justified. I will point out two different schools of thought as to what this should be taken to mean: the epistemic view and the practical view.

There has been an understandable tendency to define meta-ethics in terms suggested by the approaches and theories of its most influential figures. For many years meta-ethics was approached from the standpoint of the *language* of ethics, and it virtually became a branch of the study known as the *semantics* of natural language. It studied the meanings of the "ethical terms," such as "good," "bad," "right," and "ought," and it studied the logical or semantical structure and status of the kinds of sentence that are distinctive of ethical discourse, such as "You ought not to lie" or "Honesty is the best policy." Early in this century, G. E. Moore wrote that the "most fundamental question in all Ethics" is how the term "good" is to be defined (1903, p. 5). Forty years later, Charles Stevenson began his book *Ethics and Language* with the remark that his first object would be "to clarify the meaning of the ethical terms—such terms as 'good,' 'right,' 'just,' 'ought,' and so on" (1944, p. 1). R. M. Hare devoted the first part of *The Language of Morals* to a study of the imperative mood, arguing that "the language of morals is one sort of prescriptive language," and the ordinary imperative sentence is the simplest form of that language (1952, pp. 1–2). And Philippa Foot argued that the expression "a good action" has a "fixed descriptive meaning," at least within "a certain range."[1] It is not surprising that the semantic view of meta-ethics prevailed, for these four writers were among the most influential on meta-ethics in the first two-thirds of the century. And they spoke for the four main types of theory: intuitionism, emotivism, prescriptivism, and naturalism.[2]

Of course, there is a deeper reason for the semantic approach. As we saw, the issues in meta-ethics center around the problem of justifying morality to a rational person. Hence, if one's paradigm of a justification is the epistemic justification of a *belief* or of a *theory,* one may regard the justification of *morality* to require the justification of our moral beliefs, or of proposed moral propositions. If so, then the resources, problems, and strategies of general epistemology become germane to ethics. And one type of question will become central: What is the meaning of the sentences we use when we engage in moral discourse? What is the nature and logical status of the propositions, if any, that are expressed by us in moral discourse when we give expression to our moral convictions? Unless we can answer these questions, we will be unable to determine the exact content of the beliefs whose justification is of concern. We may not even be certain that our moral "convictions" are *beliefs,* strange as this may seem. We could put the point in more baroque language by saying that an understanding of the metaphysical or ontological commitments of morals would be prior to a moral epistemology, but then a semantics of moral discourse would be required as a condition of arriving at a reasoned appraisal of the ontology of morals. So, on the epistemic view of the problems of meta-ethics, semantic issues may seem to be central, even if not decisive.

However, the epistemic view is not mandatory, for there are non-epistemological justifications, for instance, of actions. It is fairly standard to distinguish between *theoretical* and *practical* reason: *theoretical* reason or rationality is at issue where the object of a putative justification is a belief, proposition, theory, or statement, and *practical* reason or rationality is at issue where the object of a putative justification is an action or a desire. Epistemological issues arise within the theory of theoretical reason: What counts as sound evidence or as a cogent reason for a belief? But if we are called upon to justify some *action* we have performed, or to justify how we live or what we want, then our problem is not primarily epistemological. Evidence is not at issue, nor is cogency. Instead the issue is perhaps better said to be one of propriety or appropriateness: As we saw, a rational policy or action could be characterized as one that would be decided upon after due reflection and in full cognizance of the facts. At any rate, the issue seems to be of a different kind from that involved in justifying beliefs. And one might regard the problem of justifying a morality to be of this kind, to be a problem for a theory of practical reason: A morality is justified if, roughly, choice of it, or commitment to it, would be rational (for some defined purpose and in some defined context).

This distinction between the epistemic view and the practical view was drawn by John Rawls:

> Moral philosophy includes moral theory, but takes as its main question justification and how it is to be conceived and resolved; for example, whether it is to be conceived as an epistemological problem (as in rational intuitionism) or as a practical problem (as in Kantian constructivism).[3]

Rawls views his own theory as providing a practical justification for principles of justice, following the lead of Immanuel Kant (1785). He says that "principles of justice may be conceived as principles that would be chosen by rational persons," and he adds that the theory of justice is a part of the "theory of rational choice" (1971, p. 16). But the practical conception is not restricted to Kantian and neo-Kantian approaches. For example, Thomas Hobbes's moral theory is often understood to exhibit a practical view of moral justification: In view of our interest in self-preservation, informed and rational persons would contract into a social system that included a set of social rules and the power to enforce them; this is what justifies the system and the rules that are enforced in it (1651; see Gauthier, 1979). A similar approach was taken in the 1950s by Kurt Baier (1958).

The practical conception of moral justification will seem reasonable if a morality is thought to be a set of standards or canons of behavior. On this picture, our models of morality would perhaps be gambling systems, investment strategies, and the like, although there are obvious differences between policies of this nature and a morality. A set of rules for parliamentary debate would perhaps be a better model. The point is that one would justify a policy or strategy of one of these kinds on the basis of standards of rational choice, and that the practical conception views moral justification as another problem for the theory of rational choice. On the other hand, the epistemic conception will seem reasonable if a morality is thought to be a theory as to the nature of a putative realm of fact. Psychology and astrology would be our models on this picture. If a morality is a theory, then acceptance of it would ideally be justified, if at all, on the basis of epistemic standards. The decision, then, between these two conceptions of moral justification will turn in one's conception of morality. In turn, one's conception of morality may turn on one's theory of the semantics of moral discourse.

The importance of the distinction between the epistemic and the practical perspectives can be questioned. Moreover, the distinction is sometimes blurred in people's writings, and it should also be confessed that it is not entirely sharp itself. Some theories seem to be borderline cases. Still, the epistemic approach was common to the meta-ethical theories that dominated philosophical discussion until the 1960s. Intuitionism and naturalism held what emotivism and prescriptivism denied—that an epistemic justification of moral belief could be achieved. However, emotivism and prescriptivism, and commentators on those theories, took epistemic justification as the *ideal,* as if failure to achieve it entailed a failure to provide any justification that would be of interest to the moral skeptic.

G. E. Moore held a view usually called "intuitionism" (Moore, 1903). In general terms, he held that true moral assertions pick out, or imply the existence of, moral facts. In Moore's case, these would be facts about what things are *good,* facts that are *sui generis,* and facts that can be known to obtain somehow independently of scientific or observational methods. In Moore's view, propositions about what things are intrinsically good are synthetic, but, if true, they are knowable a priori. Now so-called naturalists differ with intuitionism on both the ontological and epistemological status of morals. They agree that moral assertions express propositions or are capable of being true or false, and they agree that there are moral facts that determine the truth or falsity of moral assertions. But they hold that these facts are not *sui generis,* or special; rather, they are complexes of so-called natural facts, common or garden-variety facts of the sort investigated in the sciences, probably the social sciences. How are we to know *which* facts? How are we to know which moral statements are true or false? One strategy here, the "reductive strategy," is to hold that an analysis of the meaning of our moral assertions will show them to have a "fixed descriptive meaning" specifiable in nonmoral language and thereby enable a "reduction" of moral facts to natural facts. A kind of nonsemantic naturalism is another possibility. For instance, in his paper for this volume, Nicholas Sturgeon suggests that materialists need not suppose that moral facts are identifiable in a nonmoral ter-minology. If materialism is correct, then any moral facts are "physical," but we should not expect to confirm this by means of semantic analysis of moral assertions or by "reductive definitions" of moral terms. Our moral beliefs constitute our theory about the moral truth, and this theory is to be evaluated by applying standards that do not differ in principle from the standards we use to evaluate other theories about the world. Clearly there are significant differences of detail. For the moment, the point is that the various versions of intuitionism and naturalism fit the epistemic mold and adopt a "cognitivist" stance regarding ethics: Moral knowledge is possible.

The main critics of cognitivism have held that moral "convictions" are not beliefs properly so-called, and that moral "assertions" are non-propositional expressions that are not capable of truth or falsity. The semantic issue is joined here. What is the logical form or status of moral "assertions?" Are they propositional? Stevenson and Hare agreed basically that our moral convictions have an action-guiding or practical role that no mere belief could have, and that therefore a moral conviction is not (simply) a propositional attitude, is not (merely) an acceptance of a proposition. That is, accepting a moral judgment is not accepting a proposition. But then a moral judgment is not a proposition, and moral sentences do not express such. Emotivists like Stevenson and prescrip-tivists like Hare presented different accounts of the semantics of moral sentences, and this is not the place to enter into detail. Nevertheless, emotivism and prescriptivism do not break away from an epistemic conception of what justification of a moral conviction would consist in if it were possible. Hare's account of moral reasoning is modeled on propositional logic: We deduce specific moral judgments from more general moral principles combined with factual statements. But beyond this, justification of a moral principle, to the extent that this is possible, could consist at best only in "a complete specification of the way of life of which it is [or would be] a part." A decision to accept or reject a principle would be as justified as it could be provided only that it was made in light of such a specification. A person just has "to make up his own mind."[4]

The debate between cognitivists and noncognitivists has been thoroughly discussed in the literature, and it is not addressed in detail in these essays. But a number of essays address epistemic and semantic issues, mainly in the first section of the book. In addition, the difference between the epistemic and the practical conceptions of moral justification is illustrated: Sturgeon's essay exemplifies the former, and David Gauthier's exemplifies the latter. But before we look at the contributions to this volume, we need to notice that there is at least one important and traditional meta-ethical problem that has not yet been mentioned, but it is one that is common to both conceptions of moral justification.

Consider the question, "Why be moral?" This question can arise no matter which conception one has of moral theory, epistemic or practical. All that is required is space in one's theory sufficient to allow an individual to query the rationality of his being moral; to query the rationality of his committing himself to, or of his conforming always to, a morality justified in light of one's theory. Of course, to get the question off the ground, we must have a prior account of what it is to "be moral." This account *might* simply refer to so-called conventional morality. But it might also refer to a theory of moral truth or justification, and this could be of either type. It will be helpful to consider an example of each type.

Platonic theory manifests the epistemic view, for it can be understood to justify morality primarily on the basis of a moral ontology and epistemology: Plato postulates the existence of the "form" *The Good,* or, as we might say, he postulates the property of goodness, and he supposes that its nature fully determines what is good and bad, right and wrong. In addition, he proposes a theory of intellectual apprehension to explain how we might come to know the form. The existence of *The Good,* and of our ability to apprehend it, would explain how justified moral beliefs are possible. However, there is room in the theory for one to ask why one should pay attention to the form. In *The Republic,* Glaucon challenges Socrates to show that it is better to be just than to be unjust (358a–360e). The challenge is from the standpoint of a happiness-maximizing conception of rational choice, according to which the best or most rational course for a person is always to choose what will most contribute to his happiness. The challenge is not the self-answering query: Is it not *morally* better to be morally not-good than to be morally good? It is the rather more interesting query: Given a choice between being a morally good person and being a person who remains open to acting immorally when so acting would serve one's interests, might one not maximize one's expected happiness by choosing the latter and so be entirely rational to do so?

Glaucon's challenge can also arise within a theory that manifests a practical conception of moral justification. We have already sketched the theory of Thomas Hobbes: Our interest in self-preservation is invoked to explain why we would be rational to favor the existence of morality as a social institution in society. However, it is not obvious that certain individuals might not find it in their interest to cheat on morality. Hence, in *Leviathan*, Hobbes considers the position of the "fool," who says in his heart that he will violate the obligations of justice whenever doing so would be in his own self-interest (1651, 1958, pp. 120–122). On the face of it, a violation of morality could easily be in one's self-interest, especially if there were a low risk that it would be detected and punished. A violation could apparently be rational even in the face of a significant risk of punishment if the promised benefit to oneself were sufficiently great. Yet Hobbes argues that our uncertainty about the risk of detection, and, more generally, about the magnitude and probability of promised benefits and costs of given acts of violation, guarantees that violations of duty are not rational. The argument is discussed in detail in Gregory Kavka's contribution to this volume. The point here is just that Glaucon's challenge is relevant to theories of both the epistemic and the practical variety.

What, then, is the relationship between the issue raised by Glaucon and the problems that a theory of moral justification is meant to solve? Kurt Baier seeks to forge a connection. He argues that immorality is not necessarily *irrational*, for the minimal standards of rationally acceptable behavior do not rule it out. However, immorality does necessarily fall short of *perfect* rationality. It is contrary to reason, for reasonability is a higher standard of compliance with reason than mere rationality. If Baier is correct, then an adequate meta-ethical theory must link the concepts of justification and reason in such a way that acting immorally comes out as contrary to practical reason. There must always be a reason to avoid doing whatever morality prohibits. A theory of justification must explain the nature of this reason in a way that yields a non-question-begging response to Glaucon. Moreover, if Baier is correct, then it would seem that the practical view of moral justification has the advantage. But Baier's position is controversial, and Kai Nielsen's essay argues against it.

So far, this introduction has attempted to lay out a few compass lines to help navigation through the territory of meta-ethics. At the center is the issue whether morality, or whether *some* morality, has a basis that would permit its rational justification. However, there are different approaches to this issue. A subsidiary issue, then, is the choice among conceptions of moral justification, a major choice being between the epistemic and practical conceptions. This is not a free choice. It will be controlled by a theory of the nature of morality. Moreover, on the day of reckoning, one's meta-ethical theory must answer to a challenge of overall plausibility. It must be compatible with accepted sociological and psychological theory and with plausible philosophical theories in related fields, especially with a plausible epistemology or theory of practical reason, as the case may be. It must be compatible with a plausible account of the practical or action-guiding nature of moral conviction, with a plausible account of moral reasoning, and with a view of the semantics of moral discourse that is compatible with general semantic theory. Finally, one's theory must respond to Glaucon's challenge. So another subsidiary issue is whether practical rationality is of such a nature that there is always a reason to avoid immorality. Must a person who is perfectly rational accord to morality a privileged position in practical deliberation? That is, must he do so with respect to a morality justified by the lights of one's theory? If not, where is the sting for moral skepticism?[5]

The issues summarized in the last paragraph are those that are addressed in this book. The book does not present a favored theory. Rather, the authors discuss different areas of the meta-ethical territory, entering from different directions but meeting each other and debating the merits of their respective positions. The work published here is largely new, although of course it grows out of other work by the authors and by others in the field. If there is one sort of approach that is emphasized, it is an approach that, in Gilbert Harman's words, seeks to explain "the place of value and obligation in the world of facts as revealed by science," or "the place of values in the natural world." Harman terms this approach "naturalism."

Certain Kantian possibilities and intuitionistic possibilities are not canvassed here. The intuitionistic strategies would involve introducing types of entities or facts into one's metaphysics, or principles into one's epistemology, that are not compatible, or that are believed not to be compatible, with a naturalist view; and the Kantian strategies would consist in introducing postulates into one's account of practical reason that again are not, or are believed not to be, compatible with a naturalist view. This is not to say, however, that it would be a simple matter to state exactly what the naturalist view amounts to, nor is it meant to rule out certain novel strategies in meta-ethics that might be rendered compatible with the naturalist view in the long run. It needs to be borne in mind that the question of what *is* compatible with science and with scientific method can be a matter for research. A naturalist assumes, for instance, that science is unified, that biology, physics, and psychology are mutually compatible and interrelated in the order of explanation. However, this assumption has not been vindicated in every rich detail. Similarly, a naturalist in ethics might proceed on the assumption that ethics will be vindicated in a scientific world view without having developed a detailed scheme.

The book is divided into two parts. Part I, "Truth and Theory Acceptance in Ethics," addresses the requirements or constraints that might be imposed on a theory of moral justification, usually but not exclusively from the epistemic viewpoint. These range from the naturalist constraint already mentioned—that an adequate theory must show the place of value in the scientific world view—to a different kind of "naturalist" constraint: that an argument from the nature of mankind to a theory of morality must be informed by evolutionary biology. Part II, "Morality and Practical Reason," addresses the relationship between ethics and the theory of practical reason. The essays include an attempt to ground justice in the theory of social choice, arguments that illustrate the practical conception of moral justification, attempts to deal with Glaucon's challenge, and a sketch of an approach to the theory of practical reason from the standpoint of sociobiology.

PART I: TRUTH AND THEORY ACCEPTANCE IN ETHICS

Gilbert Harman's essay sets a major topic for the book, "Is there a single true morality?" Of course, in accord with an ecumenical attitude toward the choice between epistemic and practical conceptions of the basic issue, we might think of the topic as whether there is a single true or "maximally justified" morality. But the debate in any case concerns the truth of "absolutism," which Harman defines as the view that there is a moral law that everyone has sufficient reason to follow and that there are things that everyone has a sufficient reason to hope for or wish for. "Relativism" is simply defined as the denial of this thesis. Notice that Harman has built into his definition of absolutism the notion that reasons would be "internal" to a justified or true morality in that there would always and necessarily be a sufficient reason to avoid immorality. In this way, support for absolutism would be support for the rationality of being moral.

Harman argues that naturalism naturally leads to relativism and that absolutism will be found most plausible by those who reject naturalism in favor of "autonomous ethics." Autonomous ethics is said to differ from naturalism in that it is not dominated by a concern to find the place of ethics in the natural world. Not being dominated by this concern, autonomous ethics can pursue ethics "internally," beginning with our moral beliefs and searching for principles. Nicholas Sturgeon suggests, however, that naturalism is not incompatible with the autonomous methodology. It may be that we *need* to pursue ethics internally in order to achieve a satisfactory naturalist theory. For it may be that an explanation of the place of ethics in the natural world would require the confrontation of our best moral theory with our best theory of the (rest of the) natural world. And it may well be that, in order to arrive at a satisfactory ethical theory, we would have to engage in investigating and systematizing our moral beliefs. If this is right, then the so-called internal approach is compatible with naturalism. The fundamental issue, then, would be whether to accept the naturalist constraint—that an adequate moral theory must be compatible with a scientific world view.

Naturalism leads away from absolutism, Harman argues, given what he thinks is the philosophically favored theory of practical reason from the naturalist point of view. This theory, a "Humean" theory (attributed to Hume, 1739), links having a sufficient reason with motivation: There is warranted reasoning that would lead one to decide to do whatever one has a sufficient reason to do. But for any given thing of proposed value, or any given proposed moral principle, there are people who are not motivated appropriately, and who would fail to decide appropriately even if they were exposed to what seem to be all relevant pieces of warranted reasoning. And so there seems to be no absolute value or principle, no principle or value that could be a source of *sufficient reasons for everyone.* The key issues, then, assuming that we accept the naturalist constraint, are the theory of practical reason and the sufficient-reason requirement. Perhaps some other theories of reason are compatible with naturalism, and perhaps a morality could be justified even if it were not a source of *sufficient* reasons for *everyone.* These issues are taken up in many of the essays in the volume.

We have already mentioned some of the issues discussed by Nicholas Sturgeon. In fact, Sturgeon intends his essay as a criticism of a skeptical argument presented by Harman in *The Nature of Morality* (1977), an argument based on the view that we are justified in postulating the existence of entities or facts of a given kind only if the postulation of such entities or facts is an essential part of our best *explanation* of some of our beliefs or observations. Harman contends that we do not need to assume that there are any moral facts in order to explain observations or beliefs of any sort, and he thinks that this tends to support moral skepticism. Sturgeon thinks on the contrary that moral facts *are* components of "our best overall explanatory picture of the world." But he limits himself to arguing that we do in fact accept moral explanations of events, that at least some of these are good explanations, and that they are "not obviously undermined by anything else that we know." The burden of Sturgeon's essay is the explanation, elaboration, and defense of this view, together with a discussion of the relevance to it of views about the "reduction" of moral facts to natural facts.

The argument also is of relevance to the position taken by Harman in his essay for this volume. Harman claims that naturalism tends to support relativism, but Sturgeon argues that a scientific world view is compatible with allowing the existence of moral facts that delimit a single true morality. Still, nothing said by Sturgeon shows that such a morality would be the morality of absolutism, a source of sufficient reasons for everyone.

My co-editor, David Zimmerman, disputes Sturgeon's position, as well as certain arguments by Mark Platts and David Wiggins; he regards each of these authors as arguing in favor of "moral realism." Different authors may use the term "realism" in different ways, but Zimmerman means by it the view that "the nature of the good and the right can be explicated without essential reference" to what any moral agents "approve of or are able to commit themselves to or desire."[6] I will not attempt to summarize the debate with Sturgeon. Suffice it to say that Zimmerman assumes that Sturgeon's essay is meant as an argument for realism, and he claims that the argument fails.

Platts and Wiggins seem to be arguing that "subjectivism" about values would cause the distortion or disappearance of features of our psychology that we would not want to lose. In Platts's case, the argument is that subjectivism would lead to the erosion of our "nonappetitive desires," for motivation by a nonappetitive desire depends on the belief that the object of desire is desirable independently of the bare fact that it is desired (1981). David Wiggins argues that subjectivism forces on the theorist a distinction between an inner perspective on values, a perspective of *commitment,* and an outer perspective, from which the inner perspective is held to be *illusory.* Subjectivism would lead to the distortion of the sense of life's *meaning* that we find in the inner perspective on value (1976). Zimmerman's response is to suggest that the "subjective basis for values" consists of one's most deeply felt desires, desires that are rooted in one's psychology, desires that are rooted in "the cognitive, constitutional and historical density of the person." Desires of this sort can survive and continue to be a basis for commitment, even given the belief that subjectivism is correct. The inner perspective, so to speak, is one from which we are motivated by our nonappetitive desire of what is valuable, but we can take up this perspective without having a belief in realism.

Richard Brandt's essay pursues a version of naturalism also argued for in his recent book, *A Theory of the Good and the Right* (1979). Brandt takes up what we have called the practical conception of moral justification, developing an account of rational desire and action, and then arguing that a moral code is justified for a person if and only if the person would support it or choose it for currency in his society, were he to be "fully rational." The notion of "full rationality" is a technical one, and it is explained in detail both in his book and in the essay found here. It is criticized by Kurt Baier in the second section of this book and defended by Richmond Campbell. Briefly, the notion is that the full rationality of a person's choice depends on its having two characteristics (1979, pp. 11–13). First, the choice must be a choice of exactly what the person *would* have chosen if "every item of relevant available information" had been "present to awareness, vividly, at the focus of attention, or with an equal share of attention." Here, information counts as "relevant" if, roughly, it would have made a difference and as "available" if it is justified either by the science of the day, by publicly accessible evidence, or by the principles of logic. Second, the desires or aversions that brought about the person's choice must be as they would have been had the person undergone "cognitive psychotherapy," had the person's "motivational machinery [been] fully suffused by [relevant] available information" (pp. 111–112). So we could say that one's choice is "fully rational" just in case it is what it *would* have been had one's beliefs, desires, and aversions been corrected by one's bringing vividly to mind at the focus of attention, and perhaps repeatedly, every item of relevant available information. Brandt's proposal, then, is that justifying a moral code is a matter of justifying one's choice of it to serve as the public moral code in one's society. Of course, it is not necessarily the case—in fact it is unlikely—that the code it would be "rational" for one person to support is the same as the code it would be "rational" for another to support. So Brandt's naturalist program does not yield an absolutist theory.

Brandt unfolds this position in his essay here. He begins with the observation that there is a commonsense morality in most, if not all, societies. He holds that such a morality consists in a complex of moral attitudes and concepts, together with the terminology to express those attitudes and the thought that they are justified. Now, as we saw, the epistemic conception of moral justification gives rise to a concern with the semantics of moral language. The notion is that we can determine whether our moral judgments are epistemically justified only if we can first determine whether they are propositional, or capable of truth or falsity, and, second, only if we can determine their propositional content. It may well be that the practical conception also requires a concern with such semantic issues. At any rate, Brandt suggests that there are two traditional approaches to the issues of clarifying moral language. One aims at *describing* the ordinary meanings of moral terms or at least the meanings of moral terms as used by the theorist and the intended audience. A second aims at providing *recommendations* for the construal of moral language. This is the so-called method of reforming definitions (1979, p. 3). Brandt thinks that this second approach is the more promising of the two, and his essay attempts to work out some of the constraints on such an exercise. It is obvious that not just any reformation will do; we are after a theory of *morality*. So Brandt proposes a set of criteria for "an optimal conceptual framework for moral discourse." The key term, Brandt says, is "justified," as it occurs in the phrase "justified moral code," and Brandt sets out seven conditions for a satisfactory "explication" of this term. He then argues that his own account of moral justification is the optimal one. He goes on to propose that what we should refer to as the *facts* of morality are just the facts that constitute the truth conditions of moral assertions given the optimal conceptual framework. Here, then, we see the unfolding of a cognitivist meta-ethical theory via a set of constraints on meta-ethical theories and an argument for a practical conception of the justification of morality.

Norman Daniels discusses two of the conditions proposed by Brandt, the "empiricist constraint" and the "disalienation constraint." The former arises from the requirement that the justification of a moral code, if it is to answer practical doubts that people have about morality, must itself be value-neutral. Justification must rest on facts and logic; not these alone, as Daniels suggests, but these together with our nonmoral preferences as corrected by facts and logic through cognitive psychotherapy. The empiricist constraint is that the desires and beliefs constitutive of our *present* moral code should not be taken into account in evaluating the *justifiability* of candidate moral codes. The second constraint, the disalienation constraint, is that a successful account of justification for moral codes must close the gap between justification and motivation; it must be such that one who believed a code to be justified, in the sense specified by the theory, would find conformity to the code thereby to be *recommended*. This second constraint is obviously designed to eliminate or reduce the force of Glaucon's challenge. It says in effect that a theory of justification for moralities is unsatisfactory if it leaves (too much) conceptual space for the challenge, "Yes, but why should I conform?" Daniels argues that there is a deep tension between these two requirements. Our desires are shaped by our culture, including the morality that is part of our culture, and so we cannot "step outside our tradition," as required by the empiricist constraint, except at the cost of alienating ourselves from the result. That is, to the extent that a theory of moral justification *decreases* the effect of our prior moral views on the content of a morality it deems justified, it *increases* our alienation from that morality by increasing the distance between what it requires and what we desire, or what be believe ought to be the case.

If Daniels is right, then no theory can meet both requirements, and Daniels argues that in fact Brandt's own theory does not strictly speaking meet either. Moreover, he argues that "intuitionism," not in G. E. Moore's sense, but in that defined by John Rawls's theory of "wide reflective equilibrium," is as successful in meeting the constraints as is Brandt's theory. The wide reflective equilibrium (WRE) theory suggests that a moral code or moral principle should be deemed justified (for a person) only if it would be accepted (by the person) in a wide reflective equilibrium: a settled and coherent state of belief, where the code or principle in question is coherent with (the person's) relevant considered moral judgments, and where relevant moral or nonmoral background theories provide support for the code or principle, support that is to some degree independent of the support provided by the match with considered moral judgments. One's initial moral beliefs are "filtered" to eliminate obvious sources of error, and they may change quite radically before wide reflective equilibrium is reached. Nevertheless, it seems clear that the empiricist constraint is not met, for the content of one's equilibrium point will be affected by the content of one's moral starting point; and the disalienation constraint is not met, for one may apparently settle on a particular moral code as most coherent with the body of one's beliefs without being motivated to conform. The constraints are not met, but the thrust of Daniels's arguments is that this is no objection to WRE theory.

It is at this point that the present author enters the debate with his essay "Considered Judgments and Moral Justification." WRE theory imposes a constraint of its own on what can be deemed a justified moral code or principle, *viz.*, that to be justified, a principle must cohere with our considered moral judgments. To be sure, it is not required that there be coherence with the considered judgments with which we begin reflection; it is only required that there be coherence in the equilibrium that may ultimately be reached between a principle and a set of considered judgments. But this is enough, I argue, to call WRE theory into question. The WRE constraint is a cousin of a kind of widely accepted meta-ethical constraint, a "conservative" constraint to the effect that an adequate moral theory must conserve our considered moral judgments, those we would have, let us say, were our moral convictions to have been adequately confronted with relevant nonmoral considerations: A theory is to be rejected if it regards as justified something that is and remains "counterintuitive." This view is a basis on which many philosophers would be inclined to evaluate meta-ethical theories such as Brandt's. For, as is argued by Nicholas Sturgeon, Brandt's theory would permit quite unintuitive moral principles to be justified by its lights (1982). However, WRE theory appears to be immune to this line of attack. The meta-ethical constraint is built into it, in that it is logically impossible for a moral code or principle to be deemed justified by WRE theory unless it coheres with our considered judgments in WRE.

Some argument is required to justify the privileged status given in WRE theory, and in the common conservative constraint, to our considered judgments. Daniels holds that no epistemological *priority* is given to considered judgments in WRE theory; there is no determinate and fixed set of judgments identified in advance and treated as justified *ab initio*. And I must agree with this. However, the judgments that would be our considered judgements in WRE are given a special status as standards of justification. They are able to defeat a moral code, or in the case of the meta-ethical constraint, they are able to defeat an account of moral justification. Some argument is needed for according them this status as defeaters.

The final essay in Part I is by Ronald de Sousa. It considers the viability of arguments from our nature as humans to theories of value. Such arguments would cross the "fact-value gap," so-called, but there is an ancient tradition holding that some arguments of this sort are valid. For instance, Aristotle argued in the *Nicomachean Ethics* that if there is a *function* of humans, then the human good consists in fulfilling this function in accord with the appropriate excellences (1097b 23–1098a 19). We need not pause to consider Aristotle's conception of our function; de Sousa argues that the program suggested by the Aristotelian function argument has been undermined by modern evolutionary biology. Nevertheless, biology still does use the concept of a function, and so it seems worth investigating whether a conception of our *nature* can be constructed within the boundaries of accepted biological theory as a basis for an argument to a theory of value. This is the study carried out in detail in de Sousa's essay.

PART II: MORALITY AND PRACTICAL REASON

The essays in Part II emphasize one of the themes already introduced: the relationship between morality and practical reason. One aspect of this is the conception that a morality is to be justified, if at all, by showing the rationality of choosing it for some specified purpose in some defined context. We have seen Brandt's arguments in this direction. A second aspect arises out of Glaucon's challenge—"What reason do I have to be moral?"—and out of Brandt's notion that an adequate meta-ethical theory must close the gap between justification and motivation, disalienating people from moralities seen to be justified by its light. Recall that Harman holds also that if there is one true morality, in any sense worth discussing, then everyone has sufficient reason to conform to that morality. He defines "absolutism" as the thesis that there is such a morality. A third issue implicit in all of this is the concept of a practical reason, and its relationship to the concepts of motivation and obligation. A "Humean" view makes the relationship between reason and motivation "internal": It is logically necessary, if one has a practical reason, that one have an appropriate motivation, or that one would, in specified circumstances. Such a view is held, for instance, by both Brandt and Harman. Is the relationship between *obligation* and motivation also internal? Harman holds that it is (1975; see Copp, 1982). These are among the issues examined in the essays in Part II.

A major problem addressed in these essays is the conflict that arises in so-called prisoner's-dilemma situations, where rational self-interested behavior on the part of everyone leads paradoxically to a result that is worse from everyone's self-interested point of view than some other available result. Many situations can be of this general sort, but the example that is typically given concerns two prisoners. Suppose that two felons are arrested and held on a charge of armed robbery. They are in separate cells and cannot communicate with each other. Each is told, and told that the other is told, that their situation is as follows: the prosecution cannot secure a conviction on the charge of armed robbery unless one of them confesses. If they both refuse to confess, both will be convicted, but only of a lesser offense. Each will spend three years in prison. If one of them confesses and the other does not, then the one who cooperates and helps to secure the conviction of the other will be given a very light sentence of only one year. The other will suffer ten years in prison. If both confess, both will be convicted of the serious charge, but they will be given some credit for their cooperation. They will each spend eight years in prison. They must independently decide whether or not to confess. Whatever one chooses will affect the welfare of the other, but neither of them can affect the other's choice. They care little for each other, and, let us say, there will be no opportunity in the future for retaliation. Each of them knows that confession assures a shorter sentence for the person who confesses, regardless of what the other does, but they also know that if they both confess each will receive a longer sentence than if both do not confess. In this case, if each of them is rational to aim for a minimum sentence, then each is rational to confess, regardless of what the other does, for each of them saves two years by confessing. However, if they both confess, they both suffer for eight years, while if neither had confessed, they would only have spent three years in prison, so the optimal result for them both considered as a group, the result that each of them would rationally prefer to the outcome where both confess, is an outcome that they will not achieve if each of them aims to minimize his or her own prison sentence.

Situations with this structure are not uncommon. For example, it may be that the nuclear confrontation between the superpowers is a prisoner's-dilemma situation.[7] For our purposes, the prisoner's-dilemma suggests that there may be a formal problem for the project of justifying morality on the basis of practical reason, assuming, that is, that rationality consists in seeking to maximize one's self-interest. It calls into question this maximizing conception of reason, and suggests there may be a logical barrier to showing that the sort of cooperative behavior distinctive of morality is rational from each of our points of view.

Kurt Baier argues that the conception of practical reason developed by Richard Brandt is strongly counterintuitive. To be sure, Brandt regards his conception as a reforming suggestion for a use of "rational," not as a description of our ordinary use. Nevertheless, Brandt admits that a satisfactory account must preserve the "recommendatory force" of remarks of the form, "The rational thing to do would be . . ." It must "disalienate" us from what it would be rational for us to do (1979, pp. 160–162). Baier argues that Brandt's theory does not solve the problem of alienation. In fact, "the closer we come to solving [this] problem, the closer we are to depriving reason of its guiding function." There is a tension between the guiding function of reason and our disalienation from reason, a tension of the same nature as the tension noted by Daniels between the ability of a meta-ethical theory to take us out of our tradition and guide us to a new moral perspective and its ability to disalienate us from the moral ideal. Nevertheless, Baier does not suppose that a theory must inevitably break under this tension: He argues that "the concept of rationality embedded in our culture and our language" avoids the alienation of reason, while at the same time it preserves its guiding function.

The theory sketched by Baier is rich, complex, and highly suggestive of new approaches to dealing with the theoretical problems we have been discussing. Reason is said to be a capacity to solve problems with the aid of guidelines provided by our culture. These guidelines are not static. Their purpose is to enable us to achieve our objectives, both theoretical and practical, at a "higher aspiration level" than would otherwise be possible. The guidelines can be revised and improved over time in light of the results of their use. One must suppose that the principles of morality could also be characterized in this way, according to Baier, for he argues that, although immorality is not necessarily *irrational*, it does necessarily fall short of *perfect rationality*, being contrary to reason. But then the principles of morality must be among the guidelines of reason. Otherwise there would be no logical guarantee that actions appraised as falling short of moral requirements would also be properly appraised as falling short of perfect rationality. It follows that there must be more to practical reason than reasons of self-interest. The guidelines of a stable society must sometimes require action that runs contrary to self-interest. This is Hobbes's insight (1651), and various of our authors reinforce it by reflecting on prisoner's-dilemma situations. If we were all "rational egoists," society would be unstable. Hence, the requirements of a stable social order must be regarded as reasons that override independent self-interested reasons. However, the problem of alienation now reappears. Practical reason has been defined in terms of optimal social guidelines for the maximal fulfillment of the aspirations of each, compatible with a stable society. However, Baier says, to show that this is indeed the nature of *reason*, the "social requirements must constitute genuine reasons for everyone" in that everyone must have "adequate" independent self-interested reasons "to want there to be such social requirements and to have them regarded as overriding." To say this is to introduce the problem of alienation. Yet Baier thinks he can escape it: Suppose a social order that provides everyone with "equally good reason" to regard its reasons as overriding self-interest, a social order in which no one's reasons can be strengthened without someone's being weakened. Then "everyone has reasons as good as everyone can demand," and so everyone has adequate reasons. In such a society there is reason for each to conform to social guidelines, and so the guidelines constitute requirements of reason.

Kai Nielsen argues that Baier's enterprise fails by its own standards. Consider a person with the objective of being "a prudent free-rider with stable and sound moral institutions in place." Baier has not shown that this objective is contrary to reason. A person with this objective may successfully pursue his interests in full control of his passions, with an accurate appraisal of the facts, and making no errors of reasoning. Such a person takes into account the general cultural guidelines, manipulating them to enable maximal fulfillment of his interests. He does perhaps have sufficient reason to want general moral guidelines to be entrenched in his society and to be socialized, but Baier has not shown that our person has any reason for wanting the socialization to "stick" in his own case. Our person may be quite capable of being a free-rider who maximizes his own utility. A key point raised by Nielsen is the possibility that practical reason is not unified in a single set of guidelines: Perhaps there just are both "agent-relative" self-interested reasons and "agent-neutral" reasons such as morality entails, with no requirement that agent-neutral reasons always be given priority by a fully rational person.

Baier's view is that if morality is a source of reasons, then everyone must have an adequate reason to regard the requirements of morality as overriding self-interest; that is, everyone must have an interest, as great as is compatible with a like interest for all, in its being the case that the requirements of morality are conformed to by everyone. This idea is taken up by Jan Narveson, who sees it as supporting a *contractarian* program in ethics. For if each of us is to have an interest in everyone's conforming to morality, an interest equal to the interest of anyone else, then it would seem that morality must consist of rules that all of us could agree to in a fair bargain for mutual advantage. The problem though, given a utility-maximizing or self-interested conception of rational choice, is that our interest may lie in everyone *else's* conforming to morality. If morality is viewed schematically as a set of "rules constraining individual behavior in the direction of optimality" in prisoner's-dilemma situations, as Narveson argues, it may be in one's interest that others conform, but not in one's interest that one conform oneself. This is the free-rider problem. David Gauthier has suggested that the utility-maximizing conception of rationality should be replaced by a conception of rationality as "constrained maximization" (1975a). But Narveson proposes a different strategy for dealing with the problem. One's acceptance of morality has two aspects: a matter of one's beliefs and a matter of one's actions. The latter also has two aspects: a matter of conforming to morality and a matter of participating in activities aimed at securing general conformity. Such activities can alter the utilities of those who might otherwise find it in their interest to cheat on morality. Therefore, such activities can themselves foster rational conformity. Moreover, the rationality of everyone's participating in activities of this sort is clear, even in light of a utility-maximizing conception of rational choice, and this is all that is required for a rational underpinning of morality. A morality is "a body of principles such that any rational person would want to have them generally observed, and would accept that he should participate, at least weakly, in a social system designed to bring about that general compliance."

It is clear that Narveson's strategy leaves morality open to Glaucon's challenge, and Gregory Kavka's essay examines the merits of the challenge in abundant detail. However, before we turn to Kavka, we will examine two other essays: David Gauthier develops a contractarian theory of justice that is an example of the sort of work possible within the practical conception of justification, and Richmond Campbell examines the naturalistic credentials of the theory of practical reason that has been relied on to such a degree by our authors.

David Gauthier argues that the principles of justice are not only the solution to a problem of rational choice, as was argued by John Rawls in *A Theory of Justice*, but they are also part of the theory of rational choice. That is, they are principles for *making* rational choices, principles for making rational choices *by a society*. Now if there is a parallel between the theory of individual decision and the theory of social choice, and if an individual acts rationally by maximizing his expected utility, then we may suppose that a society acts rationally by maximizing expected "social welfare." However, Gauthier contends that social rationality does *not* parallel individual rationality in this way. A society does not pursue its "own" ends, not even a system of ends somehow derived from the ends of individuals; rather, it pursues the several individual ends to ensure *mutual advantage*. That is, this is what is pursued to the degree that social decisions are *rational*. But principles that would secure *mutual* advantage are principles to which rational individuals would agree even if they were seeking to maximize their own utility. And so the principles of justice, as principles of rational social choice, would be the solution to a problem of rational agreement for mutual advantage among self-interested individuals.

The Rawlsian theory is that principles of justice are, as it were, chosen behind a *veil of ignorance* (Rawls, 1971). But if this were right, there would be no guarantee that the principles of justice would be chosen by individuals choosing rationally in light of what *in fact* is their expected utility. But then there would be no guarantee that principles of justice would in fact secure mutual advantage. Given the conclusion that justice does or would promote mutual advantage, the Rawlsian approach must be rejected. The alternative that is developed by Gauthier exploits the notion of rational bargaining among *actual* individuals in light of their *actual* interests and capacities. There is some idealization. The privileged bargain is what would result from rational bargaining among ideally competent, informed, and rational proxies for each of us. The rationales for this, and for certain other idealizations, are stated by Gauthier.

In addition, Gauthier develops a theory of rational bargaining at least to the extent that he is able to state a set of four conditions on rational bargaining and to derive from them the result that rational bargainers will act on a principle of *minimax concession*. The idea is that each bargainer has as his *base point* the maximum that he could achieve without cooperation, and as his maximum *claim* the most he could achieve from a scheme of cooperation, consistent with its remaining advantageous for the others both to remain in the scheme themselves and not to exclude him. A rational agreement would afford each individual no more than his claim and no less than his base point; it would see each individual accept some concession, as measured by the proportion he gives up of the maximum that he claimed over the basepoint. Now Gauthier argues that rational bargainers would reach agreement on a scheme only if any alternative would require some individual to accept a greater concession than the largest required under that scheme. Rational bargainers would act on a principle of minimax concession.

Social choice plays a role in "ensuring protection" for individuals in society and in "increasing production." The principles of justice are the principles of rational social choice in this domain, and so they are principles that would result from applying the minimax concession rule. Outside of this domain, rational persons seek to maximize their expected utility. Within this domain they are to follow the principles of rational social choice, even when doing so would be a departure from expected-utility maximization. Here again we find the problem of alienation.

Perhaps the alienation problem should be avoided by amending or rejecting the view that rationality for an individual consists in maximizing expected utility. David Gauthier has argued that this is so. At any rate, it seems that if the norms of morality need to be reconciled with a scientific world view, so do the norms of rational choice and rational belief. Richmond Campbell takes up part of this task in his essay. He argues for the striking thesis that "sociobiology can have a significant role to play" in supporting a conception of rational choice within a scientific conception of the world. Suppose we begin with the expected-utility-maximizing model of rational choice, or with "rational egoism." Campbell's idea is that "empirical studies can illuminate the *normative* character of [this model of] rational motivation by making its attractiveness as a norm for behavior more intelligible."

The study of prisoner's-dilemma situations shows that cooperative or altruistic restraint for mutual advantage is not always rational, given the expected-utility-maximizing model. Campbell suggests that a formal similarity exists between the problem posed for the theory of rational egoism by the prisoner's-dilemma and the problem posed for the theory of evolution by altruistic behavior. "To ask how reciprocal altruism is possible in nature on the assumption that nature has evolved through natural selection is only superficially different from asking how reciprocal altruism is rationally possible on the assumption that rationality is rational egoism." Robert Axelrod and William Hamilton have argued that a strategy of limited cooperation, known as *Tit for Tat*, has a biological superiority over other strategies like pure cooperation and pure noncooperation: It has evolutionary stability, robustness, and viability (1981). They argue this on the basis of a model of the environment that is realistic in that it assumes a *series* of prisoner's-dilemma interactions involving individuals, where the probability of repeat interactions between the same individuals is fixed at a point between zero and one. This model "dissolves the paradox of biological altruism in PD interactions." It also "demonstrates how continued mutual cooperation in such interactions is consistent with rational egoism." Rational egoists can select *strategies,* and the Tit for Tat strategy produces more expected utility for an individual "than any of a wide variety of competing strategies." Hence, it is a rational strategy "given a series of PD's with a sufficient probability of the same individuals interacting again." Thus rational egoism is "consistent with cooperative restraint in the pursuit of individual ends—a restraint that is commonly thought to be paradigmatic of moral action."

Campbell has argued, following Axelrod and Hamilton, that certain general formal features of the interactive environment force a reconciliation between reason and altruism, and hence they eliminate the alienation problem in realistic settings. We have seen other strategies. Harman proposed that a morality should be regarded as true or justified only if it is a source of sufficient reasons for conformity. Baier argued that the norms of reason, including those of morality, are cultural guidelines with a given purpose, and so that there is a unity of practical reason, with moral standards being rational standards that override all others. These strategies, with the possible exception of Campbell's, would serve to answer Glaucon, for Glaucon demanded an *intrinsic* connection between morality and one's own good, or one's own rational choices. Gregory Kavka seeks to explore in a systematic way the nature, scope, and depth of the *extrinsic* connections between morality and practical reason.

We assume some account of morality as a background, calling it "commonsense morality," and we assume that rational conduct is self-interested conduct or "rational prudence." Given this perspective, where we assume morality is given as a set of justified requirements on actions, it may not seem a serious problem that "We cannot expect to convince a clever immoralist that it pays everyone to act morally on every specific occasion in any sort of society." Kavka's strategy, then, is to narrow the project of reconciling reason and morality by identifying some of its dimensions and selecting for discussion certain less ambitious versions of it. So we argue that *adopting the moral way of life* is consistent with self-interest, not that *all moral actions* are; we argue that a kind of "copper rule" morality of reciprocal altruism, as perhaps is modeled by Tit for Tat, is consistent with self-interest, not that the Golden Rule ideal morality is consistent with self-interest; we argue that most people in actual social circumstances find morality to be in their self-interest, not that everyone always necessarily would; we recognize that rationality embraces the pursuit of ends that are not strictly "self-interested." We aim to show that moral people have no reasons for regret, and that parents have sufficient reasons to raise moral children. And Kavka concludes, "While it is normally prudent to be moral, it is sometimes rational to be moral even if it is not prudent."

CONCLUSION

These essays carry forward the debate on meta-ethical issues, breaking new ground in some cases, cultivating and surveying older territory in others. I hope that the result will be to prompt philosophers to devote more of their attention to foundational questions in ethics, both as thinkers and as teachers. The questions are ancient in their origin, they are at the center of philosophy, and they are of great cultural importance. They demand all of the sophistication, rigor, and sensitivity that philosophers can bring to bear.[8]

NOTES

1. Foot (1967), "Introduction," p. 8. See also Foot (1978b).

2. This is the thesis of G. J. Warnock (1967). For discussion, see Warnock (1967) and Brandt (1959), chaps. 7–9.

3. Rawls (1980), Lecture 3, "Construction and Objectivity," p. 554.

4. Hare (1952), p. 69. In more recent work, Hare has attempted to retain the essentials of this view while arguing that the logic of moral discourse underwrites utilitarianism. See Hare (1981).

5. These issues are explored in Copp, *Morality and Society* (forthcoming).

6. The reader should exercise due caution throughout to ascertain the precise sense given by an author to technical philosophical terms, such as, in the case of Zimmerman's essay, the terms "realism" and "subjectivism." One should not assume that the same meaning is to be understood in every case. For instance, the reader should take care to ascertain whether the three authors discussed by Zimmerman are all realists in the sense he defines.

7. See, for example, Schelling (1960), Gauthier (1967), Lackey (1982), and Hardin (1983).

8. I am indebted to Richmond Campbell and Spencer Carr for helpful criticisms of this essay.

part one

Truth and
Theory Acceptance in Ethics

chapter one

Is There a Single True Morality?

Gilbert Harman

CONFESSION

I have always been a moral relativist. As far back as I can remember thinking about it, it has seemed to me obvious that the dictates of morality arise from some sort of convention or understanding among people, that different people arrive at different understandings, and that there are no basic moral demands that apply to everyone. For many years, this seemed so obvious to me that I assumed it was everyone's instinctive view, at least everyone who gave the matter any thought "in this day and age."

When I first studied philosophical ethics (in the 1950s), I was not disabused of this opinion. The main issue at the time seemed to be to determine exactly what form of "noncognitivism" was correct. (According to noncognitivism, moral judgments do not function to describe a moral reality but do something else—express feelings, prescribe a course of action, and so forth.)

It is true that many of the philosophers I studied seemed for some reason to want to avoid calling themselves "relativists." This was usually accomplished by defining moral relativism to be an obviously inconsistent position; for example, the view both that there are no universal moral truths and also that everyone ought to follow the dictates of his or her group, where this last claim is taken to be a universal moral truth. I wasn't sure what this verbal maneuver was supposed to accomplish. Why would anyone want to give such a definition of moral relativism? Moral relativism was obviously correct, and the philosophers I was studying seemed all to be moral relativists even if they did not want to describe themselves in that way.

In the 1960s I was distressed to hear from various people teaching ethics that students in their classes tended to proclaim themselves moral relativists until they had been shown how confused they were about ethics. I suspected that what confusions there were were not confusions of the students, but were confusions of their teachers, due perhaps to a faulty definition of moral relativism. It seemed to me that the obvious solution was to show that moral relativism can be consistently defined as a plausible view and that standard objections to moral relativism are mistaken.

So, I eventually wrote and published an essay about this (Harman, 1975), naively thinking it would clear things up and end worries about moral relativism. I was surprised to discover that this did not happen. I was also startled to find that many students in my own ethics courses resisted my attempt to make clear what I thought they instinctively believed. After some study I concluded that in fact only some of the students in my courses were instinctive moral relativists; a significant number of them were instinctive absolutists.

I had known of course that there were philosophers and friends of mine who were not moral relativists. For a long time I attributed this to their perversity and love of the bizarre and attached no significance to it. But then I discovered that some of them thought moral relativism was the perverse view, a kind of philosophical folly like skepticism about other minds or the external world (for example, Nagel, 1980). I was stunned! How could they think that when they knew so many moral relativists (like me) and no epistemological skeptics (at least none who took such skepticism seriously in ordinary life)? It then occurred to me to wonder how I could think of moral absolutism as such a perverse view when I knew so many moral absolutists.

THE ISSUE

It turns out to my surprise that the question whether there is a single true morality is an unresolved issue in moral philosophy. On one side are relativists, skeptics, nihilists, and noncognitivists. On the other side are those who believe in absolute values and a moral law that applies to everyone. Stangely, only a few people seem to be undecided. Almost everyone seems to be firmly on one side or the other, and almost everyone seems to think his or her side is obviously right, the other side representing a kind of ridiculous folly. This is strange since everyone knows, or ought to know, that many intelligent people are on each side of this issue.

Two Approaches

In this essay I want to suggest that part of the explanation for this mutual incomprehension is that there are two different ways to do moral philosophy. If one approach is taken, moral relativism, noncognitivism, or skepticism may seem obviously correct and moral absolutism may seem foolish. If the other approach is taken, absolutism may seem clearly right and skepticism, relativism, and noncognitivism may seem foolish.

The difference in approaches is, to put it crudely, a difference in attitude toward science. One side says we must concentrate on finding the place of value and obligation in the world of facts as revealed by science. The other side says we must ignore that problem and concentrate on ethics proper.

Of course, both sides agree that we must begin at the beginning with our initial beliefs, both moral and nonmoral, and consider possible modifications that will make these beliefs more coherent with each other and with plausible generalizations and other explanatory principles. Eventually, we hope to arrive at a "reflective equilibrium" (Rawls, 1971) when no further modifications seem called for, at least for the time being. This process will inevitably leave many issues unresolved; in particular, we may find ourselves with no account of the place that value and obligation have in the world of facts. This will not dismay someone who is willing to leave that question unanswered, but it will be disturbing to someone who, on the way to "reflective equilibrium," has come to think that the basic issue in moral philosophy is precisely how value and obligation fit into the scientific conception of the world.

I will use the term "naturalism" for an approach to ethics that is in this way dominated by a concern with the place of values in the natural world. I will call any approach that is not so dominated an instance of "autonomous ethics," since such an approach allows us to pursue ethics internally. Of course, autonomous ethics allows that science is relevant to ethics in as much as ethical assessment depends on the facts of the case. But unlike naturalism, autonomous ethics does not take the main question of ethics to be the naturalistic status of values and obligations.

Naturalism

I hope the terms "naturalism" and "autonomous ethics" will not be too misleading. The term "naturalism" is sometimes reserved for the thesis that moral judgments can be analyzed into or reduced to factual statements of a sort clearly compatible with the scientific world view. I am using the term "naturalism" more broadly in a more traditional and accurate sense. Naturalism in this sense does not have to lead to naturalistic reduction, although that is one possibility. Another possibility is that there is no way in which ethics could fit into the scientific conception of the world. In that case naturalism leads to moral nihilism, as in Mackie (1977). Mackie supposes that ethics requires absolute values which have the property that anyone aware of their existence must necessarily be motivated to act morally. Since our scientific conception of the world has no place for entities of this sort, and since there is no way in which we could become aware of such entities, Mackie concludes that ethics must be rejected as resting on a false presupposition. That is a version of naturalism as I am using the term.

Naturalism can also lead one to a noncognitive analysis of moral judgments. In this view, moral judgments do not function to describe the world, but to do something else—to express one's attitudes for and against things, as Stevenson (1963) argues—or to recommend one or another course of action or general policy, as Hare (1952, 1981) proposes. Or a naturalist may decide that moral judgments do make factual claims that fit in with the claims of science. This can be illustrated by some sort of naturalistic reduction. One example would be an analysis that takes moral claims to be claims about the reactions of a hypothetical impartial observer as in Hume (1739) or Firth (1952).

More complex positions are possible. Mackie (1977) argues in Chapter 1 that ethics rests on a false presupposition, but then he goes on in later chapters to discuss particular moral issues. It is almost as if he had first demonstrated that God does not exist and had then gone on to consider whether He is wise and loving. Presumably, Mackie believes that ethics as normally conceived must be or can be replaced with something else. But he does not indicate exactly what sort of replacement he has in mind—whether it is an institution of some sort, for example. Nor does he say how moral claims made within this replacement fit in with the claims of science. I suspect he would accept some sort of noncognitivist account of the judgments that are to replace the old moral judgments.

It is possible to be both a naturalist and an absolutist, although this is not very common. Firth (1952) defends an absolutist version of the ideal-observer theory and Hare (1981) defends an absolutist version of noncognitivism. But I will argue that the most plausible versions of naturalism involve a moral relativism that says different agents are subject to different basic moral requirements depending on the moral conventions in which they participate.

Autonomous Ethics

Naturalism tends toward relativism. What I am calling autonomous ethics, on the other hand, can have a very different tendency. In this approach, science is relevant, since our moral judgments depend on what we take the facts to be; but we attach no special importance to saying how obligations and values can be part of the world revealed by science. Rather, we do ethics internally. We begin with our initial moral beliefs and search for general principles. Our initial opinions can be changed to some extent so as to come into agreement with appealing general principles and our beliefs about the facts, but an important aspect of the appeal of such principles will be the way in which they account for what we already accept.

This approach normally (but not always) involves an initial assumption of moral absolutism, which in this context is of course not the thesis that there are simple moral principles that hold absolutely without exceptions, but rather the thesis that there are basic moral demands that apply to all moral agents. Autonomous ethics tends to retain that absolutist thesis. It may also involve some sort of intuitionism, claiming that each of us has immediate insight into the truths of certain moral principles. It sometimes leads to a fairly conservative morality, not much different from one's initial starting point. That is not surprising given the privileged position assigned to our initial moral beliefs.

But let me stress that conservatism is not inevitable, and autonomous ethics can and often does lead to more radical moralities too. It leads some philosphers to a radical utilitarianism, for example. It leads Rawls (1971) to principles of social justice that appear to be considerably more egalitarian than those most people accept. And Nozick (1974), using the same general approach, comes out at a very different place, in which he ends up denying that any sort of egalitarian redistribution by governments is ever morally justified. (However, the moral theory in Nozick, 1981, as contrasted with the political theory in Nozick, 1974, insists on the moral requirement of helping others.) Indeed, there are many different ways in which ethics can be pursued as an autonomous discipline with its own principles that are not reducible to the principles of any science. I can illustrate this variety by mentioning a few of the many other contemporary philosophers who accept some form of autonomous ethics: Baier (1958), Darwall (1983), Donagan (1977), Frankena (1976), Fried (1978), Gewirth (1978), Grice (1967), Nagel (1970, 1980), and Richards (1971). Each of these philosophers has a somewhat different approach, although all are absolutists who rely on some form of autonomous ethics.

I should say that it is possible to believe in autonomous ethics without being an absolutist. One might be impressed by the variety of views held by those who accept autonomous ethics and so be led to allow for relativism while continuing to accept the method of autonomous ethics, believing that naturalism must be rejected. A possible example is McDowell (1978, 1979, 1981). But the tendency of autonomism in ethics is toward absolutism. In what follows I will restrict my discussion to absolutist versions of autonomous ethics and to relativistic versions of naturalism.

Teachers of Ethics

I might also mention that ethics pursued internally, as in autonomous ethics, is more interesting to many people than ethics as pursued by naturalism. That is because autonomous ethics allows one to spend more of one's time thinking about interesting complicated moral puzzles than naturalistic ethics does, and many people find moral puzzles more interesting than "abstract" questions about the objectivity of value and its place in nature. Philosophers attracted by naturalism tend not to find ethics as interesting a subject as do philosphers attracted by autonomous ethics. So, relativists tend to be less interested in ethics than absolutists are. For example, logicians, philosphers of science, and philosophers of mathematics,who tend toward naturalism, are usually not moral absolutists and are not very interested in ethics as a philosophical subject. Philosophers who are relatively interested in ethics tend to be those who favor autonomous ethics and therefore tend to be absolutists. This is why teachers of ethics tend more than their students to be absolutists. It is not merely, as they sometimes suppose, that ethics teachers have seen through confusions that affect their students. A more important factor is that relativists tend not to become teachers of ethics.

WHY DO WE BELIEVE WHAT WE BELIEVE?

Autonomous ethics and naturalism represent very different attitudes toward the relation between science and ethics. Consider, for example, the question of what explains our believing what we in fact believe. Naturalists see an important difference between our factural beliefs and our moral beliefs. Our ordinary factual beliefs provide us with evidence that there is an independent world of objects because our having those beliefs cannot be plausibly explained without assuming we interact with an independent world of objects external to ourselves, objects we perceive and manipulate. But our having the moral beliefs we have can be explained entirely in terms of our upbringing and our psychology, without any appeal to an independent realm of values and obligations. So our moral beliefs do not provide us with evidence for such an independent realm of values and obligations, and we must choose between skepticism, noncognitivism, and relativism (Harman, 1977, chapter 1).

Autonomists disagree with this. They claim we often believe that something is good or right or obligatory in part because it *is* good or right or obligatory. They accuse naturalists of begging the question. When naturalists say that a belief cannot be explained by virtue of something's being right, unless that thing's being right consists in some psychological or sociological fact, they simply assume that all explanatory factors are part of the world revealed by science. But this is the point at issue. Autonomists argue that it is more obvious that we sometimes recognize what is right than that naturalism is correct. True, we may be unable to say how a given "moral fact" and someone's recognition of it fit into the world of facts as revealed by science. But there are always unanswered questions. To jump from our current inability to answer this question to skepticism, relativisim, or noncognitivism is to make a more drastic move than this puzzle warrants, from the point of view of autonomous ethics.

Explanation and Reduction

The naturalist seeks to locate the place of value, justice, right, and wrong, and so forth in the world in a way that makes clear how they might explain what we take them to explain. A naturalist cannot understand how value, justice, right, and wrong might figure in explanations without having some sense of their "location" in the world. We can say that this involves "naturalistic reduction," but it need not involve reductive definitions of a serious sort. Indeed, reduction rarely (if ever) involves serious reductive definitions. We identify tables with clusters of atoms in a way that allows us to understand how tables can hold up the things they hold up without having to suppose the word *table* is definable using only the concepts of physics! Similarly, we identify colors with dispositional properties of objects, namely, their tendencies to look in certain ways to certain sorts of observers in certain conditions, without having to suppose there is a satisfactory definition in these terms. Similarly for temperatures, genes, and so on. What a naturalist wants is to be able to locate value, justice, right, wrong, and so forth in the world in the way that tables, colors, genes, temperatures, and so on can be located in the world.

What is at issue here is understanding *how* moral facts might explain something, how the badness of someone's character might explain why that person acts in a certain way, to take an example from Sturgeon's essay. It is not sufficient that one be prepared to accept the counterfactual judgment that the person would not have acted in that way if the person had not had a bad character, if one does not see how the *badness* of the person's character could have such an effect. A naturalist believes one can see that only by locating badness of character in aspects of the world which one sees can have that effect.

Notice that a "naturalist" as I am here using the term is not just someone who supposes that all aspects of the world have a naturalistic location in this way, but rather someone who takes it to be of overriding importance in doing moral philosophy actually to attempt to locate moral properties. My claim is that, when one takes this attempt seriously, one will tend to become skeptical or relativistic. Sturgeon is not a naturalist in my sense, despite his insistence that he takes moral facts to be natural facts.

MORAL ABSOLUTISM DEFINED

I now want to be more specific about what is to count as moral absolutism. Various things might be meant by the claim that there are absolute values and one true morality. Moral absolutists in one sense might not be moral absolutists in other senses. We must be careful not to mix up real issues with purely verbal issues. So let me stipulate that I will take moral absolutism to be a view about the moral reasons people have to do things and to want or hope for things. I will understand a belief about absolute values to be a belief that there are things that everyone has a reason to hope or wish for. To say that there is a moral law that "applies to everyone" is, I hereby stipulate, to say that everyone has sufficient reasons to follow that law.

It is true that many philosophers pursue something that resembles autonomous ethics when they ask what principles an "ideal" moral code of one or another sort would have, quite apart from the question whether people now have any reason to follow that code. Depending on what sort of idealization is being considered, there may or may not be a unique "ideal" code of that sort. But I am not going to count as a form of moral absolutism the claim that there is a unique ideal moral code of such and such a type. Relativists and absolutists in my sense might very well agree about this claim without that having any effect at all on what I take to be the basic issue that separates them, since this claim has no immediate relevance to questions about what reasons people actually have to hope for certain things or do certain things.

Similarly, I am not going to count as a form of moral absolutism the claim that there is one true morality that applies to everyone in that everyone ought to follow it, if this is not taken to imply that everyone has a sufficient reason to follow it. I am not sure what *ought* is supposed to mean if it is disconnected in this way from reasons to do things. If what is meant is that it ought to be the case that everyone followed the one true morality—in other words that it would be a good thing if they did—then this is a version of the view that there is a unique "ideal" moral code. I am not sure what else might be meant, although a great deal more could be said here (Harman 1978a). Rather than try to say it, however, I simply stipulate that this sort of claim is not a version of what I am counting as moral absolutism.

I should note that, of the contemporary philosophers I have identified as absolutists, Baier, Darwall, Donagan, Frankena, Gewirth, Grice, Nagel, and Richards, clearly advocate moral absolutism in this sense. They all think that there are basic moral demands that in some sense every competent adult has reasons to adhere to. I *believe* the others I mentioned—namely Rawls, Nozick, and Fried—also agree with this, although they do not explicitly say so in the works I have cited.

DOES A SINGLE MORAL LAW APPLY TO EVERYONE?

Consider the issue between absolutism and relativism concerning reasons people have for doing things. According to moral absolutism about this, there is a single moral law that applies to everyone; in other words, there are moral demands that everyone has sufficient reasons to follow, and these demands are the source of all moral reasons. Moral relativism denies that there are universal basic moral demands and says different people are subject to different basic moral demands depending on the social customs, practices, conventions, values, and principles that they accept.

For example, a moral absolutist might suppose there is a basic moral prohibition on causing harm or injury to other people. This prohibition is in one sense not absolute, since it can be overridden by more compelling considerations and since it allows exceptions in order to punish criminals, for instance. But the prohibition is supposed to be universal in the sense that it applies to absolutely all agents and not just to those who happen to participate in certain conventions. The absolutist claims that absolutely everyone has sufficient reasons to observe this prohibition and to act as it and other basic moral requirements dictate.

A moral relativist denies this and claims that many people have no reasons to observe this prohibition. Many people participate in moralities that sharply distinguish insiders and outsiders and do not prohibit harm or injury to outsiders, except perhaps as this is likely to lead to retaliation against insiders. A person participating in such a morality has no reason to avoid harm or injury to outsiders, according to the relativist, and so the general prohibition does not apply to that person. Such a person may be a member of some primitive tribal group, but he or she need not be. He or she might also be part of contemporary society, a successful professional criminal, say, who recognizes various obligations to other members of a criminal organization but not to those on the outside. According to the moral relativist, the successful criminal may well have no reason at all not to harm his or her victims.

An Argument for Relativism

Let us concentrate on this case. The moral absolutist says the demands of the one true morality apply as much to this successful criminal as to anyone else, so this criminal does have a reason not to harm a given victim. The relativist denies the criminal has any such reason and so denies the relevant moral demand is a universal demand that applies to everyone. Here naturalism tends to support relativism in the following way.

Consider what it is for someone to have a sufficient reason to do something. Naturalism requires that this should be explained in terms congenial to science. We cannot simply treat this as irreducibly normative, saying, for example, that someone has a sufficient reason to do something if and only if he or she ought to do it. Now, presumably, someone has a sufficient reason to do something if and only if there is warranted reasoning that person could do which would lead him or her to decide to do that thing. A naturalist will suppose that a person with a sufficient reason to do something might fail to reason in this way to such a decision only because of some sort of empirically discoverable failure, due to inattention, or lack of time, or failure to consider or appreciate certain arguments, or ignorance of certain available evidence, or an error in reasoning, or some sort of irrationality or unreasonableness, or weakness of will. If the person does not intend to do something and that is not because he or she has failed in some such empirically discoverable way to reason to a decision to do that thing, then, according to the naturalist, that person cannot have a sufficient reason to do that thing. This is the first premise in a naturalistic argument in support of the relativist.

The other premise is that there are people, such as certain professional criminals, who do not act in accordance with the alleged requirement not to harm or injure others, where this is not due to inattention or failure to consider or appreciate certain arguments, or ignorance of certain evidence, or any errors in reasoning, or any sort of irrationality or unreasonableness, or weakness of will. The argument for this is simply that there clearly are people who do not adhere to the requirement in question and who do not *seem* to have failed in any of these ways. So, in the absence of special theoretical reasons, deriving, say, from psychology, to think these people must have failed in one of the specified ways, we can conclude they have not done so.

From these two premises it follows that there are people who do not have sufficient reasons, and therefore do not have sufficient moral reasons, to adhere to the general prohibition against harming or injuring others. In particular, a successful criminal may not have a sufficient reason not to harm his or her victims. The moral prohibition against harming others may simply fail to apply to such a person. It may fail to apply in the relevant sense, which is of course not to say that the principle makes an explicit exception for criminals, allowing them but not others to injure and harm people without restraint. Rather, the principle may fail to apply in the sense that the criminal in question may fail to have sufficient reason to act in accordance with the principle.

An Absolutist Reply

Moral absolutism must reject this argument. It can do so by invoking autonomous ethics at the place at which moral relativism invokes naturalism. Autonomous ethics does not suppose that we must give some sort of naturalistic account of having a sufficient reason to do something, nor does it suppose that only a science like psychology can discover the conditions under which someone has failed to reason in a certain way because of inattention, irrationality, unreasonableness, or any of the other causes of failure mentioned in the relativistic argument.

Autonomous ethics approaches this issue in the following way. We begin with certain beliefs. Presumably these imply that everyone has a sufficient reason to observe the prohibition against harm to others, including, in particular, the successful criminal who does not participate in or accept any practice of observing this general prohibition. At the start we therefore believe that the criminal does have sufficient reason not to harm his or her victims. Following autonomous ethics, then, we should continue to believe this unless such continued belief conflicts with generalizations or other theoretical principles internal to ethics that we find attractive because they do a better job at making sense of most of the things we originally believe. Taking this approach, the absolutist must claim that the relativistic argument does not provide sufficient reason to abandon our original absolutism. It is more plausible, according to the absolutist, that at least one of the premises of the relativistic argument is false than that its conclusion is true.

Assessing the First Premise

The first premise of the relativistic argument is that for someone to
have a sufficient reason to do something there must be warranted reasoning
available to that person that leads to a decision to do that thing, so that
if the person fails to intend to do that thing it must be because of
inattention, lack of time, failure to consider or appreciate certain arguments, ignorance of relevant evidence, an error in reasoning, irrationality, unreasonableness, or weakness of will. The absolutist might
object that this is oversimplified. If a person with sufficient reason to
do something does not do it, then something has gone wrong, and it
might be one of the things the relativist mentions, but it might be
something else as well. There might be something wrong with the *person*
in question. That person might be bad, immoral. The failure might
simply be a failure not to care enough about other people. A person
ought to care about others and there is something wrong with a person
who does not care, even if that person is not inattentive, ignorant,
rushed, or defective in any other of the particular ways the relativist
mentions. So, even if some people fail to observe the prohibition against
harming others not because of inattention, lack of time, and so forth,
but simply because of lack of concern and respect for others, such people
still do have sufficient reason not to harm others. (This response on
behalf of absolutism was suggested to me by Thomas M. Scanlon.)

The response to the relativistic argument is a response within autonomous ethics. It does not explain having a sufficient reason to do
something in terms that are acceptably factual from a naturalistic perspective. It appeals also to the notion of something's being wrong with
someone, where what might be wrong is simply that the person is bad
or immoral. It is like saying one has a sufficient reason to do something
if and only if one ought to do it, or if and only if it would be wrong
not to do it.

The relativist claims that the only plausible accounts of these normative
notions are relativistic ones. There is no prohibition on harm to outsiders
in the criminals' morality. There is such a prohibition only in some
other morality. In that other morality something is wrong with a person
who has no compunction about injuring someone else; but nothing is
wrong with such a person with respect to the criminal morality, as long
as those injured are outsiders. But how can it be a sufficient reason for
the criminal not to harm his or her victims that this is prohibited by
somebody else's morality? How can its being bad, immoral, or wrong
in this other morality not to care about and respect others give the
criminal, who does not accept that morality, a sufficient reason to do
anything?

The absolutist's answer is that failure to respect others is not just wrong according to some morality the criminal does not accept, it is also wrong, period. Something is really wrong with lack of respect and concern for others. It is not just wrong in relation to one or another morality. Of course, the relativist will not be satisfied with this answer and, appealing to naturalism, will ask what it is for something to be wrong in this way. The absolutist supposes that the failure to care about and respect others does involve something the absolutist points to by saying this failure is wrong. But what is this thing that is true of such a failure to care and that can give the criminal a sufficient reason not to harm and injure others? The relativist can see no aspect of such a failure that could provide such a reason. This of course is because the relativist, as a naturalist, considers only aspects of the failure that are clearly compatible with a scientific world view. The relativist disregards putative aspects that can be specified only in normative terms. But the absolutist, as an autonomist, can specify the relevant aspect of such a failure to care about others: It is bad, immoral, wrong not to care; the criminal ought to have this concern and respect and so ought not to harm and injure others, and therefore has a sufficient reason not to harm and injure them.

Assessing the Second Premise

We have been discussing an argument for relativism concerning moral reasons. We have seen that naturalism supports the first premise of this argument and that autonomous ethics allows the rejection of this premise. The same thing is true of the second premise, which says that there are people, such as the successful criminal, who do not observe the alleged requirement not to harm or injure others and this is not due to inattention, failure to consider or appreciate certain arguments, ignorance of relevant evidence, errors in reasoning, irrationality, unreasonableness, or weakness of will. Naturalism supports this because there do seem to be such people, and no scientifically acceptable grounds exist for thinking this is an illusion. On the other hand, autonomous ethics allows other grounds, not reducible to scientific grounds, for thinking this is an illusion. In autonomous ethics we begin by supposing that we recognize the wrongness of harming others, where this is to recognize a sufficient reason not to harm others. If that is something we recognize, then it must be there to be recognized, so the successful criminal in question must be failing to recognize and appreciate something that is there.

The absolutist might argue that the criminal must be irrational or at least unreasonable. Seeing that a proposed course of action will probably cause serious injury to some outsider, the criminal does not treat this as a reason not to undertake that course of action. This must be irrational or unreasonable, because such a consideration simply is such a reason and indeed is an obvious reason, a basic reason, not one that has to be derived in some complex way through arcane reasoning. But then it must be irrational or at least unreasonable for the criminal not to care sufficiently about others, since the criminal's lack of concern for others is what is responsible for the criminal's not taking the likelihood of harm to an outsider to be a reason against a proposed course of action. This is one way an absolutist might argue.

The relativist's reply to such an argument is that, on any plausible characterization of reasonableness and unreasonableness (or rationality and irrationality) as notions that can be part of the scientific conception of the world, the absolutist's claim is just false. Someone can be completely rational without feeling concern and respect for outsiders. But of course this reply appeals to naturalism. The absolutist who rejects naturalism in favor of autonomous ethics relies on an unreduced normative characterization of rationality and irrationality (or reasonableness and unreasonableness).

Now the argument continues as before. The relativist argues that, if rationality and irrationality (or reasonableness and unreasonableness) are conceived normatively, they become relative notions. What one morality counts as irrational or unreasonable, another does not. The criminal is not irrational or unreasonable in relation to criminal morality, but only in relation to a morality the criminal rejects. But the fact that it is irrational or unreasonable in relation to this other morality not to have concern and respect for others does not give the criminal who rejects that morality any reason to avoid harming or injuring others. The absolutist replies that relative irrationality or unreasonableness is not what is in question. The criminal is irrational or at least unreasonable, period. Not just irrational or unreasonable in relation to a morality he or she does not accept. Since it is irrational or unreasonable for anyone not to care sufficiently about others, everyone has a sufficient reason not to injure others, whether he or she recognizes this reason or, through irrationality or unreasonableness, does not recognize it.

The naturalist is unconvinced by this because the naturalist can find no aspect of the criminal the absolutist might be referring to in saying the criminal is "irrational" or "unreasonable," if this aspect is to give the criminal any reason to care about others. This of course is because the naturalist is considering only naturalistic aspects of the criminal, whereas the absolutist, as an autonomist, is thinking about an unreduced normative aspect, something the naturalist cannot appeal to.

So, as was true of the first premise of the relativistic argument about reasons, the second premise depends on an assumption of naturalism. By appealing to autonomous ethics, an absolutist can reject this premise.

An absolutist may in fact actually accept one or the other of the premises of the relativistic argument (although of course not both). A given absolutist might reject either the first premise or the second or both premises. An absolutist might even be undecided, holding merely that one or the other premise must be rejected, without saying which. There is nothing wrong with being undecided about this. Reflective equilibrium leaves many issues unresolved.

ARE THERE ABSOLUTE MORAL VALUES?

The situation is similar in the theory of value. Naturalism tends to support the conclusion that all value is relative and that something is always good for one or another person or group of people or in relation to a specified set of purposes or interests or aims. Autonomous ethics allows also for absolute values, things that are good, period, and not just good for someone or some group or for some purpose.

The issue here concerns the goodness or value of a possible state of affairs, not the goodness or value of something as a thing of a given sort. The issue is not what it is for something to be a good thing of a kind, a good knife, a good watch, a good backswing, a good apple, a good farmer, a good poem. The issue is rather what it is for an event or situation to be a good thing; what is it, for example, to be a good thing that it is raining or that Egypt and Israel signed a peace treaty.

It is uncontroversial that this sort of goodness is sometimes relational. A situation is good for someone or some group of people, good from a certain point of view, in relation to certain purposes or interests. That it is raining is a good thing for the farmer, but not for the vacationer. That Egypt and Israel signed a peace treaty might be good from their point of view, but not from the point of view of the PLO. Given a fixed point of reference, we can evaluate states of affairs as better or worse. The value of a state of affairs in relation to that reference point represents the degree to which someone with the relevant purposes and interests has a reason to try to bring about, or want, or at least hope for that state of affairs.

Now it can be argued that there is also a kind of absolute value. The claim is that states of affairs can be good or bad, period, and not merely good or bad for someone or in relation to given purposes or interests. On hearing of pointless painful experiments on laboratory animals, for example, one immediately reacts with the thought that this is bad and it would be good to eliminate such practices. Clearly, one does not simply mean that these tortures are bad for the animals involved and that these animals would benefit if such experiments were ended. A heartless experimenter might agree that what he does is bad for the animals without having to agree that it would be a good thing to eliminate this sort of experimentation. Similarly, it seems intelligible to suppose that it would be better if there were no inequalities of wealth and income in the world even though this would not be better for everyone, not for those who are now relatively wealthy, for instance. And this seems to say more, for example, than that the average person would be better off if there were no such inequalities, since an elitist might agree with that but not agree that the envisioned state of affairs would be better, period, than our present situation. Again, we can consider which of various population policies would lead to the best resulting state of affairs even though these policies would result in different populations, so that we cannot be simply considering the interests and purposes of some fixed group. It may seem, then, that we can consider the absolute value of a possible state of affairs.

Skepticism about Absolute Values

The relative value of a possible state of affairs in relation to given purposes and interests is a measure of the extent to which someone with those purposes and interests has a reason to try to bring about, or want, or hope for that state of affairs. The absolute value of a possible state of affairs is a measure of the extent to which anyone, apart from having a personal stake in the matter, has a reason to try to bring about, or want, or hope for that state of affairs. Naturalism leads to skepticism at this point. How could we ever be aware of absolute values? How could we ever know that everyone has a reason to want a certain possible state of affairs?

Further reflection along naturalistic lines suggests that apparent absolute values are often illusory projections of one's personal values onto the world. Sometimes this sort of projection yields plausible results, but usually it does not. To begin with the most plausible sort of case, in hearing about the pain involved in animal experimentation, our sympathies are immediately and vividly engaged; we immediately side with the animals against the experimenters. In saying "That is awful!" we are not just saying "That is awful for the animals," since our remark expresses our sympathetic identification with the point of view of the animals. We do not merely state a fact, we express our feelings and we expect an awareness of this state of affairs to call forth the same feelings of dismay in everyone. This expectation seems reasonable enough in this case, since it may well be, as Brandt argues, that everyone has a sympathetic reaction to suffering (1976, p. 450).

But plausibility vanishes as soon as the case becomes even a little complex. Suppose the animal experiments are not pointless but are an essential part of a kind of medical research that promises to alleviate a certain amount of human suffering. Or suppose that, although the experiments promise no practical benefit of this sort, they are relevant to a theoretical issue in psychology. A given person may still feel that it is bad that the experiments should occur and that it would be good if they were not done, the gain not being worth the cost. Again, the person is not just saying that the experiments are bad for the animals, something to which everyone would agree. He or she is also expressing overall disapproval of the experiments, expecting others also to disapprove if they consider the issue in an impartial way. The trouble is that people react differently to these cases.

Consider the question whether it is good or bad to experiment painfully on animals in order to resolve certain theoretical issues in psychology. The extent to which this is (absolutely) good is the extent to which everyone (apart from any personal stake in the matter) has a reason to try to bring it about that such experiments are done, or to want them to be done, or hope that they are done. The extent to which this is (absolutely) bad is the extent to which everyone (apart from any personal stake) has a reason to try to end the experiments, or want them to end, or hope they end. But naturalism suggests that there is no unique answer here and that what a person has a reason to want will depend on the relative value he or she attaches to animal suffering, to using animals as means, and to theoretical progress in psychology. Different people attach different values to these things without having overlooked something, without being irrational or unreasonable, and so on. So it seems that some people will have reason to be in favor of the experiments and others will have reason to be opposed to the experiments, where this is determined by the personal values of those people. If we suppose that our answer is the right answer, we are merely projecting our own values onto the world.

The Issue Joined

Of course, autonomous ethics sees nothing wrong with projecting our own values onto the world, holding in fact that that is exactly the right method! We should begin with our initial valuations and modify them only in the interests of theoretical simplicity. If we start out believing in absolute values, we should continue believing this until forced to believe otherwise.

Clearly the controversy over absolute values parallels the controversy about reasons to do things. The argument against absolute values has the same structure as the relativistic argument about reasons to do things. Its first premise is that a person has a reason to want or hope for or try to bring about a particular state of affairs only to the extent that he or she would be irrational or unreasonable not to want that state of affairs unless he or she was unaware of some relevant consideration, was confused, or had some other specified defect. Its second premise is that, except for the simplest cases, a person can fail to want a given state of affairs without being irrational or unreasonable or ignorant or whatever. The conclusion is that, except possibly for simple cases, where, for example, the only thing relevant is that a creature suffers, there are no reasons everyone has to want or hope for or try to bring about a given state of affairs. So there are no nontrivial absolute values.

As before, the two premises are defended in each case by an appeal to naturalism: We must give a naturalistic account of reasons and we must give empirical grounds for supposing someone to be irrational or unreasonable. The absolutist rejects the argument as before by invoking autonomous ethics, perhaps by rejecting the naturalistic account of reasons, perhaps by rejecting the requirement that scientific grounds must be given for a judgment of irrationality or unreasonableness, possibly remaining undecided between these alternatives.

NATURALISM VERSUS AUTONOMOUS ETHICS

So the issue between relativism and absolutism comes down to the dispute between naturalism and autonomous ethics. Which is the best approach in moral philosophy? Should we concentrate on the place of values and reasons in the world of scientific fact, as naturalism recommends, or should we start with our initial moral beliefs and look for general principles and moral theories that will eventually yield a reflective equilibrium, not putting too much weight on the question of the place of value in the world of facts.

Religious Beliefs

In thinking of the issue between naturalism and autonomous ethics, it is useful to consider analogous issues that arise in other areas. Consider religious beliefs. Our scientific conception of the world has no place for gods, angels, demons, or devils. Naturalists hold that there is no empirical evidence for the existence of such beings nor for any sort of divine intervention in human history. Naturalists say that people's religious beliefs can be explained in terms of their upbringing and psychology without any supernatural assumptions, so these beliefs provide no evidence whatsoever for the truth of religious claims. Naturalists therefore incline toward skepticism and atheism, although naturalism might also lead to a kind of religious noncognitivism which supposes that religious language makes no factual claims about a supernatural realm but has a different function, for example, in religious ritual.

Another approach to religion is for a believer to start with his or her initial religious beliefs, including beliefs in the authority of certain writings, and then to develop general principles and theories that would accommodate these beliefs, allowing modifications in the interest of more plausible general principles. This will continue until no further modifications seem useful in improving the organization and coherence of that person's views. Inevitably, many questions will remain unanswered, and these will include issues concerning the relation between that person's religious views and his or her scientific views, for example, as regards creation. But this is not a serious worry for autonomous religion, which will say this shows merely that science is not everything, or at least that there are things we do not now and perhaps never will understand.

Naturalists say there is no reason to accept religious claims, because the fact that people have the religious beliefs they have can be explained without any supernatural assumptions. Religious autonomists say there is reason to accept religious claims, at least for someone who begins with religious beliefs, since the process of generalization, systematization, and theory construction internal to religion will give that person no reason to abandon more than a few, if any, of those religious beliefs. Furthermore, certain supernatural events might be part of the correct explanation of the appearance of sacred texts, the occurrence of miracles, and particular religious experiences. There is at present no way to say how these religious explanations mesh with ordinary scientific conceptions, but that by itself is no more an objection to religion that it is an objection to science.

Naturalists in ethics might urge this religious analogy as an *ad hominem* argument against those defenders of autonomous ethics who are not willing to take the same line with respect to religion.

Beliefs about the Mind

There is another sort of issue in which an autonomous position comes off looking rather good, even in an irreligious age, namely, the so-called mind-body problem. Here the naturalistic position corresponds to the thesis of physicalism, according to which all real aspects of mind must be features of the physical brain and central nervous system, its atomic or neural structure, or some more complex structure that the brain and nervous system instantiate. This may involve behaviorism or some sort of functionalism that treats the brain as an information-processing system like a computer in a robot. A few defenders of this approach, like Skinner (1974), conclude that there are no mental events, no mind, no consciousness, no sensation. (Rorty, 1965, sympathetically describes a similar view, "eliminative materialism.") But most physicalists suppose that mental events and other aspects of mind do exist and can be identified with certain physical or structural or functional aspects of the brain and central nervous system.

On the other side is autonomous mentalism, which holds that the physicalist hypothesis clearly leaves something out. In this view we clearly know we are conscious, can initiate action, and have experiences of a distinctive phenomenological character and feeling. The physicalist hypothesis does not account for this. A computer or robot is not conscious. Although a robot can move, it does not *act* in the way people can act. And a robot has no sensuous experience. Indeed, something could have exactly the functional structure of the human brain and nervous system without being conscious. Block (1978) describes a case in which one billion people in radio communication with each other model a particular brain for an hour, each person corresponding to a particular neuron in the brain. Block takes it to be absurd to suppose that this vast collection of people would have a group consciousness that was phenomenologically the same as the consciousness of the person whose brain and central nervous system was being modeled. Nagel (1979) observes that we might know everything there was to know about the neurophysiological structure and functioning of the brain and central nervous system of a bat without knowing what the experience of the bat was like. Defenders of autonomous mentalism agree that this leaves a mind-body problem, since they are unable to say how consciousness, free will, and sensory experience can be part of the world described by physics. But they deny that this means we must stop believing in consciousness or must identify it with some aspect of physical or functional structure. For they claim, with considerable plausibility, that it is much more reasonable to believe in consciousness, free will, and sensory experience, and to believe that these are not aspects of neurophysiological functional structure, than it is to believe in physicalism.

I am not saying that autonomous mentalism *is* more plausible than physicalism. After all is said and done, I find a physicalistic functionalism more plausible than autonomous mentalism. My point is that autonomous mentalism is a perfectly respectable philosophical position.

A defender of autonomous ethics might even argue that naturalism in ethics loses much of its plausibility once autonomous mentalism is recognized as plausible. For that casts doubt on the universal applicability of the naturalistic approach and therefore casts doubt on the naturalist's argument that a belief that something is right cannot be explained by that thing's being actually right unless that thing's being right consists in some psychological or sociological fact. The naturalist's only argument for this, it might be said, depends on accepting the general applicability of naturalism. But it is not obvious that this approach is generally applicable, since it is not obviously correct as compared with autonomous mentalism. There is at least some plausibility to the claim that one's awareness of what red looks like is to be explained by appeal to an experience of redness that does not consist entirely in some neurophysiological event. It might be said that the naturalist has no argument against autonomous ethics, since the naturalist cannot take for granted the general applicability of naturalism.

Ethics

Defenders of autonomous ethics argue that their approach represents the only undogmatic way to proceed. They say that naturalism begs the question in supposing that everything true must fit into a scientific account of the world and by supposing that the central question about morality is how, if at all, morality fits into such a scientific account.

Defenders of naturalism reply that naturalism itself is the result of following the method of reflective equilibrium, and that autonomous ethics begs the question by assigning a specially protected status to initial moral beliefs as compared, say, with initial beliefs about the flatness of the earth or the influence of the stars on human history. Naturalists say that, starting with our initial beliefs, we are led to develop a scientific conception of the world as an account of everything there is. In doing so, we also acquire beliefs about how we learn about the world and about how errors can arise in our thinking. We come to see how superstition arises. We begin to worry about our moral views: Are they mere superstitions? We note certain sorts of disagreement in morality and extreme differences in moral customs. We observe that some people are not much influenced by what we consider important moral considerations. All this leads us to raise as a central question about morality how morality fits in with our scientific conception of the world. Naturalism is no mere prejudice in favor or science; it is an inevitable consequence of intelligent thought. This, at least, is what a defender of naturalism will say.

A defender of autonomous ethics will reply that moral disagreements, differences in custom, and the behavior of criminals prove nothing. All these things are compatible with moral absolutism.

The naturalist retorts that any view can be made *compatible* with the evidence; astrology, for example, is perfectly compatible with the evidence. The issue is not what is compatible with the evidence, but what best accounts for it. The naturalist argues that relativism accounts for the evidence better than absolutism does, since relativism is able to say how reasons and values are part of the world science describes, whereas absolutism is not able to do that.

The defender of autonomous ethics replies that such an argument is no better than the corresponding argument for behaviorism. Behaviorism is able to say how mental states (as it conceives them) are part of the world physics describes and autonomous mentalism is not able to say how mental states (as *it* conceives them) are part of the world physics describes; but one should not for this reason alone abandon one's initial view that one is conscious, makes decisions, has feelings, and so on, where this is not just being disposed to act in various ways (since something could have the dispositions without being conscious and could be conscious without having the dispositions). Similarly, one should not accept the naturalistic argument and give up one's belief in absolute values and universal moral reasons.

I see no knockdown argument for either side. A question of judgment is involved, "Which view is more plausible, all things considered?" To me, the relativistic naturalist position seems more plausible. Others find the absolutist position of autonomous ethics more plausible. I have not tried to show that one side is correct. I have tried to bring out the central issue.

chapter two

Moral Explanations

Nicholas L. Sturgeon

There is one argument for moral skepticism that I respect even though I remain unconvinced. It has sometimes been called the argument from moral diversity or relativity, but that is somewhat misleading, for the problem arises not from the diversity of moral views, but from the apparent difficulty of *settling* moral disagreements, or even of knowing what would be required to settle them, a difficulty thought to be noticeably greater than any found in settling disagreements that arise in, for example, the sciences. This provides an argument for moral skepticism because one obviously possible explanation for our difficulty in settling moral disagreements is that they are really unsettleable, that there is no way of justifying one rather than another competing view on these issues; and a possible further explanation for the unsettleability of moral disagreements, in turn, is moral nihilism, the view that on these issues there just is no fact of the matter, that the impossibility of discovering and establishing moral truths is due to there not being any.

I am, as I say, unconvinced: partly because I think this argument exaggerates the difficulty we actually find in settling moral disagreements, partly because there are alternative explanations to be considered for the difficulty we do find. For example, it certainly matters to what extent moral disagreements depend on disagreements about other questions which, however disputed they may be, are nevertheless regarded as having objective answers: questions such as which, if any, religion is true, which account of human psychology, which theory of human society. And it also matters to what extent consideration of moral questions is in practice skewed by distorting factors such as personal interest and social ideology. These are large issues. Although it is possible to say some useful things to put them in perspective,[1] it appears impossible to settle them quickly or in any a priori way. Consideration of them is likely to have to be piecemeal and, in the short run at least, frustratingly indecisive.

These large issues are not my topic here. But I mention them, and the difficulty of settling them, to show why it is natural that moral skeptics have hoped to find some quicker way of establishing their thesis. I doubt that any exist, but some have of course been proposed. Verificationist attacks on ethics should no doubt be seen in this light, and J. L. Mackie's recent "argument from queerness" is a clear instance (Mackie, 1977, pp. 38–42). The quicker argument on which I shall concentrate, however, is neither of these, but instead an argument by Gilbert Harman designed to bring out the "basic problem" about morality, which in his view is "its apparent immunity from observational testing" and "the seeming irrelevance of observational evidence" (Harman, 1977, pp. vii, viii. Parenthetical page references are to this work). The argument is that reference to moral facts appears unnecessary for the *explanation* of our moral observations and beliefs.

Harman's view, I should say at once, is not in the end a skeptical one, and he does not view the argument I shall discuss as a decisive defense of moral skepticism or moral nihilism. Someone else might easily so regard it, however. For Harman himself regards it as creating a strong *prima facie* case for skepticism and nihilism, strong enough to justify calling it "the problem with ethics."[2] And he believes it shows that the only recourse for someone who wishes to avoid moral skepticism is to find defensible reductive definitions for ethical terms; so skepticism would be the obvious conclusion for anyone to draw who doubted the possibility of such definitions. I believe, however, that Harman is mistaken on both counts. I shall show that his argument for skepticism either rests on claims that most people would find quite implausible (and so cannot be what constitutes, for *them,* the problem with ethics); or else it becomes just the application to ethics of a familiar *general* skeptical strategy, one which, if it works for ethics, will work equally well for unobservable theoretical entities, or for other minds, or for an external world (and so, again, can hardly be what constitutes the distinctive problem with *ethics*). In the course of my argument, moreover, I shall suggest that one can in any case be a moral realist, and indeed an ethical naturalist, without believing that we are now or ever will be in possession of reductive naturalistic definitions for ethical terms.

I. THE PROBLEM WITH ETHICS

Moral theories are often tested in thought experiments, against imagined examples; and, as Harman notes, trained researchers often test scientific theories in the same way. The problem, though, is that scientific theories can also be tested against the world, by observations or real experiments;

and, Harman asks, "can moral principles be tested in the same way, out in the world?" (p. 4)

This would not be a very interesting or impressive challenge, of course, if it were merely a resurrection of standard verificationist worries about whether moral assertions and theories have any testable empirical implications, implications suitable in some relatively austere "observational" vocabulary. One problem with that form of the challenge, as Harman points out, is that there are no "pure" observations, and in consequence no purely observational vocabulary either. But there is also a deeper problem that Harman does not mention, one that remains even if we shelve worries about "pure" observations and, at least for the sake of argument, grant the verificationist his observational language, pretty much as it was usually conceived: that is, as lacking at the very least any obviously theoretical terminology from any recognized science, and of course as lacking any moral terminology. For then the difficulty is that moral principles fare just as well (or just as badly) against the verificationist challenge as do typical scientific principles. For it is by now a familiar point about scientific principles—principles such as Newton's law of universal gravitation or Darwin's theory of evolution— that they are entirely devoid of empirical implications when considered in isolation.[3] We do of course base observational predictions on such theories and so test them against experience, but that is because we do *not* consider them in isolation. For we can derive these predictions only by relying at the same time on a large background of additional assumptions, many of which are equally theoretical and equally incapable of being tested in isolation. A less familiar point, because less often spelled out, is that the relation of moral principles to observation is similar in *both* these respects. Candidate moral principles—for example, that an action is wrong just in case there is something else the agent could have done that would have produced a greater net balance of pleasure over pain—lack empirical implications when considered in isolation. But it is easy to derive empirical consequences from them, and thus to test them against experience, if we allow ourselves, as we do in the scientific case, to rely on a background of other assumptions of comparable status. Thus, if we conjoin the act-utilitarian principle I just cited with the further view, also untestable in isolation, that it is always wrong deliberately to kill a human being, we can deduce from these two premises together the consequence that deliberately killing a human being always produces a lesser balance of pleasure over pain than some available alternative act; and this claim is one any positivist would have conceded we know, in principle at least, how to test. If we found it to be false, moreover, then we would be forced by this empirical test to abandon at least one of the moral claims from which we derived it.

It might be thought a worrisome feature of this example, however, and a further opening for skepticism, that there could be controversy about which moral premise to abandon, and that we have not explained how our empirical test can provide an answer to *this* question. And this may be a problem. It should be a familiar problem, however, because the Duhemian commentary includes a precisely corresponding point about the scientific case: that if we are at all cautious in characterizing what we observe, then the requirement that our theories merely be *consistent* with observation is an astoundingly weak one. There are always many, perhaps indefinitely many, different mutually inconsistent ways to adjust our views to meet this constraint. Of course, in practice we are often confident of how to do it: If you are a freshman chemistry student, you do not conclude from your failure to obtain the predicted value in an experiment that it is all over for the atomic theory of gases. And the decision can be equally easy, one should note, in a moral case. Consider two examples. From the surprising moral thesis that Adolf Hitler was a morally admirable person, together with a modest piece of moral theory to the effect that no morally admirable person would, for example, instigate and oversee the degradation and death of millions of persons, one can derive the testable consequence that Hitler did not do this. But he did, so we must give up one of our premises; and the choice of which to abandon is neither difficult nor controversial.

Or, to take a less monumental example, contrived around one of Harman's own, suppose you have been thinking yourself lucky enough to live in a neighborhood in which no one would do anything wrong, at least not in public; and that the modest piece of theory you accept, this time, is that malicious cruelty, just for the hell of it, is wrong. Then, as in Harman's example, "you round a corner and see a group of young hoodlums pour gasoline on a cat and ignite it." At this point, either your confidence in the neighborhood or your principle about cruelty has got to give way. But the choice is easy, if dispiriting, so easy as hardly to require thought. As Harman says, "You do not need to *conclude* that what they are doing is wrong; you do not need to figure anything out; you can *see* that it is wrong" (p. 4). But a skeptic can still wonder whether this practical confidence, or this "seeing," rests in either sort of case on anything more than deeply ingrained conventions of thought—respect for scientific experts, say, and for certain moral traditions—as opposed to anything answerable to the facts of the matter, any reliable strategy for getting it right about the world.

Now, Harman's challenge is interesting partly because it does not rest on these verificationist doubts about whether moral beliefs have observational implications, but even more because what it does rest on is a partial answer to the kind of general skepticism to which, as we have seen, reflection on the verificationist picture can lead. Many of our beliefs are justified, in Harman's view, by their providing or helping to provide a reasonable *explanation* of our observing what we do. It would be consistent with your failure, as a beginning student, to obtain the experimental result predicted by the gas laws, that the laws are mistaken. That would even be one explanation of your failure. But a better explanation, in light of your inexperience and the general success experts have had in confirming and applying these laws, is that you made some mistake in running the experiment. So our scientific beliefs can be justified by their explanatory role; and so too, in Harman's view, can mathematical beliefs and many commonsense beliefs about the world.

Not so, however, moral beliefs: They appear to have no such explanatory role. That is "the problem with ethics." Harman spells out his version of this contrast:

> You need to make assumptions about certain physical facts to explain the occurrence of the observations that support a scientific theory, but you do not seem to need to make assumptions about any moral facts to explain the occurrence of the so-called moral observations I have been talking about. In the moral case, it would seem that you need only make assumptions about the psychology or moral sensibility of the person making the moral observation. (p. 6)

More precisely, and applied to his own example, it might be reasonable, in order to explain your judging that the hoodlums are wrong to set the cat on fire, to assume "that the children really are pouring gasoline on a cat and you are seeing them do it." But there is no

> obvious reason to assume anything about "moral facts," such as that it is really wrong to set the cat on fire. . . . Indeed, an assumption about moral facts would seem to be totally irrelevant to the explanation of your making the judgment you make. It would seem that all we need assume is that you have certain more or less well articulated moral principles that are reflected in the judgments you make, based on your moral sensibility. (p. 7)

And Harman thinks that if we accept this conclusion, suitably generalized, then, subject to a possible qualification I shall come to shortly, we must conclude that moral theories cannot be tested against the world as scientific theories can, and that we have no reason to believe that moral facts are part of the order of nature or that there is any moral knowledge (pp. 23, 35).

My own view is that Harman is quite wrong, not in thinking that the explanatory role of our beliefs is important to their justification, but in thinking that moral beliefs play no such role.[4] I shall have to say something about the initial plausibility of Harman's thesis as applied to his own example, but part of my reason for dissenting should be apparent from the other example I just gave. We find it easy (and so does Harman [p. 108]) to conclude from the evidence not just that Hitler was not morally admirable, but that he was morally depraved. But isn't it plausible that Hitler's moral depravity—the fact of his really having been morally depraved—forms part of a reasonable explanation of why we believe he was depraved? I think so, and I shall argue concerning this and other examples that moral beliefs commonly play the explanatory role Harman denies them. Before I can press my case, however, I need to clear up several preliminary points about just what Harman is claiming and just how his argument is intended to work.

II. OBSERVATION, EXPLANATION, AND REDUCTION

(1) For there are several ways in which Harman's argument invites misunderstanding. One results from his focusing at the start on the question of whether there can be moral *observations*.[5] But this question turns out to be a side issue, in no way central to his argument that moral principles cannot be tested against the world. There are a couple of reasons for this, of which the more important[6] by far is that Harman does not really require of moral facts, if belief in them is to be justified, that they figure in the explanation of moral observations. It would be enough, on the one hand, if they were needed for the explanation of moral beliefs that are not in any interesting sense observations. For example, Harman thinks belief in moral facts would be vindicated if they were needed to explain our drawing the moral conclusions we do when we reflect on hypothetical cases, but I think there is no illumination in calling these conclusions observations.[7] It would also be enough, on the other hand, if moral facts were needed for the explanation of what were clearly observations, but not moral observations. Harman thinks mathematical beliefs are justified, but he does not suggest that there are mathematical observations; it is rather that appeal to mathematical truths helps to explain why we make the physical observations we do (p. 10). Moral beliefs would surely be justified, too, if they played such a role, whether or not there are any moral observations.

So the claim is that moral facts are not needed to explain our having any of the moral beliefs we do, whether or not those beliefs are observations, and are equally unneeded to explain any of the observations we make, whether or not those observations are moral. In fact, Harman's view appears to be that moral facts aren't needed to explain anything at all: although it would perhaps be question-begging for him to begin with this strong a claim, since he grants that if there were any moral facts, then appeal to other moral facts, more general ones, for example, might be needed to explain *them* (p. 8). But he is certainly claiming, at the very least, that moral facts aren't needed to explain any nonmoral facts we have any reason to believe in.

This claim has seemed plausible even to some philosophers who wish to defend the existence of moral facts and the possibility of moral knowledge. Thus, Thomas Nagel has recently retreated to the reply that

> it begs the question to assume that *explanatory* necessity is the test of reality in this area. . . . To assume that only what has to be included in the best explanatory picture of the world is real, is to assume that there are no irreducibly normative truths.[8]

But this retreat will certainly make it more difficult to fit moral knowledge into anything like a causal theory of knowledge, which seems plausible for many other cases, or to follow Hilary Putman's suggestion that we "apply a generally causal account of reference . . . to moral terms" (Putnam, 1975, p. 290). In addition, the concession is premature in any case, for I shall argue that moral facts do fit into our explanatory view of the world, and in particular into explanations of many moral observations and beliefs.

(2) Other possible misunderstandings concern what is meant in asking whether reference to moral facts is *needed* to explain moral beliefs. One warning about this question I save for my comments on reduction below; but another, about what Harman is clearly *not* asking, and about what sort of answer I can attempt to defend to the question he is asking, can be spelled out first. For, to begin with, Harman's question is clearly not just whether there is *an* explanation of our moral beliefs that does not mention moral facts. Almost surely there is. Equally surely, however, there is *an* explanation of our commonsense nonmoral beliefs that does not mention an external world: one which cites only our sensory experience, for example, together with whatever needs to be said about our psychology to explain why with that history of experience we would form just the beliefs we do. Harman means to be asking a question that will lead to skepticism about moral facts, but not to skepticism about the existence of material bodies or about well-established scientific theories of the world.

Harman illustrates the kind of question he is asking, and the kind of answer he is seeking, with an example from physics which it will be useful to keep in mind. A physicist sees a vapor trail in a cloud chamber and thinks, "There goes a proton." What explains his thinking this? Partly, of course, his psychological set, which largely depends on his beliefs about the apparatus and all the theory he has learned; but partly also, perhaps, the hypothesis that "there really was a proton going through the cloud chamber, causing the vapor trail, which he saw as a proton."

We will *not* need this latter assumption, however, "if his having made that observation could have been equally well explained by his psychological set alone, without the need for any assumption about a proton" (p. 6).[9] So for reference to moral facts to be *needed* in the explanation of our beliefs and observations, is for this reference to be required for an explanation that is somehow *better* than competing explanations. Correspondingly, reference to moral facts will be unnecessary to an explanation, in Harman's view, not just because we can find some explanation that does not appeal to them, but because *no* explanation that appeals to them is any better than some competing explanation that does not.

Now, fine discriminations among competing explanations of almost anything are likely to be difficult, controversial, and provisional. Fortunately, however, my discussion of Harman's argument will not require any fine discriminations. This is because Harman's thesis, as we have seen, is *not* that moral explanations lose out by a small margin; nor is it that moral explanations, although sometimes initially promising, always turn out on further examination to be inferior to nonmoral ones. It is, rather, that reference to moral facts always looks, right from the start, to be "completely irrelevant" to the explanation of any of our observations and beliefs. And my argument will be that this is mistaken: that many moral explanations appear to be good explanations, or components in good explanations, that are not obviously undermined by anything else that we know. My suspicion, in fact, is that moral facts are needed in the sense explained, that they will turn out to belong in our best overall explanatory picture of the world, even in the long run, but I shall not attempt to establish that here. Indeed, it should be clear why I could not pretend to do so. For I have explicitly put to one side the issue (which I regard as incapable in any case of quick resolution) of whether and to what extent actual moral disagreements can be settled satisfactorily. But I assume it would count as a defect in any sort of explanation to rely on claims about which rational agreement proved unattainable. So I concede that it *could* turn out, for anything I say here, that moral explanations are all defective and should be discarded. What I shall try to show is merely that many moral explanations look reasonable enough to be in the running; and, more specifically, that nothing Harman says provides any reason for thinking they are not. This claim is surely strong enough (and controversial enough) to be worth defending.

(3) It is implicit in this statement of my project, but worth noting separately, that I take Harman to be proposing an *independent* skeptical argument—independent not merely of the argument from the difficulty of settling disputed moral questions, but also of other standard arguments for moral skepticism. Otherwise his exposition is entirely misleading

(and his argument, I think, not worth independent discussion). For *any* of these more familiar skeptical arguments will of course imply that moral explanations are defective, on the reasonable assumption that it would be a defect in any explanation to rely on claims as doubtful as these arguments attempt to show all moral claims to be. But if *that* is why there is a problem with moral explanations, one should surely just cite the relevant skeptical argument, rather than this derivative difficulty about moral explanations, as the basic "problem with ethics," and it is that argument we should discuss. So I take Harman's interesting suggestion to be that there is a *different* difficulty that remains even if we put other arguments for moral skepticism aside and *assume,* for the sake of argument, that there are moral facts (for example, that what the children in his example are doing is really wrong): namely, that these assumed facts *still* seem to play no explanatory role.

This understanding of Harman's thesis crucially affects my argumentative strategy in a way to which I should alert the reader in advance. For it should be clear that assessment of this thesis not merely permits, but *requires,* that we provisionally assume the existence of moral facts. I can see no way of evaluating the claim that *even if* we assumed the existence of moral facts they would still appear explanatorily irrelevant, without assuming the existence of some, to see how they would look. So I do freely assume this in each of the examples I discuss in the next section. (I have tried to choose plausible examples, moreover, moral facts most of us would be inclined to believe in if we did believe in moral facts, since those are the easiest to think about; but the precise examples don't matter, and anyone who would prefer others should feel free to substitute his own.) I grant, furthermore, that if Harman were right about the outcome of this thought experiment—that even after we assumed these facts they still looked irrelevant to the explanation of our moral beliefs and of other nonmoral facts—then we might conclude with him that there were, after all, no such facts. But I claim he is wrong: Once we have provisionally assumed the existence of moral facts, they *do* appear relevant, by perfectly ordinary standards, to the explanation of moral beliefs and of a good deal else besides. Does this prove that there *are* such facts? Well of course it helps support that view, but here I carefully make no claim to have shown so much. What I *show* is that any remaining reservations about the existence of moral facts must be based on those *other* skeptical arguments, of which Harman's argument is independent. In short, there may still be a "problem with ethics," but it has *nothing* special to do with moral explanations.

(4) A final preliminary point concerns a qualification Harman adds himself. As I have explained his argument so far, it assumes that we could have reason to believe in moral facts only if this helped us "explain

why we observe what we observe" (p. 13); but, he says, this assumption is too strong, for we can have evidence for the truth of some beliefs that play no such explanatory role. We might, for example, come to be able to explain color perception without saying that objects have colors, by citing certain physical and psychological facts. But this would not show that there are no colors; it would show only that facts about color are "somehow reducible" to these physical and psychological facts. And this leaves the possibility that moral facts, too, even if they ultimately play no explanatory role themselves, might be "reducible to certain other facts that can help explain our observations" (p. 14). So a crucial question is: What would justify a belief in reducibility? What makes us think color facts might be reducible to physical (or physical and psychological) facts, and what would justify us in thinking moral facts reducible to explanatory natural facts of some kind?

Harman's answer is that it is still the *apparent* explanatory role of color facts, or of moral facts, that matters; and hence that this qualification to his argument is not so great as it might seem. We know of no precise reduction for facts of either sort. We believe even so that reduction is possible for color facts because even when we are able to explain color perception without saying that objects are colored,

> we will still *sometimes* refer to the actual colors of objects in explaining color perception, if only for the sake of simplicity. . . . We will continue to believe that objects have colors because we will continue to refer to the actual colors of objects in the explanations that we will in practice give.

But Harman thinks that no comparable point holds for moral facts. "There does not ever seem to be, even in practice, any point to explaining someone's moral observations by appeal to what is actually right or wrong, just or unjust, good or bad" (p. 22).

Now I shall argue shortly that this is just wrong: that sober people frequently offer such explanations of moral observations and beliefs, and that many of these explanations look plausible enough on the evidence to be worth taking seriously.[10] So a quick reply to Harman, strictly adequate for my purpose, would be simply to accept his concession that this by itself should lead us to regard moral facts as (at worst) reducible to explanatory facts.[11] Concern about the need for, and the role of, reductive definitions has been so central to meta-ethical discussion in this century, however, and has also proved enough of a sticking point in discussions I have had of the topic of this essay, that I should say a bit more.

As a philosophical naturalist, I take natural facts to be the only facts there are.[12] If I am prepared to recognize moral facts, therefore, I must take them, too, to be natural facts: But which natural facts? It is widely thought that an ethical naturalist must answer this question by providing reductive naturalistic definitions[13] for moral terms and, indeed, that until one has supplied such definitions one's credentials as a *naturalist* about any supposed moral facts must be in doubt. Once such definitions are in hand, however, it seems that moral explanations should be dispensable, since any such explanations can then be paraphrased in nonmoral terms; so it is hard to see why an ethical naturalist should attach any importance to them. Now, there are several problems with this reasoning, but the main one is that the widely held view on which it is based is mistaken: mistaken about where a scheme of reductive naturalistic definitions would be found, if there were to be one, but also about whether, on a naturalistic view of ethics, one should expect there to be such a thing at all. I shall take up these points in reverse order, arguing first (a) that it is a mistake to require of ethical naturalism that it even promise reductive definitions for moral terms, and then (b) that even if such definitions are to be forthcoming it is, at the very least, no special problem for ethical naturalism that we are not *now* in confident possession of them.

(a) Naturalism is in one clear sense a "reductionist" doctrine of course, for it holds that moral facts are nothing but natural facts. What I deny, however, is that from this metaphysical doctrine about what sort of facts moral facts are, anything follows about the possibility of reduction in another sense (to which I shall henceforth confine the term) more familiar from the philosophical literature: that is, about whether moral explanations can be given reductive definitions in some distinctive nonmoral vocabulary, in which any plausible moral explanations could then be recast. The difficulty with supposing naturalism to require this can be seen by pressing the question of just what this distinctive vocabularly is supposed to be. It is common to say merely that this reducing terminology must be "factual" or "descriptive" or must designate natural properties; but unless ethical naturalism has already been ruled out, this is no help, for what naturalists of course contend is that moral discourse is *itself* factual and descriptive (although it may be other things as well), and that moral terms themselves stand for natural properties. The idea, clearly, is supposed to be that the *test* of whether these naturalistic claims about moral discourse are correct is whether this discourse is reducible to some other; but what other? I consider two possibilities.

(i) Many would agree that it is too restrictive to understand ethical naturalism as requiring that moral terms be definable in the terminology of fundamental physics. One reason it is too restrictive is that philosophical naturalism might be true even if physicalism, the view that everything is physical, is not. Some form of emergent dualism might be correct, for example. A different reason, which I find more interesting (because

I think physicalism *is* true), is that physicalism entails nothing in any case about whether even biology or psychology, let alone ethics, is reducible to physics. There are a number of reasons for this, but a cardinality problem noted by Richard Boyd is sufficient to secure the point (Boyd, forthcoming a). If there are (as there appear to be) any continuous physical parameters, then there are continuum many physical states of the world, but there are at most countably many predicates in any language, including that of even ideal physics; so there are more physical properties than there are physical expressions to represent them. Thus, although physicalism certainly entails that biological and psychological properties (and ethical properties, too, if there are any) are physical, nothing follows about whether we have any but biological or psychological or ethical terminology for representing these particular physical properties.

(ii) Of course, not many discussions of ethical naturalism have focused on the possibility of reducing ethics to physics; social theory, psychology, and occasionally biology have appeared more promising possibilities. But that facts might be *physical* whether or not all the disciplines that deal with them are reducible to *physics*, helps give point to my question of why we should think that if all ethical facts are *natural* (or, for that matter, *social* or *psychological* or *biological*), it follows that they can equally well be expressed in some other, nonmoral idiom; and it also returns us to the question of just what this alternative idiom is supposed to be. The answer to this latter question simply assumed in most discussions of ethical naturalism, I think, is that there are a number of disciplines that we pretty well know to deal with a single natural world, for example, physics, biology, psychology, and social theory; that it is a matter of no great concern whether any of *these* disciplines is reducible to some one of the others or to anything else; but that the test of whether ethical naturalism is true *is* whether ethics is reducible to some (nonmoral) combination of *them*.[14]

But what rationale is there for holding ethics alone to this reductive test? Perhaps there would be one if ethics appeared in some salient respect strikingly dissimilar to these other disciplines: if, for example, Harman were right what whereas physics, biology, and the rest offer plausible explanations of many obviously natural facts, including facts about our beliefs and observations, ethics never does. Perhaps ethics could then plausibly be required to earn its place by some alternative route. But I shall of course argue that Harman is wrong about this alleged dissimilarity, and I take my argument to provide part of the defense required for a naturalistic but nonreductive view of ethics.

(b) A naturalist, however, will certainly want (and a critic of naturalism will likely demand) a fuller account than this of just where moral facts are supposed to fit in the natural world. For all I have shown, moreover, this account might even provide a scheme of reduction for moral discourse: My argument has been not that ethical naturalism could not take this form, but only that it need not. So where should one look for such a fuller account or (if it is to be had) such a reduction? The answer is that the account will have to be derived from our best moral theory, together with our best theory of the rest of the natural world—exactly as, for example, any reductive account of colors will have to be based on all we know about colors, including our best optical theory together with other parts of physics and perhaps psychology. If hedonistic act-utilitarianism (and enough of its associated psychology) turns out to be true, for example, then we can define the good as pleasure and the absence of pain, and a right action as one that produces at least as much good as any other, and that will be where the moral facts fit. If, more plausibly, some other moral theory turns out to be correct, we will get a different account and (if the theory takes the right form) different reductive definitions. It would of course be a serious objection to ethical *naturalism* if we discovered that the *only* plausible moral theories had to invoke supernatural facts of some kind, by making right and wrong depend on the will of a deity, for example, or by implying that only persons with immortal souls could have moral obligations. We would then have to choose between a naturalistic world view and a belief in moral facts. But an ethical naturalist can point out that there are familiar moral theories that lack implications of this sort and that appear defensible in the light of all we know about the natural world; and any of them, if correct, could provide a naturalistic account of moral facts and even (if one is to be had) a naturalistic reduction of moral discourse.

Many philosophers will balk at this confident talk of our discovering some moral theory to be correct. But their objection is just the familiar one whose importance I acknowledged at the outset, before putting it to one side: For I grant that the difficulty we experience in settling moral issues, including issues in moral theory, is a problem (although perhaps not an insuperable one) for any version of moral realism. All I contend here is that there is not, in addition to this acknowledged difficulty, any special further (or prior) problem of finding reductive definitions for moral terms or of figuring out where moral facts fit in the natural world. Our moral theory, if once we get it, will provide whatever reduction is to be had and will tell us where the moral facts fit.[15] The suspicion that there must be more than this to the search for reductive definitions almost always rests, I believe, on the view that these definitions must be suited to a special epistemic role: for example, that they will have to be analytic or conceptual truths and so provide a privileged basis for the rest of our theory. But I am confident that moral reasoning, like reasoning in the sciences, is inevitably dialectical and lacks a priori foundations of this sort. I am also sure that no ethical naturalist need think otherwise.[16]

The relevance of these points is this: It is true that if we once obtained correct reductive definitions for moral terms, moral explanations would be in principle dispensable; so if ethical naturalism had to promise such definitions, it would also have to promise the eliminability in principle of explanations couched in moral terms. But note three points. First, it should be no surprise, and should be regarded as no special difficulty for naturalism even on a reductionist conception of it, that we are not now in possession of such definitions, and so not *now* in a position to dispense with any moral explanations that seem plausible. To be confident of such definitions we would need to know just which moral theory is correct; but ethics is an area of great controversy, and I am sure we do not yet know this. Second, if some moral explanations do seem plausible, as I shall argue, then one important step toward improving this situation in ethics will be to see what sort of theory emerges if we attempt to refine these explanations in the light both of empirical evidence and theoretical criticism. So it is easy to see, again even on a reductionist understanding of naturalism that promises the eliminability of moral explanations in the long run, why any naturalist will think that for the foreseeable short run such explanations should be taken seriously on their own terms.

The third and most important point, finally, is that the eliminability of moral explanations for *this* reason, if actually demonstrated, would of course not represent a triumph of ethical skepticism but would rather derive from its defeat. So we must add one further caution, as I promised, concerning Harman's thesis that no reference to moral facts is *needed* in the explanation of moral beliefs. For there are, as we can now see, two very different reasons one might have for thinking this. One— Harman's reason, and my target in the remainder of this essay—is that no moral explanations even seem plausible, that reference to moral facts always strikes us as "completely irrelevant" to the explanation of moral beliefs. This claim, if true, would tend to support moral skepticism. The other reason—which I have just been considering, and with which I also disagree—is that any moral explanations that *do* seem plausible can be paraphrased without explanatory loss in entirely nonmoral terms. I have argued that it is a mistake to understand ethical naturalism as promising this kind of reduction even in principle; and I think it in any case absurd overconfidence to suppose that anyone can spell out an adequate reduction now. But any reader unconvinced by my arguments should note also that this *second* reason is no version of moral skepticism: For what anyone convinced by it must think, is that we either are or will be able to say, in entirely nonmoral terms, exactly which natural properties moral terms refer to.[17] So Harman is right to present reductionism as an alternative to skepticism; part of what I have tried to show is just that it is neither the only nor the most plausible such alternative, and that no ethical naturalist need be committed to it.

III. MORAL EXPLANATIONS

With these preliminary points aside, I turn to my arguments against Harman's thesis. I shall first add to my example of Hitler's moral character several more in which it seems plausible to cite moral facts as part of an explanation of nonmoral facts, and in particular of people's forming the moral opinions they do. I shall then argue that Harman gives us no plausible reason to reject or ignore these explanations; I shall claim, in fact, that the same is true for his own example of the children igniting the cat. I shall conclude, finally, by attempting to diagnose the source of the disagreement between Harman and me on these issues.

My Hitler example suggests a whole range of extremely common cases that appear not to have occurred to Harman, cases in which we cite someone's moral character as part of an explanation of his or her deeds, and in which that whole story is then available as a plausible further explanation of someone's arriving at a correct assessment of that moral character. Take just one other example. Bernard DeVoto, in *The Year of Decision: 1846,* describes the efforts of American emigrants already in California to rescue another party of emigrants, the Donner Party, trapped by snows in the High Sierras, once their plight became known. At a meeting in Yerba Buena (now San Francisco), the relief efforts were put under the direction of a recent arrival, Passed Midshipman Selim Woodworth, described by a previous acquaintance as "a great busybody and ambitious of taking a command among the emigrants."[18] But Woodworth not only failed to lead rescue parties into the mountains himself, where other rescuers were counting on him (leaving children to be picked up by him, for example), but had to be "shamed, threatened, and bullied" even into organizing the efforts of others willing to take the risk; he spent time arranging comforts for himself in camp, preening himself on the importance of his position; and as a predictable result of his cowardice and his exercises in vainglory, many died who might have been saved, including four known still to be alive when he turned back for the last time in mid-March. DeVoto concludes: "Passed Midshipman Woodworth was just no damned good" (1942, p. 442). I cite this case partly because it has so clearly the structure of an inference to a reasonable explanation. One can think of competing explanations, but the evidence points against them. It isn't, for example, that Woodworth was a basically decent person who simply proved too weak when thrust into a situation that placed heroic demands on him. He volunteered, he put no serious effort even into tasks that required no heroism, and it seems clear that concern for his own position and reputation played a much larger role in his motivation than did any concern for the people he was expected to save. If DeVoto is right about this evidence, moreover, it seems reasonable that part of the explanation of his believing that Woodworth was no damned good is just that Woodworth *was* no damned good.

DeVoto writes of course with more moral intensity (and with more of a flourish) than academic historians usually permit themselves, but it would be difficult to find a serious work of biography, for example, in which actions are not explained by appeal to moral character: sometimes by appeal to specific virtues and vices, but often enough also by appeal to a more general assessment. A different question, and perhaps a more difficult one, concerns the sort of example on which Harman concentrates, the explanation of judgments of right and wrong. Here again Harman appears just to have overlooked explanations in terms of moral character: A judge's thinking that it would be wrong to sentence a particular offender to the maximum prison term the law allows, for example, may be due in part to her decency and fairmindedness, which I take to be moral facts if any are. But do moral features of the action or institution being judged ever play an explanatory role? Here is an example in which they appear to. An interesting historical question is why vigorous and reasonably widespread moral opposition to slavery arose for the first time in the eighteenth and nineteenth centuries, even though slavery was a very old institution; and why this opposition arose primarily in Britain, France, and in French- and English-speaking North America, even though slavery existed throughout the New World.[19] There is a standard answer to this question. It is that chattel slavery in British and French America, and then in the United States, was much *worse* than previous forms of slavery, and much worse than slavery in Latin America. This is, I should add, a controversial explanation. But as is often the case with historical explanations, its proponents do not claim it is the whole story, and many of its opponents grant that there may be some truth in these comparisons, and that they may after all form a small part of a larger explanation.[20] This latter concession is all I require for my example. Equally good for my purpose would be the more limited thesis that explains the growth of antislavery sentiment in the United States, between the Revolution and the Civil War, in part by saying that slavery in the United States became a more oppressive institution during that time. The appeal in these standard explanations is straightforwardly to moral facts.

What is supposed to be wrong with all these explanations? Harman says that assumptions about moral facts seem "completely irrelevant" in explaining moral observations and moral beliefs (p. 7), but on its more natural reading that claim seems pretty obviously mistaken about these examples. For it is natural to think that if a particular assumption is completely irrelevant to the explanation of a certain fact, then the fact would have obtained, and we could have explained it just as well, even if the assumption had been false.[21] But I do not believe that Hitler would have done all he did if he had not been morally depraved, nor, on the assumption that he was not depraved, can I think of any plausible alternative explanation for his doing those things. Nor is it plausible that we would all have believed he was morally depraved even if he hadn't been. Granted, there is a tendency for writers who do not attach much weight to fascism as a social movement to want to blame its evils on a single maniacal leader, so perhaps some of them would have painted Hitler as a moral monster even if he had not been one. But this is only a tendency, and one for which many people know how to discount, so I doubt that our moral belief really is overdetermined in this way. Nor, similarly, do I believe that Woodworth's actions were overdetermined, so that he would have done just as he did even if he had been a more admirable person. I suppose one could have doubts about DeVoto's objectivity and reliability; it is obvious he dislikes Woodworth, so perhaps he would have thought him a moral loss and convinced his readers of this no matter what the man was really like. But it is more plausible that the dislike is mostly based on the same evidence that supports DeVoto's moral view of him, and that very different evidence, at any rate, would have produced a different verdict. If so, then Woodworth's moral character is part of the explanation of DeVoto's belief about his moral character.

It is more plausible of course that serious moral opposition to slavery would have emerged in Britain, France, and the United States even if slavery hadn't been worse in the modern period than before, and worse in the United States than in Latin America, and that the American antislavery movement would have grown even if slavery had not become more oppressive as the nineteenth century progressed. But that is because these moral facts are offered as at best a partial explanation of these developments in moral opinion. And if they really *are* part of the explanation, as seems plausible, then it is also plausible that whatever effect they produced was not entirely overdetermined; that, for example, the growth of the antislavery movement in the United States would at least have been somewhat slower if slavery had been and remained less bad an institution. Here again it hardly seems "completely irrelevant" to the explanation whether or not these moral facts obtained.

It is more puzzling, I grant, to consider Harman's own example in which you see the children igniting a cat and react immediately with the thought that this is wrong. Is it true, as Harman claims, that the assumption that the children are really doing something wrong is "totally irrelevant" to any reasonable explanation of your making that judgment? Would you, for example, have reacted in just the same way, with the thought that the action is wrong, even if what they were doing *hadn't* been wrong, and could we explain your reaction equally well on this assumption? Now, there is more than one way to understand this counterfactual question, and I shall return below to a reading of it that might appear favorable to Harman's view. What I wish to point out for now is merely that there is a natural way of taking it, parallel to the way in which I have been understanding similar counterfactual questions about my own examples, on which the answer to it has to be simply: It depends. For to answer the question, I take it, we must consider a situation in which what the children are doing is not wrong, but which is otherwise as much like the actual situation as possible, and then decide what your reaction would be in that situation. But since what makes their action wrong, what its wrongness *consists* in, is presumably something like its being an act of gratuitous cruelty (or, perhaps we should add, of intense cruelty, and to a helpless victim), to imagine them not doing something wrong we are going to have to imagine their action different in this respect. More cautiously and more generally, if what they are actually doing is wrong, and if moral properties are, as many writers have held, supervenient on natural ones,[22] then in order to imagine them not doing something wrong we are going to have to suppose their action different from the actual one in some of its natural features as well. So our question becomes: Even if the children had been doing something else, something just different enough not to be wrong, would you have taken them even so to be doing something wrong?

Surely there is no one answer to this question: It depends on a lot about you, including your moral views and how good you are at seeing at a glance what some children are doing. It probably depends also on a debatable moral issue; namely, just *how* different the children's action would have to be in order not to be wrong. (Is unkindness to animals, for example, also wrong?) I believe we can see how, in a case in which the answer was clearly affirmative, we might be tempted to agree with Harman that the wrongness of the action was no part of the explanation of your reaction. For suppose you are like this. You hate children. What you especially hate, moreover, is the sight of children enjoying themselves; so much so that whenever you see children having fun, you immediately assume they are up to no good. The more they seem to be enjoying themselves, furthermore, the readier you are to fasten on any pretext for thinking them engaged in real wickedness. Then it is true that even if the children had been engaged in some robust but innocent fun, you would have thought they were doing something wrong; and Harman is perhaps right[23] about you that the actual wrongness of the action you see is irrelevant to your thinking it wrong. This is because your reaction is due to a feature of the action that coincides only very accidentally with the ones that make it wrong.[24] But, of course, and fortunately, many people aren't like this (nor does Harman argue that they are). It isn't true of them that, in general, if the children had been doing something similar, although different enough not to be wrong, they would still have thought the children were doing something wrong. And it isn't true either, therefore, that the wrongness of the action is irrelevant to the explanation of why they think it wrong.[25]

Now, one might have the sense from my discussion of all these examples—but perhaps especially from my discussion of this last one, Harman's own—that I have perversely been refusing to understand his claim about the explanatory irrelevance of moral facts in the way he intends. And perhaps I have not been understanding it as he wishes. In any case, I agree, I have certainly not been understanding the crucial counterfactual question, of whether we would have drawn the same moral conclusion even if the moral facts had been different, in the way he must intend. But I am not being perverse. I believe, as I said, that my way of taking the question is the more natural one. And more important, although there is, I grant, a reading of that question on which it will always yield the answer Harman wants—namely, that a difference in the moral facts would *not* have made a difference in our judgment—I do not believe this can support his argument. I must now explain why.

It will help if I contrast my general approach with his. I am addressing questions about the justification of belief in the spirit of what Quine has called "epistemology naturalized" (Quine, 1969a, pp. 69–90. See also Quine, 1969b). I take this to mean that we have in general no a priori way of knowing which strategies for forming and refining our beliefs are likely to take us closer to the truth. The only way we have of proceeding is to assume the approximate truth of what seems to us the best overall theory we already have of what we are like and what the world is like, and to decide in the light of *that* what strategies of research and reasoning are likely to be reliable in producing a more nearly true overall theory. One result of applying these procedures, in turn, is likely to be the refinement or perhaps even the abandonment of parts of the tentative theory with which we began.

I take Harman's approach, too, to be an instance of this one. He says we are justified in believing in those facts that we need to assume to explain why we observe what we do. But he does not think that our knowledge of this principle about justification is a priori. Furthermore, as he knows, we cannot decide whether one explanation is better than another without relying on beliefs we already have about the world. Is it really a better explanation of the vapor trail the physicist sees in the cloud chamber to suppose that a proton caused it, as Harman suggests in his example, rather than some other charged particle? Would there, for example, have been no vapor trail in the absence of that proton? There is obviously no hope of answering such questions without assuming at least the approximate truth of some quite far-reaching microphysical theory, and our knowledge of such theories is not a priori.

But my approach differs from Harman's in one crucial way. For among the beliefs in which I have enough confidence to rely on in evaluating explanations, at least at the outset, are some moral beliefs. And I have been relying on them in the following way.[26] Harman's thesis implies that the supposed moral fact of Hitler's being morally depraved is irrelevant to the explanation of Hitler's doing what he did. (For we may suppose that if it explains his doing what he did, it also helps explain, at greater remove, Harman's belief and mine in his moral depravity.) To assess this claim, we need to conceive a situation in which Hitler was *not* morally depraved and consider the question whether in that situation he would still have done what he did. My answer is that he would not, and this answer relies on a (not very controversial) moral view: that in any world at all like the actual one, only a morally depraved person could have initiated a world war, ordered the "final solution," and done any number of other things Hitler did. That is why I believe that, if Hitler hadn't been morally depraved, he wouldn't have done those things, and hence that the fact of his moral depravity is relevant to an explanation of what he did.

Harman, however, cannot want us to rely on any such moral views in answering this counterfactual question. This comes out most clearly if we return to his example of the children igniting the cat. He claims that the wrongness of this act is irrelevant to an explanation of your thinking it wrong, that you would have *thought* it wrong even if it wasn't. My reply was that in order for the action not to be wrong it would have had to lack the feature of deliberate, intense, pointless cruelty, and that if it had differed in this way you might very well *not* have thought it wrong. I also suggested a more cautious version of this reply: that since the action is in fact wrong, and since moral properties supervene on more basic natural ones, it would have had to be different in *some* further natural respect in order not to be wrong; and that we do not know whether if it had so differed you would still have thought it wrong. Both of these replies, again, rely on moral views, the latter merely on the view that there is *something* about the natural features of the action in Harman's example that makes it wrong, the former on a more specific view as to which of these features do this.

But Harman, it is fairly clear, intends for us *not* to rely on any such moral views in evaluating his counterfactual claim. His claim is not that if the action had not been one of deliberate cruelty (or had otherwise differed in whatever way would be required to remove its wrongness), you would still have thought it wrong. It is, instead, that if the action were one of deliberate, pointless cruelty, but this *did not make it wrong*, you would still have thought it was wrong. And to return to the example of Hitler's moral character, the counterfactual claim that Harman will need in order to defend a comparable conclusion about that case is not that if Hitler had been, for example, humane and fair-minded, free of nationalistic pride and racial hatred, he would still have done exactly as he did. It is, rather, that if Hitler's psychology, and anything else about his situation that could strike us as morally relevant, had been exactly as it in fact was, but this had *not constituted moral depravity,* he would still have done exactly what he did.

Now the antecedents of these two conditionals are puzzling. For one thing, both are, I believe, necessarily false. I am fairly confident, for example, that Hitler really was morally depraved[27]; and since I also accept the view that moral features supervene on more basic natural properties,[28] I take this to imply that there is no possible world in which Hitler has just the personality he in fact did, in just the situation he was in, but is not morally depraved. Any attempt to describe such a situation, moreover, will surely run up against the limits of our moral concepts— what Harman calls our "moral sensibility"—and this is no accident. For what Harman is asking us to do, in general, is to consider cases in which absolutely *everything* about the nonmoral facts that could seem morally relevant to us, in light of whatever moral theory we accept and of the concepts required for our understanding of that theory, is held fixed, but in which the moral judgment that our theory yields about the case is nevertheless mistaken. So it is hardly surprising that, using that theory and those concepts, we should find it difficult to conceive in any detail what such a situation would be like. It is especially not surprising when the cases in question are as paradigmatic in light of the moral outlook we in fact have as is Harman's example or as is, even more so, mine of Hitler's moral character. The only way we could be wrong about this latter case (assuming we have the nonmoral facts right) would be for our whole moral theory to be hopelessly wrong, so radically mistaken that there could be no hope of straightening it out through adjustments from within.

But I do not believe we should conclude, as we might be tempted to,[29] that we therefore know a priori that this is not so, or that we cannot understand these conditionals that are crucial to Harman's argument. Rather, now that we have seen how we have to understand them, we should grant that they are true: that if our moral theory were somehow hopelessly mistaken, but all the nonmoral facts remained exactly as they in fact are, then, since we do *accept* that moral theory, we would still draw exactly the moral conclusions we in fact do. But we should deny that any skeptical conclusion follows from this. In particular, we should deny that it follows that moral facts play no role in explaining our moral judgments.

For consider what follows from the parallel claim about microphysics, in particular about Harman's example in which a physicist concludes from his observation of a vapor trail in a cloud chamber, and from the microphysical theory he accepts, that a free proton has passed through the chamber. The parallel claim, notice, is *not* just that if the proton had not been there the physicist would have thought it was. This claim is implausible, for we may assume that the physicist's theory is generally correct, and it follows from that theory that if there hadn't been a proton there, then there wouldn't have been a vapor trail. But in a perfectly similar way it is implausible that if Hitler hadn't been morally depraved we would still have thought he was: for we may assume that our moral theory also is at least roughly correct, and it follows from the most central features of that theory that if Hitler hadn't been morally depraved, he wouldn't have done what he did. The *parallel* claim about the microphysical example is, instead, that if there hadn't been a proton there, but there *had* been a vapor trail, the physicist would still have concluded that a proton was present. More precisely, to maintain a perfect parallel with Harman's claims about the moral cases, the antecedent must specify that although no proton is present, absolutely *all* the nonmicrophysical facts that the physicist, in light of his theory, might take to be relevant to the question of whether or not a proton is present, are exactly as in the actual case. (These macrophysical facts, as I shall for convenience call them, surely include everything one would normally think of as an observable fact.) Of course, we shall be unable to imagine this without imagining that the physicist's theory is pretty badly mistaken[30]; but I believe we should grant that, *if* the physicist's theory were somehow this badly mistaken, but all the macrophysical facts (including all the observable facts) were held fixed, then the physicist, since he does accept that theory, would still draw all the same conclusions that he actually does. That is, this conditional claim, like Harman's parallel claims about the moral cases, is true.

But no skeptical conclusions follow; nor can Harman, since he does not intend to be a skeptic about physics, think that they do. It does not follow, in the first place, that we have any reason to think the physicist's theory *is* generally mistaken. Nor does it follow, furthermore, that the hypothesis that a proton really did pass through the cloud chamber is not part of a good explanation of the vapor trail, and hence of the physicist's thinking this has happened. This looks like a reasonable explanation, of course, only on the assumption that the physicist's theory is at least roughly true, for it is this theory that tells us, for example, what happens when charged particles pass through a supersaturated atmosphere, what other causes (if any) there might be for a similar phenomenon, and so on. But, as I say, we have not been provided with any reason for not trusting the theory to this extent.

Similarly, I conclude, we should draw no skeptical conclusions from Harman's claims about the moral cases. It is true, I grant, that if our moral theory were seriously mistaken, but we still believed it, and the nonmoral facts were held fixed, we would still make just the moral judgments we do. But *this* fact by itself provides us with no reason for thinking that our moral theory *is* generally mistaken. Nor, again, does it imply that the fact of Hitler's really having been morally depraved forms no part of a good explanation of his doing what he did and hence, at greater remove, of our thinking him depraved. This explanation will appear reasonable, of course, only on the assumption that our accepted moral theory is at least roughly correct, for it is this theory that assures us that only a depraved person could have thought, felt, and acted as Hitler did. But, as I say, Harman's argument has provided us with no reason for not trusting our moral views to this extent, and hence with no reason for doubting that it is sometimes moral facts that explain our moral judgments.

I conclude with three comments about my argument.

(1) I have tried to show that Harman's claim—that we would have held the particular moral beliefs we do even if those beliefs were untrue—admits of two readings, one of which makes it implausible, and the other of which reduces it to an application of a general skeptical strategy, which could as easily be used to produce doubt about microphysical as about moral facts. The general strategy is this. Consider any conclusion *C* we arrive at by relying both on some distinguishable "theory" *T* and on some body of evidence not being challenged, and ask whether we would have believed *C* even if it had been false. The plausible answer, *if* we are allowed to rely on *T*, will often be no: for if *C* had been false, then (according to *T*) the evidence would have had to be different,

and in that case we wouldn't have believed *C*. (I have illustrated the plausibility of this sort of reply for all my moral examples, as well as for the microphysical one.) But the skeptic intends us *not* to rely on *T* in this way, and so rephrases the question: Would we have believed *C* even if it were false *but* all the evidence had been exactly as it in fact was? Now the answer has to be yes, and the skeptic concludes that *C* is doubtful. (It should be obvious how to extend this strategy to belief in other minds, or in an external world.) I am of course not convinced: I do not think answers to the rephrased question show anything interesting about what we know or justifiably believe. But it is enough for my purposes here that no such *general* skeptical strategy could pretend to reveal any problems peculiar to belief in *moral* facts.

(2) My conclusion about Harman's argument, although it is not exactly the same as, is nevertheless similar to and very much in the spirit of the Duhemian point I invoked earlier against verificationism. There the question was whether typical moral assertions have testable implications, and the answer was that they do, so long as you include additional moral assumptions of the right sort among the background theories on which you rely in evaluating these assertions. Harman's more important question is whether we should ever regard moral facts as relevant to the explanation of nonmoral facts, and in particular of our having the moral beliefs we do. But the answer, again, is that we should, so long as we are willing to hold the right sorts of *other* moral assumptions fixed in answering counterfactual questions. Neither answer shows morality to be on any shakier ground than, say, physics: for typical microphysical hypotheses, too, have testable implications, and appear relevant to explanations, only if we are willing to assume at least the approximate truth of an elaborate microphysical theory and to hold this assumption fixed in answering counterfactual questions.

(3) Of course, this picture of how explanations depend on background theories, and moral explanations in particular on moral background theories, does show why someone already tempted toward moral skepticism on other grounds (such as those mentioned at the beginning of this essay) might find Harman's claim about moral explanations plausible. To the extent that you already have pervasive doubts about moral theories, you will also find moral facts nonexplanatory. So I grant that Harman may have located a natural symptom of moral skepticism; but I am sure he has neither traced this skepticism to its roots nor provided any independent argument for it. His claim that we do not *in fact* cite moral facts in explanation of moral beliefs and observations cannot provide such an argument, for that claim is false. So, too, is the claim that assumptions about moral facts seem irrelevant to such explanations, for many do not. The claim that we *should* not rely on such assumptions

because they *are* irrelevant, on the other hand, unless it is supported by some independent argument for moral skepticism, will just be question-begging: for the principal test of whether they are relevant, in any situation in which it appears they might be, is a counterfactual question about what would have happened if the moral fact had not obtained, and how we answer that question depends precisely upon whether we *do* rely on moral assumptions in answering it.

A different concern, to which Harman only alludes in the passages I have discussed, is that belief in moral facts may be difficult to render consistent with a naturalistic world view. Since I share a naturalistic viewpoint, I agree that it is important to show that belief in moral facts need not be belief in anything supernatural or "nonnatural." I have of course not dealt with every argument from this direction, but I *have* argued for the important point that naturalism in ethics does not require commitment to reductive definitions for moral terms, any more than physicalism about psychology and biology requires a commitment to reductive definitions for the terminology of those sciences.

My own view I stated at the outset: that the only argument for moral skepticism with any independent weight is the argument from the difficulty of settling disputed moral questions. I have shown that anyone who finds Harman's claim about moral explanations plausible must already have been tempted toward skepticism by some other considerations, and I suspect that the other considerations will always just be the ones I sketched. So that is where discussion should focus. I also suggested that those considerations may provide less support for moral skepticism than is sometimes supposed, but I must reserve a thorough defense of that thesis for another occasion.[31]

NOTES

1. As, for example, in Gewirth (1960), pp. 311–330, in which there are some useful remarks about the first of them.

2. Harman's title for the entire first section of his book.

3. This point is generally credited to Pierre Duhem (1906, 1954). It is a prominent theme in the influential writings of W. V. O. Quine. For an especially clear application of it, see Putnam (1977a).

4. Harman is careful always to say only that moral beliefs *appear* to play no such role; and since he eventually concludes that there *are* moral facts (p. 132), this caution may be more than stylistic. I shall argue that this more cautious claim, too, is mistaken (indeed, that is my central thesis). But to avoid issues about Harman's intent, I shall simply mean by "Harman's argument" the skeptical argument of his first two chapters, whether or not he means to endorse all of it. This argument surely deserves discussion in its own right in either case, especially since Harman himself never explains what is wrong with it.

5. He asks: "Can moral principles be tested in the same way [as scientific hypotheses can], out in the world? You can observe someone do something, but can you ever perceive the rightness or wrongness of what he does?" (p. 4)

6. The other is that Harman appears to use "observe" (and "perceive" and "see") in a surprising way. One would normally take observing (or perceiving, or seeing) something to involve *knowing* it was the case. But Harman apparently takes an observation to be *any* opinion arrived at as "a direct result of perception" (p. 5) or, at any rate (see next footnote), "immediately and without conscious reasoning" (p. 7). This means that observations need not even be true, much less known to be true. A consequence is that the existence of moral observations, in Harman's sense, would not be sufficient to show that moral theories can be tested against the world, or to show that there is moral knowledge, although this *would* be sufficient if "observe" were being used in a more standard sense. What I argue in the text is that the existence of moral observations (in either Harman's or the standard sense) is not *necessary* for showing this about moral theories either.

7. This sort of case does not meet Harman's characterization of an observation as an opinion that is "a direct result of perception" (p. 5), but he is surely right that moral facts would be as well vindicated if they were needed to explain our drawing conclusions about hypothetical cases as they would be if they were needed to explain observations in the narrower sense. To be sure, Harman is still confining his attention to cases in which we draw the moral conclusion from our thought experiment "immediately and without conscious reasoning" (p. 7), and it is no doubt the existence of such cases that gives purchase to talk of a "moral sense." But this feature, again, can hardly matter to the argument: Would belief in moral facts be less justified if they were needed only to explain the instances in which we draw the moral conclusion *slowly*? Nor can it make any difference for that matter whether the case we are reflecting on is hypothetical. So my example in which we, quickly or slowly, draw a moral conclusion about Hitler from what we know of him, is surely relevant.

8. Nagel (1980), p. 114n. Nagel actually directs this reply to J. L. Mackie.

9. It is surprising that Harman does not mention the obvious intermediate possibility, which would occur to any instrumentalist: to cite the physicist's psychological set *and* the vapor trail, but say nothing about protons or other unobservables. It is *this* explanation that is most closely parallel to an explanation of beliefs about an external world in terms of sensory experience and psychological makeup, or of moral beliefs in terms of nonmoral facts together with our "moral sensibility."

10. In his essay in this volume, Harman says that some philosophers, those he calls "autonomists," who pursue ethics "internally" without much concern about how moral facts could fit into a scientific world view, regard our moral beliefs as explained by corresponding moral facts; whereas "naturalists," who accept a scientific viewpoint and are concerned about how moral facts fit in, reject such explanation. So he now concedes that some philosophers offer moral explanations. My claim, however, is that these explanations seem plausible to many people with no philosophical axe to grind, and I agree with Harman (in his book, not in this essay) that the plausibility of these explanations, together with the plausibility of a naturalistic metaphysics, should lead these people *toward* ethical naturalism, not away from it.

Harman's distinction among philosophers is puzzling in any case, for it appears to get things largely backward. I have already quoted Thomas Nagel, one of Harman's autonomists, professing indifference as to whether moral facts explain anything. And, by contrast, it seems that any naturalist who believes that there *are* moral facts (as she may but need not, as Harman defines naturalism) should regard those facts as helping to explain our moral beliefs. On Harman's own (much debated) version of naturalism, for example, the wrongness of owning slaves just consisted, to a good first approximation, in the fact that this practice was implicitly contrary to conventions accepted by the slaveowners and their society (pp. 91–133, esp. pp. 94–95). But if *that* is what the wrongness of slavery consisted in, isn't it almost certain that its wrongness played a role—in fact, quite a large role— in producing the widespread belief that it was wrong? It would be remarkable if this were not so, and Harman offers no evidence that it was not.

11. And it is hard to see how facts could be reducible to explanatory facts without being themselves explanatory. Opaque objects often look red to normally sighted observers in white light because they *are* red; it amplifies this explanation, but hardly undermines

it, if their redness turns out to be an electronic property of the matter composing their surfaces.

12. Some of what I say could no doubt be appropriated by believers in supernatural facts, but I leave the details to them. For an account I could largely accept, if I believed any of the theology, see Adams (1981), pp. 109–118.

13. Or, at any rate, a reductive scheme of translation. It surely needn't provide explicit term-by-term definitions. Since this qualification does not affect my argument, I shall henceforth ignore it.

14. *Nonmoral* because ethics (or large parts of it) will be trivially reducible to psychology and social theory if we take otherwise unreduced talk of moral character traits just to be *part* of psychology and take social theory to *include*, for example, a theory of justice. As an ethical naturalist, I see nothing objectionable or unscientific about conceiving of psychology and social theory in this way, but of course this is not usually how they are understood when questions about reduction are raised.

15. So I am again puzzled by Harman's distinction (this volume) between naturalism and what he calls autonomous ethics. I see that one can do ethics "autonomously" without being a naturalist, for one's ethical views might be influenced by belief in the supernatural; and one can be a philosophical naturalist without engaging in autonomous ethics if one is an ethical skeptic or nihilist. But unless a nonskeptical naturalist is required, unrealistically, to *begin* with a set of reductive definitions (or unless autonomous ethics requires *ignoring* some natural facts—which ones?), I do not see how a naturalist, concerned about where moral facts fit in the natural world, can begin to answer this question except by engaging in what Harman calls autonomous ethics.

16. For more on this view of moral reasoning, see Sturgeon (1982). On scientific reasoning see Boyd (1982; forthcoming b).

G. E. Moore (1903) thought that the *metaphysical* thesis that moral facts are natural facts entailed that moral theory would have a priori foundations. For he took the metaphysical thesis to require not merely that there be a reductive scheme of translation for moral terminology, but that this reduction include explicit property-identities (such as "goodness = pleasure and the absence of pain"); and these he assumed could be true only if analytic. I of course reject the view that naturalism requires any sort of reductive definitions; but even if it required this sort, it is by now widely acknowledged that reductive property-identities (such as "temperature = mean molecular kinetic energy") can be true without being analytic. See Putnam (1977b; 1981, pp. 206–7).

17. Nor does this view really promise that we can do without reference to moral facts; it merely says that we can achieve this reference without using moral terms. For we would surely have as much reason to think that the facts expressed by *these* nonmoral terms were moral facts as we would for thinking that our reductive definitions were correct.

18. DeVoto (1942), p. 426; a quotation from the notebooks of Francis Parkman. The account of the entire rescue effort is on pp. 424–444.

19. What is being explained, of course, is not just why people came to think slavery wrong, but why people who were not themselves slaves or in danger of being enslaved came to think it so seriously wrong as to be intolerable. There is a much larger and longer history of people who thought it wrong but tolerable, and an even longer one of people who appear not to have gotten past the thought that the world would be a better place without it. See Davis (1966).

20. For a version of what I am calling the standard view about slavery in the Americas, see Tannenbaum (1947). For an argument against both halves of the standard view, see Davis (1966), esp. pp. 60–61, 223–225, 262–263.

21. This counterfactual test no doubt requires qualification. When there are concomitant effects that in the circumstances could each only have been brought about by their single cause, it may be true that if the one effect had not occurred, then neither would the other, but the occurrence of the one is not relevant to the explanation of the other. The test will also be unreliable if it employs backtracking or "that-would-have-had-to-be-because" counterfactuals. (I take these to include ones in which what is tracked back to is not so much a cause as a condition that partly constitutes another: as when someone's winning a race is part of what constitutes her winning five events in one day, and it is true that

if she hadn't won five events, that would have had to be because she didn't win that particular race.) So it should not be relied on in cases of either of these sorts. But none of my examples falls into either of these categories.

22. What would be generally granted is just that *if* there are moral properties they supervene on natural properties. But, remember, we are assuming for the sake of argument that there are.

From my view that moral properties *are* natural properties, it of course follows trivially that they supervene on natural properties: that, necessarily, nothing could differ in its moral properties without differing in some natural respect. But I also accept the more interesting thesis usually intended by the claim about supervenience—that there are more basic natural features such that, necessarily, once they are fixed, so are the moral properties. (In supervening on more basic facts of some sort, moral facts are like *most* natural facts. Social facts like unemployment, for example, supervene on complex histories of many individuals and their relations; and facts about the existence and properties of macroscopic physical objects—colliding billiard balls, say—clearly supervene on the microphysical constitution of the situations that include them.)

23. Not *certainly* right, because there is still the possibility that your reaction is to some extent overdetermined, and is to be explained partly by your sympathy for the cat and your dislike of cruelty, as well as by your hatred for children (although this last alone would have been sufficient to produce it). We could rule out this possibility by making you an even less attractive character, indifferent to the suffering of animals and not offended by cruelty.

Of course, it may now be hard to imagine that such a person (whom I shall cease calling "you") could retain enough of a grip on moral thought for us to be willing to say he thought the action *wrong,* even if only on a pretext, as opposed to saying that he merely pretended to do so. This difficulty is perhaps not insuperable, but it is revealing. Harman says that the actual wrongness of the action is "completely irrelevant" to the explanation of the observer's reaction. Notice that what is in fact true, however, is that it is *very hard* to imagine someone who reacts in the way Harman describes, but whose reaction is *not* due, at least in part, to the actual wrongness of the action.

24. Perhaps deliberate cruelty is worse the more one enjoys it (a standard counterexample to hedonism). If so, the fact that the children are enjoying themselves makes their action worse, but presumably isn't what makes it wrong to begin with.

25. That the wrongness is relevant does not settle just *how* important it is to the explanation; that will depend on the extent to which it is the very features that *make* the action wrong that explain the belief in its wrongness. People who accept my argument for the relevance of the wrongness may differ on this further issue, moreover, if they disagree about which features matter and why. A moral relativist and a consequentialist, for example, might disagree about why the cruelty of the action matters, the one tracing this to the local moral conventions, the other to the normally bad consequences of cruelty given the general circumstances of human life. They could agree that if the action hadn't been wrong most ordinary people wouldn't have thought it wrong, and hence with my claim about the *relevance* of the wrongness to the explanation of the belief. For of possible worlds in which the action (on these views) is not wrong, the nearer, presumably, are those in which it differs in ways to which ordinary moral judgment is in fact obviously responsive, not those in which the conventions of society or the general conditions of human life are changed. In assessing the *importance* of the wrongness to the explanation of the belief, however, proponents of either of these views may well want to know how sensitive ordinary moral judgment would be, and would have been, to changes along these (as they think) more fundamental dimensions.

I believe this point (suggested to me, though not in just this form, by some comments from Harman) is correct: The assessment of the relative importance of the relevant moral facts in the explanation of moral beliefs will be even more highly theory-dependent than is the initial judgment as to which ones are relevant. (And the extent to which these judgments of relevance are themselves theory-dependent is a central point of the rest of my essay.) Notice, though, that *no* moral theory will make the moral facts look unimportant in the explanation of *all* moral beliefs, for no theory will have this result when applied to beliefs formed by conscious application of that theory itself. And we must, in any case, beware demanding of moral explanations of moral beliefs more than we require of nonmoral explanations of nonmoral beliefs. When Lavoisier took something to be an acid this was often enough, and importantly, because it really was an acid; but of course his conception of what an acid is was not accurate or complete enough to guarantee that in every actual case, let alone every possible one, he could correctly distinguish acids from other substances. For so long as people have classified animals into kinds there have surely been clear cases in which part of the explanation of someone's thinking something a cat has been that it *is* a cat, but we can hardly attribute to people in general a conception of cats sensitive, especially in counterfactual circumstances, to all the features contemporary theory uses to define species membership. Indeed, we know it is a good bet that even contemporary physical theory is not exactly right in everything it says about, for example, protons; so Harman, when he says that a contemporary physicist may have believed a proton was present partly because a proton really was present, is accepting this explanation as adequate for his epistemological purposes, even though there are (almost certainly) circumstances in which that physicist's conception of a proton would have led him into mistakes. In a similar vein, I see no problem in principle with supposing it *quite* important to the explanation of someone's belief in, say, the injustice of slavery, that slavery really was unjust, even if (from the point of view of some better theory that we accept) his conception of injustice is relatively unsophisticated and not entirely accurate, and therefore leaves him unable correctly to distinguish justice from injustice in every actual or possible case.

26. Harman of course allows us to assume the moral facts whose explanatory relevance is being assessed: that Hitler was depraved, or that what the children in his example are doing is wrong. But I have been assuming something more—something about what depravity *is*, and about what *makes* the children's action wrong. (At a minimum, in the more cautious version of my argument, I have been assuming that *something* about its more basic features makes it wrong, so that it could not have differed in its moral quality without differing in those other features as well.)

27. And anyway, remember, this is the sort of fact Harman allows us to assume in order to see whether, if we assume it, it will look explanatory.

28. It is about here that I have several times encountered the objection: but surely *supervenient* properties aren't needed to explain anything. It is a little hard, however, to see just what this objection is supposed to come to. If it includes endorsement of the conditional I here attribute to Harman, then I believe the remainder of my discussion is an adequate reply to it. If it is the claim that, because moral properties are supervenient, we can always exploit the insights in any moral explanations, however plausible they may seem, without resort to moral *language*, then I have already dealt with it in my discussion of reduction: The claim is probably false, but even if it is true, it is no support for Harman's view, which is not that moral explanations are plausible but reducible, but that they are totally implausible. And doubts about the causal efficacy of supervenient facts seem misplaced in any case, as attention to my earlier examples (note 22) illustrates. High unemployment causes widespread hardship, and can also bring down the rate of inflation. The masses and velocities of two colliding billiard balls causally influence the subsequent trajectories of the two balls. There is no doubt some sense in which these facts are causally efficacious *in virtue of* the way they supervene on—that is, are constituted out of, or causally realized by—more basic facts, but this hardly shows them *in*efficacious. (Nor does Harman appear to think it does: For his *favored* explanation of your moral belief about the burning cat, recall, appeals to psychological facts (about your moral sensibility), a biological fact (that it's a cat), and macrophysical facts (that it's on fire)—supervenient facts all, on his physicalist view and mine.) If anyone does hold to a general suspicion of causation by supervenient facts and properties, however, as Jaegwon Kim appears to (1979, pp. 47–48), it is enough here to note that this suspicion cannot diagnose any special difficulty with *moral* explanations, any distinctive "problem with ethics." The "problem," arguably, will be with every discipline but fundamental physics.

29. And as I take it Philippa Foot (1978a), for example, is still prepared to do, at least about paradigmatic cases.

30. If we imagine the physicist *regularly* mistaken in this way, moreover, we will have to imagine his theory not just mistaken but hopelessly so. And we can easily reproduce the other notable feature of Harman's claims about the moral cases, that what we are imagining is *necessarily* false, if we suppose that one of the physicist's (or better, chemist's) conclusions is about the microstructure of some common substance, such as water. For I agree with Saul Kripke that whatever microstructure water actually has is essential to it, that it has this structure in every possible world in which it exists. (Kripke, 1980, pp. 115–144.) If we are right (as we have every reason to suppose) in thinking that water is actually H_2O, therefore, the conditional "If water were not H_2O, but all the observable, macrophysical facts were just as they actually are, chemists would still have come to *think* it was H_2O" has a necessarily false antecedent; just as, if we are right (as we also have good reason to suppose) in thinking that Hitler was actually morally depraved, the conditional "If Hitler were just as he was in all natural respects, but not morally depraved, we would still have *thought* he was depraved" has a necessarily false antecedent. Of course, I am not suggesting that in either case our knowledge that the antecedent is false is a priori.

These counterfactuals, because of their impossible antecedents, will have to be interpreted over worlds that are (at best) only "epistemically" possible; and, as Richard Boyd has pointed out to me, this helps to explain why anyone who accepts a causal theory of knowledge (or any theory according to which the justification of our beliefs depends on what explains our holding them) will find their truth irrelevant to the question of how much we know, either in chemistry or in morals. For although there certainly are counterfactuals that are relevant to questions about what causes what (and, hence, about what explains what), these have to be counterfactuals about real possibilities, not merely epistemic ones.

31. This essay has benefited from helpful discussion of earlier versions read at the University of Virginia, Cornell University, Franklin and Marshall College, Wayne State University, and the University of Michigan. I have been aided by a useful correspondence with Gilbert Harman; and I am grateful also for specific comments from Richard Boyd, David Brink, David Copp, Stephen Darwall, Terence Irwin, Norman Kretzmann, Ronald Nash, Peter Railton, Bruce Russell, Sydney Shoemaker, and Judith Slein.

chapter three

Moral Realism and Explanatory Necessity

David Zimmerman

I. THE QUESTION OF MORAL REALISM

At least since Descartes, philosophers have been convinced that there is an intimate dialectical connection between questions of reason or justification and questions of truth, realism, and reduction. The connection works in both directions. Since the logic of justifying a certain class of statements depends on what they are about, getting clear on what would count as a justification requires getting clear on their ontology. On the other hand, since the very possibility of a justification (once one knows what would count) also depends so heavily on what the statements are about, justificatory concerns can place crucial constraints on the account of this ontology. For example, skeptical worries have often motivated the avoidance of realism about material objects and abstract entities. On the face of it, there is reason to think that this two-way connection is just as intimate where the statements are ethical,[1] so in my contribution to this volume I want to clarify the idea of moral justification by tackling a cluster of issues involving the nature of moral truth and the ontology of moral theories.

There is a class of meta-ethical theories that reduce the good and the right to subjective stances of various kinds. Examples are noncognitivist theories like emotivism and prescriptivism, but also naturalist theories like Harman's reduction of certain "oughts" to a commitment to social conventions; Brandt's reduction of rightness to the set of rules that would be selected by a person whose desires would survive a process of cognitive purification; Firth's analysis of "right" in terms of the responses of an ideal observer; and perhaps Rawls's account of value as the object of desires that satisfy the constraints of deliberative rationality.[2] Opposed to these is the ontological conviction that the truth conditions of moral statements are essentially independent of subjective stances, and that the nature of the good and the right can be explicated without any essential reference to what moral agents or judges approve of or are able to commit themselves to or desire. Call this opposing conviction moral realism. The intuitive idea is that moral reflection and moral judgment are a matter of discovery, rather than of invention, projection, expression, or even self-discovery, because the good and the right are "in the world." Whereas realism about numbers or physical objects or theoretical entities is the view that the ontology of statements about these things transcends their epistemic *recognition*-conditions, moral realism in the sense that concerns me is preeminently the view that the ontology of moral statements transcends their motivational *acceptance*-conditions.[3]

Characterized in this fashion, moral realism and the meta-ethical subjectivism that contrasts with it are not the same as cognitivism and noncognitivism.[4] Subjectivists who take moral sentences to state facts about stances like approval, desire, and commitment are cognitivists, but some subjectivists are noncognitivists; namely, those who take moral sentences to express or otherwise evince these stances. Some philosophers concerned with moral justification make much of this distinction among nonrealist theories, but they are wrong to do so.[5] The real issues for that part of meta-ethics concerned with matters of truth and existence turn on the question of whether moral properties are part of the fabric of the world (including the human world, a point I shall come back to), rather than being human inventions. With respect to problems like moral relativism and the force of moral obligation, or value and the meaning of life, moral philosophers who agree that moral sentences are fact-stating may not agree sufficiently about the sorts of facts stated to arrive at common solutions. The issue that divides them is realism, not cognitivism.

In this essay I consider a kind of dispute between moral realists and antirealists that turns on the explanatory necessity (or, anyway, effectiveness) of supposing that goodness and rightness exist. For example, some moral realists insist that the reduction of rightness to subjective stances cannot accommodate the *prima facie* logical features of normative discourse, notably the fact that "*x* is right" and "it is not the case that *x* is right" appear to be genuine contradictories. Some antirealists reply that moral conflicts are best modeled on conflicts of desire, not of belief, and are thus not only consistent with a nonrealist ontology, but require one.[6] I will consider two other disputes over explanatory necessity. In his contribution to this volume, Nicholas Sturgeon argues that reference to moral properties is unavoidable in explanations of actions, events, and beliefs. The argument turns on his rejection of the idea that ethical naturalism requires the term-by-term reduction of moral properties, *a fortiori* their reduction to subjective stances. His model for such a nonreductive naturalism is the functionalist program in the philosophy of mind, motivated in large part by the demands of explanatory generality. I argue that the model is inappropriate and that this argument for nonreductive moral realism fails.

Not all *explananda* in the dispute over explanatory necessity between moral realists and antirealists are so unproblematic and uncontested as actions, events, and moral beliefs. For example, some realists insist that the identification of value with subjective stances like desire or approval drastically distorts the "inner view" of intrinsic values; that is, what it is like to confront value in the world. They conclude that the rejection of realism undermines the meaning intrinsic value brings into life.[7] Antirealists, on the other hand, are tempted to reply that this is all very well as a piece of phenomenology, but (like all phenomenology) it leaves all the important questions about the existence and nature of the good unanswered. I will consider this and one other dispute in which the very phenomena to be explained are themselves essentially contested. I begin by suggesting that antirealists should try to resist the temptation to dismiss out of hand the realist's *explananda*. Instead, they should adopt the more fruitful strategy of taking seriously the contested phenomena and trying to show that the data can indeed be accommodated within a subjectivist framework (cf. Blackburn, 1971). I argue that they can be, and that sometimes the moral realist is inclined to suppose the contrary because he has an excessively narrow conception of the antirealist program. I end the paper with the suggestion that broadening the antirealist program in the most appropriate way reduces the importance of the split between moral realists and nonrealists, at least where it is a matter of accommodating the essentially contested phenomena.

II. EXPLANATORY NECESSITY AS THE TEST OF EXISTENCE

Before discussing these issues I want to consider one recent attempt to circumvent the whole question of realism by rejecting explanatory necessity as the crucial constraint. Moral realism can arise in two ways, which differ primarily in their attitude toward explanatory necessity as a measure of reality. Moral realists who accept this constraint are very much in the position of those mathematical realists who believe we ought to countenance the existence of numbers because they are necessary ingredients in the explanatory schemes of physical science—who are realists, that is, because they accept a naturalist constraint on ontological commitments. (I use "naturalist" here roughly in Harman's sense.) I am more concerned here, however, with those moral realists who reject, or at least proclaim that they reject, this explanatory constraint. Consider, for example, Thomas Nagel's reply to John Mackie's "argument from queerness" against the idea that there are entities in the world the knowledge of which alone generates motivations to instantiate them (see Mackie 1977, pp. 38–42; Nagel, 1979). Nagel acknowledges that Mackie intends this argument to count not just against a Moorean or Platonic realism, which takes values to be some sort of occult entity, but also against a realism about reasons themselves. But he replies:

> It begs the question to assume that *explanatory* necessity is the test of reality in this area. The claim that certain reasons exist is a normative claim, not a claim about the best explanation of anything. To assume that only what has to be included in the best explanatory picture of the world is real is to assume that there are no irreducibly normative truths. (1979, p. 114)

As Nagel himself notes, there is much more to be said on both sides of the issue. I will limit myself to two points. First, an observation *ad hominem:* it is not clear that Nagel himself escapes all commitment to the explanatory constraint, for consider these remarks about how one is to go about discovering whether anything has value:

> An objective method has more to go on, for its data include the appearance of value to individuals with particular perspectives, including oneself. In this respect, practical reason is no different from anything else. Starting from a pure idea of a possible reality and a very impure set of appearances, we try to fill in the idea of reality so as to make some partial sense of the appearances, using objectivity as a method. (1979, p. 115)

Add to this his remarks about how "reality in detail can be confirmed by appearances," and it begins to look as though Nagel is committed to something like "inference to the best explanation" as a methodological constraint on arguments about the reality of values and reasons.[8] This suggests a second, more general point: Contrary to what Harman suggests,[9] meta-ethical naturalists are not the only ones who can employ inference to the best explanation as a methodological tool. We have already seen that realism about numbers can arise from explanatory considerations. It may be replied that this does involve a kind of naturalism, since the *explananda* are certain empirical facts about the material world. But in the present case the *explananda* are (in Nagel's phrase) "appearances of values" (1979, p. 113), and it can be left quite open initially whether the reference to values in this description is to receive an ultimate reduction. Thus Nagel is quite wrong to suggest that acceptance of the explanatory constraint commits one *ab initio* to the reducibility of values and practical reasons. A naturalistic reduction might issue from a consideration of explanatory necessity, but then again it might not, as in the case of mathematical realism generated from the needs of physical theory. If the world includes the appearance of value, as Nagel assumes it does, then it is legitimate and non-question-begging to ask whether one needs to assume the existence of irreducible values and practical reasons in order to explain these appearances.

III. UNCONTESTED EXPLANANDA: STURGEON'S MORAL EXPLANATIONS

In pursuing this question I first want to consider contexts in which the *explananda* themselves are not contested by realists and antirealists. In "Moral Explanations," Nicholas Sturgeon heartily accepts explanatory necessity as a test of existence, and he argues on this basis that hypotheses citing moral properties frequently have a role in the explanation of actions, events, and beliefs not possessed by any theoretical framework that aims at their reduction or elimination. For example, we might explain Hitler's extermination of the European Jews by citing his depraved moral character, or we might explain the emerging opposition to slavery in North America in the nineteenth century (even though the institution had existed long before this) by appealing to the fact that it had become morally much worse by then.

Against this, one might urge, as Harman does (1977, chap. 1), that it is possible to explain such actions or events directly in terms of factors that make no explicit reference to morality at all. For example, one might explain Hitler's actions in terms of a certain set of beliefs and character traits (Hitler believed that Jews are human vermin and wanted to kill such people), where character traits are taken to be action-tendencies that can be specified in nonmoral terms. The nonmoral explanatory model would then be a straightforward application of the want-belief framework. Or, one might explain why opposition to slavery arose only in the nineteenth century by specifying those respects in which the institution became worse (perhaps families tended to be separated more frequently, or conditions of servitude became more painful, or there was a decrease in certain kinds of freedom of action), and then conjoining these factual claims with statements about the character traits and beliefs of the abolitionists (they had a strong aversion to social institutions with these features and believed that slavery had come to embody them more thoroughly). To be sure, the person offering the explanation might also believe that Hitler's traits of character and beliefs were indeed morally depraved, but citing this moral fact adds nothing to the explanation of his actions, nothing which is not already there in the nonmoral specification of the content of these traits and beliefs. Similarly, although the abolitionists' distinctly moral beliefs about slavery do indeed enter into the explanation of the rising opposition, the reference to moral properties occurs only in oblique contexts. Therefore, the *explanans* itself is no more committed to the existence of moral properties than is an explanation of the rising interest in alchemy committed to the existence of a chemical process that turns base metal into gold.

We should note that two distinct antirealist claims are possible: (1) there are no moral facts because they are not required to do any explanatory work; and (2) even if there were moral facts, they would not be required to do any explanatory work because they can be reduced to nonmoral facts. The first is a straightforward eliminativism. The second, however, is probably closer to the view Harman wants to defend and Sturgeon wants to criticize (see Sturgeon, this volume, note 28). As Sturgeon points out, the reductionist version of antirealism does not completely deprive moral facts of an explanatory role, since they still can enter into explanations via the reduction sentences. The question, of course, is whether they are indispensible in these explanations. If a reduction of the moral to the nonmoral is possible, then they are not indispensible, since the reduction relation is asymmetrical with respect to explanatory power. That is, if M enters into the explanation of D, but M can be reduced to N (say via bilateral reduction sentences), then M can be dispensed with in the explanation of D (even if we are not eliminativists with respect to facts of this kind), because the complete explanation of what an M is can be given in terms of facts of type N. The issue dividing moral realists and most antirealists, therefore, is reductionism, Sturgeon agrees (see this volume, pp. 58ff). When trying to explain actions and events like Hitler's destruction of the Jews or the rising opposition to slavery, is it always possible to specify the relevant set of character traits and beliefs and institutional features in nonmoral terms? For example, can we reduce "morally depraved" to some set of character traits and "morally worse" to some set of institutional changes?

This large question has absorbed a lot of philosophical energy in the meta-ethical battles of the century, and while I do not intend to try to refight them here, one aspect of the issue can be handled manageably in the context of explanatory necessity. Virtually everyone agrees that moral properties supervene upon nonmoral ones (although there are disagreements about the precise nature of this relationship). Suppose that this supervenience is one-many, so that each moral property supervenes upon a number of distinct nonmoral properties. In this case, even though supervenience is asymmetrical, there would still be explanatory work for moral facts to do, because only they would operate at the appropriate level of generality.

This appeal to explanatory generality appears to be the strongest argument Sturgeon has for the explanatory indispensibility of moral facts. The key premise is the claim that the reduction of moral to nonmoral properties is at best one-many. What can be said in its defense? From the way he develops his case, it is clear that Sturgeon is quite impressed by the parallel between theoretical accounts of the nature of moral properties and functionalist programs in the philosophy of mind, which are physicalistic in ontology but nonreductionist in execution.[10] For functionalists, the essence of the mental is captured at an appropriately abstract level of description required mainly because these functional states can be realized in a variety of nonequivalent physical systems. Since the main argument for this kind of functionalism and against a type-identification of mental states with physical states appeals to the phenomenon of multiple realization, the modeling of one's meta-ethics on this philosophy of the mental will work only if there is some analogue of multiple realization in the moral sphere.

There are two broad possibilities, one corresponding to a nonreductive moral realism, which takes the nonmoral right- and good-making properties as the bases of multiple realization, the other to an antirealist subjectivism, which takes certain subjective stances as the base. Let us consider the realist theory first. For Sturgeon's parallel to hold, moral properties must be multiply realized in nonmoral criteria of application. The analogy has two distinguishable aspects, multiplicity and realizability. It might seem that multiplicity comes only if some form of moral pluralism turns out to be the correct account of right- and good-making properties; otherwise there would be no multiplicity to do the realizing. Since this requirement would rule out theories of obligation like utilitarianism and theories of value like hedonism, it might appear that to sustain the parallel between nonreductive realism and functionalism one must also reject the moral neutrality of meta-ethics.

Sturgeon may in fact believe that a naturalist account of ethics depends on what the ultimately best moral theory turns out to be, and he may wish to put his money on pluralism. He need not make his own analogy hostage to such uncertainty, however, for he only has to hold that some form of moral pluralism is possible, not that it is actually true. After all, arguments for functionalism often appeal to the mere possibility of the multiple realization of mental states in nonequivalent physical structures (for example, the possibility of "martian pains"). The possibility of moral pluralism is all the analogy requires, but it is not clear that Sturgeon himself can make this move, for there is a lot of evidence that he believes certain (all?) moral claims are necessarily true, if true at all, on a parallel with Kripke's treatment of certain statements involving natural kinds (for example, his thesis that "water is H_2O" is necessarily true if true at all). This emerges clearly in Sturgeon's discussion of the crucial counterfactuals to be employed in testing the explanatory necessity of moral properties.[11] But since I take up some independent doubts about this necessity claim a bit later, and since the claim creates problems (of consistency) more for Sturgeon rather than for the analogy itself, I will move right along to a deeper reason for being doubtful about it.

The analogy holds that a mental state stands to its nonequivalent physical realizations as a moral property stands to its nonmoral criterion of application, but actually there are three terms to the functionalist account, the third being the idea of functional realization. This is quite central in the nonreductive account of the mental. Most important, it provides a unifying way of characterizing all those states that count as pain or as belief even though they are realized in nonequivalent physical structures; that is, it gives the "essence" of pain or of belief, over and above their simply being pain and belief. Indeed, the fact that these states are realized functionally is just about all that gives the idea of realization its purchase in this context: The mental states are realized in the physical structures by virtue of the fact that these structures are the media in which the states play certain causal roles. Without functional role one might just as well speak of "instantiation" as of "realization," in which case one would have a kind of (mental) type- (physical) token dualism, rather than a theory that can claim to be physicalistic in spirit.

Similarly, without any analogue for functional role on the meta-ethical side of the analogy, one has a kind of nonreductive dualism, not unlike Moorean intuitionism, for there is nothing to unify the instantiations of the moral properties in the distinct nonmoral conditions, except the fact that they are all instantiations of, say, rightness. I am at a loss to think what this unifying analogue might be, but without it the analogy is considerably weakened.

Let us link up these doubts about the analogy with a point about explanatory generality. As Sturgeon sees it, the issue is whether the nonmoral explanation is as "general and illuminating as the moral explanation purports to be."[12] His answer is that nonmoral explanations are frequently "too specific"; for example, the original hypothesis is that opposition grew because slavery got worse; the particular facts cited will constitute the "particular way" it got worse, but it is irrelevant (or anyway not as illuminating) to say that the institution got worse in just that way.[13] This is directly parallel to the sort of defense functionalists frequently give for their reluctance to identify mental with physical properties; namely, that physicalistic explanations fail to capture an important generality about the mental and are thus (in Ned Block's phrase) too "chauvinistic" (Block, 1980).

It cannot be denied that many nonmoral aspects of slavery are irrelevant for the explanation of the emerging opposition: that a certain type of chain or whip was used, and so on. But Sturgeon is insisting that sometimes no set of nonmoral facts is sufficiently general, not even those facts that would be offered by the abolitionists themselves as justification for the claim that the institution of slavery got morally worse. I find this hard to accept. First, note that the actuality or possibility that "morally worse" is "multiply realized" in a number of different nonmoral properties (or sets of such properties) is irrelevant to the issue at hand, for the explanation of why opposition to slavery intensified is that it became morally worse in a certain respect (say because the overseers became more cruel), even though this opposition might also have emerged if (counterfactually) the institution had become worse in some other respect (say because fewer liberties were allowed). Generality is a two-edged sword in explanatory contexts: Too much is as bad as too little. The moral explanation of why opposition to slavery emerged only in the nineteenth century is too general. One wants to know in what respect it became morally worse; that is, to which of its features opponents were reacting. Similar remarks apply to the moral explanations of why Hitler exterminated the European Jews cast in terms of his moral depravity. Surely a more perspicuous explanation delves more deeply into his psychology and tells us considerably more about those features of his personality that led to the Holocaust. The crucial question is whether it is ever necessary to appeal to moral facts in achieving an appropriately general explanation of actions, events, attitudes, and beliefs. I have no conclusive argument for the thesis that appeal to the nonmoral right- and good-making properties is always sufficient, but perhaps I have said enough to indicate how unpersuasive Sturgeon's own examples are to the contrary.

I do not want to leave the issue there, however, for Sturgeon's target throughout most of "Moral Explanations" is not a moral realism that tries to reduce moral properties to nonmoral criteria of application, but rather the kind of moral subjectivism that reduces them to subjective stances. Indeed, his explicit target is Harman (1975), who reduces certain moral "oughts" to commitments to social conventions. Oddly, Sturgeon does not explicitly press the generality argument for the explanatory indispensibility of moral facts against this kind of nonrealist reductionism, but it is worth asking whether the crucial analogy between the moral and the mental-as-functional is any easier to sustain here. Is it plausible to argue that moral properties are not one-one reducible to subjective stances like desires, attitudes, and commitments because, even if such a subjectivism were essentially correct, the moral properties would be "multiply realized" in the stances? Many subjectivist theories aim at a comprehensive reduction of the good and the right at just the level of generality as the moral properties themselves. A prominent example is Firth, who argues (unsuccessfully) that the responses of ideal observers are necessarily uniform; another is Brandt, who would accept a multiplicity of reforming definitions of "good" and "right" only with the greatest reluctance. If these meta-ethical theories are workable, then the analogy depending on multiple realization fails. Of course, some subjectivists like Harman are frank relativists, so on their theories there is a kind of multiple realization of moral properties in nonequivalent subjective stances. But if Sturgeon (1982) argues strenuously against versions of subjectivism with absolutist ambitions, he argues even more strenuously against the relativist variety. Clearly, this is not the route to a nonreductionist naturalism he would choose for himself.

Even if his argument from generality fails or is less than conclusive, Sturgeon still has another line of argument to fall back on, which appeals to a kind of moral essentialism, akin to a Kripkean treatment of natural kind terms. Recall his counterfactual test for determining explanatory dispensibility, the schema of which is something like this: Hypothesis H is irrelevant to the explanation of fact F only if "the fact could have obtained and we could have explained it just as well, even if the hypothesis had been false" (this volume, p. 65). Applying this to the explanation of Hitler's extermination of the jews, we get the result that his moral depravity is explanatorily irrelevant only if he would have exterminated the Jews, and we could have explained that fact just as well, even if everything else had been the same except that Hitler was not morally depraved. Sturgeon insists that in construing the "even if . . ." clause of this counterfactual, we are not to imagine everything's being the same, except that Hitler has a different kind of character (and perhaps different beliefs). We are to imagine, rather, that *every* nonmoral feature of the situation is held constant, including all of Hitler's traits of character and beliefs, nonmorally specified, that is; the very set of conditions that a reductionist would offer in a non-moral explanation of what Hitler did (this volume, p. 68).

Now consider how Sturgeon's application of this schema is supposed to yield moral essentialism. He has trouble with a counterfactual like "if Hitler's psychology in all non moral respects, and everything else about his situation that strikes as morally relevant, had been exactly as it in fact was, but this *had not constituted moral depravity,* he would still have done exactly as he did" because the antecedent clause seems to him *necessarily* false (this volume, p. 69). The following rather compressed argument provides his defense of this claim:

I am fairly confident, for example, that Hitler really was morally depraved; and since I also accept the view that moral features supervene on more basic natural properties, I take this to imply that there is no possible world in which Hitler had just the personality he in fact did, in just the situation he was in, but is not morally depraved (this volume, p. 69).

If the argument is sound then moral truths are essential truths; and if they are essential truths then the counterfactual schema cannot be used to demonstrate the explanatory irrelevance of moral hypotheses.

I have two doubts about this argument, one about how Sturgeon hopes to establish the crucial essentialist thesis, the other about his use of the counterfactual schema. First, Sturgeon's argument requires that the necessity entering into the analysis of supervenience be logical or metaphysical, but judging from some recent work on the concept,[14] it is not at all clear that this is so. Moreover, some have suggested that moral supervenience in particular can be explicated within the framework of a subjectivist or non-realist metaethics roughly as follows: moral property M supervenes on a non-moral criterion of application N by virtue of the fact that N is the object of some (suitably constrained) subjective stance (attitude, motivation, or convention) that enters into the reductive account of the nature of moral properties.[15] If Sturgeon's argument from generality (and other arguments against the very possibility of such non-realist reductions) fail, then this explanation may just work. But if so, there is no route from moral supervenience to essentialism.

Some remarks of Sturgeon suggest that he has in mind a moral essentialism modeled on a Kripkean treatment of natural kind terms, but how does one discover that minimizing pain or keeping one's promises is essentially right (if right at all) on the model of discovering that water is H_2O (if H_2O at all)? To aid one's intuitions about the metaphysical necessity of statements about natural kinds there are the *a posteriori* methods of scientific discovery and validation conjoined with the technique of "Twin-Earth" parables as deployed by Putnam (1975). Sturgeon's remarks about epistemology naturalized as a model for moral theory indicate that he would have us employ something like the method of reflective equilibrium to set about discovering moral truths; the real question, however, is how to establish their metaphysical necessity. Perhaps Sturgeon believes that something analogous to Twin-Earth parables can aid our intuitions. We need further illumination.

My second worry about the argument from essentialism concerns Sturgeon's use of the counterfactual schema for determining explanatory relevance. He suggests that what the reductionist (*a fortiori* the eliminativist) asks us to suppose "will surely run up against the limits of our moral concepts . . . so it is hardly surprising that, using the moral theory and those moral concepts, we should find it difficult to conceive in any detail what such a situation would be like" (this volume, p. 69). But this is to presuppose that the reductionist and eliminativist are asking us to make distinctly substantive moral suppositions which run up against the limits of whatever particular substantive theory we hold, but this is not so. Whether pressing the reductionist or eliminativist version of the counterfactual test runs up against "the limits of our moral concepts" is still an open question, and one to be closed only by independent arguments bearing on the viability of these meta-ethical programs (like the argument from generality just considered). This suggests that the counterfactual schema ought to be augmented. Understanding it in the way Sturgeon insists upon strongly suggests that Hitler would have exterminated the Jews even if the nonmorally specified traits of character and beliefs had constituted moral benevolence instead or had at least been morally neutral. But as I understand the reductionist's position, he is not suggesting that there is an alternative explanation which does not appeal to Hitler's moral depravity but instead to some other moral status of his character (I take moral neutrality to be a moral status), but rather that there is an alternative explanation which makes no essential reference to moral properties at all. Eliminativists and reductionists would therefore wish to augment the counterfactual schema in this fashion: hypothesis H is irrelevant to the explanation of fact F only if the fact could have obtained and we could have explained it just as well, even if the hypothesis had been false, *or* its key theoretical terms had been referentially vacuous (eliminativist), *or* its key theoretical concepts had been reducible without remainder (reductionist). But if the schema is understood in this fashion, and the argument from essentialism fails, then all the weight is placed on the argument from generality. And we have seen that there is reason to be dubious about its force.

IV. ESSENTIALLY CONTESTED EXPLANANDA

Still, there may be good reasons for embracing moral realism if there are other aspects of rightness and goodness which can be best explained by a realist ontology. The phenomena that concern Sturgeon are themselves all relatively unproblematic: actions, events of other kinds, and beliefs both moral and nonmoral. But disputes over the explanatory adequacy of moral ontologies do not always begin with such uncontested data; sometimes the very conceptions of the phenomena up for explanation seem to be deeply ladened with meta-ethical theory. I have already mentioned the dispute over how the phenomenon of moral conflict is best explained. Another example is the dispute over how best to accommodate certain logical features of moral discourse. Realists sometimes complain that a subjectivist account of moral judgment has relativist implications that prevent it from accommodating the fact that '*A* ought to be done under condition *C*' and 'It is not the case that *A* ought to be done under condition *C*' are genuine contradictories. But it is open to the nonrealist to reply that these logical features are mere appearances that themselves presuppose a realist construal of the truth conditions of moral statements.[16] To be sure, something like this may happen in science too. If there is any truth to the various Kuhn-Feyerabend[17] incommensurability theses, then a term used to record observations about physical objects, say "motion," may receive incommensurable interpretations from Aristotelian and Newtonian and Einsteinian theories. Consequently, there is no one set of descriptions of the motion of bodies up for competing explanation by the theories, but rather three sets, one for each theory. The situation in ethics, however, may be even more desperate. Critics of the idea of observational incommensurability in science point out that there may be enough referential stability to ensure sufficient theory-neutrality of the observational language (see, for example, Scheffler, 1967). Aristotelians, Newtonians, and Einsteinians at least agree that bodies do move, and referential stability may be enough to give them a common phenomenon to explain; but moral realists and antirealists often cannot even agree on whether their contested *explananda* exist.

In the face of this difficulty, what are the disputants to do? As noted earlier, the anti realist ought to be the one to make the provisional concession. To get the dialectic off the ground, he ought to take very seriously the phenomena the realist cites and try to show that a nonrealist moral ontology can in fact accommodate and explain them, and that where it cannot, the price to be paid is not so high as the realist fears. This bears a resemblance to the strategy a compatibilist on the free-will question employs to reassure the incompatibilist that in a determined world he can have almost everything he says he wants, and that the rest is not worth having.

I will consider two closely related disputes involving essentially contested *explananda*. It has been argued that "[F]or a reflective being with a nature like ours, the price of abandoning moral realism can be the end of desire" (Platts, 1980, p. 79). It has also been argued that subjectivist ontologies of value distort the "inner, participant" perspective we have on them and on the meaning they bring into life (Wiggins, 1976, Section IV). The *explananda* here are essentially contested because it is open to the antirealist to insist that precisely because nothing objectively matters we ought to surrender all desires that presuppose the contrary, and to insist, moreover, that the inner, participant perspective on values and meaning is illusory, however psychologically compelling.

But, as just indicated, pressing this short answer would be a mistake. There is a lot more to be said if a nonrealist takes these phenomena seriously and tries to accommodate them.

Mark Platts insists on the conceptual priority of the objectively desirable over the desired out of fear that the rejection of realism about values leads to the erosion of our nonappetitive appetites by making them hostage to contingency (1980, p. 79). I take this as the claim that antirealism places a reflective person in a difficult dilemma: either to immerse himself as a desiring participant in a world containing values, but at the price of supposing falsely that these values are objective; or to shed this illusion of objectivity, but at the price of surrendering all but his appetitive desires. Platts suggests that while it is easy to make intelligible the motivating force of appetites, like the aversion to pain or the desire for sex, the nonappetitive desires by contrast do not force themselves on us in the same way (mainly because they lack the distinctive phenomenological feels that characterize the appetites). Therefore, something must stand in for these phenomenological features and thereby sustain the motivating force of these nonappetitive desires. The only real possibility, he suggests, is for their propositional content to contain the thought that their objects are independently desirable. For, suppose that I desire that p. If desire were conceptually prior to desirability, then it is logically possible that I might have desired that not-p instead and thus might have considered not-p desirable instead. Platts insists, however, that it is

> a brute human fact about human motivation and human desires that if this agent, at the point of action, considers this other possibility in his own terms, then he will cease to be motivated by his desire that p . . . reflection will eliminate the motivating force of his desire; and since *ex hypothesi* his desire lacks any phenomenological quality, his desire will then cease to be as the motivating force ceases to be. (1980, p. 79)

Thus the abandonment of realism about values is the end of nonappetitive desire; and since this is such a large and humanly central class of desires, its loss is a high price to pay.

In response, it should be noted that there is an important sense in which one can abandon realism about values and still acknowledge the conceptual priority of the desirable over the desired, for on any plausible version of subjectivism the desirable is not simply the desired: The desires or pro-attitudes that constitute values will be highly constrained. At the very least they will be epistemically rational.[18] We must therefore suppose that the antirealist allegedly in Platts's quandary reflects on the fact that his nonappetitive desire that p is (at least) epistemically rational. If he is truly reflective, in the sense of wanting to avoid irrationality, then this thought will dispell at least some of the mystery as to why he wants that p. Therefore, we can concede Platts's suggestion that the content of nonappetitive desires contains the thought that their object is independently desirable but give this a nonrealist reading.

At this point, the antirealist may begin to reflect on the fact that he might have found not-p desirable instead, which on the subjectivist reading is the thought that the desire that not-p might have been among his epistemically rational desires instead. Must *this* lead to the end of desire? That depends on what happens when he reflects upon the general desire that all his desires be epistemically rational. Barring some kind of transcendental argument for its necessity, it is possible that he might not have had this desire, in which case the desirability of p is hostage to the contingency of his desire that all his desires be epistemically rational. (At this crucial point, desire *is* conceptually prior to desirability for the nonrealist.) Must his reflection on *this* possibility lead to the end of his desire that p? . . . or to the end of his desire that his desires be rational?

These queries lead the antirealist to a second kind of reflection: upon the causal origins of his nonappetitive desires. He will ask how he came to want all his desires to be rational, and what in his constitution explains why acting on this desire brings about that he wants that p. Must these reflections lead to the erosion of his nonappetitive desires? How much contingency can a reflective person take about his own desires? Or, to put the question the other way around, how much self-delusion must an antirealist about values engage in to sustain his desires? Can he experience the "pull" of values in the world while at the same time believing that he himself is the source of those values?

The answers to these questions depend on how the nonrealist about values conceives of the states of the subject that constitute certain states of affairs as values. If he considers the genesis of value to be a matter of radical *decision*, on the model of existentialists and some noncognitivists, then I think there is a lot to Platts's depiction of the dilemma that follows the abandonment of realism. For consider the situation as it presents itself to the radical decisionist. He reflects on the fact that he desires that p, and that it is among his epistemically rational desires, and that he wants all his desires to be epistemically rational. But when he comes to the point of reflecting upon the causal origins of these nonappetitive desires, he comes up against a blank. They have no causal origins: He simply *decided* that having epistemically rational desires and that p should count as values. Now this is too much contingency for a clear-eyed nonrealist, committed to the "pull" of values, to take. Decision is simply too thin a basis to support a subjectivist account of values.[19]

In settling upon a better subjective basis for values, the antirealist should take quite seriously Platts's explanation of the motivating force of appetitive desires and turn it to his own advantage. Recall Platts's claim that appetitive desires have phenomenological qualities that make intelligible why they should motivate an agent. In answer to the challenge "why seek (or avoid) *that?*" one can only, as it were, display this quality ("that is just what pain, sex, eating chocolate, are like"). But the question is whether these phenomenological qualities are the crucial ingredient in the explanation or just the *involuntary, presented* quality of their appeal (or lack of appeal) to creatures with a certain kind of constitution and/ or history. Compare a similar challenge and response involving decidedly nonappetitive desires: "Why seek out Cezanne paintings?" "Because *that* . . . is what they are like?" To be sure, there are crucial differences in the kinds of "display" relevant in the two kinds of cases (no doubt closely related to the fact that nonappetitive desires lack a distinct phenomenology). For one thing, the display of the Cezanne painting will be (to put it mildly) considerably more articulate, for the simple reason that there is more to be articulate about. And this explains (in part) other differences. The having (if not the acting upon) nonappetitive desires is generally more under a person's rational control; they are more cognitively charged; they are generally (always?) culturally articulated and thus less simply a matter of biology or low-level learning; moreover, they can be elaborated, transformed, and placed into ensembles that confer new significance upon the individual desires. (Think of the effect upon aesthetic appreciation of learning about the history of a style.) These are inadequate comments on some crucial differences, but rather than try to fill out the picture here, I want to stress what appetitive and nonappetitive desires have in common. After all (or much) of the cultural and personal articulation, elaboration, and so on of nonappetitive desires is completed, they, too, present themselves to the individual. At this boundary the motivational account of the genesis of values also employs the framework of discovery (as opposed to decision or invention), usually more characteristic of its realist opponent. After (and probably also while) confronting the object or state of affairs, living with it, learning about it, the individual discovers in himself a desire for it. (I do realize that desire is an inadequate term for the sort of nonappetitive affinities to artworks, friends, work, and the other sorts of values at issue here.)

Desire or motivation itself is a much better basis for a subjectivist account of values because it reaches much deeper into the person himself and is thus amenable to some kind of explanation. In confronting values the agent, therefore, confronts part of himself, not an utterly gratuitous part that could just as well light upon *p* as upon not-*p*, but a part with a biological and/or cultural history that is usually not transparent to the person himself, but there to be explored, often not unlike other parts of the world. For, human motivation is a part of the natural world, a fact that should impress realist critics of subjectivism more than it does, because it can enter into an explanation of why values seem to have a "pull" upon us, something that the radical decisionist is at a loss to account for.

If desire rooted in the cognitive, constitutional, and historical density of the person is placed at the center of a subjectivist account of values, then Platts's dilemma can be escaped. Heartily embracing values does not force the subjectivist into some kind of self-imposed delusion; and honestly facing the implications of subjectivism does not lead to the erosion of all his (nonappetitive) desires. For it is generally just not true that one's desires could just as easily have lighted upon p as upon not-p. Human motivation has firmer contours than that. To be sure, the only necessity here is psychological necessity, but that is the only thing required if value is to have a firm place in the world.

If Platts were right that the end of realism is the end of desire, then the reflective agent would face a dilemma. But although this would be terrible, it would still be mainly a practical problem. Subjectivism would still be intact as a theoretical option, its supporters still in a position to insist that philosophical honesty compels us to take the hard road and acknowledge that the price must be paid. A deeper challenge to a nonrealistic account of values would aim at showing that it is incoherent in some way, for incoherence is the most serious explanatory failure of all.

Both radical decisionism and the kind of grounded motivational subjectivism just sketched hold that objectively speaking, abstracting from all human stances toward the world, nothing matters, nothing has value or meaning. David Wiggins suggests that this conception forces a distinction between an inner, participant perspective on values and meaning and an outer, theoretician perspective, a distinction that leads to trouble:

> The trouble is that, if we want to preserve any of the distinctive emphases of this particular [subjectivism], then we will find that, for purposes of the validation of any human concern, the [subjectivist] view must always readdress the problem to the inner perspective without itself adopting that perspective.[20]

The problem seems to be this. The experience of value and the deep, unthinking conviction that life has meaning characterize the inner perspective. Taking up the outer perspective, subjectivism insists that these are mere appearances: Nothing has objective value or meaning. But even from the external perspective this sounds too harsh, so to reinvest the world with meaning the subjectivist points to the inner perspective and the availability of the role of participant. But he cannot himself take up this perspective, precisely because he insists that what is revealed there is mere illusion. Thus he is caught between his own eliminativist ontology of value ("from the objective point of view, nothing matters") and his reluctance to leave it at that and simply dismiss out of hand the idea of value.

An obvious move here is to retreat from an austere eliminativism to a more tolerant reductionism ("values just are permanent possibilities of motivational commitment"). Putting to one side the difficulties in getting clear on how to determine whether a particular program is eliminativist or reductionist, there will be problems with this move if a subjectivist reduction also distorts the inner perspective by failing to save the appearances manifest there. This involves a considerable retreat from the charge that subjectivism involves a kind of incoherence, but it is serious nonetheless. What appearances are supposed to be distorted? Wiggins suggests that there are two. First, "it makes too little difference to the meaningfulness of life how well or badly our strivings are apt to turn out, but I object that that is not how it feels to most people from inside. . . . The will itself, taking the inner view, craves objective reasons" (1976, pp. 340–341). Second, we are keenly interested from the inner perspective in the difference between circular, static practical reasonings and life plans (like that of the hog farmer who buys more land to grow more corn to feed more hogs to buy more land) and noncircular acts of *poesis* and exercises of *phronesis,* and the life plans they constitute (1976, pp. 342–343).

Each of these criticisms assumes that subjectivism rules out certain substantive values and sources of meaning, but this is not so: It rules out neither the importance of the success of our strivings nor the noncircularity of our life plans. Perhaps Wiggins means to be pointing up intellectual tendencies in subjectivism rather than its essential features; but however this may be, it should be emphasized that subjectivism is an account of what value and meaning are and is thus not committed to any particular substantive account of what are values and meanings, certainly not a kind of Benthamite conception, holding that only states of consciousness are intrinsically valuable. Meta-ethical subjectivism can admit anything as a substantive value, however highly articulated, however remote from human consciousness. What it does insist on, of course, is that the condition specifying what constitutes states of affairs as valuable must make reference to subjective states. Thus the crucial distinction is between those states of affairs (including states of consciousness) that have value and those states of consciousness that confer or constitute value.

Can this distinction bear the weight the subjectivist places on it? This is precisely the point where it is crucial that the subjectivist distance himself from the radical decisionist, for if he does not, Wiggins's criticism that the subjectivist account of the realtionship between constituting state and intentional object is entirely too fortuitous will have considerable force. For the radical decisionist, it is true that the requisite state "could just as well have lighted upon any other object (even any other kind of object)" (1976, p. 347), but if the states constituting value are motivations or pro-attitudes deeply rooted in human psychology or in culturally articulated patterns of response, then they are not so fortuitously tied to their intentional objects, for these deeply rooted states can enter into explanations as to why people have certain desires but not others.[21] Since I have dwelt on this point already in my comments on Platts's dilemma, I will move on to consider another alleged problem.

It might be argued that the subjectivist accounts of value and meaning are incoherent in another way because they assume a sharp distinction between the inner and outer perspectives, a distinction that cannot be sustained. The outer perspective is preeminently that of the meta-ethical theorist, the inner view that of the moral participant, so one way to show that the distinction between perspectives cannot be sustained is to show that the uncommitted neutrality of the theorist is impossible. The question of the substantive neutrality of meta-ethics has been debated for some time, but Wiggins has recently employed a novel argument that deploys the framework of radical interpretation.[22] The basic idea is that there are certain a priori constraints on any attempt to assign content to the propositional attitudes of another, nontrivial constraints that guarantee some large degree of intersubjective agreement between the beliefs, desires, and so forth of interpreter and interpreted. The crucial constraint is some version of the principle of charity, which counsels the interpreter to minimize the number of inexplicably irrational or false propositional attitudes assigned to the interpreted, as measured against the principles of rationality of the interpreter. If the meta-ethical theorist is the interpreter attempting to analyze the moral discourse of the moral participant, then his first step will be to identify the latter's heartfelt moral utterances. But if charity dictates that the theorist minimize inexplicable disagreement between his own beliefs and concerns and those of the participant, then the theorist must project many of his own heartfelt moral beliefs onto the participant. But this entails that in the very process of assigning content to moral beliefs he must evince his own commitment to moral beliefs, which is to say that he cannot remain the uncommitted theorist.[23] But if the very attempt to do meta-ethics brings with it heartfelt moral commitments, then the integrity of the other perspective on values as objectively arbitrary is seriously undermined, and with it subjectivism itself, since this meta-ethical theory just is the outer perspective.

This is a fascinating argument (the idea of radical interpretation is fascinating), but there is much to question in it. First, it is unclear just how much pressure the a priori constraint of charity places on the meta-ethical theorist to take up the commitments of the participant. Charity counsels that he assign a minimum of *inexplicably* irrational and/or false attitudes, a qualification that may be compatible with more than a little intersubjective disagreement between interpreter and interpreted. Let us waive this point, however, because there is a second problem that does not require us to deal with such difficult questions about the general project of radical interpretation. The argument seems to assume that the subjectivist is committed to the idea that the inner and outer perspectives on value must be kept distinct, at least to the extent that one who takes up the outer perspective cannot also wholeheartedly embrace values. If the considerations I advanced against Platts's dilemma are sound, however, this rigid distinction between inner and outer is not an essential feature of subjectivism, at least not of the variety that casts deeply grounded desires in the value-constituting role. For as I argued there, reflection on the theoretical belief that values are a matter of our deepest (epistemically rational) motivational commitments need not drive out those value-constituting motivations. In confronting value, we confront (an important part of) ourselves; a realization that need not drive us to despair of the fact that nothing "objectively" matters. For a reflective person prepared to explore the deepest springs of his nature and to sharpen his sensitivity to the world, the abandonment of moral realism can be the awareness of desire, and therefore of value.

V. EXPLAINABLE SUBJECTIVISM AND MORAL REALISM

The considerations raised by Platts and Wiggins are not the only worries one might have about the rejection of moral realism, but they are among the central ones. If the considerations offered in the last section are convincing, however, the conflict between realist and nonrealist accounts of morality is not nearly as important as many have thought. Here is the reason. On some substantive moral theories, right- and/or good-making properties are themselves subjective states amenable to the same sorts of explanations as the states cited in subjectivist meta-ethical theories. For example, a preference-utilitarianism holds that the crucial right-making property is the maximization of preference-satisfaction; certain meta-ethical theories hold that rightness is to be reduced to the preferences of a certain class of agents. As far as ontology goes, neither the substantive nor the meta-ethical theory is any more committal than the other. I have argued that the key to allaying the sorts of worries expressed by Platts and Wiggins lies in the depth of our explanations of the subjective states that figure one's nonrealist meta-ethics. Now I want to argue that if deep explanations are available, there is no good reason to struggle over the issue of moral realism, at least not with respect to the range of issues considered here.[24]

Take the subjectivist scheme for analyzing or reducing moral concepts, "x is _____" if and only if x is the object of subjective state _____ (where the first blank is filled in with the moral term in question and the second with the meta-ethically relevant and no doubt highly constrained subjective state). For example, Rawls argues for a conception of goodness as desire constrained by deliberative rationality; Brandt argues for a conception of rightness as embodied in the set of rules that would be selected by an agent with nothing but desires that would survive a certain kind of purifying cognitive psychotherapy; and Harman argues for a conception of a certain class of moral obligations as grounded in commitment to social conventions. As near as one can tell, none of them is attracted to the idea that these subjective stances are gratuitously or arbitrarily chosen. It will be convenient to have a name for the kind of nonrealist meta-ethics that rejects radical decisionism, so let us adopt the ungainly label "explainable subjectivism" to convey the idea that the meta-ethically significant subjective states are open to empirical investigation. On such theories it is an open question how best to explain how people acquire their rational desires or their propensity to make certain commitments.

Some of these explanations will be "deep," some "shallow." Oversimplifying considerably, we can distinguish between two contrasting explanatory frameworks, those that cast the explanations in terms of "innate," or anyway relatively enduring features of persons, and those that appeal primarily to environmental variables. Examples of the first are Piagetian and Freudian accounts of moral development and of course sociobiological theories. Examples of the second are classical and operant conditioning theories, as well as the somewhat more complex models building on them, like social learning theory. The distinction is crude because any plausible explanatory framework will appeal to explanatory variables of each kind. There is really a continuum of theories, differing in the relative explanatory importance of innate structrue and environmental influence, something that obviously comes in degrees. Piagetian theories of moral development, for example, place great explanatory emphasis on stages in the child's innate cognitive development, but they also acknowledge that environmental factors, like the opportunity to play certain social roles, interact with innate factors to produce the child's moral capacities at a given point. Even the most extreme of the innate variable frameworks, sociobiology, can admit the cultural elaboration of our genetic endowment. Indeed, environmental pressure is a crucial factor in all natural-selection explanations. Environmental-variable theories, on the other hand, allow a place for innate factors. Even the most extreme of these conditioning models, which explain the acquisition of a morality primarily in terms of patterns of environmental reinforcement, must allow that the person has some innate structure, if only a capacity for the association of ideas and of course a set of unconditioned responses to build upon.

Both kinds of accounts are compatible with many degrees of convergence or divergence in basic desires or attitudes or responses, although, all things considered equal, there will probably be more convergence if some innate-variable theory is closer to the truth, because we can expect there to be more similarity of innate structure than of environment. And even where there is enough similarity of environmental patterns of reinforcement to produce convergence of desire, attitude, or response, this convergence is less stable, because the factors producing it are themselves less stable and enduring. The point to be emphasized, however, is that it is an empirical question whether relatively deep or evanescent factors produce basic human desires, attitudes, and responses, and thus just how much convergence there will be. Subjectivist meta-ethical theories ground morality in rational desire, attitude, or commitment, but they leave these empirical questions open.

Now let us shift attention to those versions of moral realism that adopt a generally naturalistic conception of morality but reject the subjectivist reduction of the good and the right to desires, attitudes, or commitments, however rational, reducing them instead to the natural good- and right-making properties themselves. As we have seen, one important reason for the rejection stems from the fear that anything short of realism leaves morality and moral response hostage to the contingency of mere subjectivity. This fear may be misplaced, however, for consider how many good- and right-making properties themselves involve states of subjects and are thus similarly hostage to contingency. I have already mentioned preference-utilitarianism, but there are many other obvious examples—hedonistic utilitarianism, certain forms of perfectionism, any theory of value or obligation that stresses human flourishing or the fulfillment of human interests or needs. There are also some less obvious examples, like rights-based theories designed to protect ends such as interests or needs, and perhaps even some side constraint rights-based theories. (The only kind of substantive moral theory not likely to be hostage to the contingency of making states of subjects central in the substantive account of goodness and rightness is a duty-based ethics.) Because of this, any realist form of naturalism that reduces the good or the right to one of these substantive conceptions faces just the problems of contingency thought to plague antirealist subjectivism. If the subjectivist reduction of rightness to a commitment to social conventions cannot guarantee that all will commit themselves to the same convention, neither can the realist reduction to utility-maximization guarantee that there will be sufficient coherence in the social-welfare function to yield a coherent theory of the right. If the reduction of rightness to the set of rules preferred by an agent with none but rational desires cannot guarantee that all such agents will settle on the same set of rules, neither can an ethics of human flourishing guarantee that there will be enough uniformity in human nature to produce a nontrivial basis for moral obligations. One could go on. For every worry about the possible relativistic consequences of a subjectivist meta-ethics, there is a parallel worry about the fragmentation and disunity of the good and the right in realist theories that give an account of these notions in terms of good- and right-making properties involving states of subjects. But this includes virtually all realist theories. And perhaps more to the point, for every worry about the sheer contingency of those states to which subjectivists reduce the good and the right, there is a parallel worry about the contingency of those states figuring in the moral realist's favored account, whether it involves welfare, interests, needs, or human flourishing.

The real issue, it appears, is how contingent these states turn out to be; that is, how deep are the factors that explain them. But this is an empirical question that cannot be settled by any meta-ethical theory; moreover, subjectivists are as entitled as realists to whatever framework, at whatever level of depth, provides the ultimate explanation of how moral agents acquire and sustain their desires and attitudes, their interests and needs.[25]

NOTES

1. Some, however, have doubted this dependence of moral justification on moral ontology. For an example of such doubts, see the early chapters of David Copp's *Morality and Society* (forthcoming). I will not try to deal with this complex issue here.

2. Harman (1975; 1977; and this volume); Brandt (1980 and this volume); Firth (1952); and Rawls (1971).

3. Cf. the characterizations of moral realism in Petit (1981), Platts (1980), and Quinn (1978). Philipa Foot (1983) takes moral realism to be exclusively a view about the transcendence of moral truth over epistemic recognition-conditions, on a parallel with Dummett's treatment (1978) of realism in mathematics. I prefer to take it as a view about the transcendence of truth over motivational acceptance-conditions, because that is where the central controversies about justification in ethics arise.

4. These two distinctions are sometimes conflated. See, for example, Williams (1973a and 1973b) and Blackburn (1971).

5. For an opposing view, see Hare (1976). Part of his reason for defending the distinction between cognitivist and prescriptivist versions of nonrealism springs from his particular conception of moral reasoning. For criticism of the most recent version of Hare's prescriptivism, see Zimmerman (1984).

6. See, for example, Williams (1973a and 1973b). For effective criticism of his position, see Foot (1983).

7. Wiggins (1976). It should be noted that Wiggins is not an unalloyed moral realist, but he adopts instead an intermediate position that parallels in tantalizing respects Kant's conception of objectivity in the First Critique.

8. But see also Nagel's remark about *perceiving* that there are certain reasons for action (1979), and his insistence that (for him) another's being in pain is "self-evidently" an objective reason for action (1979), both of which suggest that he believes that statements about reasons for acting are not arrived at by inference at all.

9. Harman (this volume). There is an important ambiguity in Harman's characterization of the distinction between ethical naturalism and autonomism. The naturalist may be viewed as one who insists that moral properties are either to be identified with natural properties or are nothing at all; or as one who is willing to employ the explanatory constraints of science in order to carry out their reduction to (or elimination in favor of) natural properties. On the second construal (but not on the first), an ethical naturalist could end up believing in unreduced moral properties—if there is some explanatory work that a naturalistic reduction (or elimination) leaves undone.

10. Sturgeon (this volume), p. 60. The classic papers on functionalism are by Putnam; see, for example (1967). I infer Sturgeon's attraction to this parallel from his references to Boyd's treatment of the mental in (forthcoming c). In the following discussion I ignore Boyd's point about the cardinality problem (invoked by Sturgeon in this volume, p. 60) mainly because the major reductive programs in ethics need not hold out for a reduction of moral to physical properties.

11. Sturgeon (this volume), note 30. The Kripkean treatment of natural-kind terms emerges in Putnam (1975).

12. Sturgeon, correspondence with Harman.

13. Ibid.

14. For some relevant discussion of the kinds of necessity that may enter into the analysis of supervenience, see Kim (1978).

15. For an elaboration of this idea, see Blackburn (1971).

16. Still another example is the dispute over the reality of "strong evaluation." See Taylor (1977), who acknowledges that there is opposition to the very concept of strong evaluation in note 3.

17. As articulated, for example, in Kuhn (1962) and Feyerabend (1965).

18. For one account of this kind of constraint, see Brandt's discussion of "cognitive psychotherapy" (1979); for another, see Rawls on deliberative rationality (1971, section III).

19. For some rather different criticisms of radical decisionism, see Taylor (1977).

20. Wiggins (1976). Wiggins takes noncognitivism as his target. For reasons hinted at in note 5, I believe that nothing substantial changes if we broaden his target to include cognitivist but nonrealist theories (thus I substitute "subjectivism" in the passage quoted in the text).

21. For a subjectivist, the tie between value-constituting psychological states and their intentional objects will be merely causal, and thus they lack the kind of necessity the realist wants and that seems to be a feature of the inner perspective on values and meaning that he is trying to save.

22. The idea of radical interpretation has been deployed in an argument against moral relativism in Cooper (1978). For some critical comments directed against this approach to the problem, see Zimmerman (1983).

23. Here is the way Wiggins describes the situation: "To see itself and its object in the alien manner of the outer view, the states as experienced would have to be prepared

to suppose that it, the state, could just as well have lighted on any other object (even any other kind of object), provided only that the requisite attitudes could have been induced. But of this conception of such states we are entitled to complain that nothing remains that we can recognize or which the inner perspective will not instantly disown" (Wiggins, 1976, p. 347). Note the similarity to Platts's argument discussed above.

24. In working out the basic argument of this section, I have been greatly stimulated by Richard Boyd (forthcoming c). Boyd's title indicates, however, that he takes this line of argument in a somewhat different direction from the one explored here. I should also note that if the argument of this section has force, then I must qualify, and perhaps take back, certain conclusions about the importance of the distinction between normative and meta-ethics urged in Zimmerman (1980).

25. This essay was written while the author enjoyed the support of a National Endowment for the Humanities Fellowship at the Hastings Center, Hastings-on-Hudson, New York. I would like to thank the Center for providing both the Fellowship and a stimulating intellectual home in 1982–83. Thanks are also due to Simon Fraser University for providing a sabbatical leave, which afforded the leisure necessary for undertakinig this study. I am also grateful to my co-editor, David Copp, for several stimulating conversations on this cluster of issues (although in fairness I should note that the stimulation did not come from agreement).

chapter four

The Explanation of Moral Language

Richard B. Brandt

What follows is concerned primarily with specifically moral terms: 'moral duty', 'moral obligation', 'morally ought', 'morally reprehensible', and the like; and there are implications for expressions like 'is a good thing'.

It is doubtful whether every language has words with the same meaning as these, or even that these English terms are used with the same meaning among all contemporary native speakers of English. Many classical scholars think the Greeks (such as Achilles and Aristotle) did not have moral concepts like ours (mine?), and it seems hard to separate the most nearly corresponding concepts in the Judaeo-Christian tradition from the concept of God's requirements on human conduct. John Gay, in a work first published in 1731 (and typical of the major theological utilitarians), said that "obligation" is just "the necessity of doing or omitting any action in order to be happy: i.e., when there is such a relation between an Agent and an action that the Agent cannot be happy without doing or omitting that action, then the Agent is said to be obliged to do or omit that action." This passage is consistent with thinking, as he later goes on to suggest, that moral obligation is just being required, on pain of future punishment by God, to do or omit something. This concept of moral obligation seems very different from ours (mine?). But Elizabeth Anscombe seems to think Gay's view of "moral obligation" is the only one that makes sense. Indeed, she holds that it and "morally wrong" make sense only in the context of belief in divine commands; in the absence of such belief, she says, these terms make no more sense than "if the notion 'criminal' were to remain when criminal law and criminal courts have been abolished and forgotten" (1958, 1968, pp. 193, 204). She thinks other usages, of speakers devoid of theological convictions (like probably usages of most contemporary writers on ethics), are "fishy."[1] One suspects there is even more reason to doubt that our (my?) moral concepts appear in China, Japan, and India, not to mention primitive societies. Is "morally reprehensible" the same as "losing face"? If John Ladd is right, the Navaho have only one "moral" term: *babadzid*, meaning "imprudent" or "dangerous" (1957). There is a priori reason to doubt the universality of moral concepts if we think that the meanings of these terms are affected by and bound up with the total conceptual scheme of speakers.

This (possible) absence of uniformity of concepts is consistent with there being a commonsense *morality* (with variable content) in most, if not all, societies. At least it is if we say a society "has a morality" if most adult members (a) are motivated to some extent to do or avoid *doing* some things for no further reason and particularly not for reason of self-interest; (b) tend to feel guilty (at least, uncomfortable) to some extent independently of expectations about disapproval by others, if they fail to conform their conduct accordingly (there may or may not be concepts of justification and excuse), and (c) tend to be indignant at and criticize others when their conduct shows substandard motivation in this respect. Let us call this complex "moral attitudes" with respect to some forms of conduct. It may also be that every or nearly every language contains terminology to *express* these attitudes, and to claim or imply that they are in *some appropriate way justified*.

It must be left open what kind of justification is thought appropriate. Beliefs about this clearly vary, appeal to what the gods approve is one way. My suggestion that morality in this loose sense is at least nearly universal I confess is motivated in good part by my belief that resentment of deliberate injury must be at least nearly universal, and that some sympathy also is at least nearly universal either because it contributes to the survival of either small societies or the gene-type of the altruist, or, perhaps also, through conditioning from situations universal to early childhood. Anyway, Achilles seems to have been indignant when Agamemnon took away his prisoner Briseis, and I speculate from his speech that he thought his anger was justified. If some morality in this sense is universal, it does not follow that any (much less every) precise moral *concept* is universal.

Various moral philosophers, however, have thought there is in some sense a standard ordinary meaning of moral terms and have made

---

[1] Professor Frankena has suggested, in lectures, that Samuel Clarke was the first philosopher to have used "obligation" in the sense she regards as fishy, when Clarke said there is an obligation to do what is fitting—an obligation independent of commands or sanctions or of relation to the agent's own interest (see Clarke, 1705; 1738, pp. 487, 492; 1897, pp. 9, 16).

proposals purporting to be descriptions of what that meaning is. G. E. Moore, in *Principia Ethica*, held that "is wrong" just means "produces less good than some other act open to the agent," whereas in *Ethics* he thought that when people use "wrong" they have in mind some un-analyzable property or relation. Richard Price, Samuel Clarke, and W. D. Ross seem to share this latter view. Roderick Firth and, I think, Hume suppose that some "ideal observer" account renders the actual meaning, in some sense or other, of these moral terms; and the same appears to be true of R. M. Hare's universal-prescription account. (At least, he thinks his account describes his own usage, and he thinks others' meanings are probably the same.) Now, *whose* meanings are these philosophers purporting to describe? Hardly John Gay and his contemporaries. St. Paul? The most convincing course for them to take is to represent their accounts as explications of the meanings of themselves and some of their *readers*; to do this successfully would be a substantial achievement.

There is another tradition in philosophy, of proposals about how moral language should be "construed," which does not purport to describe ordinary meanings. W. K. Frankena has said that the problems of meta-ethics demand "clarity and decision about the nature and functions of morality, of moral discourse, and of moral theory, and this requires not only small-scale analytic inquiries but also studies in the history of ethics and morality, in the relation of morality to society and of society to the individual, as well as in epistemology and in the psychology of human motivation" (1958, p. 80). Anscombe seems to recommend that the word *ought* in its "emphatic" sense be dropped by persons who do not subscribe to the notion of a divine law-giver. A somewhat similar recommendation apparently would be made by Philippa Foot. Rawls, in the passage where he discusses the status of his explanation of "morally wrong" or "just," in terms of what would be chosen in the "original position," does not claim that his account replicates what ordinary English speakers mean by these terms, but he says he is offering a *replacement* that serves the same purposes and does not suffer from the problems surrounding the original terms (1971, p. 111).

Should we also perhaps include Kant in this group? Immediately after the first formulation of the categorical imperative in the *Grundlegung*, he writes:

> Now if all the imperatives of duty can be derived from this one imperative as their principle, then even although we leave it unsettled whether what we call duty may not be an empty concept, we shall still be able to show at least what we understand by it and what the concept means [. . . was wir dadurch denken und was dieser Begriff sagen wolle]. (1785, 1964, p. 88)

Is it being alleged this is the meaning of the ordinary concept, or is it what Kant is alleging would be a sensible one? He might mean that morality can command respect only if its principles are binding on all rational beings, and if the content of its prescriptions for conduct is the same as the conduct that actually would take place in a purely rational being (one not guided by desires or inclinations). If he had this in mind, his theory might be construed as *recommending* a certain concept of "moral obligation," not just claiming to report what concept people already have in mind. Kant thought that the moral philosopher had best begin with the morality of common sense, but he did not think it superfluous to move on to a metaphysics of morals.

Another person who may belong in this group is J. S. Mill. In the fifth chapter of *Utilitarianism* he makes a statement important for his normative ethics:

> We do not call anything wrong unless we mean to imply that a person ought to be [it is desirable that he be] punished in some way or other for doing it—if not by law, by the opinion of his fellow creatures; if not by opinion, by the reproaches of his own conscience. This seems the real turning point between morality and simple expediency.

So Mill concludes that a morally wrong act is not identical with an inexpedient act, but is one it is expedient for the legal/moral system to sanction by legal punishment, public opinion, or the pangs of conscience. Thus Mill opts not for moral rightness being fixed directly by the relative utility of an act being morally appraised, but by whether it would be punished by an optimal legal/moral system. A great deal, then, turns on this point. Does Mill think that the point is one about "our" actual concepts? Perhaps he does mean that in ordinary use the predication of "wrong" carries with it the *implication* that it is desirable that the act be punished in some way. Or perhaps he intends to report just what he thinks is a widespread *belief*—that wrong acts ought to be punished in some way. Or, perhaps, might he be moved by the thought that, if one wants to produce happiness in the world, one had better sanction act-types that tend to cause unhappiness and mark these by calling them "wrong?" That would be a *recommendation* of a use of "wrong" in view of what Mill thinks is the function of morality and of the necessary place of sanctions in making it work. He could agree with what Frankena said.

Thus there are two main traditions of philosophical thinking about how moral language should be construed. One is that everybody's or somebody's (maybe just the reader's or the writer's) moral meanings are reasonably definite, and that a description of what these are can be given precise enough to be a helpful guide in moral thinking. The other tradition is that, irrespective of how diverse or confused the meaning or use of moral terms may be, around the world, or even at various stages of the usage of a given individual, there is a certain pattern of concepts it is useful or important for there to be, when the functions of morality in society and of moral discourse in morality, and the psychology of individual morality, are taken into account. The first of these has not achieved convincing results: The nonnaturalist philosophers have not convinced other philosophers that people do have some un-analyzable nonempirical concept in mind when they use these terms. Nor have the naturalists (or prescriptivists) been convincing that ordinary ethical usage is properly described in the ways that have been proposed— although it is always possible some naturalist may come forth with a convincing account. Possible, but unlikely.

My suggestion is that the more promising line of thinking for moral philosophers to take is to work out the details of showing that a certain pattern of concepts is important because of the clarity and other benefits it would make possible for moral discourse. Unfortunately, philosophers of this persuasion have not offered precise accounts how one is to identify the purportedly optimal or clarifying conceptual scheme. Rawls's remarks are helpful, but he lays down a restriction that the optimal set of concepts must yield as analytic moral principles, which, when taken in conjunction with observable facts, lead deductively to the person's own moral principles in 'reflective equilibrium,' a view that seems to lean heavily toward revision of moral concepts in the direction of maintaining the moral status quo. In what follows I will attempt to identify criteria for an optimal conceptual framework for moral discourse that is more open to serious revision of a person's moral commitments. I proposed such an account in a recent volume (1979), but without a connected explanation and justification of the criteria for identification of the ideal conceptual framework for moral discourse. I will try to fill this gap, to some degree, by explaining the reasons for a certain conceptual framework for moral discourse. How are we to motivate, or recommend, the selection of certain explications for moral terms when we do not provide a description of some ordinary-language meaning of these terms?

I. A PARTIAL EXPLANATION OF
SOME NECESSARY MORAL CONCEPTS

We may begin with what seems to be the most important thing about morality: the motivational system that comprises people's personal moral codes. Compared with this, moral discourse is relatively an epiphenom-enon. What is it for a person to have a motivational moral code? First, he will have aversions to some act-types for no further reason and in particular no reason of self-interest, such as an aversion to breaking a promise. Second, when more than one of these aversions is engaged by a single contemplated action, he will incline pro or con performing the action, depending on the strength of the various aversions and something analogous to a vector sum. Third, if he thinks he acted contrary to these aversions, he will tend to feel guilty unless there was some "excusing" factor present, such as mistake of fact, inability to act otherwise, and so on. Fourth, if a judge thinks another has acted contrary to the aversions the judge has, he will tend to disapprove of this agent for what he did, unless, again, there was an "excuse." Fifth, he will tend to admire and favor certain act-types, even when he is not inclined to disapprove of their omission; and it may be he will disfavor and feel some contempt for persons because they act in certain ways (such as refusing a match when someone has requested one politely), even if he would hardly disapprove of the person in the sense of feeling indignant with him (and might not feel remorseful if he offended himself). Sixth, he will disapprove of the absence of the aversions referred to; in fact, it is precisely when he finds it necessary to attribute someone's conduct to the absence of one or more of these aversions that he thinks the action is "without excuse." Finally, he believes about all these attitudes/ dispositions on his part that they are justified in some appropriate way. Doubtless there is much more to be said (e.g., about what exactly it is to feel guilty). What one would like to provide is a complete phenomenology of the "moral life."

We know a good deal about individual "moral codes" in this sense. We know that individual moral systems normally make life more tolerable in society. We know that various factors play a role in the development of individual moral codes: knowing that certain act-types tend to cause harm, sympathetic concern—native or acquired early in life by conditioning—for the welfare of others, the observation of "models," conditioning from criticism of one's conduct by others, and so on (Hoffman, 1970, 1981). We also know that there are differences among the moral codes of individuals in the same society (for instance, the dispute about the morality of abortion), and much more when the individuals come from quite different types of culture.

Not everyone would agree to the above account of what it is to have a "personal moral code." Not so very many decades ago matters would have been described (and still are in some circles) in a very different way. It would have been said that what it is for a person to have a moral code is for him to have beliefs about what kind of conduct God requires of man (either because He wants people to behave so as to contribute to the social welfare, or for some other reason), and for him to think that God will severely punish those who knowingly flout his commands, and hence that the person will, out of prudent regard for his own future welfare, be strongly motivated to conform his behavior to these requirements. Alternatively, it might be said that what it is for a person to have a personal moral code is for him to have various theoretical beliefs about which types of action are fitting or unfitting (have a certain property or relation), and, if the person has a general desire to conform his behavior to what is fitting, he will find himself motivated to behave in what he thinks the most fitting way, in whatever circumstances. Doubtless there are other ways in which having a "personal moral code" might be described. The account I gave strikes me as most realistic and compatible with what we know at the present time, so I shall stick with this account of what it is to have a personal moral code. I do not at all deny that many persons have had a moral code in the sense described in terms of theological beliefs, or that many still do; but at present it seems more fruitful to think of a moral code as I have suggested. Actually, it seems likely that many persons have a personal moral code in the sense I explained, and also in the theological sense, at the same time.

It is useful to think of people's moral codes as, like the law, an instrument for guiding behavior so as normally to bring about a desirable end-state for society. The various aversions toward act-types are normally aversions to conduct unfavorable to the welfare of society. The guilt feelings and disapproval of others function to strengthen the basic aversions when these have been too weak to control conduct. But since it is pointless for a person to be "punished" by guilt feelings or the disapproval of others when his aversions are already of standard strength, a person's objectively objectionable behavior will be "excused" when there is not reason to think it derived from a substandard level of the moral aversions; that is, from a defect of character. This feature of moral systems again has its analogue in the law. Incidentally, there have been moral codes with no provision for "excuses"—moral codes that we might call codes of "strict liability."

While it is useful to think of moral codes as instruments for bringing about desirable states of society, one *need* not think of them in this way. One may view them as just phenomena, to be understood and appraised; certainly one need not think of them as a product of a process of social evolution that favored the survival of societies that managed somehow to develop moral codes among their members, any more than one need view them as a result of biological evolution.

But what has all this about motivational moral codes to do with moral *concepts*? If there are motivational moral codes, is moral *discourse* necessary at all? Much less, need there be any particular conceptual framework for moral discourse? The answer, perhaps obviously, is that moral discourse *is* necessary, or at least it is highly desirable. For one thing, if the system is to work, it must be possible to express one's disapproval of what has been done, if not to the agent himself, then at least to one's friends. And if there is communication among observers about whether an agent is to be disapproved of for his behavior, or his behavior excused, it must be possible to discuss whether the behavior was compatible with a standard level of aversions in the agent; in other words, with his being virtuous. So much communication in the group is necessary. Moreover, since an agent will often find situations unclear and confusing, agents will want to ask for moral advice from others, and if advice is to be given, again there must be moral discourse and terminology that makes moral advice-giving possible.

But moral symbolism—a convenient terminology indicating the status of acts in relation to a thinkers' own presumed-justified moral code—is needed not just for interpersonal communication, but for an agent's own moral reflection. Suppose an agent is averse to promise-breaking, but in a particular case he happens to know that keeping a promise will be costly to him but of no benefit to the promisee; or perhaps he knows that he gave the promise originally on the basis of a deliberate misrepresentation of fact by the promisee. Now it may be that his moral code (or "intuitions") is so fine-tuned that when he calls these special circumstances to mind, his hesitation to break that promise dissipates—or perhaps better, he finds he has no standing aversion to breach *that* kind of promise at all. But it may well be that his moral code does not provide such automatic guidance. The agent has to think. Moreover, he may have a higher-order aversion to aversions of his own that he thinks are socially counterproductive; in other words, he has attitudes about moral attitudes. For the purpose of bringing the higher-order attitude to bear on the lower-order one, he requires symbolic processes. Much the same when his moral aversions conflict in a given case. His motivational code may not be fine-tuned enough automatically to guide him, everything considered, in favor of one course of action. Again he may need to think; and again he may need to reflect on what relative weighting of moral aversions would be socially most beneficial. Thinking may thus give direction to his first-order attitudes. Still again, a person may wonder if he really should feel guilty about something he did, say, something hurtful to someone. Perhaps he had had too many drinks. Is that an excuse? Is it an excuse to lose one's temper and do something one would not otherwise have done? To answer these questions, reflection is needed about what level of moral aversion should be standard in the society—and for this it may be that reflection is needed about what level of moral aversion it is socially beneficial to bring about by criticism, and so on. None of this reflection can occur without a framework enabling one to make the various distinctions.

There is actually an effective moral system in our society, and there obviously is interpersonal discussion of moral issues and intrapersonal moral reflection. So we must anticipate that there is a set of concepts, capable of making the distinctions to which I have been referring, already in our conceptual scheme. As indeed there is. We have the terminology: "Everything considered, what he morally ought to do—or is morally bound to do—is so-and-so." Then there is "he has some (or a *prima facie*) obligation to do so-and-so." and "doing that was reprehensible." Or, "he didn't do what morally he ought to have done, but his failure has to be excused on account of his misunderstanding of the situation." Or, "his behavior has no excuse; if he had been as careful of the welfare of others as he should have been, he would never have done it." And so on. Morality needs such a conceptual framework.

I have not so far proposed any complete analysis of any of these terms but have merely suggested that, for an effective moral system, there must be a certain type of motivational framework and a corresponding conceptual framework.

What have philosophers to contribute to all this? Well, it is one thing for there to be roughly a certain conceptual framework available for moral discourse, but it is another thing for the concepts to be sharp, and for speakers to understand just which distinctions they are designed to make and how they are important for the functioning of the moral system. So a philosopher may be performing a valuable service if he does something to get these distinctions and their importance recognized by speakers of the moral language of his society.

II. FILLING IN THE DEFINITION: THE OPTIMAL PROCEDURE

So far I have argued that a framework of concepts is requisite for a morality: the concepts of *prima facie* obligation, obligation overall everything considered, excuse, reprehensibility everything considered, the praiseworthy or supererogatory, perhaps also moral rights and "offenses," and so on. These notions must have certain connections with one another. I have not, however, argued for any complete account of the meaning or function of any of them.

The major historical controversies among writers on meta-ethics have not been directed at the points I have been making so far. There is, or should be, agreement among naturalists and noncognitivists and non-naturalists that the terms we have been discussing are needed for the effective functioning of a moral system, although they might not put the matter in just these terms. All will or should agree that we need to distinguish "morally ought not to," "reprehensible," and "excuse," in roughly the way suggested. The meta-ethical wars have been about something else. They have been about how the above terms should be explained by an account that goes to the bottom of matters. We must now turn our attention to this. Fortunately, we do not need to worry about proposing and supporting a separate explication for each of the terms we have been discussing. For we can follow a strategy proposed some years ago by A. C. Ewing, to the effect that all these terms can be construed by means of just one fundamental ethical concept, one called "fittingness," plus commonsense nonmoral notions. We can agree, except that in place of his concept of fittingness, which Ewing conceived to name a simple unobservable relation, we can take the term "justified" as our basic concept, as it is used when we speak of a *justified* moral code. It will be recalled that I said that what it is to have a moral code is for one to have certain desires/aversions and to view them as *justified* in some appropriate sense (the sense being left a bit vague).

To see how this works, let us consider how "is reprehensible" might be explained in this way. Ewing would have said something like this: For X to be reprehensible for his act A is for it to be *fitting* that persons disapprove of X on account of A. Whereas my suggestion would be that "X is reprehensible for his act A" be construed as "Anyone who subscribed to a *justified* moral system would disapprove of X for his action A." These proposals seem not to be controversial. What *is* controversial is how "justified moral system" is to be construed. A nonnaturalist like Ewing will say that a person "subscribes to a justified moral system" if and only if his approvals and disapprovals are *fitting*, where "fitting" names an unobservable but intellectually inspectable relation. A noncognitivist like Stevenson would say that a "justified moral system" is one that condemns those actions that "I hereby condemn and recommend that others condemn." And so on. The problem, then, is this. Suppose we assume as agreed that proposals about a common *actual* meaning of "justified moral system" in ordinary speech, like other moral expressions, are to be ignored as unsuccessful. We also assume there is no such thing as a nonempirical property of fittingness, such as Ewing thought he had in mind, and we may therefore just ignore nonnaturalism. How, then, are we to pick reasonably among various possible explications of "justified," presumably along naturalist lines or along prescriptivist lines or some combination thereof?

It will be reassuring and helpful to remind ourselves at this point just what we are looking for. In the first place, we are not looking for some concept, or property, to which a person's moral attitudes might be a natural response in the way fear is a natural response to what is considered dangerous. Many philosophers have thought there are such concepts: That we may apprehend the supposed fact that some action or state of affairs has some property *P*, and that we then naturally respond to this by a desiring, or approving, or admiring attitude. This has generally been the view of nonnaturalist writers. But my suggestion here is that we look at matters from the opposite end, that we take as our basic fact that people subscribe to moral codes in the motivation sense I have sketched—that they have aversions to certain act-types, that they have dispositions to feel guilt or to disapprove, and so on. Our question, then, is: If some such moral system were in place in a given person or society, in what sense might it be *justified*? One might then ask, What is the *importance* of knowing whether an effective moral code is *justified*? What is the function of raising such questions?

I believe the importance of the concept of justification depends on the fact that most people have practical problems about their own moral codes and those of others, partly for the reason that they are well aware of the fact of divergences among moral codes. People do ask themselves: What kind of moral code am I to teach myself, subscribe to, prefer, support for the educational system? (These questions are all closely related, and we may take them as coming to the same thing for present purposes.) So a person, along with subscribing to a moral code, may entertain practical doubts about it. Nor are such doubts restricted to a society like our own, with all its information about divergences, better- or worse-founded beliefs about how people come by their moral codes; for instance, from prestige-suggestion, modeling by parents or teachers, and so on. Such doubts were present among the Greeks and, I speculate, among primitive peoples. (One old Hopi Indian, who decided not to try to answer my own queries about his moral views, said: "Those are very hard questions you are asking, and I will never know the answers to them.") So people do want to know whether their own moral codes are subject to well-founded criticism, whether there are considerations that can give them assurance rather than self-doubt.

What we want to do, then, is to spell out a conception of "justified" that will do this job—that is, will answer this practical doubt when it is shown that some moral code is justified in that sense. The request for such a conception may still seem indeterminate. But let me point out that there are several properties that such a concept of justification must have, or which an explanation giving a meaning to "justified" must have. First, the concept, or explanation, must be clear; there is no point in an explanation of "justified" that is no clearer than "justified" in ordinary use. Second, there are some epistemological restrictions. "Justified" is not to be explained so that we can know if a moral code is justified only if there is a priori intuitive knowledge of synthetic propositions in ethics. Again, "justified" is not to be construed in terms merely of *coherence* of ethical commitments. If no single commitment has a justified claim to be accepted, then neither does a set of them, however large or coherent. This requirement must be admitted to be somewhat controversial, but the most serious defenders of the coherence theory of justification of theoretical beliefs at present would agree that coherence need not lead toward truth unless the system includes reports of experience that are themselves independently credible. It is plausible to make the same demand for "justification" in the context of moral codes.

Third, our explanation for "justified" must be evaluatively neutral. We may not propose, for instance, that "a moral code is justified" is to be construed just as, "The acceptance of that code would maximize happiness" as a utilitarian might have it, and as Mill may have thought when he said that the goal of happiness must be the test of actions and morality alike. The reason for this is that the function of the concept of justification is to help us discriminate among warring moral codes and to criticize our own. It would fail in this function if everyone is free to define "justified" in terms of his own preferred moral system. Fourth, the explanation for "justified" should not simply authorize everyone to follow whatever attitudes or desires he happens to have. It may not simply say, in effect, "If you believe something is right, then it *is* right." If a person raises a practical question he presumably wants some more perspicuous, helpful answer than this. Fifth—and this is a difficult requirement to meet—it must be true of any explained meaning for "justified" that *any* person who comes to believe that a moral code is justified in that sense will find that this moral code is thereby *recommended* to him, that his ambivalences are at least partly resolved, that he is made more content or satisfied with that moral code. So, if it is shown that a utilitarian moral code is justified in the explained sense, everyone will be thereby more disposed to be a utilitarian. One trouble with some conceptions of "justified"—say those that embody talk of "a moral point of view"—is that they would not recommend the so-explained "justified" moral code to anyone with egoistic inclinations.

Of course, once we have settled on a *conception* of "justification," a lot more argument is likely to be needed in order to show that some type of moral code is justified in that sense, say a utilitarian or egoist or contractarian type.

I shall want to add two more conditions for a satisfactory explication of "justified," but it is convenient to postpone that briefly.

Is there any explanation of "moral code justified for X" that meets those conditions? I have been able to think of only one, and it turns out not to be very simple when we try to spell it out. The proposal is that a moral code is justified for a person X if he would choose or support it for his society if he were *fully rational*. This proposal may seem a bit hollow, because the term "rational" itself does not enjoy a clear and agreed meaning, and we have to spell that out with still another explanation. I have the temerity, however, to attempt this, while conceding that my proposal possibly needs some refinements. It goes as follows. Suppose I say, "It is rational for X to support moral system S." I propose we mean by this: "I hereby recommend that X support S, (1) taking as my objective maximizing satisfaction of the ultimate desires of X as corrected to form a transitive system, be mood-independent, and capable of surviving repeated vivid reflection on relevant facts; and (2) having as my beliefs the ones X is justified in having on the basis of his evidence; (3) in view of the fact that support of S implements a strategy that in the long run will satisfy X's corrected desires as effectively as any other strategy and is coherent with what we know, especially the psychology of motivation."

What in effect this explanation implies for how a person is to identify a rational choice for him is that he lay out the options available (the moral systems among which he may choose), determine the probable consequences of the support of (adoption of) each and how probable the consequence is, and invite him to consider how much he "truly" wants these several consequence-sets—the degree of wanting being written down to correspond with the improbability of the consequence given that the option is taken. A "true" preference is identified as one corrected in the ways suggested. The consequences of supporting one moral system rather than another might be changes in general welfare, in the distribution of welfare, in one's own welfare, in promises being kept, the truth spoken, and so on. We invite the individual to make up his mind which set of consequences he "truly" prefers.

I believe that an explanation of "the moral code justified for X" in terms of "the moral code X would support if he were fully rational" meets all the conditions I have listed as necessary if it is to be helpful in moral reflection. So far as I can see, the conception is value-neutral. What it does require is that a moral code be chosen so as to take account of all the facts that are known, or at least knowable to the agent; I do not see that as incompatible with value-neutrality. Most important, however, I suggest that a person coming to see that a certain moral code is the one he would support if he were fully rational will recommend it to him, that any ambivalences about it will be resolved.

One might object to this proposal on the ground that it is apt just to affirm the moral commitments the agent already has, since his *present* moral preferences will fix his desires for the outcomes of a given moral system. This objection, however, would be mistaken. For the preferences on the basis of which a moral system is justified are preferences for the *consequences* of the operation of a moral system, and not desires/aversions for certain act-types for no further reason, desires/aversions which are constitutive of an agent's moral code. Thus it is one thing to be averse to *hurting* others—and that is part of one's moral code—but it is quite another thing to want people to be welloff, healthy, happy, and so on, and it is this preference that is involved in the selection of a justified moral code. So the selection of a moral system is made by reference to a person's *nonmoral* preferences for some consequences.

There is another restriction one might want to lay on the selection of a moral system, in order to assure that one is not choosing on the basis of merely conventional desires. I think myself this restriction is already implied in my definition of "rational choice," but if one disagrees about this, something should be done to make sure one can step outside one's own tradition and appraise it somewhat afresh. One might do this by insisting that the chooser's preferences not be merely what he has acquired from his parents or TV or the newpapers, but that they be ones acquired only through sensitive interaction with the environment— finding what is satisfying and what is not—and that would not be extinguished by learning that they rest causally on false assumptions about facts. The conception that desires/aversions can be criticized in this way is controversial and difficult, and I have discussed it as fully as I can elsewhere (1979, pp. 10–15, 24, 70ff., 113, 149ff.). At any rate, the present restriction implies that we are to ask a person which moral system he would support, in view of his preferences for its expectable consequences—preferences that would survive the cognitive criticism I have elsewhere called "cognitive psychotherapy."

Some persons may feel that we should not call a moral system justified for a person unless it can be shown that the very same moral system is justified for everybody. They may feel we should not speak of "justification" unless we can say something is justified, *period*. And, of course, it does not follow from the fact that a certain moral system *S* is justified in the sense sketched for *P*, that it is so for everybody. I am inclined to think that such persons want more than probably it is possible to get, and the result of their linguistic stipulation is that the word "justified" would have use only for some parts of moral systems, but not for all that we think important.

If we introduce the term "justified" with my foregoing (relativistic) explanation, then it would be convenient to explain "*X* is morally obligated to do *A*," as uttered by *me*, to mean, "The moral system which *I* would support, if I were fully rational and expected to live in *X*'s society, would call on *X* to do *A*," where "calls on *X*" would be spelled out in terms of aversions to act-types, tendencies to feel guilt, and so on. Similarly, for the other moral terms like "It was reprehensible of *X* to have done *A*" or "*X* has a *prima facie* obligation to do *A*."

It would be an important objection to this line of thinking if it turned out that thoughtful people, familiar with the science of today, and with serious acquaintance with the theory of knowledge, including the necessity of avoiding moral premises in a justification, felt that our explication will not do as a replacement for "justified moral system," if "is morally wrong" is to be construed as "would be prohibited by the justified moral system." Would some such persons find that, to determine what they would normally call "morally wrong action" or disapprove morally, they must raise questions this explication does not imply one need raise? Or contrariwise, would they find that the explication requires them to assure themselves of points that they are confident are irrelevant to whether some course of action is right or wrong, to be morally approved or disapproved of? Of course, it is not easy to know what thoughtful people would think. My speculation is that persons who understand what social moral systems are and what they accomplish, and who understand what kinds of criticism of moral aversions are possible given what we know about human psychology, would be content with the reflection on how to determine which actions are right or wrong, of the sort that is required by my explication.

What would be the effect if people came to accept these explications in the sense that they would attach these meanings to the several moral terms much as they attach a meaning to the term "electron?" One might say, very little at all, on the ground that the important thing is the kind of motivational moral system people have, and the psychological processes that institute such systems will go on irrespective of the meanings attached or moral terms, especially "justified." But that is too simple. The acceptance of these definitions into ordinary thinking would serve to avoid aimless reflection—reflection one would discard if one thought deeply about the matter but otherwise might be time-consuming and misleading. Again, it would have the effect of channeling moral thinking so that facts and logic are used maximally to control moral commitments and decisions, and it would serve to raise doubts and stimulate more reflection when this has not been done. A third effect is that it would be clear that morality is a "rational" phenomenon, not exactly in the economists' sense (although this enters into it), but in the sense in which we think some desires/aversions are foolish and irrational; the explication makes clear in what sense this is so. (The question is not, however, answered whether it is always rational to act morally.) These facts, are no mean reasons in support of influencing language to embody the explication.

If we select a conceptual scheme for moral discourse in this way, there is a parallel between it and the status of contemporary concepts in science. Let us suppose that English speakers have been using "morally wrong" in roughly the present ordinary sense since around 1700, about the same length of time as "electricity," first used in 1646. We might then say that the proposals of various naturalistic/prescriptive/nonnaturalist theories of moral terms have been proposals for understanding "morally wrong" in an optimal way—in a way that takes into account all the facts mentioned above. We might then think that philosophers who have made these proposals (Hutcheson, Hume, Smith, Moore, Firth, Hare, Rawls) have improved the conceptual scheme of educated people much as there has been improvement, among scientists, in the conception of electricity as a result of experiment and theoretical development in physics. We might then take what is referred to by the *optimal* use of "morally wrong" as the *fact* of moral wrongness and hold that, rather gropingly, this same fact has been referred to all along by users of the term "morally wrong." So we could then say that there is an optimal conceptual framework for ethics, and these earlier theories of philosophers have been gradually improving approximations to it. In a corresponding sense we might say that there are "facts" of ethics, and we might then say that one who recognizes this is a "realist" about ethics.

chapter five

Two Approaches to Theory Acceptance in Ethics[1]

Norman Daniels

1. "INTUITIONISM" VS. "MORAL EMPIRICISM"[2]

Just what role should be assigned to moral judgments or moral intuitions in the process of selecting among or justifying moral theories is a matter of ancient controversy. Egoists and utilitarians, for example, have always had to do battle with those who urge a tribunal in which a moral theory must match commonly held moral judgments. Proponents of such tribunals have been hard pressed, in turn, to provide credentials for these judgments. This old debate has taken on a modern form in the contrast between two recent proposals for solving the problem of theory acceptance or justification in ethics, the method of wide reflective equilibrium, which derives from Rawls, and the moral empiricism advocated by Brandt. My intention is to contrast these methods to see what lessons we may draw about the role of moral judgments in theory acceptance.

It is fair to construe these two recent proposals as major alternatives. Indeed, Brandt elaborates his own view in response to the "intuitionism" he thinks undermines the method of wide reflective equilibrium, and specifically, Rawls's use of the method in constructing his contractarian approach to the problem of choosing among competing moral conceptions. I shall concentrate on Brandt's methodological proposals, both

This article is based on the author's "Can Cognitive Psychotherapy Reconcile Reason and Desire?", *Ethics* 93 (July 1983): 772-785, and published here with the permission of *Ethics* and the University of Chicago Press.

because of their intrinsic interest and because I have discussed the strengths and weaknesses of wide reflective equilibrium in detail elsewhere (1979a, 1979b, 1980a, 1980b). I will, however, offer a brief sketch of the method of wide reflective equilibrium so that some points of contrast with Brandt's approach will be clear.

I shall argue that Brandt's strategy is an attempt to comply with two main methodological constraints, which he views as conditions of adequacy on any account of justification in ethics. Both of these constraints, an *empiricist constraint* and a *disalienation constraint,* are advanced by Brandt to correct what he takes to be fatal flaws in Rawlsian "intuitionism." The fact that Brandt's own proposal runs afoul of his own constraints points to some serious questions both about the plausibility of the constraints themselves and the adequacy of Brandt's proposal, viewed as an alternative to wide reflective equilibrium.

2. WIDE REFLECTIVE EQUILIBRIUM[3]

A wide reflective equilibrium is a coherent triple of sets of beliefs held by a particular person; namely, (a) a set of considered moral judgments; (b) a set of moral principles; and (c) a set of relevant background theories, which may include both moral and nonmoral theories. We collect the person's initial moral judgments, which may be particular or general, and filter them to include only those of which he is relatively confident and which have been made under conditions generally conducive to avoiding errors of judgment. We propose alternative sets of moral principles which have varying degrees of "fit" with the moral judgments. Rather than settling immediately for the "best fit" of principles with judgments, which would give us only a narrow equilibrium, we advance philosophical arguments that reveal the strengths and weaknesses of the competing sets of principles (that is, competing moral conceptions). I construe these arguments as inferences from relevant background theories (I use the term loosely). Assume that some particular set of arguments wins and the moral agent is thus persuaded that one set of principles is more acceptable than the others (and perhaps than the conception that might have emerged in narrow equilibrium). The agent may work back and forth, revising his intial considered judgments, moral principles, and background theories, to arrive at an equilibrium point that consists of the triple—(a), (b), and (c).

There must be more structure here. The theories in (c) must show that the principles in (b) are more acceptable than alternatives on grounds to some degree independent of (b)'s match with relevant considered moral judgments in (a). Without such independent support, the principles have no support which they would not already have had in a corresponding narrow equilibrium where no special appeal to (c) is made. I can raise this point another way: How can we be sure that the moral principles that systematize considered moral judgments are not just "accidental generalizations" of the "moral facts," analogous to accidental generalizations we want to avoid confusing with real scientific laws? In the scientific case, we have evidence that we are not stuck with accidental generalizations if we can derive the purported laws from a body of interconnected theories, provided these theories reach beyond the "facts" the laws generalize in a diverse and interesting way.

The analogy suggests one way to ensure independent support for the principles in (b) and to rule out their being mere accidental generalizations of the considered judgments in (a). We should require that the theories in (c) not just be reformulations of the set of considered moral judgments (a) to which we seek to "fit" the principles in (b). The background theories should have a scope reaching beyond the range of the judgments in (a). Suppose some set of considered moral judgments, (a′), plays a role in constraining the background theories in (c). Then we are asking that some interesting, nontrivial portion of (a′) should be disjoint from the set (a) that constrains the principles in (b). The *independence constraint* is the requirement that (a′) and (a) be to some significant degree disjoint.[4]

It is important to note that the acceptability of the theories in (c) may thus in part depend on some moral judgments. We are not in general assuming that (c) constitutes a reduction of the moral in (b) and (a) to the nonmoral. Thus the independence constraint may be satisfied if the background theories in (c) incorporate different moral notions (say, fairness and certain claims about the nature of persons) from those (say, rights and entitlements) employed by the principles in (b) and judgments in (a).[5]

Wide reflective equilibrium as I have described it is not a standard form of moral intuitionism because it is not foundationalist. Despite the care taken to filter initial judgments to avoid obvious sources of error, no special epistemological priority is granted to considered moral judgments. We are missing the little story that intuitionist theories usually provide, explaining why we should pay homage to those judgments and indirectly to the principles that systematize them. Without such a story, we have no foundationalism and so no standard form of moral intuitionism.

Nevertheless, it might be thought that reflective equilibrium involves an attempt to give us the effect of intuitionism without any fairy tales about epistemic priority. The effect is that a set of principles gets "tested" against a determinate and relatively fixed set of moral judgments. We have, as it were, foundationalism without foundations. Once the foundational claim about moral judgments is removed, however, we have nothing more than a person's moral opinion, however considered. Since such opinions are often the result of self-interest, self-deception, historical and cultural accident, hidden class bias, and so on, just systematizing some of them hardly seems a promising way to provide justification for them or for the principles that order them.

This objection rests on two distinct complaints: (1) that reflective equilibrium merely systematizes some relatively determinate set of moral judgments; and (2) that the considered moral judgments are not a proper foundation for an ethical theory. The first complaint is unfounded. Wide reflective equilibrium does not merely systematize some determinate set of judgments. Rather, it permits extensive revision of these moral judgments. There is no set of judgments that is held more or less fixed as there would be on a foundationalist approach, even one without foundations.[6] In seeking wide reflective equilibrium, we are constantly making plausibility judgments about which of our considered judgments we should revise in light of theoretical considered judgments at all levels. Wide reflective equilibrium keeps us from taking considered moral judgments at face value, however much they may be treated as starting points in our theory construction.

The second complaint, that considered moral judgments are an inappropriate foundation for moral theory, brings us to the heart of Brandt's rejection of wide reflective equilibrium as a form of intuitionism. In seeking reflective equilibrium, Brandt argues, we begin with a set of moral judgments or intuitions to which we assign an *initial credence level* (say from 0 to 1 on a scale from things we believe very little to things we confidently believe). We filter out judgments with low initial credence levels to form our set of considered judgments. Then we propose principles and attempt to bring the system of principles plus judgments into equilibrium, allowing modifications wherever they are necessary to produce the system with the highest overall credence level.

But why, asks Brandt, should we be impressed with the results of such a process? We should not, he argues, unless we have some way to show that "some of the beliefs are initially *credible*—and not merely initially believed—for some reason other than their coherence" (1979, p. 20, emphasis added) in the set of beliefs we believe the most. For example, in the nonmoral case, Brandt suggests that an initially believed judgment is also an initially credible judgment when it states (or purports to state) a fact of observation. "In the case of normative beliefs, no reason has been offered why we should think that initial credence levels for a person correspond to *credibilities*," (p. 20).[7] The result is that we have no reason to think that increasing the credence level for the system as a whole moves us closer to moral truth rather than away from it.

Coherent fictions are still fictions, and we may only be reshuffling our prejudices.

I believe some of the force of Brandt's argument derives from an inappropriate analogy between considered moral judgments and observation reports in science. But since I have responded to Brandt's argument in some detail elsewhere, and since David Copp has discussed my arguments in this volume, I shall not defend wide reflective equilibrium directly here. Rather, I shall turn to the alternative methodology Brandt proposes to see if it really does avoid problems facing reflective equilibrium.

3. BRANDT'S METHODOLOGICAL CONSTRAINTS

Brandt insists that moral intuitionism, even in its more sophisticated Rawlsian version, wide reflective equilibrium, is worse than hopeless: "We must avoid intuitionism even if this were to mean (as it does not) that we must end up as complete skeptics in the area of practice" (p. 3). The problem, as we have seen, is that we have no positive account of why we should grant initial credibility to these data, and we have excellent reason to be skeptical of moral intuitions, influenced as they often are by cultural tradition, social class, and other sources of bias. Consequently, Brandt argues, appeals to intuitions prevent our adopting an adequately objective critical perspective. "What we should aim to do is *step outside our own tradition* somehow, see it from the outside, and evaluate it, separating what is only the vestige of a possibly once useful moral tradition from what is justifiable at the present" (pp. 21–22, emphasis added).

Anti-intuitionism is not surprising coming from a utilitarian like Brandt. But if we must not appeal to moral judgments in answering the fundamental questions of moral theory—like "What is good?" and "What is right?"—then where are we to turn? Brandt answers that we must see "how far facts and logic alone carry us in criticism of a moral system: this is the question my conceptual framework has been designed to answer" (p. 244; cf. p. 10). To make facts and logic maximally relevant, these fundamental questions must be reformulated so that they are "sufficiently clear and precise for one to answer them by some mode of scientific or observational procedure" (p. 2). Such reformulation must not be based on mere appeals to linguistic intuitions, since ordinary usage is vague and conflates important distinctions.

Brandt argues that we must adopt a method of "reforming definitions." These do not mean the same as the expressions they replace, but they let us address more effectively the central issues raised by the original questions. Specifically, Brandt proposes that the term "rational" be taken to "refer to actions, desires, or moral systems which survive maximal criticism and corrections by facts and logic" (p. 10).[8] He then replaces "What is the best thing (for a given agent) to do?" with the reforming question, "What is the fully rational thing to do?" (pp. 14–16). Finally, he replaces "good" by "rationally desired" (pp. 126–129) and "morally wrong" by the following: "would be prohibited by any moral code which all fully rational persons would tend to support, in preference to all others or to none at all, for the society of the agent if they intended to spend a life-time in that society" (p. 194).

Two constraints emerge as central in Brandt's repudiation of intuitionism and his advocacy of reforming definitions. Brandt believes that if justification in ethics is to be possible, it must rest on facts and logic alone. Call this requirement the *empiricist constraint*. As we shall see, we may need to distinguish weak and strong versions of the empiricist constraint, governing explicit and implicit moral influences, respectively, but for now it will suffice to refer to the exclusion of moral judgments or intuitions from the process of justification as the empiricist constraint. Brandt insists on a second constraint as well. He wants to close the gap between justifying a moral theory or code and motivating someone to accept its requirements. For him, no justification will be significant if it is not also motivating. Consequently, a moral code must appeal to the agent's actual desires or to his rational desires (in a sense of "rational" to be explained). This is the *disalienation constraint* (pp. 186–187).

These two constraints are viewed by Brandt as conditions of adequacy on a successful theory of justification in ethics. They are clearly violated by the method of wide reflective equilibrium as it is used in Rawls's hands to construct his contractarian argument for justice as fairness. The appeal to considered moral judgments, both in the design of the Original Position and in the constraint on principles selected there, violates the empiricist constraint. For example, it is a moral ideal of persons as free and equal that underlies the design of the constraints on choice in the Original Position. Moreover, since the selection of a moral conception in the contract situation depends on the *hypothetical* interests of agents in it, then there appears to be a straightforward violation of the disalienation constraint. Indeed, Rawls's arguments about the "reasonable" vs. the "rational," and his solution to the problem of moral motivation by positing a "sense of justice" as a fundamental moral power of persons, constitute an alternative to the disalienation constraint only at the cost of directly violating the empiricist constraint.

That wide reflective equilibrium violates both constraints when used by Rawls is a problem only if the constraints are themselves really conditions of adequacy on methods of theory acceptance in ethics. I think they are not, but I shall try to raise problems for these constraints not by direct argument, but by examination of the way in which Brandt's own method is forced to violate them. Specifically, I shall argue that Brandt fails to justify his reforming definition of "the good," since he simply substitutes the new problem, "Why should I be rational?" for the traditional problem, "Why should I be moral?" This means that he cannot guarantee that the disalienation constraint will be satisfied when we pursue his method for choosing moral codes. Second, the rational desires that provide the bedrock facts motivating the choice of moral codes do not in any way let us "step outside our own tradition" and achieve the "objective" stance Brandt promises. This violates at least some form of the empiricist constraint. The combined force of these criticisms is to suggest that a more enlightened approach to theory acceptance in ethics may result if we abandon these methodological constraints.

Before it is possible to take up these criticisms, we must discuss Brandt's treatment of rational choice. His method of theory selection in ethics depends critically on the details of his account of rational choice, and some of my criticisms will therefore turn on these details. Still, certain general features of the approach underlie other criticisms, which bodes ill for attempts to improve on Brandt's approach by modifications of its details.

4. RATIONAL DESIRE AND COGNITIVE PSYCHOTHERAPY

The boldest feature of Brandt's discussion of rational action and rational agents is his attempt (p. 110) to supplant the Humean view that reason cannot criticize desire. Brandt offers an account of rational desire, and indeed an operational definition of rational desire. He argues that "cognitive psychotherapy" is the appropriate operation to use in such a definition. This is the process of "confronting desires with relevant information by repeatedly representing it, in an ideally vivid way, and at an appropriate time. . . . The process relies simply upon reflection on available information, without influence by prestige of someone, use of evaluative language, extrinsic reward or punishment, or use of artificially induced feeling—states like relaxation" (p. 113). Accordingly, desires that result from or survive cognitive psychotherapy are rational; those that are extinguished are irrational.

What motivates Brandt to go beyond Hume's purely instrumental view of rationality is that he does not want what is good and what is right to be held hostage by what are intuitively bizarre or crazy desires. However, his reforming definitions of "good" and "right," which turn on what is best for a rational agent to choose, risk just such moral terrorism. If we search for a way to sort the acceptable desires from the unacceptable, we face serious problems. Had we an acceptable teleological theory of the ultimate function or ends of man, we might be able to derive constraints on the set of desires that can be counted as rational. But without this account, any other such "theory" is really a value-laden ideal,[9] an appeal to which would violate Brandt's restriction that we rely on facts and logic alone in the justification of moral beliefs.

Brandt's appeal to cognitive psychotherapy is an attempt to meet just this constraint: "It is," he suggests, "*value-free reflection*" (p. 113). His underlying idea is that many of the desires we think irrational are not consonant with important facts about the world and ourselves. These desires are "mistaken" not because it is a mistake to think we can act on them, but because we have such desires via beliefs about the world and ourselves that are mistaken. Hume viewed a passion, such as hope or fear, grief or joy, as "unreasonable" when it is "founded on the supposition of the existence of objects which really do not exist."[10] Brandt extends this view to desires. He suggests that someone may have an aversion to a certain food because he mistakenly believes it will make him ill (p. 115); he may desire that blacks be denied prestigious jobs because he believes they are less intelligent. A related group of mistaken desires or aversions is based not on false beliefs, but on generalizations from untypical examples: aversion to eating all fish after not liking cod (p. 120) or aversion to all on welfare because some are "cheaters." Another category of example seems to depend on a different relation to "the facts": I may desire something (food, money, attention) "too strongly" because I am overcompensating for an earlier deprivation (p. 133). Brandt's "artificial" desires are even more complex: I may have an aversion to entering a nonprestigious occupation or interracial marriage (p. 117) because I have acquired my parents' negative attitudes, although I might otherwise find the occupation or marriage satisfying.[11]

Brandt's central idea, then, is that we are generally reliable desire-acquisition devices. We tend to acquire nonmistaken desires and to shed mistaken ones when we are suffused with adequate representations of relevant truths. We have, in short, an account of rational desire "naturalized." Brandt's proposal can be summarized as follows: (1) the "mistaken" desires are a significant portion of the desires we intuitively or pretheoretically view as irrational; moreover, it is the only category of intuitively irrational desires we can pick out by reference to facts and logic alone; (2) cognitive psychotherapy is a value-free procedure for eliminating most of these mistaken desires; (3) the operational definition that involves cognitive psychotherapy is a reasonable refinement of the intuitive notion of irrational desires. We may now ask, are the mistaken desires an adequate refinement of the intuitively irrational ones? And is cognitive psychotherapy adequate to the task Brandt sets it?

The category of mistaken desires seems too narrow. Some desires we intuitively consider irrational are not clearly based on false beliefs. Certain obsessive or fetishist desires may not rest on false beliefs or on false estimates of the happiness produced by satisfying them. The Humean example Brandt cites (p. 110) when he promises to go beyond Hume ("It is not contrary to reason to prefer the destruction of the whole world to the scratching of my finger") may also not be mistaken in Brandt's sense, although some would view it as irrational. (Of course, the irrationality here cannot turn on some notion of gross evil without violating Brandt's methodological constraints.)

The category of mistaken desires is too broad, including desires that are not intuitively irrational. In Brandt's view, a desire is mistaken if it is based on beliefs that it would be unjustified to hold in light of all relevant information available to society (pp. 12, 70, 113); it is then a legitimate target for cognitive psychotherapy. But I may lack some of that information and still be justified in holding certain false beliefs. Desires based on these beliefs will then be mistaken, but they are not (at least intuitively) irrational. Brandt is led to this counterintuitive result because he wants our choices of what is good and what is right to be as informed as possible, without requiring the impossible, that we be omniscient—thus the "all relevant information available" criterion.[12] But by defining the category of mistaken desires through reference to such a strong criterion, Brandt idealizes the concept of rationality in a way that invites trouble.

The situation is even worse for Brandt. We are likely to call a mistaken desire irrational only if someone clings to it despite becoming aware that there is information that falsifies its underlying beliefs. Astonishingly, it is just when such a mistaken desire resists cognitive psychotherapy that Brandt calls it rational! Because of the disalienation constraint, Brandt wants actual outcomes of the therapeutic process to determine what is rational, not outcomes that "ought to" take place. So, if I am so "hung up" on a mistaken desire that it survives cognitive psychotherapy, it counts as rational. Now, I may fail to extinguish a mistaken desire if I cannot draw all the relevant inferences from the information presented in therapy, or if I am in some other way very stupid. But then, the more dense I am, the more my mistaken desires will count as rational, give Brandt's operational definition.[13]

This point brings us to the question whether cognitive psychotherapy is the appropriate technique for ridding ourselves of mistaken desires. Brandt admits that it will fail to extinguish some mistaken desires, such as those acquired in early childhood. Incidentally, Brandt does not consider the opposite problem: I might extinguish desires that are not mistaken (such as the desire to make love or to complete this essay) if I vividly repeat to myself all relevant information at the appropriate time, say at the occurrence of the desire. The price of letting mistaken desires slip through is high, for we fail to dispel our worry that the good and the right will be hostage to irrational desires. Yet Brandt does not strengthen cognitive psychotherapy so that the purification process brings more powerful techniques to bear. We cannot resort to psychotherapy by an expert, or to drugs, or to behavior modification techniques involving reward or punishment (cf. p. 113). All we may do is vividly and repeatedly represent the relevant truths to ourselves.[14]

The unrestricted use of more powerful techniques, like behavior modification, is presumably barred on two counts. Not only might they smuggle in the therapist's prior values, but also, they are powerful enough to extinguish both mistaken and nonmistaken desires and so cannot be used to sort them from each other. Yet if some mistaken desires are unconscious, they will surely escape detection without expert help.[15] Brandt may fear that we will err in identifying a given belief as mistaken, but if we do not supplement cognitive psychotherapy with more powerful techniques, too many mistaken desires will slip through. An intermediary approach would use more powerful techniques on clearly mistaken desires. These points about the adequacy of cognitive psychotherapy are connected to deeper worries: The classical learning theory underlying Brandt's account may be only a fragment of an adequate learning theory.[16]

5. WHY SHOULD I BE RATIONAL?

If Brandt's reforming definition for "good" is to work, then he must show that there is recommendatory force to my knowing that some of my desires or actions are (or would be) rational and others irrational. Such a demonstration is both a condition of adequacy on the reforming definition (pp. 14–15, 151–152) and an important step toward satisfying the disalienation constraint. If knowing that a certain choice would be the rational one for me does not recommend it to me, then there is little hope that I can be disalienated from (what would be) my rational choice of a moral code.

Brandt's argument that there is recommendatory force rests on claiming that people have certain second-order aversions and desires. Specifically, he suggests that we are made uncomfortable by the awareness that we have irrational desires and aversions (p. 157). These desires, moreover, are inefficient sources of happiness: Satisfying them is likely to make us less happy than we would be made by satisfying rational desires (p. 157). Since "probably everyone with an adequate conceptual scheme (with the concept of long-range happiness) will take a positive interest in his net happiness over a lifetime" (p. 158), people will disfavor such inefficient desires and aversions. As Brandt points out, however, "if you are uninterested in happiness or avoiding dissonance, the 'argument' does not work" (p. 159).[17]

Brandt's argument proves too much. Suppose my initial desires include some irrational desires and aversions. Brandt wants to show that, if I know some of my desires are irrational, I have a reason or motivation to want to acquire the rational set by undergoing cognitive psychotherapy. But suppose someone shows me that there is another, superior set of desires, one which would be an even more efficient source of happiness than my rational set. This superior set might even contain some irrational desires. Now I have a reason or motivation to seek the superior set over the rational set—the very same motivation that leads me to prefer the rational set to my initial set. The rational set is at best only one among many sets of desires that commend themselves to me, once I let my hedonistic desire to maximize happiness carry the weight that it does in Brandt's argument.[18]

There may be a way around this problem for Brandt. After all, we often think there is a point to modifying our desires to make ourselves happier, but this modest fact does not compel us to strive to be, or to become, whatever person is constituted by a superior happiness-producing set of desires.[19] We hold some things more dear than that. Specifically, we tend to define ourselves through the systems of long-term desires that form our life plans. Accordingly, Brandt might suggest that abandoning initial desires in favor of rational desires does not threaten our sense of self or integrity, whereas abandoning original desires for the superior set might.

Unfortunately, even if this appeal to integrity is on the right track, it is unclear how far it carries us. I might now *resist* the suggestion that I undergo cognitive psychotherapy and give up my quirky and irrational desires because I view them as part of what makes me quirky old *me*. My integrity in this case prevents me from becoming rational, and Brandt's argument proves too little. A middle-course for Brandt's argument must tell us just when and how the concern for integrity modifies the desire to maximize happiness. Since Brandt does not address this issue, I do not know which, if any, of my rationalized desires are recommended to me.

If the argument about recommendatory force fails, there is little hope of meeting the disalienation constraint. Knowing that a moral code would be the best one for me to choose were I rational (were I to undergo cognitive psychotherapy) is irrelevant if I have prevailing irrational desires that lead me to choose a different code. The fully rational me might just as well be another person for all the grip *his* motives have on me.

6. CAN A FULLY RATIONAL AGENT STEP OUTSIDE HIS TRADITION?

I have suggested that Brandt adopts an empiricist constraint on justification in ethics: No appeal to moral intuitions or judgments may play a role in the justification of moral principles or codes. Does Brandt's own procedure for selecting moral codes respect the spirit or just the letter of that constraint? To answer this question and the one raised in the next section about the role of consensus, we must be clear about the procedure for selecting among alternative moral codes.[20]

The rational agents in Brandt's choice problem are intended to contrast sharply with both the traditional "ideal observer" and Rawls's hypothetical contractors. Brandt's fully rational agents know less than omniscient observers, but they know far more than Rawlsian contractors, who operate behind a veil of ignorance. In the process of becoming fully rational agents by undergoing cognitive psychotherapy, they appeal to all relevant information available in the society. They have all relevant information about themselves—their skills, talents, abilities, social position, sex, and so on—and all available information about the society they will live in. No special assumptions are made about their degree of benevolence or selfishness. Their rational desires, whatever they are, all play a role, with the important exception: Explicitly moral desires and aversions are not to play a role in the choice. Including these would violate the empiricist constraint.[21] Each rational agent is then asked to consider which social moral code he would choose to govern the society he will live in. Finally, the area of convergence, if any, among codes chosen by all fully rational agents gives us the content of the notions of "the right" (p. 194).

Brandt suggests that his code-selection procedure offers an important advantage lacking in such alternatives as Rawls's. A central constraint on the outcome of Rawls's contract procedure is that principles have to match "our" considered moral judgments in reflective equilibrium. This constraint, Brandt argues, traps us in our own tradition (pp. 21–22, 186, 236). It takes the perspective of our own tradition as the ultimate one for critical purposes. Yet once we realize that there is diversity among moral codes, we are led to inquire "which of these codes is 'correct'—that is, criticized by facts and logic as far as possible. We do not like to think that our moral thinking is confined to making our intuitions coherent; we should like to step outside our tradition, look at it from the outside, and see where more basic kinds of criticism would lead. Now identifying the moral code that a fully rational person would support does just this" (p. 185; see also pp. 186–187).

Does Brandt's version of the choice problem allow us to step outside our tradition in the ways these passages suggest? Brandt believes that cognitive psychotherapy allows the fully rational agent to do so because value judgments have played no role in purifying his desires. Moreover, all of the actual results of cognitive psychotherapy play a role in the choice: There is no value-laden filter screening out some of them (in the manner of Rawls's veil of ignorance) and there are no special assumptions about the degree of benevolence moral agents ought to exhibit (p. 138). Rather, the desires that emerge after cognitive psychotherapy are among the "facts" that must be reconciled with the choice of a moral theory. Here Brandt's goal of disalienating people from morality reinforces his qualms about letting prior moral judgments influence the justificatory process. But has the purified, fully rational agent been lifted outside his own tradition merely by avoiding such value-laden filters? Pretty definitely not. The agent is still the product of his culture and the social institutions in it. Consequently, he is a product of its implicit and explicit social moral code, for this code presumably shapes the basic institutions that in turn shape the desires individuals acquire. Merely excluding the desires that are explicitly moral from the deliberation, as Brandt does (p. 203), does not remove the imprint of the social setting upon desires.

Consider an example. Suppose that the society from which one comes is highly benevolent and pays considerable attention to inculcating benevolent attitudes in children from an early age. It reinforces these attitudes with highly egalitarian distributions and tends to play down competitive individualism. Such societies may produce more persons approximating Brandt's perfectly benevolent agents than would societies like ours, which have highly inegalitarian distributions along class, race, and sex lines. Toleration for these unequal distributions and nonbenevolent attitudes is greatly enhanced by an ideology and accompanying emotional structure that glorifies competitive individualism. At the extreme, we find societies with highly entrenched—even stable—race or caste structures. The rational desires, in Brandt's account, of superior caste persons from such societies may well include desires to be treated better than members of the inferior race or caste. Such desires may be inculcated in the early phases of childhood and be reinforced throughout youth. Brandt might object that any ideology that justifies such practices is likely to rest on false beliefs about the inferiority of the low-caste group, and so the corresponding desires should be extinguished with cognitive psychotherapy. But such ideologies are highly resistant to extinction merely through exposure to "all the relevant facts." Witness the difficulty in eradicating the "blaming the victim" ideologies that help "justify" American racism (Ryan, 1976).

This sketch suggests that the likelihood of producing persons who are highly benevolent, rather than benevolent only toward an "in" or preferred group, depends very much on prior moral judgments—specifically on those operating as the social moral code in the society that produced the rational agent. The desires that play a role in theory (code) selection thus bear the imprint of such prior moral judgments. Brandt operates under an illusion: He believes that, since moral desires do not explicitly play a role in the selection of the code, only "facts and logic" do. Brandt's apparent lack of concern for the social structuring of desires in a morally laden way is indeed surprising; my complaint is but a version of the traditional criticism that utilitarianism is biased toward the status quo. This complaint points to a deep tension between the empiricist and disalienation constraints.

There is also a deep irony here. Brandt argues that the imposition of Rawls's thick veil of ignorance is equivalent to making special assumptions about benevolence (p. 244) and thus violates the empiricist constraint. But a central justification that Rawls gives for the thick veil is that it corrects for the way in which existing basic social institutions shape the desires of moral agents. Its intended effect is to eliminate the hidden influences of prior moral values that are embedded in the social structures that shape the chooser. Brandt's fear of allowing moral judgments to play any role in the justificatory process, his empiricist constraint, may thus make his procedure more subject to the charge of failure to step outside of tradition than Rawls's is. That is, the known moral influence may be less dangerous than the unknown one.

Given Brandt's concern for stepping outside tradition, it is surprising to discover that we must rely on tradition to construct the pluralist ideal moral code (pp. 289–290). Brandt urges us to take existing legal and moral rules as our starting point. We then modify them according to their ability to maximize happiness. Strictly speaking, Brandt is not committing the same error as the one that he ascribes to Rawls. For the process of constructing—or discovering—the ideal code is not itself a justificatory process. Thus he is not relying on accepted moral judgments to justify other moral judgments. Even if Brandt restricts his empiricist constraint to "contexts of justification," not "contexts of discovery," two problems arise. First, the ultimate structure of the moral code will probably be affected by the fact that the existing code is taken as a starting point (p. 293 not withstanding). This parallels the objection to reflective equilibrium; that even if considered moral judgments are revisable, the equilibrium is going to be a function of the starting point. We need some account of why the starting point is a plausible one. Yet

Brandt seems to believe that the existing moral and legal code is a good place to start. It reflects society's experience in regulating certain kinds of behavior and conflict. It is a heritage we dare not ignore. But this very respect for the existing social moral code is quite out of keeping with the near contempt Brandt expresses when he worries about the problem of choosing a general moral position. Why give credibility to the code for one task but not the other?

7. WHERE DOES BRANDT'S METHODOLOGY TAKE US?

Is there any moral code that all fully rational agents would prefer for the society in which they live? If there are such codes, "is morally wrong" should be replaced by "would be prohibited by any such code," which fixed its descriptive meaning. However, if there is no such code, then we need a relativized definition for "is morally wrong," one that fixes its descriptive meaning for each agent. To determine whether "wrong" has the force of "wrong according to everyone" or just "wrong according to me," we must know what moral codes rational agents will choose.

Brandt seems undecided among three possible outcomes of such choices, which yield strong, modest, and minimal conclusions, respectively. The *strong* conclusion is that "roughly, and in the long run, rational selfish persons will support a happiness-maximizing moral system, not intentionally, but inadvertently, since of course each rational selfish person will support his best—his expectable welfare-maximizing—option among the viable ones open to him" (p. 220). The strong conclusion immediately follows Brandt's argument that "the moral principles which will be most viable will be those which arouse least total resentment, counting both numbers and intensity; and hence equalitarian principles will tend to be more viable" (p. 219). Brandt implies that even selfish, fully rational persons would choose a comprehensive, relatively egalitarian moral code and not just the minimal self-protections of what Brandt calls the "Hobbesian core." If this conclusion could be sustained, "is morally wrong" would presumably have the content "is prohibited by the egalitarian code."

But Brandt backs away from the strong conclusion because selfish persons enjoying advantageous social positions might not accept a happiness-maximizing egalitarian code (p. 221). He retreats to the *modest* conclusion that a "central [Hobbesian] core—the protective system roughly supportive of the criminal law—can be justified to all selfish persons alike, and indeed to persons of any degree of benevolence; but various possible additions to this might not, any of them, be justifiable to all selfish persons" (p. 221). Indeed, if anything is "wrong according to everyone," it is only what falls in this core.

Brandt hints at the need to retreat still further. After his discussion of egoism, he remarks, "neither will a selfish person want an egoist moral system, unless he is in a special position of power, in which case he may not care about a moral system at all" (p. 270). This admission, nowhere else remarked on, suggests the *minimal* conclusion, that some fully rational moral agents, who are both selfish and especially well situated, may not even find that the Hobbesian core is in their long-run interests. Perhaps the lackluster selfish person will support the Hobbesian core, but the bold and powerful will not.

Brandt may feel justified in ignoring the minimal conclusion because of the rarity of such fortunate, selfish people. But it is important to see that, if we do not ignore it, and if we also insist that the replacement expressions refer to a code that all rational persons prefer, then we are left with vacuous definitions of "morally right" and "morally obligatory." Brandt's mention of the relativized reforming definition ("wrong according to my code") thus implies that we may not be moved beyond the minimal conclusion. Definitions aside, there is another problem: The function of a moral code—to serve as a public and final court of appeal in resolving a broad range of conflicting claims—is undermined if the core is very thin. Even the modest Hobbesian core may not provide enough of a basis of agreement to sustain real cooperative social effort. Brandt seems unworried about such lack of consensus (p. 242), but it may be more than the social fabric can bear.

Just what is the importance of agreement on a code? Suppose I have undergone cognitive psychotherapy and my irrational desires have been eliminated. Suppose further that I am benevolent and am concerned as much about the happiness of persons in other groups, say blacks, as I am about my own happiness. Unfortunately, the society in which I am to live has a long tradition of racial discrimination, on the model of the Jim Crow laws of the South. Unlike the case of the South, however, the black population is quite small. Nevertheless, the racist expectations and desires of the white population are deep and strong, and not everyone in the society is likely to shed them even with cognitive psychotherapy. So it is reasonable to anticipate the instability of any social moral code that does not cater to these desires and expectations.[22] Even allowing for some black noncompliance with a Jim Crow code, we would expect it to be far more stable. It is even possible that such a code would in fact maximize happiness, given the respective population sizes. Consequently, the Jim Crow code might be the best one for me to support, given my high level of benevolence.

Of course, this code may not be chosen by everyone. At the risk of appearing selfish, fully rational blacks might not choose it. But, *ex hypothesi,* this lack of support does not make the code unstable, so Brandt cannot insist on unanimity on these grounds. Nor can Brandt insist on unanimity in the way Rawls does, through the veto available to agents in his Original Position. Indeed, Brandt is quite disparaging about this unanimity requirement (pp. 242–243), which in any case needs a justification. For Rawls, the justification depends on moral assumptions about free and equal moral agents.[23] But Brandt's empiricist constraint bars any such justification, and he insists that the appropriateness of the reforming definition of "morally right" should depend on the actual outcomes of the justificatory choice procedure. So Brandt is left with the problem of assigning a status to the Jim Crow code given that it meets these conditions: (1) it is stable compared to alternatives; (2) it would be chosen by enough of the population (say 90 percent) to make it generally current; and (3) it is happiness-maximizing. Should we now say that this code gives us the content of "it is morally right and wrong" because the overwhelming majority would choose it, were they rational? Or do we retreat to the relativistic "right according to the majority" but "wrong according to the minority?" Brandt insists that "we let the chips fall where they will" [(p. 3)] but either result seems unacceptable to me.

Indeed, Brandt's problem here (if it is a problem) brings to mind a criticism that David Lyons has made of Rawlsian contractarianism: We have no reason to think the outcome of such a rational choice procedure determines what is *moral* rather than merely what is *prudential* (Lyons, 1975). Of course, the outcome of the Rawlsian choice procedure is also constrained by the requirement that the preferred principles match considered moral judgments in reflective equilibrium. This constraint gives some assurance that the outcome is moral. But Brandt rejects any such constraint: It would be completely counter to his empiricist constraint. So if it is prudent for the majority of fully rational agents to choose the Jim Crow code, there is no further requirement that the outcome match moral judgments. Thus Lyons's criticism has a far greater bite when directed against Brandt than against Rawls.

8. SOME LESSONS

The question was asked, in Section 6, whether Brandt's own procedure for selecting moral codes respects the spirit, and not just the letter, of the empiricist constraint. We may now clarify that question in light of the problems raised for Brandt's methodology in the last two sections. Brandt's method, it appears, at best conforms to a *weak* version of the empiricist constraint: No *explicit* appeal to moral intuitions or judgments may play a role in the process of justifying a moral code. But conformity with the weak empiricist constraint is compatible with the presence of at least two types of moral influence on the justificatory process.

First, it is possible that explicit moral beliefs or desires can act causally, but in undetected ways, to affect our other desires. Merely ruling out appeal to such explicit desires will not then eliminate their other effects on our desires and choices (see notes 15 and 21). Second, our desires, even after cognitive psychotherapy, are a product of the social structures in which we are raised. Consequently, moral codes that influence the design of those social structures will leave their imprint—overt or covert—on our rational desires. As a result, Brandt's method is likely not to conform to a *strong* version of the empiricist constraint: Prior moral judgments or intuitions may play neither an explicit nor implicit role, inferential or causal, in influencing the outcome of the justificatory process.

The failure of Brandt's method to conform to the strong empiricist constraint, even it it complies with the weak one, violates the spirit in which the empiricist constraint is advocated by him. The point behind Brandt's repudiation of intuitionism was (1) that appeals to such moral judgments trapped us in our tradition and lacked objectivity, and (2) that they lacked "credibility" as a basis for moral-theory construction or justification. In contrast, Brandt sought a method that relied on facts and logic alone. But now we see that the desires that survive cognitive psychotherapy are not free from important moral influences. They are not "just facts," but facts that reflect the influence of prior moral choices. These desires, too, trap us in our own traditions. And their "credibility" as bases for moral-theory construction or justification will be neither greater nor less than the credibility of the moral judgments that are embodied in the moral codes that have causally influenced their content and structure.

It might be argued that there is some advantage to conforming to the weak empiricist constraint even if the strong one is violated. At least one source of bias, one source of skeptical objection, is removed. But if we are in a rowboat, the unseen leaks will wet our feet as thoroughly as the visible ones, and at least we can patch the ones we see. Brandt seems to be in basically the same leaky boat as Rawls, although at least Rawls is clear that we must do some bailing.

Even if Brandt is in the same boat as Rawls, perhaps some modest modification of his strategy would permit us to find a way to purify desires of moral influences. This suggestion brings us to a point noted in Section 6—that there is a tention between the empiricist and disalienation constraints. The disalienation constraint requires that, in the procedure for choosing moral codes, we employ only those desires we *actually* have, or at least those it is "recommendatory" for us to have. This constraint imposes severe limits on the degree to which we can "purify" our desires. But the stricter our compliance with the disalienation constraint, the more likely our violation of the strong empiricist constraint. Suppose, for example, we could correct, at least hypothetically, for the influence of prior moral codes on our desire sets by determining just which desires are morally influenced. We could make these corrections in "our" choice of an ideal moral code only if we resorted to hypothetical choices, which would violate the disalienation contraint, or if we could show that each correction can be "recommended" to us, which seems totally implausible. So any strategy for conforming to the strong empiricist constraint would probably have to abandon the disalienation constraint. This is no minor concession for Brandt.

There is another constraint on the ways in which Brandt might try to modify his basic strategy. If conformity to the strong empiricist constraint is to be achieved, it must be complete: *All* moral influences on the desires that play a role in justification must be eliminated. In contrast, if only some such influences are eliminated, and others are viewed as "acceptable," then it begins to look as if we are invoking moral distinctions in another guise. But to seek the elimination of all moral influences on desires may leave us with too small a desire set to permit any "rational" choice of a moral code.

If Brandt is forced to concede violation of the strong empiricist constraint, then the issue between his method and the method of wide reflective equilibrium—for example, in Rawls's use of it—becomes one of degree and not principle. It becomes the issue of how best to correct for the possibility that prior moral judgments that influence moral theory acceptance may be biased or otherwise epistemologically worrisome. What is then needed is a comparison of the resources for criticism and the pressures for revision that are present in both methods. We will have to abandon the illusion that there is a knockdown epistemological objection to one method to which the alternative is immune. Of course, there is another alternative open to Brandt, which is hinted at in his remark quoted earlier: "We must avoid intuitionism even if this were to mean (*as it does not*) that we must end up as complete skeptics in the area of practice" (p. 13, emphasis added).

NOTES

1. This essay, especially sections 4–7, is to a significant extent based on my "Can Cognitive Psychotherapy Reconcile Reason and Desire?" in *Ethics* (1983). I wish to thank Hugo Bedau, Charles Beitz, Judith Wagner DeCew, and Susan Wold for provocative

discussion of Brandt's work during the fall of 1979, Richard Brandt for helpful comments on an early draft, and David Copp and David Zimmerman for suggestions about this version. All references to Richard Brandt's *A Theory of the Good and the Right* (1979) will be indicated parenthetically in the text.

2. The term moral empiricism is taken from Nicholas Sturgeon's (1982) review essay.

3. This section is based on material from Daniels (1979b), pp. 265–268, and (1980a), pp. 85–88.

4. My formulation is not adequate as it stands, since there will even be trivial truth-functional counterexamples to it unless some specification of 'interesting' and 'nontrivial' is given. I also say nothing about how to measure the scope of a theory. The problem is a standing one in the philosophy of science. I am indebted to George Smith for helpful discussion of this point.

5. Rawls's contract argument is a feature of a particular wide reflective equilibrium. The contract apparatus is not self-evidently acceptable. It contains complex 'formal' (publicity), motivational, and knowledge constraints on contractors and principles. Philosophical argument must persuade us that it is a reasonable device for selecting between competing conceptions of justice. These arguments are inferences from a number of background theories—of the person, of procedural justice, of the role of morality in society. Principles chosen must be in a (partial) reflective equilibrium with a relevant set of considered judgments and must yield a feasible, stable, well-ordered society. General social theory tells us what is feasible.

6. I believe that if this point is taken seriously, it undercuts the force of David Copp's claim that wide reflective equilibrium is a "conservative" theory. He argues that if j is a considered moral judgment of which a person remains confident, and j does not fit with the rest of the otherwise-coherent package of beliefs and theories held by the person, then j remains justified for the person. I am inclined to say that such a person has not achieved wide reflective equilibrium and j is not necessarily justified for the person. See David Copp's essay.

7. Brandt's discussion draws on early characterizations of justification by Nelson Goodman (1952) and Israel Scheffler (1954). In Scheffler's discussion, the method is described using the notion of 'initial credibility,' which is not explicated for us. Later in the article we are told that initial credibility is only an indication of our "initial commitment to . . . acceptance" (p. 187). Perhaps Brandt's argument should be construed as the objection to assuming, as Scheffler is willing to do, that initial credibility and initial commitment to acceptance (Brandt's 'credence level') correspond in the moral case in the way they do in the nonmoral case.

8. More specifically, there are three senses of "rational": (1) an action is rational to the first approximation if and only if, taking desires and aversions as a given, it reflects optimal use of "all relevant available information" concerning means and ends and weighted probabilities of satisfaction; (2) a desire or aversion is rational if and only if "it is what it would have been had the person undergone *cognitive psychotherapy*"; and (3) an action is fully rational if and only if it is based on rational desires and is rational to the first approximation (p. 11). A fully rational agent is one in a position to carry out fully rational actions.

9. Rawls's "model conception" of persons as free and equal moral agents has such a status. Persons are "free" to form and revise conceptions of the good and "equal" in their possession of a sense of justice. Such complexity in the theory or ideal of the person—human nature, if you will—is not only absent in Brandt's account, but it is ruled out by Brandt's methodological constraints. John Rawls (1980); cf. also Daniels (1979a).

10. See (1739), bk. II, sec. 3, and Brandt (1979), pp. 110–111. Brandt, incidentally, credits Rashdall with giving an approximation to cognitive psychotherapy (p. 209). In the passage Brandt cites, however, Rashdall suggests that we can ferret out the truly moral content from our intuitions. These cleansed intuitions then form the foundation of our moral system, contra Brandt. See Hastings Rashdall (1924), vol. I, p. 212.

11. Brandt defines a desire as artificial if it "could not have been brought about by experience with actual situations which the desires are for and the aversions against (p. 117). The counterfactual is problematic. If it permits major changes in a person's system

of desires, then some changes will make the same test desire natural, whereas others will make it artificial. If it involves only minimal alteration of his desires, changing only the test desire, then artificiality depends on quite incidental facts about him. Some aversions that then intuitively seem artificial will turn out to be natural.

12. Brandt wants "relevance" to be both a *causal* notion (p. 12) and a *content* notion (p. 112). Unfortunately, some information that ought to count as relevant by the content criterion may not count as such because it fails to have the proper causal effect. So although we (in contrast to Brandt) might want to call a desire irrational because it resists extinction when exposed to relevant information, Brandt is free to conclude that the information is not relevant.

13. Brandt's problem here is part of a more general problem with idealized views of rationality. Cf. Cherniak (1980, 1981).

14. Paul Meehl has pointed out to me that Brandt's version of cognitive psychotherapy should not be confused with the more aggressive therapist-guided techniques usually known by the same name.

15. Although the problem of unconscious desires is a problem for Brandt's approach, he does not mention it. Instead, he makes an entirely inappropriate criticism of Rawls's veil of ignorance, which, he says, cannot block the operation of unconscious desires (p. 240). Rawls's construction is here an analytic or formal construction, not an empirical process to be foiled in the way Brandt suggests.

16. For example, Brandt makes little effort to connect his account of learning theory to recent work in cognitive psychology, especially the developmental literature.

17. The higher-order desire to maximize happiness is a requirement of the motivational and learning theory Brandt sketches (p. 154). The strong claim on page 154 takes desire as given and does not avoid the argument above.

18. Indeed, if some behavior-modification method much more powerful than cognitive psychotherapy would lead me to the superior set and increased enjoyment, I would be foolish not to try it. For Brandt's considered remarks on hedonism, see pp. 132–138.

19. As part of a general argument that "satisfaction" is an inappropriate criterion for well-being in important moral contexts, Rawls suggests that the deep social-utility functions needed for maximizing satisfaction interpersonally commit us to the view that persons are just containers. See Rawls (1982), especially pp. 173–179.

20. Brandt devotes Chapter IX to "psychologizing" the notion of a moral code, so that a code is not a set of principles, but a set of underlying desires and aversions. Yet the entire argument about choosing moral codes is conducted as if we are talking about principles. I adhere to this "intellectualist" approach throughout, despite its "disastrous problems" (p. 171).

21. Excluding them, however, exposes Brandt to a criticism he raises (implausibly) against Rawls; namely, whether we can simply ignore desires it is posited that we have (p. 240). If so, we may be violating the disalienation constraint (see note 15).

22. Brandt's use of the term "intrinsic" desire or aversion does not exclude us from having a nonmistaken and possibly nonartificial desire to have blacks treated in discriminatory ways. Nor does he turn to a restriction to "self-regarding" desires like Dworkin's. See Ronald Dworkin (1977).

23. See Rawls (1980) for explicit claims about the centrality of the ideal or "model conception" of the person to the design of the original position. See also Daniels (1980a).

chapter six

Considered Judgments and Moral Justification: Conservatism in Moral Theory

David Copp

"Conservatism" involves giving a privileged place in moral theory to our moral convictions, or to those we would have under specified hypothetical circumstances. Our "considered judgments," as they are called, may be invoked, on the one hand, as providing a standard against which theories of moral justification can be assessed. There is a common assumption that a theory may be undermined if it can be shown to imply that some of our considered judgments are not justified. On the other hand, our considered judgments may themselves figure in theories of moral justification, as, for instance, in typical coherence theories of moral justification. In both cases we see a form of conservatism.

Conservatism of one kind or another is widely accepted by moral theorists, partly because of an idea that there is no alternative. If the convictions we have do not provide a standard against which we can assess our theories, then what standard have we? This idea is reinforced by the view that conflict between a theory and our convictions provides us with a justification for rejecting the theory. These considerations support one type of conservatism, the type that treats our considered judgments as a standard against which theories of moral justification are tested. Conservatism has also gained from recent attacks on foundationalist epistemologies and the resulting rise in the fortunes of coherence theories. If we are to restructure and refine Neurath's boat as it sails through the skeptical storm, then, in ethics, it seems that we must hammer our considered judgments into place in a network of supporting principles and theories. If this is our view of moral justification, then we accept a conservative coherentism.

I will distinguish between two types of conservative theory, and I will begin by providing a rough characterization, leaving complications and necessary qualifications for later. Roughly, a "type-one" conservative theory is a theory of moral justification according to which a *moral judgment's*, or a *morality's*, being justified depends at least in part on its being appropriately related to our considered moral judgments in ideal circumstances. A "type-two" conservative theory is a view regarding the justification of *theories* of moral justification themselves, rather than, as with type-one theories, the justification of moral *judgments* or *moralities*. A type-two conservative theory may be characterized roughly as a theory according to which the tenability of a *theory of moral justification* depends at least in part on its implying that our considered moral judgments in ideal circumstances would be justified. I will contend that conservative theories of both types are mistaken.

1. SKEPTICISM AND MORAL JUSTIFICATION

A theory of moral justification is a response to moral skepticism. However, a wide variety of views about morality could be called skeptical in one sense or another. I will regard skepticism as consisting in the view that morality ought rationally to be discarded along with (other) false theories, such as astrology, or (other) unwarranted systems of behavioral standards, such as courtly love. Skepticism suggests that morality has no role to play in governing the life or actions of a rational and informed person or society. I assume that the task of providing an adequate response to moral skepticism is the central task of moral theory. I also assume that it would not be adequate simply to throw the burden of proof to the skeptic, or simply to examine individual skeptical arguments and to show where they can be resisted. The root issue is one of overall plausibility. An adequate response to skepticism would require supporting the overall plausibility, in the light of other philosophical and empirical theories, and of other propositions that we accept, either of skepticism or of some nonskeptical position. It would require supporting what I will call a *theory of moral justification*.

Given the radical nature of skepticism, a response to it need not contend that there are moral facts, or that there is or could be moral knowledge. Theories that did make such a contention would be counted as theories of moral justification; thus intuitionistic theories, naturalist theories, and certain contractarian theories would be so counted. But noncognitivist theories and certain types of relativism would also be counted as theories of moral justification, even though they would not imply the existence of moral facts or knowledge. Skepticism itself should be counted as a theory of moral justification, as, in general, should any theory that speaks to the issue of moral skepticism. As a first approximation, we could say that a theory of moral justification is a theory that provides an account of the circumstances (if any) under which a morality or a moral judgment is *justified,* either *simpliciter* or in relation to some person or group.

More happily, we could say: A theory of moral justification is a theory about moralities, or about moral judgments, that provides an account of the conditions (if any) under which some moralities, or moral judgments (perhaps in relation to some person or society), are intellectually or rationally to be preferred to some other moralities or moral judgments, and are intellectually or rationally worthy of being subscribed to, given what is known.

Theories of moral justification must be distinguished from two other sorts of theory with which they are easily confused. Later, in discussing conservatism, I will point out places where these confusions could become important.

First, a theory of moral justification is a theory as to when a morality or moral judgment *itself* may be justified, not an account of the circumstances under which a *person* is justified *in* his moral views.[1] Let us call theories of the former sort theories of "objective justification," and theories of the latter sort theories of "personal justification." The difference between these two kinds of theory can be clearly brought out if we notice that a moral skeptic need not deny that we may be justified *in* our moral views. What he denies is that our moral views are justified *themselves.* Similarly, a skeptic about religion could consistently hold both that Aquinas was justified *in* his religious views and that Aquinas's views were themselves unjustified. Matters of personal justification have to do with whether *people* can be faulted for some kind of irrationality given the *genesis* of their views; but skepticism raises issues about the existence of a rational warrant for those views themselves. The relationship between these types of issues is complex, but an account of personal justification in ethics would not directly yield a position on moral skepticism.[2]

Second, we need to distinguish between theories of moral justification and *systematizing* or *descriptive* moral theories. Systematizing theories are theories as to what principles would systematize some person's or group's considered moral views.[3] Thus utilitarianism is typically advanced as a theory that systematizes our views. Systematizing theories do not speak to the issue of skepticism, unless they are combined with conservative assumptions. For instance, there is the view that the derivability of a moral judgment from a systematizing theory, together with true factual premises, is sufficient to justify that judgment,[4] regardless of whether the systematizing theory has any independent justification or any property to recommend it other than its systematizing property. This view would reflect a kind of conservative coherence theory of moral justification. We will examine the credentials of such theories below. The present point is that conservative theories of justification, such as John Rawls's and Norman Daniels's accounts of wide reflective equilibrium theory, sometimes can also be interpreted as systematizing theories.[5] The distinction between these kinds of theory must be kept clearly in mind.

Theories of moral justification themselves need to be supported, for there are competing theories. I will call theories of moral justification "type-one" theories. An account of the justification of theories of moral justification would provide a basis for choosing on a principled basis between rival type-one views. I will call such accounts "type-two" theories. We need to distinguish between theories of moral justification (that is, type-one theories) and theories of the justification of theories of moral justification (that is, type-two theories). No doubt one could carry on this series of meta-theories indefinitely, at least notionally. But the problem of justifying a theory of moral justification is part of the problem of theory justification in general. Any danger of a vicious regress is avoided by imposing the constraint that a tenable general theory of theory justification be self-supporting in the sense that it itself meet the conditions it imposes on justified theories in general.

In summary, I have claimed that the central task of moral theory is to provide an adequate response to moral skepticism. I have suggested that accomplishing this task would require one to devise a theory of moral justification, or a type-one theory, and to support this theory on the basis of a type-two theory, which, in turn, would be part of a general account of the justification of theories.

2. TWO TYPES OF CONSERVATISM

Conservative theories give an essential role in their account of justification to the considered moral judgments that some person or persons would make in hypothetical ideal circumstances of some specified kind. I call theories of this sort "conservative" because they tend to preserve as justified our considered judgments in ideal circumstances, or our "idealized" considered judgments. I hope my use of the term "conservative" will not be misleading. Of course, conservative theories of justification need not support political or moral views that are "conservative" in the sense commonly given to the term in political debate. They are conservative only in the one way I am about to explain.

Conservative theories can differ in the account they give of the nature of "considered" moral judgments. However, I think a Rawlsian account would generally be accepted: One's considered moral judgments are roughly those moral judgments of which one is fully and nontemporarily confident, or would be, if one carefully considered them in a situation devoid of factors known in general to interfere with deliberation and judgment (cf. Rawls, 1971, pp. 47–48). Among factors of this kind are haste, bias, inattention, intoxication, lack of information, and states of emotional upset. Factors such as this interfere with epistemic judgment, and they usually can be avoided or are relatively temporary, so I will characterize them as "occasional epistemic distorting factors." Being a considered judgment is a matter of having a complex psychological and relational property, the property a judgment has in relation to a person when that person would be fully and nontemporarily confident of the judgment if he were carefully to consider it in a situation devoid of occasional epistemic distorting factors.[6]

A conservative theory can allow for a good deal of theoretically motivated change in our considered views. Rawls pointed out that our considered judgments prior to philosophical reflection might be different from our considered judgments after reflection. Being nontemporarily confident does not imply permanent confidence, and carefulness does not imply philosophical sophistication. Hence, as Rawls pointed out (1971, pp. 48–50), one might come to question one's original judgments if one were made aware of their implications, or their systematizing principles, and of alternatives that might be theoretically more attractive. One's views might then change, until one came to have considered judgments that were a better match to the principles one favored and that had implications one could accept. Rawls assumed that this process would cease in a "reflective equilibrium," and he assumed that it is the considered moral judgments one would make in reflective equilibrium that are germane to assessing a moral theory (p. 48). They are the data against which a theory is to be checked (p. 51). Of course, I do not want to tie conservatism to the Rawlsian notion of reflective equilibrium. I will write generally of the considered moral judgments that would be made under relevant "ideal circumstances." These judgments may be quite different from our initial considered judgments.

Some constraints must be imposed on this notion of ideal circumstances. One, in particular, is most important for my argument, a constraint I will call the *nonvacuousness constraint:* A conservative theory must specify the notion of an ideal circumstance, and other relevant notions, such that the conservative condition the theory imposes on the justification of the objects of its concern, be they moralities or theories of moral justification, is not either satisfied by all such objects or failed by all such objects alike.

In a conservative theory, justification of an object depends on its being appropriately related to idealized considered moral judgments.

This is the conservative condition. If *all* objects alike either are so related, or are not so related, then the theory is not worth taking seriously as a conservative theory: It may imply that *none* of the objects of its concern is justified. Then it is not a serious alternative to skepticism. Or it may imply that *all* of the objects of its concern are justified. Then the theory is too generous to be taken seriously. Finally, despite failing to meet the nonvacuousness constraint, it may allow that some of the objects of its concern are justified and some are not. Then the conservative condition does not play an *essential* role in the theory, and the theory should not be regarded as conservative. In short, a theory that fails to meet the nonvacuousness constraint either is not worth taking seriously at all or is not to be considered a conservative theory.

There are two basic kinds of conservative theory: (1) conservative theories of moral justification, and (2) conservative theories regarding the justification of theories of moral justification.

Type-One Conservative Theories: A theory of moral justification is conservative just in case it implies that a moral judgment's or a morality's being justified, either *simpliciter* or in relation to some person or group, depends on, or is in virtue of, at least in part, that judgment's or that morality's standing in some appropriate justificatory relation to the considered moral judgments that would be made in specified ideal circumstances either by everyone or by that person or that group, and depends on, or is in virtue of, at least in part, their being considered judgments.[7]

Type-Two Conservative Theories: A theory of the justification of theories of moral justification is conservative just in case it implies that the tenability of a theory of moral justification, either *simpliciter* or in relation to some person or group, depends on, or is in virtue of, at least in part, that theory's implying to be justified the considered moral judgments that would be made in specified ideal circumstances either by everyone or by that person or that group, and depends on, or is in virtue of, at least in part, their being considered judgments.[8]

Conservative theories differ with respect to which agents' considered judgments are taken to be relevant. In general, I will ignore this complication and write of "our" considered judgments.

It should be clear how type-one and type-two conservative theories differ: They are theories about the justification of different, though related, things. Type-one theories, whether or not conservative, are about the justification of moralities or moral judgments; and type-two theories are about the justification of type-one theories, or theories of moral justification. Type-two conservatism does not imply type-one conservatism. That is, a type-two conservative theory typically would allow the possibility that some nonconservative type-one theory is justified. For a theory of moral justification could imply that our considered moral judgments in ideal circumstances would be justified, but it could imply this without making the justification depend on their being considered. Such a theory would meet the type-two conservative constraint while not itself being a conservative theory of moral justification. What is typical of type-two theories is the view that theories of moral justification can be defeated or undermined by marshaling counterexamples supported by considered judgments.

Let us now begin to assess the credentials of conservatism. Different considerations may support or undermine the different types of conservatism, but I will attempt to focus on issues that bear on conservatism in general.

3. SKEPTICISM AND CONSERVATISM

At root, conservatism relies on taking our confidence in certain moral judgments to be an index of justification. There are refinements in the view, to be sure, for our confidence is only regarded as an index when it survives reflection, and when it would exist in the absence of occasional distorting factors and in some specified circumstance, such as Rawls's wide reflective equilibrium. Nevertheless, conservatism does not give equal weight to all of the beliefs we would have after careful consideration, in the absence of epistemic distorting factors, and in otherwise ideal circumstances. Only the beliefs in which we would have full and non-temporary *confidence* are dubbed considered judgments, and they play an essential role in conservative theories of justification. This is why I say that conservatism can be seen as taking our confidence as an index of justification, albeit our confidence in ideal circumstances. What would lead a philosopher to this view?

This question is particularly pressing given that type-two conservative theories beg the question against skepticism. Type-two theories entail that a tenable theory of moral justification must imply to be justified the considered moral judgments that would be made in ideal circumstances by relevant persons; and it is to be assumed that there are such judgments. Thus type-two theories entail that a theory of moral justification is not tenable if it implies that *no* moral judgment is justified. But moral skepticism is precisely a theory of moral justification, or a family of such theories, according to which no moral judgment is justified. Obviously, then, type-two theories imply that moral skepticism is not tenable. This means that considerations that count in favor of skepticism count against the type-two conservative constraint. It also means that, in the absence of an independent argument in favor of the constraint, or against skepticism, the constraint begs the question against skepticism. This is a serious objection to second-order conservatism.

One might reply that second-order conservatism simply consists in applying standard philosophical methodology to the problem of assessing theories of moral justification. It may be thought that we are entitled to rely on our considered moral judgments in moral theory, just as we are entitled to rely on our "intuitions" about knowledge in assessing epistemological theories. This line of thought raises issues of philosophical methodology that I cannot adequately discuss here. To be sure, it is standard in epistemology to begin with the assumption that epistemological skepticism is wrong, and to use the skeptic's arguments to learn about the nature of knowledge and justification.[9] However, the analogous strategy in ethics would imply rejection of the assumption I began with—the assumption that the central task in ethics is to provide a response to moral skepticism. Moreover, the analogy with epistemology is weak. Epistemological skepticism has very little theoretical plausibility. If we held it to be justified, we would have to hold our scientific theories to be unjustified; yet scientific theories are paradigmatic of justified theories. Ethical skepticism, on the other hand, does not conflict with holding science to be justified. In short, there is no reason to think that a strategy that would be adequate for dealing with epistemological skepticism would also be adequate for dealing with ethical skepticism.

If it is agreed that responding to skepticism is the chief task of moral theory, then the objection we are discussing is serious. In light of it, we must be wary of type-two conservatism unless we have *independent* grounds for rejecting skepticism. Unfortunately, many philosophers are inclined to reject skepticism *because* it conflicts with their "intuitions." It is therefore important to realize that our grounds for rejecting skepticism must not presuppose conservatism in this way.

4. REASONS FOR CONSERVATISM

I do not know of any arguments that are formulated explicitly as arguments in favor of conservatism. However, four considerations should be discussed.

I think the most deeply rooted consideration that leads philosophers to conservatism is the idea that there is no methodological alternative. Thomas Nagel reflects this idea in his suggestion that we have *no option* but to begin with the set of moral convictions we find initially credible and to try to construct a moral theory on that basis (Nagel, 1980, p. 104). The fact is, however, that conservatism goes beyond this methodological claim. Conservatism holds that *justification* depends, at least in part, on an appropriate relationship to our idealized considered moral judgments. Nagel's claim about the options we have implies nothing about the plausibility of conservatism. Nagel's method could lead us to a nonconservative theory of moral justification and does not even imply acceptance of the type-two conservative constraint. Even if Nagel is right, conservatism does not follow.

A second consideration is the idea that if a morality or theory conflicts with our firmly held convictions, convictions we hold in the absence of occasional epistemic-distorting factors and in otherwise ideal circumstances, then we have a reason to reject the morality or the theory. This may well be so, but it has no direct bearing on the question we are interested in. I have urged the importance of distinguishing between theories of moral justification and accounts of personal justification. Where a person's confidence in a set of moral views, or in a theory, persists after careful thought in an epistemically ideal situation, his confidence *may* bear on the question whether *he* is justified *in* those views. But a person's *confidence* has no obvious bearing on the question whether that theory, or those views, are *themselves* justified in any sense that would imply a response to the skeptic. Clarity in this area requires that we insist on the distinction between theories of the justification of *persons in* their beliefs and theories of the justification of theories and of moralities *themselves*. It is the latter that concern us here. Nevertheless, a failure to make this distinction, or a confusion between the two sorts of theory, could explain the conservative idea that our confidence in a set of judgments in ideal circumstances has a bearing on justification.

A third consideration is suggested by the dichotomy that Gilbert Harman finds between "naturalism" in ethics and "autonomous ethics" (this volume). Perhaps, if Harman is correct, the rejection of naturalism would lead to autonomous ethics. And autonomous ethics can seem to be a kind of conservatism. If so, then any of the arguments that have been mooted against naturalism could be a basis for a conservative position.

Harman suggests that the term "naturalism" traditionally refers to a kind of second-order constraint on theories of moral justification; namely, that an adequate theory must show "precisely how value and obligation fit into the scientific conception of the world" (this volume). He contrasts naturalism in this sense with "autonomous ethics," an approach that attaches "no special importance" to such a showing but pursues ethics by beginning with our initial moral beliefs and searching for fundamental moral principles that agree with our beliefs about the facts and with the moral opinions we are convinced of after reflection. Described in this way, autonomous ethics may sound like conservatism, and it may seem that conservatism is a form of antinaturalism. However, on the one hand, an autonomous theory may be, but need not be, type-two conservative: A type-two theory could reject *both* the naturalist *and* the conservative constraints, and regard as acceptable a theory, such as Kantian theory, that meets neither of the constraints. Moreover, on the other hand, a type-two theory could be *both* conservative *and* naturalist: Nothing prevents a naturalist type-two theory from demanding that an adequate theory of moral justification not only explain how ethics fits into the natural world but also justify our considered judgments in ideal circumstances. Hence, an antinaturalist autonomous theory could be either conservative or not, and so could a naturalist theory be either conservative or not. When naturalism is understood as Harman suggests, neither it nor its denial commits one to a position on conservatism.

The term "naturalism" is sometimes used differently. Sometimes it is used to label type-one theories that meet Harman's type-two naturalist constraint *by* implying that moral judgments can be "reduced to" factual statements that plainly fit the scientific conception of the world. A kind of analytic utilitarianism would be a naturalist theory, as is Brandt's psychologism (1979). However, on the one hand, a naturalist theory of this kind could also be type-one conservative. I think that a variation of an ideal-observer theory could be devised that would have both characteristics. Moreover, a commitment to the existence of some adequate type-one naturalist theory could be combined with a commitment to the type-two conservative demand that an adequate theory must justify our idealized considered judgments. Hence, type-one naturalism is compatible with conservatism. More obviously, on the other hand, the acceptance of a type-one theory that is *not* naturalist is compatible with the *rejection* of conservatism. For instance, Kantian moral theory and Moorean intuitionism are neither type-one naturalist nor type-one conservative.[10] I conclude that when naturalism is understood to involve commitment to a type-one reductionist theory, neither it nor its denial commits one to a position on conservatism.

It seems, then, that both forms of conservatism are logically independent of both forms of naturalism. If this is right, then both naturalists and antinaturalists may embrace conservatism. But both may reject it equally well.

Finally, one might think that an adequate general epistemological theory, when applied to the problem of moral justification,[11] would yield a conservative theory. Two models are available. A conservative *foundationalism* would portray our idealized considered moral judgments as epistemically basic beliefs that, together with other basic beliefs, provide the basis for any other justified beliefs but are justified themselves without the need of grounding. I will argue that a conservative foundationalism is a nonstarter quite apart from the question of whether foundationalism is generally plausible. A conservative *coherence* theory may seem more plausible, for it would acknowledge that our considered moral judgments need to be justified and propose that they may be justified by being brought into coherence with our other beliefs. Moreover, coherentism might seem to support conservatism in ethics, for it would seem to regard our moral beliefs as standing in no greater need of justification than, say, our ordinary beliefs about our immediate physical environment. I will argue that this appearance is misleading and that coherentism actually undermines conservatism. However, these epistemological theories need to be discussed in some detail.

5. CONSERVATISM AS A FOUNDATIONALISM

A conservative foundationalism would regard our considered moral judgments in ideal circumstances as epistemically basic. That is, it would regard such judgments as justified, but not on the basis of any evidence or of any other considerations. It would regard them as justified just in virtue of being our considered judgments in ideal circumstances, or in virtue of their alleged possession of some other property, such as their being indicators of moral reality. A theory of this sort would be a nonstarter. It would beg the question against skepticism. Its view of our idealized considered judgments would be unsubstantiated. And, finally, it would be undermined by psychological explanations of our moral attitudes.

To begin with, a conservative foundationalism would maintain exactly what moral skepticism denies; namely, that some moral judgments are justified. Moreover, it would deny that any argument is *needed* to show that our idealized considered judgments are justified. And it would not make available any such argument because the availability of such an argument would undermine its view that such judgments are epistemically *basic*. Clearly then, it would beg the question, unless it were accompanied by an independent argument against skepticism.

However, there is no reason to believe that our idealized considered moral judgments are epistemically basic, so even if we had an independent reason for rejecting skepticism, foundationalism would be implausible. The key point is that a conservative foundationalism would regard certain judgments as certified simply by the *confidence* we would have in them if we carefully considered them in a situation where we were not subject to occasional epistemic-distorting factors and which was otherwise ideal. This would be to place too great a reliance on our confidence. We often hesitate to place much reliance on the confidence of others, and we know that what we are confident of can change from time to time. It would seem sensible to remain skeptical about our own confidence, even about our confidence in ideal circumstances. There is no reason, for instance, to believe that our confidence is an indicator of a "moral reality."

Typical foundationalist views provide no adequate basis for regarding idealized considered judgments as basic. A moral-sense theory would regard our considered judgments as analogous to observation reports and as similarly reliable. An intuitionism would regard them as self-evident. However, our considered judgments are not plausibly regarded in either light. We typically support moral judgments, even considered judgments, by citing reasons. This is unlike the way we support observation reports (Daniels, 1979b, pp. 270–71). It would be unnecessary if considered judgments were self-evident, and if they were epistemically basic. I see no way of making plausible the idea that certain judgments are certified simply by the fact that they would be among our considered judgments in ideal circumstances.

Finally, conservative foundationalism is directly challenged by a common kind of argument to the effect that we accept nonmoral theories that provide adequate explanations of our having the moral views that we have. Such explanations do not require that we suppose our moral views to indicate a moral reality, or to be justified in any way that would answer the skeptic (Brandt, 1979, p. 20; Harman, 1977, pp. 6–9). These theories would explain not only our having a given set of actual views but also the fact that we might have a different set of views were we to be free of occasional epistemic distorting factors and in otherwise ideal circumstances. Therefore, a conservative theory cannot escape the challenge by linking justification to the considered judgments we *would* make in ideal circumstances, rather than to those we initially accept.

One's sincere, complete, and nontemporary confidence in a judgment can be explained by psychological mechanisms having to do with one's moral training and one's personality, and by sociological factors having to do with the culture of one's group, one's class background, and so on. We have every reason to believe that human psychology is plastic with respect to the moralities that can successfully be instilled. Recent efforts to show that evolutionary theory, or psychological theory, places limits on the plasticity do not alter this fact. Moreover, one's ability and willingness to alter one's moral views, and the likelihood of one's views altering, in hypothetical circumstances, also can be explained by similar psychological and sociological factors. Thus psychological and sociological factors seem to determine whether the moral views of which one is fully and nontemporally confident would change if one carefully considered them in a situation devoid of occasional epistemic distorting factors. This certainly undermines the plausibility of the conservative view that one's considered moral judgments in hypothetical ideal circumstances are *ipso facto* justified.

What is more, the *kind* of psychological factor that plays a role in determining what moral judgments we would accept in various hypothetical idealized circumstances should be of particular concern to a foundationalist. I will call them "suspicious formative factors" to distinguish them from what I have called "occasional epistemic distorting factors." The nature of the judgments we would make in hypothetical circumstances depends partly on the flexibility of our views. But the degree to which one's views are flexible is influenced by, for instance, the degree to which one's early moral training and environment were authoritarian, the degree to which one is stubborn, the degree to which one is intellectually self-confident, or has intellectual courage, the degree to which one is able to admit error to others and to oneself, the degree to which one is influenced by authority, and the degree to which one's interests and the interests of one's fellows depend on the general acceptance of one's views. Formative factors such as these influence the nature of the judgments one would accept in hypothetical circumstances that, in various ways, are different from one's actual situation. Their influence undermines the plausibility of conservative theories that take certain hypothetical judgments as a standard of justification.

It might seem that conservatism has an obvious reply to this objection. Considered judgments are, by stipulation, judgments one would accept in a situation devoid of factors known to interfere with deliberation and judgment. Moreover, I have left it largely open how a conservative theory might specify the nature of the hypothetical ideal circumstances in which our considered judgments are taken to constitute a standard of justification. To avoid the objection, a conservative theory need only provide an adequate account of ideal circumstances, an account that ensures that our considered judgments in ideal circumstances are free of influence by distorting factors.

However, typical proposals regarding the notion of ideal circumstances do not escape the objection. For instance, one might propose to exploit Kohlberg's (1973) suggestion that the most advanced level of moral sensibility is exhibited by people who have reached the most advanced stage of cognitive development. A conservative theory could take as a standard of justification the considered moral judgments we would make at the most advanced level of cognitive development and in possession of all relevant information. This would be a kind of ideal-observer theory. However, it would not escape the objection. Kohlberg's suggestion does not imply that every person at the highest level of cognitive development would have the same considered judgments, nor does it imply that any one such person would have the same considered judgments at all times. We know, for instance, that two philosophically sophisticated medical doctors can reach conflicting considered judgments about controversial issues such as abortion. They could be at the same level of cognitive development, be equally well informed, and be equally free of occasional distorting factors. The explanation for their difference of opinion would presumably make reference to different formative influences on their moral attitudes, and this means that Kohlberg's suggestion is compatible with the kind of influence on our views that fueled the objection under discussion. It would be wrong to suppose that our considered judgments in Kohlbergian ideal circumstances would be free of influence by suspicious formative factors.

It still may seem that there is an obvious response to the objection: Specify that our considered judgments are a standard of justification only in circumstances where they *are* free of influence by distorting factors. That is, to avoid the objection, a conservative theory need only specify that ideal circumstances are circumstances in which our considered judgments have not been influenced by *any* distorting factors.

But this reply violates the nonvacuousness constraint. A conservative theory must specify the notion of an ideal circumstance, such that the conservative condition the theory imposes on the justification of the objects of its concern is not either satisfied or failed by all such objects alike. I think that there is no fact of the matter as to what moral judgments would be our considered judgments in circumstances where, not only are we not subject to occasional epistemic distorting factors, but also our views are not explained by formative factors of the sort already mentioned. That is, there is no fact of the matter as to what our considered judgments would be like were our early moral training not to have been at all authoritarian, and were our moral views not to have been at all influenced by anyone's self-interest, by our class background, or by the culture of our society. Further, there is no psychologically possible world in which we are free from influence by all factors of the sort in question and yet have some considered moral judgments. The set that contains all and only the considered moral judgments we would make in circumstances free of all influences of these kinds is *empty*. But all that I need is agreement that there is *no fact of the matter* as to *which* set of moral judgments is the relevant set. For given this, then no matter what relation is to hold between a justified morality or theory and the set of idealized considered judgments, since there is no fact as to which set *is* this set, there is no fact as to whether anything is appropriately related to *it*. Given this, every morality or moral theory fails in the same way to be appropriately related to *the* set of idealized considered judgments. It follows that the nonvacuousness constraint would be violated by a conservative theory that based justification on considered judgments that are specified to be free of influence by any distorting factors.

I do not see any escape from the objection. A conservative theory faces a dilemma. If its specification of the notion of ideal circumstances ensures that any considered judgment made in ideal circumstances would be free of influence by distorting factors, then it violates the nonvacuousness constraint. However, if its specification of this notion does not ensure this, then there is reason to think that considered judgments, even in ideal circumstances, might fail to be justified. Hence, there is reason to think that they are not epistemically basic.

I conclude that a conservative foundationalism would be implausible. It would beg the question against moral skepticism. No explanation has been given as to why moral judgments that would be considered judgments in ideal circumstances (specified in a non-question-begging way) would be *ipso facto* justified. Finally, there is independent reason to think that even our considered judgments in appropriately specified ideal circumstances might fail to be justified.

6. CONSERVATISM AS A COHERENTISM

A conservative coherence theory, unlike a foundationalism, would acknowledge that our considered moral judgments, even in ideal circumstances, need to be justified. It would propose that they are justified just in case they are coherent with the rest of our views. It would seem, therefore, that a coherence theory would be immune to the above objections. Moreover, it may seem that conservative coherentism draws its credibility from the strength of general coherence theories in epistemology. A general coherence theory would assert that a judgment is justified for a person just in case it coheres appropriately with the overall idealized and coherent set of the person's beliefs. Conservative coherentism may seem simply to draw the corollary of this for the case of our moral judgments. However, I will argue on the contrary that a conservative coherence theory would treat our idealized considered judgments as constituting a *standard of justification*. Because of this, even conservative coherence theories are liable to most of the objections that undermine foundationalism. Moreover, because of this, a conservative coherence theory would not be merely a corollary of a general coherence theory. In fact, conservative coherentism would be *undermined* by a plausible general coherence theory.[12]

In order to be specific, let us consider Norman Daniels's theory of "wide reflective equilibrium" (1979b). It is the most sophisticated type-one conservative theory to be found in the literature. Basically, it is a generalization of John Rawls's (1971) coherentist methodology. Daniels holds that a moral judgment is justified for a person only if it is one that he would accept in "wide reflective equilibrium."[13] Wide reflective equilibrium is achieved when there is "coherence in an ordered triple of sets of beliefs held by a particular person, namely, (a) a set of considered moral judgements, (b) a set of moral principles, and (c) a set of relevant background theories" (1979b, p. 258).

The theory is actually more complicated than appears in this statement of it. The background theories include both a body of social theory and a set of moral or general normative theories that themselves are constrained by a set of considered judgments (pp. 259–260). Wide reflective equilibrium actually demands a structured coherence in an ordered quintuplet of sets of beliefs held by a person. The inclusion of sets of considered judgments in the quintuplet ensures that the theory is conservative. Nevertheless, Daniels's theory allows for quite extensive revision of a person's initial moral judgments, and it demands a quite complex relationship among the various classes of beliefs that are to be brought into coherence (p. 266). Theoretical considerations may lead to changes in *any*, and perhaps *all*, of the moral judgments one initially accepts (p. 267). In fact, Daniels suggests, the answer to the question, which judgments must be found to be coherent with principles and theories in wide equilibrium, may emerge *"only when* reflective equilibrium is reached, and still is revisable in the light of further theory change" (pp. 267–268, fn. 17).

The important point is that Daniels's theory, like any conservative theory, treats our considered moral judgments in ideal circumstances as constituting a standard of justification.

Daniels claims, on the contrary, that his theory, unlike a foundationalism, grants to considered judgments "no special epistemological priority" (p. 265), and it allows for "drastic *theory-based* revisions of moral judgments" (p. 266). In a conservative coherence theory, considered judgments are justified only if in a coherent package with moral principles.

However, there is an important asymmetry between considered judgments and the other judgments that are to be brought into coherence. In particular, suppose that one's judgments and beliefs constitute a coherent package except that a single moral judgment j does not "fit" the package. Under this circumstance, j is not justified because it is not part of a wide reflective equilibrium. Nevertheless, j can undermine the credentials of the rest of one's view on the *sole* condition that it be a considered judgment. This is an unhappy result, to say the least. To see that it obtains, suppose, on the one hand, that j is a considered moral judgment. Suppose that one remains fully confident of j despite the failure of fit. Suppose that one's confidence in j is not shaken by any theoretical considerations finding their source in the theories included in the coherent package. Then the lack of fit with j impugns the coherent package as insufficiently comprehensive, and the existence of the package does not show its constituent judgments to be justified. In Daniels's theory the lack of fit with *j* shows that one has not achieved wide reflective equilibrium. The package is not justified. Things would be worse if one would remain confident in *j,* come what may. Then *j* would be part of *any* wide equilibrium that one did achieve. The package is shown to be *unjustifiable.* On the other hand, suppose that *j* is a moral judgment that one accepts, but that is not a *considered* judgment because one is not sufficiently confident of it. Then the lack of fit between *j* and the coherent package impugns *j* as unjustified, but it does *not* undermine the claim to be justified of the moral judgments that are constituents of the coherent package. In Daniels's theory, the lack of fit with *j* is compatible with the achievement of wide reflective equilibrium, and it is compatible with counting the bulk of one's moral views as justified, *unless j* is a considered moral judgment. A conservative coherence theory is marked by the ability of a judgment to impugn the claim to be justified of the constituents of a coherent package, even though it is not itself justified, simply on the basis that it is and would remain a *considered* moral judgment. In this respect, even a conservative *coherence* theory takes considered judgments to be a *standard* of justification.

One might propose a relaxation of conservatism, requiring only that *most* of one's considered judgments enter a wide reflective equilibrium, and allowing that the existence of a few recalcitrant judgments is not sufficient to undermine the rest of one's view. However, the present point would remain, for we can let *j* in the argument represent a *set* of unruly moral judgments, a set containing just more than a few judgments. On the one hand, suppose *j* to represent a set of *considered* judgments, and on the other hand, a set of unruly moral beliefs of which one is not sufficiently confident for them to count as considered judgments. Neither set is justified, but the former undermines the bulk of one's moral beliefs simply because its members enjoy one's confidence. Clearly then, even the relaxed conservative position treats considered judgments as a standard of justification.

It follows that even a conservative coherentism is liable to some of the objections discussed in the last section. It owes us an explanation of why our considered judgments in ideal circumstances should be regarded as constituting a standard of justification. This is especially so given that there is reason to believe that our idealized considered judgments might fail to be justified.

It also follows that one can dispute conservative coherence theories without needing to dispute coherence theories in general. I have no desire to enter into a debate about the merits of theories of epistemological justification. It may be that our best account of theory justification is coherentist, and so it may be that our best type-two theory is coherentist.

The issue here is whether it, and whether our best theory of moral justification, are both coherentist and *conservative*. To reject conservatism while retaining a coherence theory would be to allow that the "best" achievable coherent structure, given one's beliefs, may exclude certain beliefs one remains confident of, and so it may exclude certain considered moral judgments, perhaps even more than a few. Given Daniels's terminology, it would be to allow that the "best" achievable coherent structure may not be in wide reflective equilibrium with our considered moral judgments.

I wish to argue that one who accepts a plausible general coherence theory of justification should reject conservatism. A plausible coherence theory of justification would undermine conservative coherentism because it would imply that no kind of judgment should be accorded *ab initio* the status that a conservative theory accords to our idealized considered judgments, the status of a standard of justification. That is, a plausible coherence theory would not demand of a justified set of beliefs coherence with some type of belief specified *ab initio* in the theory, and specified partly in terms of its content. Thus a plausible coherence theory could not be conservative.

Conservative coherence theories of moral justification face a dilemma. On the one hand, unless there is a prior reason to think that considered moral judgments in ideal circumstances would be credible, there is no reason to treat them as a standard of justification. To be sure, a conservative theory would imply that our considered judgments are justified only if they appropriately cohere with our other beliefs, but this does not distinguish them from any other judgments, and it does not justify treating them as a standard of justification. In the absence of a prior justification of this treatment, there is no basis for specifying *ab initio* in a theory of justification that a moral theory or morality is justified only if it is coherent with our idealized considered moral judgments. On the other hand, if there is a justification of them that is prior to the account provided in the conservative theory, then the theory is not a fully general account of the justification of moral judgments. Hence, even if such a prior justification is available, it would be an error to build a conservative constraint into a theory that is intended as a general theory of moral justification.

I find it doubtful that a coherence among our beliefs, including our considered moral beliefs, would be sufficient to justify our moral beliefs. But that is not the present issue. Not even a relationship among our beliefs and theories of the complexity demanded in Daniels's theory would be sufficient. To see this, suppose that we have achieved a reflective equilibrium among our nonmoral beliefs, including relevant empirical social theories, and so on. Now, add to this equilibrium a set M of beliefs that is internally coherent, coherent with the rest of the beliefs in the equilibrium, and whose nature is somehow constrained by the theories in the equilibrium. Let M include a theory of moral justification, moral background theories, and some moral principles and considered judgments. I doubt that the set is thereby justified. After all, an *arbitrary* set M' of propositions that is internally coherent, coherent with the rest of the beliefs in the equilibrium and constrained somehow by relevant theories, could also be added to the equilibrium. The set M' could represent a putative history and social science of an unknown planet. It would not thereby be justified, no matter how complex. But that is not the present issue.

Daniels considers an argument that is similar to my argument from the need for a prior justification of considered judgments. His reply is that it "reduces either to a burden-of-proof argument, which is plausible but hardly conclusive, or to a general foundationalist objection to coherence accounts of theory acceptance (or justification)" (1979b, p. 273). Since he thinks that a general foundationalist attack would not be plausible, given the difficulties of foundationalist theories of justification (p. 273), he regards the objection as at best a burden-of-proof-shifting argument (pp. 271–272). Daniels also suggests two other replies to the argument, but I will pass over them because they are not really pertinent.[14]

However, it is fatal for Daniels to admit that conservative coherence theories must accept the burden of providing an account of the reliability of considered moral judgments (p. 272). This is to admit that the theory of wide reflective equilibrium and other similar theories are not general accounts of moral justification. In effect, it is to admit that conservative coherence theories yield a theory of moral justification only given a prior account of the reliability of considered moral judgments. But this is simply to raise again the problem of moral justification. One might think that conservative theories have succeeded at least in reducing the general problem to the specific problem of justifying considered moral judgments in wide reflective equilibrium. But this is illusory; the fundamental problem remains, as is shown by the fact that we have no reason to expect that an adequate theory of justification will support, rather than undermine, the claim that considered judgments are largely justified.

In reply, one might invoke the idea that the best available account of *nonmoral* theory justification is coherentist. Daniels suggests a reply along these lines (p. 273): To be plausible, the present attack must be limited to *conservative* coherence theories *in ethics*. But then our nonmoral theory must be able to escape any analogue of the argument. It can do so, Daniels thinks, because it allows us "to assign initial credibility to nonmoral observation reports" (p. 272). We have a "causal story" that explains why "the reports are generally reliable, though still revisable" (p. 270). However, this "credibility story about nonmoral observation reports is itself only the product of a nonmoral wide reflective equilibrium" (p. 272). Therefore, if the *nonmoral* theory can escape the no-credibility objection with an account of the credibility of observation reports that derives from "component sciences constrained by coherence considerations" (p. 273), then the *moral* theory can escape in an analogous way. An account of the reliability of considered judgments is needed, "but it too will derive from component theories in wide equilibrium" (p. 273). That is, if the no-credibility argument does not also impugn our nonmoral theory, then it merely assigns to the wide reflective equilibrium theory the burden of anchoring the theory in an account of the credibility of considered judgments.

However, a plausible nonmoral coherence theory would not demand coherence with observation reports *ab initio* in the way that conservative coherence theories demand coherence with considered judgments. Rather, coherentist considerations would be relied upon to generate an account of the justification of observation reports. The analogy with nonmoral theories does not support conservatism.

It is worth briefly responding to Daniels's suggestion that an account of the reliability of considered judgments will derive *only* from an acceptable theory in wide reflective equilibrium (p. 271). I take it that he does not mean by this merely that an account will flow from other theories held by the theorist, if at all. This is not controversial. Rather, I take him to mean that an adequate account of the reliability of our considered moral judgments will *itself* have to be in equilibrium with our considered moral judgments, for considered moral judgments are included in the relevant equilibria, and will *itself* have to show to be justified our considered moral judgments in wide reflective equilibrium. In effect, this is to embrace the type-two conservative constraint on theories of moral justification. But we have been given no reason to accept this constraint. For all that we know, an adequate theory might show our considered judgments *not* to be justified, and so they might *not* be in wide equilibrium with our considered judgments. In fact, we have some reason to think this *will* be so.

I conclude that in the absence of an account of the credibility of our considered moral judgments, there is no warrant for treating these judgments as constituting a standard of justification. Therefore, we can reject type-one conservative theories that purport to be general theories of moral justification, and according to which a moral judgment, or a morality, that is justified is so (partly) in virtue of its being appropriately related to our considered moral judgments. At best, such a theory depends on a logically prior account of the credibility of considered judgments. We also can reject type-two conservative theories that purport to be general accounts of the tenability of type-one theories, and according to which a theory of moral justification is tenable (partly) in virtue of its showing to be justified our considered moral judgments. At best, such a theory is also incomplete. But the rationale of conservatism depends on the plausibility of taking our considered judgments to provide a standard against which moral judgments, moralities, or theories of moral justification may be tested. Our conclusion is that this standard is at best a derivative one.

7. THE DYNAMICS OF MORAL BELIEF

I have argued that both foundationalist and coherentist versions of conservatism are undermined by the need for an account of the credibility of considered moral judgments that would justify treating them as constituting a standard of justification. At best, they constitute a derivative standard. My final argument is intended to undermine more directly the plausibility of conservatism. It turns on three claims. First, the considered judgments we would make in ideal circumstances at one time can be different from those we would make at another time. Second, the cause of the change in our views may be such that the change could not plausibly be supposed to have any bearing on the justifiability of any moral judgment, morality, or theory of moral justification. Third, this is contrary to what is implied by conservatism.

Conservative theories grant that the judgments that would qualify as our considered judgments can be different at different times, for they suppose that our considered judgments in ideal circumstances could be different from those we would make in less than ideal circumstances. My argument depends on the claim that changes in a person's basic attitudes can occur without there being any change in morally pertinent general facts about the world and human society, and that the result could be that the considered moral judgments the person would make in ideal circumstances *before* the change are different from those he would make in ideal circumstances *after* the change. Such a change in a person's views could not sensibly be supposed to have any bearing on the status as justified of any morality or moral theory, given that pertinent general facts remain unchanged. But any conservative theory would treat such a change in a person's views as pivotal.

To take a simple example, suppose that a charismatic person of strong moral views persuades us that, *S,* it is morally appropriate to execute thieves. Suppose that we would not have thought so before, not even in ideal circumstances, but that we are now fully convinced that it is so, and we would remain convinced in any realizable circumstances, however ideal. There has been a shift in our basic attitudes, and the shift is reflected in a change in the judgments we would make in ideal circumstances. We need not suppose that the shift in our views is without suitable rationalization. We may imagine that the change is due to a change in our responsiveness to certain arguments. However, we do need to suppose that there has been no change in pertinent general facts.

Conservative theories would imply that, given a shift of this kind in our basic views, there would be a corresponding shift in the status as justified of various moralities and moral theories. For example, consider a theory of moral justification T that implies that S is unjustified, and consider a morality M that is inconsistent with S. Suppose that *before* the shift in our views T satisfied the type-two conservative constraint,[15] implying that all our idealized considered judgments are justified, and M satisfied a type-one conservative theory, being coherent with all our considered moral judgments. *After* the shift in our views, T would no longer satisfy the type-two constraint, and M would no longer be coherent with all of our considered moral judgments. Consequently, a type-two conservative theory would entail that T is untenable, and a type-one conservative theory would presumably imply that M is unjustified. But it is implausible to suppose that a morality or a theory of moral justification would be justified at one time but unjustified at another, where there is no explanation for this except that our moral views have changed. Whatever general theoretical considerations counted in favor of T and M still do so, with the single exception that T and M no longer cohere with all of our considered judgments. It is implausible to suppose that these considerations are discredited simply by the fact that S would now be among our idealized considered judgments. Hence, the most plausible view is that the existence of the new considered judgment does not show the theory or the morality to be unjustified.

It should be clear that the argument does not turn on the claim that if a moral code or theory of moral justification is justified (relative to certain persons) at one time, it cannot fail to be justified (relative to those persons) at all other times. It depends only on the weaker claim that if a moral code or a theory does lose its status as justified, this cannot be the result simply of a change in the moral views of certain persons, not even a change in the considered judgments they would make in ideal circumstances.

It should also be clear that the kind of change we have imagined is not different in principle from the kind of change in our views that occurs in our early moral training. Thus it would not do to require of a considered judgment in ideal circumstances that it not owe its existence to a process of the kind that is involved in my hypothetical case. Otherwise, it is unlikely that any judgment in psychologically realizable circumstances would qualify. But the *interest* of a conservative theory depends on the psychological possibility of a person's being in ideal circumstances and having considered judgments in those circumstances. Otherwise, the theory could not be *used* to test the justifiability of moralities or moral theories. Also, otherwise there would be a danger of there being no *fact* of the matter as to what judgments would be a person's considered moral judgments in ideal circumstances.[16] And if there were no fact of the matter, the theory would violate the nonvacuousness constraint.

One might reply to the argument that if the notion of *ideal circumstances* were suitably defined in a conservative theory, then, for any given set of pertinent general empirical conditions, there would be a definite set of moral judgments that would qualify at all times as a given person's idealized considered judgments. Given a suitable definition of ideal circumstances, a conservative theory would not imply that a change in our moral views could change the status of a morality or moral theory unless there were also a change in pertinent empirical facts.

In effect, this reply accepts the burden of providing an account of ideal circumstances that would allow a conservative theory to escape the objection. However, the burden will not be easy to discharge. There is nothing in the description of the case to ensure that our new judgment about thieves owes its acceptance to some occasional epistemic distorting factors. Moreover, the best developed type-one conservative theory in the literature is subject to the objection, for, as Daniels admits, a set of moral principles and background theories may be in wide reflective equilibrium with our considered judgments at one time but not be in wide reflective equilibrium with the considered judgments we would make at a later time, after a shift in our moral views (1979b, p. 281). Because of this, even if the principles were justified before the shift in our views, and even though pertinent general facts remain unchanged and the nonmoral background theories we accept remain unchanged, Daniels's theory would judge the principles not to be justified after the shift, merely on the implausible ground that the shift occurred.

My argument depends on the assumption that the burden of providing an adequate account of ideal circumstances cannot be discharged. It depends on the following assumption: For any specification of the notion of ideal circumstances in a conservative theory, provided that the specification is noncircular and does not violate the nonvacuousness constraint, and provided that circumstances of the specified kind are psychologically realizable, it is logically possible that the considered judgments a person would make in circumstances of the specified kind would change, say, under the influence of a charismatic person, even though it is not the case that the status as justified of a morality or moral theory would also have changed. That is, it is logically possible that the set of judgments that would qualify as a person's idealized considered judgments before a change in his attitudes would be different from the set that would so qualify after the change. I think that this assumption is plausible, but I do not know how to prove that it is true.

This central assumption is logical or conceptual rather than empirical. The conservative claims that the *justification* of a morality or moral theory *depends on* the existence of an appropriate relation between the object of justification and our considered judgments in ideal circumstances. For this claim to be plausible, there must not be a logically possible circumstance in which a morality or moral judgment is justified, despite the lack of an appropriate relation to our considered judgments in ideal circumstances. Hence, it is not enough for the conservative to claim that, *as a matter of fact,* in circumstances of some specified kind, our considered judgments would not change under the influence of a charismatic person. It is sufficient for me to make a claim about the logical possibility that our idealized considered judgments should change in a situation where it is not plausible to suppose that the status as justified of a morality or moral theory would also have changed.

To forestall misunderstanding, it is important to distinguish between a morality's or a moral theory's being *itself* justified and a *person's* being justified *in* accepting it. General theoretical considerations may support a theory of moral justification that implies that a particular morality is justified. For all that I have said, if this morality is inconsistent with judgments that would be among our considered moral judgements in ideal circumstances, it may be that we would be justified *in* rejecting the morality and the theories that support it. This may be so; however, it seems to me that a person may be justified in holding a moral principle, or a theory of moral justification, given the considerations that support it, even if he accepts some considered moral judgment that the theory or principle implies to be unjustified. True, the person would then be in a state of "cognitive dissonance,"[17] but there is no reason to conclude on this basis that he would not be justified in accepting the theory or principle. Perhaps he would not be justified in his considered judgment. In any case, his cognitive dissonance would not bear on the question whether the moral principle, or the theory of moral justification, is justified itself. It seems that a theory of moral justification or moral principle may be justified *itself,* even if it does not imply that our considered moral judgments are justified.

Our moral views are not sufficiently *static* for the needs of conservatism. If we regard the considered moral judgments we would make in ideal circumstances as indicating a psychological property we have, this property is not static. From time to time, under the influence of ratiocination, of pressure to conform, or what have you, our moral views change, and at the same time there may be a change in the considered moral judgments we would make in ideal circumstances. This undermines the plausibility of taking our considered moral judgments to constitute a standard of justification, for it shows the putative standard to be a drifting one.

8. CONCLUSION

My arguments are meant to undercut the plausibility of taking our considered judgments in ideal circumstances to constitute a standard of justification. A conservative foundationalism would be implausible, for it is implausible to suppose that certain judgments would be justified simply in virtue, of the fact that we would be confident of them in suitable circumstances. A conservative coherentism would also be implausible because it would take our considered judgments in ideal circumstances to be a standard of justification *ab initio,* while admitting that they need to be justified. If they have no prior justification, it is a mistake to treat them as a standard of justification; but if they do have a prior justification, it is a mistake to treat them as a standard *ab initio* in a theory that purports to be a *general* account of moral justification, or of moral theory justification. Finally, the dynamics of our confidence in moral views does not correspond to any plausible view of the dynamics of justification.

My arguments leave open the possibility that morality can be justified. Let us suppose that our best general account of theory justification is basically coherentist. Applied to theories of moral justification, it presumably would demand that a theory be coherent with theories of moral psychology, with sociological accounts of the nature of morality, with any other relevant empirical theories, and also with philosophical theories we accept. It is left open by my arguments that there are pertinent theoretical considerations that support a theory of moral justification and, hence, a moral code. However, the rejection of conservatism allows that we may regard a moral theory and a moral code to be justified even if they fail to justify certain moral judgments of which we remain confident.[18]

NOTES

1. I am indebted to Ali Akhtar and Robert C. Richardson for showing me the need to make this distinction. Norman Daniels draws the distinction at (1979b), p. 257, fn. 1.

2. Similarly, we need to distinguish between theories of the justification of inductive reasoning and accounts of when a person would be justified in his inductive practices. For relevant discussion, see Stitch and Nisbett (1980). I owe this reference to Steven Savitt.

3. John Rawls (1971, p. 51; see pp. 46–47) suggests that the classical conception of moral theory sees the task as that of providing a systematization of our considered judgments in reflective equilibrium. He quotes Henry Sidgwick as having said that the history of moral philosophy is a series of attempts to state "in full breadth and clearness these primary intuitions of Reason, by the scientific application of which the common moral thought of mankind may be at once systematized and corrected" (p. 51, fn. 26; Sidgwick, 1907, p. 373). However, Sidgwick's use of the term "corrected" here suggests that moral theory has more than a descriptive or systematizing task. With this of course I agree.

4. Or to justify it in relation to the set of persons whose considered judgments are systematized by the theory.

5. In *A Theory of Justice*, Rawls seemed ambivalent—between regarding the principles of justice he proposed as justified by a proposed theory of moral justification (see, for instance, 1971, pp. 77–81), and regarding them as justified simply as a descriptive or systematizing theory of our views (see for instance, pp. 46–51). More recently, he suggests that he sees his arguments as justifying them in the stronger sense, even though only in relation to us (1980, p. 554).

Daniels's theory (1979b) could be read either as a theory of moral justification or as a theory as to what justifies the claim that a given set of principles, a putative systematizing moral theory, best systematizes the considered moral judgments of a person. I assume he intends the former. He says (p. 257, fn. 1) that the problem addressed in his paper is "strictly analogous to the general and abstract problem of theory . . . justification posed in the philosophy of science with respect to non-moral theories." See also pp. 273–282, and Daniels (1980b), p. 21.

6. Hence, moral principles may qualify as considered judgments along with judgments about particular situations.

7. Any theory that allows the possibility of moral justification can appear to be conservative. For any such theory implies that if a morality is justified, then it stands in *some* relation to the convictions we would have in *certain* circumstances. Any such theory implies that if a morality is justified, then the considered moral judgments we would make in *circumstances in which we fully accepted, and judged only successfully in accord with*, that morality would be *implied* by that morality, together with certain of our nonmoral beliefs. However, appearances are deceiving, for *any* morality, justified or not, stands in *this* relation to the judgments we would make in circumstances of the suggested kind. A corollary of the nonvacuousness constraint can therefore be relied upon: If a theory is type-one conservative, then it specifies a justificatory relation and a type of circumstance such that it is *not* the case that *any* morality would stand in the specified justificatory relation to the considered moral judgments we would make in circumstances of the specified kind. The phrase, "depends on, or is in virtue of," and the final clause in the account given in the text, together with the nonvacuousness constraint, ensure that some theories of moral justification are not conservative.

The final clause in the account given in the text helps to ensure that the category of conservative theory is not too broad. Consider, for instance, the "Platonic" view that the considered moral judgments we would make when acquainted with the form, The Good, are *ipso facto* justified. This theory implies that a morality's being justified depends on its being *consistent with* the considered moral judgments we would make *when acquainted with The Good*. It is not genuinely conservative, however, because the fact that the moral judgments in question are *considered* is irrelevant. For instance, even if we were not fully and nontemporally confident of those judgments, they would still be justified. The final clause ensures that this Platonic view is not mistakenly counted as type-one conservative.

8. *Any* theory that allows the possibility of justifying a theory of moral justification can appear to be conservative. For any such theory implies that if a theory of moral justification T is itself justified, then T implies to be justified the considered moral judgments we would make in *circumstances in which we fully accepted, and judged only*

successfully in accord with, a morality that is justified according to *T.* Yet some theories are not genuinely conservative. A corollary of the nonvacuousness constraint can be relied on here: If a theory is type-two conservative, then it specifies a kind of circumstance such that it is *not* the case that *any* theory of moral justification would imply to be justified the considered moral judgments we would make in circumstances of the specified kind. See note 7 for further elaboration of an analogous point that arises for my account of type-one conservatism.

Some putative conservative theories may simply beg the question in favor of a preferred theory of moral justification. The final clause in the account given in the text should rule out their being counted as type-two conservative.

9. For example, see Harman (1973), Introduction.

10. Moore's (1903) theory is not conservative, since judgments of which we are certain "in a psychological sense" may not be self-evident, and so they may not be intuitions in the proper sense, and since intuitions in the proper sense are not justified even partly in virtue of being considered judgments (pp. 148–149).

11. It should be recalled in this connection that our search in ethics for a theory of moral *justification* is not primarily a search for a theory that underwrites moral knowledge, or that underwrites *cognitivism* in ethics. The typical moral skeptic does deny moral knowledge, but he is more concerned to deny the rationality of morality. So the skeptic could be answered by a theory that fell short of underwriting cognitivism. Still, if there could be *knowledge* of moral truths, then some forms of skepticism would be wrong. Morality would have a place at least in the beliefs of a rational person.

Nevertheless, the relevance of theories of epistemological justification is not clear. It may be that such theories are best regarded as accounts of *personal* justification, as accounts of the criteria for a *person's* being justified *in* believing a proposition, rather than as accounts of the criteria for a proposition's being objectively justified. If so, then theories of epistemological justification are not germane. However, although knowledge may require that a person be justified in his beliefs, it may also require objective justification of the belief. The issue is not settled, and so the relevance of epistemology is not clear.

Accounts of theory confirmation in the philosophy of science may also be suggestive. They, at least, are theories of objective justification. Conservative theories that may be suggested by analogy with the philosophy of science are discussed in the text. What needs to be emphasized here is that our need is for a theory of objective justification that can be applied in ethics

12. In what follows, I make claims about what a general coherence theory of justification *should* allow or imply. Of course, some coherence theories may fail to allow or imply the relevant things. I do not have the space to argue for my claims here.

13. Actually, Daniels writes of justifying "moral theories," where a moral theory seems to be, for him, a set of moral principles, perhaps together with a set of "background" moral views. But he thinks that a moral theory is justified (for one) only if it would be accepted (by one) in wide reflective equilibrium (1979b, pp. 256–257, 268–273, 277). He presumably would generalize this to a view about the justification of moral judgments and of moralities.

14. The objection Daniels considers is different from the one I have been proposing. Still it is worth pointing out that his replies would not be pertinent, if directed to my argument. First, he thinks the objection he is concerned with is based on an inappropriate analogy between considered judgments and observation reports (1979b, pp. 270–271). But it is not part of my objection that a conservative coherence theory needs an account of the credibility of considered judgments that is analogous in its content to the account we can give of the credibility of observation reports. I merely maintain that a conservative coherence theory needs to be anchored in an account of the reliability of considered judgments, just as a coherence theory of nonmoral justification, if it treated observation reports as a standard of justification, would need to be anchored in an account of the reliability of observation reports. Second, he contends that there is good reason for "starting from considered moral judgments in our theory construction" (p. 272). But, again, this would miss the point of my argument. It may or may not be that the method of wide reflective equilibrium would be *useful* as a *method* for discovering a satisfactory theory of

moral justification, or a plausible moral view. However, my argument purports to defeat the claim of Daniels's theory to be *more* than a useful method, to be itself a satisfactory account of the conditions under which moral judgments or moralities are justified.

15. Of course, different type-two theories impose different constraints, but the argument could be run for any such theory where the notion of ideal circumstances is specified in non-question-begging and noncircular terms.

16. Unless the theory specified the notion of ideal circumstances in question-begging or circular terms, such as "circumstances in which one judges only in accord with morality *M*, but not as a result of distorting formative processes."

17. This is a term that Brandt (1979, p. 21) attributes to Leon Festinger (1957).

18. A version of this paper was read to the Department of Philosophy at the University of British Columbia, and sections of it were read to the 1981 meeting of the Western Canada Philosophical Association and to the 1982 meeting of the Pacific Division of the A.P.A. I would like to thank those who contributed to the discussions for their helpful suggestions and comments. I am also indebted to Richmond Campbell, Norman Daniels, and Robert C. Richardson for very stimulating and useful discussions. I wrote this essay while on sabbatical leave from Simon Fraser University, with the aid of a Leave Fellowship from the Social Sciences and Humanities Research Council of Canada. I am grateful for the opportunity given me by these institutions.

chapter seven

Arguments from Nature

Ronald de Sousa

The first duty in life is to be as artificial as possible.

Oscar Wilde

"No thank you. I don't think Nature intended us to drink while flying."

New Yorker *cartoon*

One truth is clear: whatever is, is right.

Alexander Pope

1. NATURALISM, ANTINATURALISM, NEUTRALISM: SOME PRELIMINARY BOTANY

"It's good because it's natural." This argument, which apparently entitles health-food stores to charge more for organic vegetables, is also found in Aristotle: "What is by nature proper to each thing will be at once the best and the most pleasant for it" (*Nicomachean Ethics*, 1178a 6–7). I'll call it the *Positive Naturalist* argument.

The *Negative Naturalist* argument is the one offered by the Catholic church (and others) against buggery or contraception: "It's bad because it's unnatural."

The two arguments are independent. You could believe that what is natural is to be commended while being quite indifferent about the unnatural, or conversely. But both are "naturalist" in preferring the natural to the unnatural. In this they contrast with corresponding variants of *Antinaturalism*.

This article was first published in *Zygon*, volume 15 (June 1980):169–191.

A *Negative Antinaturalist* argument is offered by Katherine Hepburn to Humphrey Bogart in *African Queen*: "Nature, Mr. Alnut, is what we were put in the world to rise above." This conception of a corrupt nature is also honored in the Christian tradition. Some atheists like Schopenhauer have agreed that "Man is at bottom a savage, horrible beast" (1897, 1957, p. 18); and perhaps something like the badness of nature is involved in the argument from evil against atheism.

The *Positive Antinaturalist* argument also has a tradition behind it, although not such an influential one. It is represented by the aestheticism of Oscar Wilde and Huysmans's *Against Nature.*

That all these positions have actually been held[1] suggests that either humans are naturally perverse or a number of different conceptions of nature are involved. At least the latter is true. Nature has been contrasted with the human, the learned, the cultural, the social, the artificial. But in its most general meaning it contrasts only with *what is not*: The natural is merely the *factual.*

In this last sense, most of us were brought up to think that no argument from nature (AN) is valid. Ironically, it is a small step from this view to the construction of a new kind of AN: "It's natural, therefore it's neither good nor bad." On this view nothing in the world has intrinsic value: Good or bad are mere projections of our will onto the morally inert screen of natural fact.[2] But although the step is small, it is fallacious. From the invalidity of Naturalist and Antinaturalist arguments (call it *Weak Neutralism*), it does not follow that no fact of nature has intrinsic value (*Strong Neutralism*). The fallacy is the obvious one of going to (p $\sim$q) from $\sim$(p q). Yet the weak doctrine is a powerful motive for the strong. For epistemologically they are equivalent: If we cannot argue from fact to value, what remains to ground judgments of value in but the pure subjective will?

A value judgment must be grounded in something. And, as Socrates might add, in something that is, not something that is not. At the very least, the widely adopted maxim that *ought implies can* requires that we discover what is "humanly possible." This brings in another common pattern of AN: "It's impossible, so we shouldn't try it," or "You can't change human nature." Call this the *Negative Argument from Impossibility.* It's acquired rather a bad press, for in practice, what those who use this argument generally mean by "Nature" is the *status quo.* It's rare that something is positively *known* to be impossible, surprisingly enough to be news fit to print. So this argument finds an obvious home in dubious propaganda. But when it's really known to be true, as well as surprising, that something is impossible, then this pattern of argument constitutes one clearly valid form of AN. For example: "Perpetual motion machines are impossible, so don't waste your time trying to construct one." So it's to be expected that arguments of this form will be popular at those periods (from the 18th century on) when science seems to have provided some novel and unshakable insight into human nature. But although all ANs aspire to the condition of this impossibility pattern, few attain it. The *very improbable* is not enough: "ought" does not imply "is not unlikely to succeed."

Quite the opposite, in fact: It's been held, apparently, that *"unlikely to succeed implies ought."* Or so I interpret Sir Edmund Hilary's explanation of why he climbed Everest. Vesuvius, after all, was there too. We might label this the *Positive Argument from Possibility.* Whether this and the Negative Argument from Impossibility are to be classed as Naturalist, I leave the reader to decide. A *Positive Argument from Impossibility,* "try because it is impossible," is perhaps exemplified by Tertullian's "Credo quia absurdum," and by Camus's "Sisyphean" ethics. And to complete our botanizing, we might list as the *Negative Argument from Possibility* the view—perhaps at last this is one that has never been held—that if something is possible it is not worth attempting.

2. THE IMPOSSIBILITY OF RATIONAL ETHICS

Any ethics must posit a ground of preference between possible alterations of the *status quo.* The very concept of an action necessarily requires at the outset two conceptions of nature. For as Mill put it, "While human action cannot help conforming to nature in one meaning of the term, the very aim and object of action is to alter and improve nature in the other meaning" (1874). But neither of these conceptions of nature is one from which we can seek *guidance.* So it seems we need *three* concepts of nature:

Nature$_1$: the status quo; or the condition of the world as it would subsequently be without the intervention of human beings (or of a given agent.)

Nature$_2$: whatever is a fact, without counterfactual qualification.

Nature$_3$: that subset of N_1 and N_2 that contains the reasons for preferring a particular difference between them.

Now it cannot be merely arbitrary, for a rational ethics, that some r is a reason for preferring A to B. It must be a *fact.* So N_2 will contain the differences between N_1 and N_2, as well as the reasons for preferring some such differences to others. But if so, N_2 must contain all hypothetical facts about N_1 too: In other words, N_2 must contain all practically accessible possible worlds. "All possible worlds lie within the actual one" (Goodman, 1965, p. 57), and N_2 must include N_1, Mill's "other meaning." But on what basis are we to select the members of N_3? By hypothesis, N_3 contains all the facts that constitute *reasons* for preferences. So the basis for deciding what goes into N_3 must lie in N_3 itself, and rational Ethics is impossible.

The problem is quite general, and it affects antinaturalists no less than naturalists. To those who would fight nature or improve on her, the aspiration to do so—even if divinely inspired—is also a fact about humans, something contained in N_2. And therefore they, too, need a principle of selection, something to sort moral fact from corrupt nature. They may have a worse problem than the naturalists, if they insist that their principle of selection must come from outside N_2 altogether. But at best, the antinaturalist is in the same logical position as the naturalist, and in the sequel I shall mostly ignore the former.

At this point the advocates of ANs will protest in the name of utilitarian good sense. The argument for the impossibility of ethics is as silly as it is preposterous, they will say. For there *is* a principle of selection too obvious to need grounding: What ANs need as premises are facts about the needs, aspirations, wants, and capacities of human beings. "The sole evidence it is possible to produce that anything is desirable," says Mill, "is that people do actually desire it" (1863, 1957, p. 44).

But *which* ones are the relevant desires? Nothing seems more characteristic of human nature than to desire one's desires to be other than they are (Frankfurt, 1971). In practice, our second-order desires are as often celebrated as deplored in the name of Nature. So we can't escape the need for a principle of selection.

3. FUNCTIONS: THE ARISTOTELIAN SOLUTION

Perhaps if we look the problem squarely in the face, it will suggest its own solution. The paradox we are faced with involves the need to select among merely possible facts some that are more factual than others: to select a class of more factual nonfacts. Well, Aristotle had just the name for what we need: *potentiality,* or teleological facts. To find guidance in ethics you should look neither to the actual facts alone, whatever they may be, nor to possibilities in the abstract, but for the *function* of the human being. But how is this to be discovered? This is where the work starts. One might give a minimal answer: "Be just what you are," or a maximal one: "Become whatever you can." But a minimal answer won't do; "simply living," as Aristotle points out, "we share even with plants" (*Nicomachean Ethics,* 1097b 30). Our principle of discrimination doesn't lead far enough. A maximal answer is no better off. If we are to actualize all our potentialities, then again the principle of discrimination has told us nothing. For whatever we do is an exercise of some potentiality and takes time out from the exercise of another.

Aristotle's solution to this problem invokes two principles. One is that the relevant potentialities must be the ones that belong to us *as human beings,* that is as beings of a certain *kind.* The other is that these potentialities are to be ones that belong to humans *alone:* "We are looking," he continues in the passage from which I have just quoted, "for something peculiar to humans."

The second principle is often dismissed with an allusion to Aristotle's obsession with definition by genus and differentia: as if it were only the differentiae that gave the true nature of the species. But this explanation fails to note that what we share with plants and other animals, for Aristotle, has its own standards of vegetative and subrational excellence, which Aristotle simply took for granted. It was not there that the ethical choice among distinctly human possibilities could lie. More important is the first assumption: that individual potentialities must be understood in terms of the potentialities of the *kind.* If you were to investigate the potentialities of an individual in isolation, you could only wait around and see what they did. And by the time you had your evidence it would seem otiose to encourage self-actualization. The supreme moral injunction would have to be "Whatever you're doing, carry on." (Or, for the antinaturalist, what parents tell their children: "Whatever you're doing, don't.") Aristotle escapes the problem: He can examine some specimens, and especially specimens of a "complete" life—"for one swallow does not make a spring" (1098a 18)—and thereby gain insight into the nature of the others. On this model, the nature of a species is both *fixed in time* and *determinate* in character. Individuals have natures in virtue of belonging to certain kinds, and the variations between them are explained away at best as inessential, or at worst as teratology—monsters outside the regular order of Nature.

This implies a two-step program for the discovery of individual natures: At the first step, the collection of instances yields insight into their common essence; at the second step, any individual's nature is *deduced* from its membership in the kind.

In the light of Darwinian natural selection, we have lost faith in this program. Species are not fixed in time, and what we allow as the norm for a given species at a given time is only a matter of convenient statistics. Individual variation is the fundamental fact: The degree of uniformity within a species is what stands in need of explanation, as Darwin signaled by the title of his book. If we want to know the nature of an individual, we can no longer make the same use of the evidence we gather from the observation of others. There are two crucial differences.

The first difference is that the two-step program for the discovery of individual essences is no longer available. We are left with a more pedestrian brand of statistical induction, implementing the expectation that resemblances of certain sorts are likely to go together to a certain degree. Second, the deductive step in Aristotelian induction no longer makes sense, since there is no first step in which a fixed essence is discovered.

The second difference is that while Darwinism loosens the connection between members of the species, it establishes a new kinship between members of different species. We need no longer be confined to looking at what is exclusively human. The range of evidence that is *prima facie* relevant is thus vastly increased. If DNA is the same everywhere, perhaps even behavior is similar in more quarters than we thought. (On the other hand, the vegetative and animal functions may be more *different* among species than we thought.) Moreover, the notion of *function*— the teleological notion that is so vital to the Aristotelian scheme—shows no signs of being abandoned in modern biological talk. The hope might therefore seem reasonable that modern evolutionary biology can reconstruct a useful conception of nature on which evaluative arguments can get a grip. In the rest of this essay, I shall consider whether this hope can be fulfilled.

When we appeal to biology to guide us, we can do one of two things. We can look at the biological *facts of life*, to gain power and multiply our options by understanding its mechanisms. We require only minimal ethical assumptions to infer from the existence of a vaccine that we ought to use it unless it has deleterious side effects, or to believe that educational methods can be improved by more knowledge of the facts of human development. Such arguments generally fall into the class of impossibility or possibility arguments. Here I shall have little to say about them. The principal disputes arise from attempts to look to biological nature for some deeper levels of human fact. It is here that references to the concepts of evolutionary theory come in. The most common strategies are three:

1. Look for the *general direction of evolution* for a reconstruction of the notion of higher and lower forms of life.
2. Look to *adaptation* (or fitness, or survival) for a criterion of *biological value.*
3. Look to the conditions prevailing at the time our adaptive mechanisms were selected (the Environment of Evolutionary Adaptedness, EEA) for clues to the deeper nature of our wants as they are rooted in natural *needs* and *capacities.*

Let's look at these three strategies in turn.

4. THE DIRECTION OF EVOLUTION

Some biologists have been sanguine about plotting the course of evolutionary progress:

> When we look at evolution as a whole, we find, among the many directions which it has taken, one which is characterized by introducing the evolving world stuff to progressively higher levels of organization and so to new possibilities of being, action, and experience. . . . I do not feel that we should use the word purpose save where we know that a conscious aim is involved; but we can say that this is the *most desirable* direction of evolution, and accordingly that . . . it is ethically right to aim at whatever will promote the increasingly full realization of increasingly higher values. (Huxley and Huxley, 1947, 1969, p. 125)

In this version, which is Julian Huxley's, the argument seems to recoil from its own thrust right in the middle, when it turns out that evolution offers us not so much a menu as a cafeteria. But for some evolutionists Nature herself will prescribe the dish if we will listen. Witness G. G. Simpson:

> Man has certain basic diagnostic features which set him off most sharply from any other animal. . . . Interrelated factors of intelligence, flexibility, individualization, and socialization . . . occur rather widely in the animal kingdom as progressive developments, and all define different, but related sorts of evolutionary progress. In man all four are carried to a degree incomparably greater than in any other sort of animal. . . . Even when viewed within the framework of the animal kingdom and judged by criteria of progress applicable to that kingdom as a whole and not peculiar to man, man is thus the highest animal. (Munson, 1971, pp. 270–271)

Not all biologists are on the naturalist side. Here, for example, is T. H. Huxley:

> Let us understand, once for all, that the ethical progress of society depends, not on imitating the cosmic process, still less in running away from it, but in combating it. (Huxley and Huxley, 1947, 1969, p. 82)

That sounds like the trumpet of antinaturalism. But T. H. Huxley, for good measure, also presented the neutralist position, variety Strong:

> The propounders of what are called the 'ethics of evolution' . . . adduce a number of more or less interesting facts and more or less sound arguments, in favour of the origin of the moral sentiments . . . by a process of evolution . . . but as the immoral sentiments have no less been evolved, there is, so far, as much natural sanction for the one as the other. (p. 80)

To discover whether we should side with the older and tougher evolutionist or with the younger generation, we must ask whether biology is able to construct a credible concept of the *function* or *teleology* of evolution.

What tempts us to teleology is the improbable. That's when we say: This can't be just coincidence. That's what makes the force of the Argument from Design for the existence of God. The intricacy of adaptations in nature seems so intrinsically improbable as to demand a planner. Chance variation and natural selection remove the sting from the improbability. Now the Designer hypothesis is no longer attractive, but can we still speak of *functions*? We can, if a definition of them can be found that is sufficiently general to fit both the products of natural selection and those of intelligent plans. Such a definition is available because of Larry Wright, Charles Taylor, and others. On their proposal, a fact, thing, or event is teleological, *if its existence can be explained by its tendency to produce a certain result* (Wright, 1973). A designer's artifact is obviously teleological because the designer's conception of its effects caused him to produce it. But so is an adapted organ: To say that it is *adapted* is to say that it was differentially spared by the axe of selection because of its effects. Whether some character has a function, as well as what it is, are difficult biological questions. But their meaning is clear. They are questions about the character's effect on differential reproduction in the ancestors of the organisms in question.

The virtue of this analysis is that it explicates the notion of goal without presupposing it.[3] This is exactly what we need if we are to ground our ethical goals in natural functions. But it immediately follows that while we can legitimately attribute functions to organs and characteristics on this basis, no such sense can be made of the "function" or "direction" of evolution as a whole. It was not brought about by its effects since it only happened once, unless designed by God. So those evolutionists who insist on reading a function into evolution as a whole are most consistent if, like Teilhard de Chardin, they hold on to God.

5. THREE PARADOXES OF ADAPTATION-AS-VALUE

Still, perhaps there is another way to squeeze some sense out of the notion of the function of evolution without abandoning biology for theology. In this spirit one sometimes hears it said that the basic biological "virtue" is *fitness*.[4] Fitness is reproductive success, called *adaptation* when it is considered in relation to a given environment, and perhaps "adaptability" when considered in relation to ecological change. For example, G. G. Simpson refers to humans as "the most adaptable of animals." The only aseptic meaning I can give to this is that insofar as we can make any reasonable predictions about the durability of the species, it is likely to be among the highest. Yet if we keep our notion cleanly biological in this way, it won't give us the results we might hope for. We must face three paradoxes:

(i) To say that we are extraordinarily *adaptable* seems extremely plausible. We can even survive on the moon, for a while. But the only real test of adaptation is long-term survival: By that test only actual seniority can earn the high rungs of the evolutionary ladder. Our special talents may spur lofty aspirations; but in terms of achievements we are very far below the rat, the shark, and the cockroach—not to mention the amoeba.

(ii) Nor can we even celebrate the survival in us of our ancestors' prehominidoidal genes. For they, unlike those of the cockroaches' ancestors, have *not* survived intact: "They are changed, changed utterly." When a species has done some adapting, it isn't *that species* anymore. This is the equivalent for the species of the question whether what "survives" in the afterlife will be sufficiently like me to count as *me*. The question arises with a vengeance for the survival of a species. For the identity of a species over time is made particularly obscure by the fact that the usual test of species difference—reproductive isolation—is trivially satisfied across distant generations:

If Adaptation be Nature's Grand Prize
The Winner fades in our evolving eyes.

(iii) The third paradox lies in the antithesis that may be conjured between adaptation and evolution. If a species is adapted, it doesn't *need* to change. But without change, there is no evolution.[5] So if, as has been claimed, we are now so very well adapted, our superiority amounts to the fact that we need *no longer evolve*. But that's where the cockroach is already. Does our superiority then lie merely in having taken longer to get there? To be sure, an objector will say, we are still evolving, but culturally, not biologically. This is what is always pointed out in the last chapters of books on evolution.[6] But there's no getting away from the fact that *biologically* our capacity to adapt culturally can be considered a merely longer route to a genetic constancy that the cockroach and the shark achieved a good deal faster.

6. OSCAR WILDE'S BOOMERANGS: SPECIES-NORMS AND THE EEA

I conclude from the preceding considerations that neither the notion of a direction of evolution nor the mechanism of adaptation yields a coherent grounding for an evolutionary concept of value. But perhaps my mistake was to seek criteria of value too far afield in nature: too far outside the individual consciousness—or perhaps too far inside to the still inaccessible genes. The Utilitarian will protest again: Look to pleasure and pain. The contribution of a philosophy of nature may only be to help in sorting natural pleasures from unnatural, not because natural is good, but because natural is more pleasant and pleasant is good. Thus Hume speaks of

> these sentiments that spring up naturally in my present disposition. . . . Should I endeavour to banish them by attaching myself to my other business or diversion, I feel I should be a loser in terms of pleasure. (1739, 1968, p. 271)

The assumption here is that those pleasures that "spring up naturally" will be deeper and stronger, although not necessarily finer—Plato, Freud, and perhaps Mill agree[7]—than those that arise from an acquired taste in "higher," mental, or sublimated pleasures. The only trouble is, we simply can't tell by introspection which of our pleasures are the natural ones, and which are conditioned by perversion, self-deception, or honest-to-goodness Civilization. So here's where biologists can help us: Not with the construction of criteria of value, but by telling us which pleasures are the natural ones. If we could understand the origin of our various impulses and desires, we would then at least know how to "follow nature" if we wanted to. The biological notion of adaptation can help us if we *don't* assume that we were made for the life we lead now.

> The only relevant criterion by which to consider the natural adaptedness of any particular part of present day man's behavioural equipment is the degree to which and the way in which it might contribute to population survival in man's primeval environment, i.e., the one that man inhabited for two million years until changes of the past few thousand years led to the extraordinary variety of habitats he occupies today. . . . his environment of evolutionary adaptedness [EEA]. (Bowlby, 1969, p. 59)

In this way, suggests Mary Midgley, we might be able to understand, and implicitly justify, the universal horror of parricide: "Why is parricide . . . *unnatural*? Because we are brood-tending creatures, of a sort that forms bonds of affection, gratitude and cooperation in infancy" (Midgley, 1978, p. 274).

This argument is hard to assess, principally because our attitude to the "naturalness" or otherwise of parricide may well be clouded by some inklings of its other drawbacks. Better consider something not inherently criminal, say, the argument often made by psychoanalysts that the choice of a career to the exclusion of motherhood is for women an "unnatural" choice, or that homosexuality is wrong because it is unnatural. Such arguments present a number of difficulties.

First, an *ad hominem*: That some behavior is instinctual, in Freud's own thinking, is far from a sufficient reason for enjoining it. Quite the contrary. His view of the relation of ethics to instinct is not too far from that of T. H. Huxley: The repression of instinct is the price that must be paid for civilization. The nuance of difference is that for Freud the energy for the repression is also of instinctual origin—and thus in some sense *natural* (1957–73, vol. 22, p. 77). But even if sociality itself has roots as deep as the aggression it requires us to repress, still, on the Freudian scheme, some natural wants in the EEA must have had to be curbed for the sake of others. Besides, not all our instincts need have sprung fully armed from the conditions of our EEA. Paul MacLean's hypothesis of the "triune brain" makes excellent evolutionary sense: Bred in different environments to perform different but now overlapping functions, the "reptilian," "early mammalian" or limbic brain, and the "advanced mammalian brain" continue to function together—but not always in harmony (MacLean, 1969). Not all of our inner conflicts spring from the pull between instinct and culture. Some may lodge among different evolutionary layers of instinct itself. And when there is conflict at the heart of "Nature," which voice does Nature require us to attend to?

The question admits of no coherent answer. We may want to say the EEA-generated voice matters most because it is closest to our own (who cares what we thought before we split off from the crocodiles?). But in that case why not look at our own present environment directly—it's even more like itself. No, the answer will come, for we are looking to illuminate our nature, and we can do that while appealing only to strategies of survival that are not too remote from our emotional imagination. Let's look more closely, for an example, at E. O. Wilson's sociobiological speculation about "homosexual genes" (1978, pp. 149–150): They were adaptive in the EEA by promoting cooperative and avuncular behavior. This argument might have the effect of reassuring us as to the value of homosexuality in terms of its evolutionary credentials. But this consideration appears to presuppose that homosexual behavior stands in *prima facie* need of such justification. And this need may in fact be merely the product of pseudobiological myths in the first place. (Besides, what of the backlash from the antinaturalists? This is Oscar Wilde's First Boomerang: Imagine his reaction on being told that his homosexuality was *only natural*. Would we have changed his sexual preference on the spot?) As Gould observes, "The strategy is a dangerous one, for it backfires if the genetic speculation is wrong . . . for the behavior then becomes unnatural and worthy of condemnation (Gould,

1977, p. 267). Strictly speaking this doesn't follow, since as we saw the two naturalist arguments—positive ("natural therefore good") and negative ("unnatural therefore bad")—are independent. But the rhetorical slide is nonetheless tempting. Is there any more than rhetoric on the side of sociobiological comfort?

Not if we mean to privilege the EEA, or any epoch other than our own. For every behavior could be matched with some niche, past or possible, in which it would be adaptive. Mary Midgley has compared this difficulty to the problem of deciding how long a run Economic Man must be given before he does his accounting:

> Changes long after an individual's death can bring his hitherto unwelcome genes into sudden demand; webbed feet or a silent habit become necessary in new circumstances. But they might not have done, and it is idle to say "then he was fitter than we supposed";—after all, we might have to reverse the judgment again later on. (Midgley, 1979, p. 433)

Indeed, the argument can be turned on its head: Every adaptive innovation was an *abnormality* in the light of evolution so far. Its value therefore *must* have derived from its adaptive value not in the past, but for the future. This is Wilde's Second Boomerang: *Nothing is more natural than the abnormal.* Freaks are the fuel of evolution.

7. STATISTICAL NORMALITY, AND A LITTLE BIT ABOUT SEX

More must be said about whether we can infer something about a trait's value from its conditions of acquisition. I shall return to this in a moment. But, first, some troubles caused by the statistical nature of "normality."

The problem is this. What we are ultimately interested in are *individual* natures and norms. And until we are able to read an individual's genetic code straight off the DNA, we can construct cases, under plausible assumptions, in which (i) "conforming to the statistical norm" does not provide a sufficient condition of individual normality. Worse, we can also imagine situations where (ii) a high degree of uniformity around a statistical norm might be a sign of widespread pathology. Let me explain.

Sociobiological arguments presuppose that there are basically two sources of individual variation among the organisms of a single gene pool: genetic endowment and environmental influence. A notion of biological normality must be specifiable in terms of these two classes of factors. Whatever the criteria turn out to be, there will be a range of normal variation within each set of factors. The geometry of this will

Figure 1.

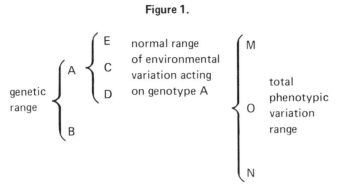

be enormously complicated; for there will be many ranges of variation with various degrees of mutual independence. But consider a single dimension, in which a range of environmental conditions will act on each point in a range of genetic variation. These two together will determine a total range of phenotypic variation (*Fig. 1*). Now, it is a natural assumption that the extreme points on the scale of phenotypic possibilities will be pathological, and the middle points will be paradigmatically "normal." But this assumption is false. For consider the range E-D of environmental possibilities acting on point A, the uppermost point in our chosen dimension of the genetic range of variation A-B. E-D will determine a range of nonpathological phenotypes. Outside that range of phenotypes, individuals of that particular genetic constitution (but not of some very different genetic makeup) will be pathological. Take physical size, for example. A given genome A will determine phenotypes at the upper end of variation found in any particular environment; another, at B, will result in individuals at the bottom end of any particular environmental constant. But some environmental factors—a severe vitamin deficiency at a crucial stage of growth, for example—will result in a pathologically small individual in relation to genome A, who might yet be taller than average individuals of genome B. Whether any purely biological notion of pathology can be constructed is a matter of dispute[8]; but the advocate of ANs must assume that we can. Then the two possibilities I have mentioned arise:

(i) In some cases where a phenotype that is exactly at the midpoint of the total phenotypic variation range (say, at point O in *Fig. 1*), and who is therefore *statistically normal*, will be outside the range of nonpathological variation for genome A. All that is needed is that the range of normal environmentally generated variation in genotype A fail to overlap with the corresponding range for genotype B.

Figure 2.

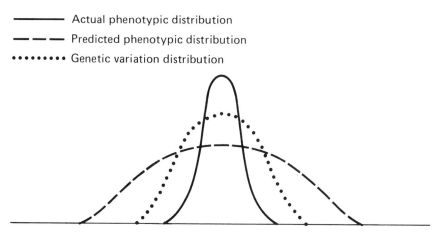

——————— Actual phenotypic distribution
— — — Predicted phenotypic distribution
• • • • • • • Genetic variation distribution

(ii) Common sense suggests that statistical normality will in general be definitionally incompatible with pathology. If a bell curve is narrow and symmetrical, then it would seem to be evidence that the population consists in the main of normal individuals. But imagine that we have evidence (perhaps obtained indirectly, by looking at a control population where the gene pool is roughly similar) that genetic variability is high—has a flattish bell curve—and that the environmental variance is low. Then the expectation would be, on the same assumptions as before, that the observed phenotypes would also arrange themselves along a flat bell curve. If the curve is narrow, with a very large proportion of the population close to the statistical mean, this may well mean that most individuals are in the pathological range for their genome (*Fig. 2*).

It's conceivable that circadian patterns of wakefulness might provide an example. Suppose they're determined quite closely by genetic factors and that they vary all around the clock. Imagine further (what many people's experience seems to confirm) that having to make peak demands on one's metabolism more than two or three hours away from the midpoint C leads to pathological losses in efficiency (see *Fig. 1*). Then a society in which everyone rises, works, and sleeps in synchrony might be one where most people are pathologically abnormal.

My point here is not to deny the distinction between genetic endowment and environment, and still less to deny the relevance of facts about both these aspects of our "natures" to questions of value. It is that the epistemological difficulties in the way of arguments *to* nature are such as to enslave them to ideology. Two politically significant examples can be found in the race and IQ controversy, and in discussions of sex roles.

The IQ and race controversy in the past decade has been fueled by A. R. Jensen's contention that the differences between races in average IQ are not to be accounted for in terms of environmental differences. But Dobzhansky has pointed out that an impoverished environment might be pathological in that it does not allow genetic differences to be manifested in the phenotypes:

> Genetic differences may manifest themselves conspicuously in people who develop in favorable and stimulating environments, and remain undisclosed in adverse or suppressive environments. Carriers of genetic endowments who could unfold high IQs under favorable conditions will fare no better than genetically less well endowed people in suppressive environments. (Dobzhansky, 1973, pp. 21–22)

The same hypothesis suggests itself to explain the long-popular view that "women depart less from the normal than man" (Shields, 1977, p. 23). Far from supporting the claim that there is less genetic variability in women than in men (which anyway makes no genetic sense), such lesser variance among women, if it is a fact, supports the feminist argument that the social imposition of sex roles—the existence of gender as we know it—is a source of widespread pathology *even if* there are statistically significant differences between the genetic components of male and female aptitude or temperaments. For as Trebilcott has said, the imposition of roles "tends to force some individuals into roles for which they have no natural inclination and which they might otherwise choose against" (Trebilcott, 1978, p. 292).

8. THE AMBIGUITY OF "NEED" AND "POTENTIAL," AND A BIT MORE ABOUT SEX

The foregoing arguments have proceeded as if we could isolate single dimensions of variablity. In fact, the only characteristics for which this is true are likely to be uninteresting ones, such as eye color or body size. Those that affect behavior are likely to interact in such a way that a high degree of development of one potential may ride on or interfere with that of another. "Our nature fits us to operate as a whole," says Mary Midgley (1978, p. 265). We must integrate the development of our various capacities and sometimes pay a price for the hypertrophy of one with the hypo-(or hyper-)trophy of others. Do we pay for sublimation with sexual repression? Do we pay for the hypertrophy of left-hemispheric functions with diminished right-brain functions? Must we choose between Art and Life? And if we must, is that bad? The previous considerations suggest that this is possibly so for some individuals, but that it is almost impossible to tell. The answer presupposes a notion of individual need; that is, of what is "natural in the strong sense":

> If it is natural, in the strong sense, it fills a need, and one that cannot easily be filled with a substitute. What we need is not necessarily something we die without, but it is something without which we shall be worse off. (Midgley, 1978, p. 186)

Let us continue to waive the question of how much "worse off" we must be to count as pathological and assume that criteria could be found. To say that something is a need is to say that in some way there is a biological ground to it. But this can be so in two significantly different ways. I shall say that our needs can be *primary* or *secondary*.

The need for food is primary. Not just for some food, without which we die, but for nutritionally adequate food, without which we do not thrive. It's primary because it isn't merely a *consequence* of some adaptation in some distant EEA: We need food now, for its own sake. Secondary needs may feel equally imperative to the individual, but we have them only because they served some primary need that our ancestors had but we no longer do. Suppose, for example, that Lionel Tiger is right about men "needing" to get together in groups. This is a speculation based on (a) the observation that men seem to want to get together in groups, and (b) the reconstruction of an EEA in which our ancestors needed to be programmed to want to band together for survival (Tiger, 1970). It serves no conceivable purpose right now and may cause considerable harm. So the only sense in which they need to is that they want to, although such wants may once have had a selective advantage.

Whether a need is primary or secondary may not be easy to tell. Take sleep, for example. It *feels* like a primary need if anything does. And most people display severe pathology if deprived of sleep. But no one has found what sleep actually does for us, what it "restores" or whether indeed it restores anything (Webb, 1977, p. 375). Carl Sagan, following Webb and Meddis, has suggested that the original function of sleep was to keep us quiet. "It is conceivable that animals who are too stupid to be quiet on their own initiative are, during periods of high risk, immobilized by the implacable arm of sleep (Sagan, 1977, p. 131). This would make our present need for sleep *secondary*: Our bodies now need sleep because our ancestors' bodies were, as it were, fooled into thinking that they did.

Most of the needs on which our sociality is built are secondary. We are free to speculate that those "natural needs" which social taboos and sanctions aim to normalize are those that are both *secondary* and *imperfectly programmed.* Mill points out, in a famous passage of *The Subjection of Women,* that "the anxiety of mankind to interfere in behalf of nature, for fear lest nature should not succeed in effecting its purpose, is an altogether unnecessary solicitude" (1869, p. 154; Trebilcott, 1978, p. 291). But in the case of imperfectly programmed secondary needs, it is quite understandable: Biology is supposed to tell us that the need is really there even if we don't feel it, so it's logical to try and meet it. But the results are likely to be paradoxical. While there is a primary biological need for a process of selection, the social sanction will *slow* it down. It is only when the need has become *secondary* that the social sanctions may activate a selection that, by now, serves no useful purpose. Consider, for example, the relation between the biological fact of *incest avoidance* and the sociological fact of *incest taboos.*[9] Assume a selective advantage to exogamy. This will favor individuals with an instinctive disposition to avoid mating with close kin. But suppose this gets reinforced (perhaps through the secondary need to promote social conformity) by a social taboo. Then the selection will not get a chance to favor the "naturally exogamous," since the social taboo will cover up the genotypic difference between them and the "naturally endogamous." Hence, the proportion of incestuous genes will remain relatively constant. Yet a few individuals, under these conditions, may be incorrigibly incestuous: The taboo and the sanctions implied may lessen their reproductive success, but this will be a very marginal effect. It will continue, however, when by the separation of sex from reproduction the need for incest avoidance is adaptively obsolete. So the incest taboo is perfectly counterproductive. It slows the process of selection when it might be useful and accelerates it when it is useless.[10]

In short, the analysis of secondary needs leads to the same conclusion as the paradoxes of adaptation. Difficult though it is to tell by inspection how to rank our apparent needs, the long way around through ancestral biology seems hardly worth the journey. It is not that our secondary needs don't matter, or that light thrown on their adaptive origins is without *explanatory* value. But if they are secondary needs, they matter only as *wants*. To be rid of the desire is to be rid of the need. For now all there is to the need is "the need to satisfy that want."

This distinction between primary and secondary needs may throw some light onto some of the perennial arguments surrounding sexual morality and normality. The "vaginal orgasm," for example, may be seen as the *myth of a primary need*, based on a *speculation about a secondary one*. The rationale would go something like this: Because reproduction is effected by copulation, nature must have "programmed" women as well as men for copulation. But the vaginal orgasm is the only form of pleasure that could directly reward copulation, so it must be the only "natural" pleasure of sex. Feminists have pointed out that if we attend to the present facts of pleasure and desire we get a very different picture of female sexuality:

> There is no apparent physiological condition in the human female to stimulate simple, direct reproductive behavior, and . . . since the clitoris is the center of female sexual response, the phallus is less relevant to female sexuality than is a finger or a tongue. . . . it becomes clear that women don't need men for satisfaction. (Rotkin, 1972, pp. 155, 157)

This disconnects the observable facts about the sexuality of (at least some) women from any biological speculation about its origins. And why should it not? Why should we attend more closely to biology than to the phenomenology of desire and satisfaction?

Because, the conservatives will say, nature is too complex to "second guess." We know that sex *must* have had a reproductive function even if the need for it is now only secondary. So if we keep it that way, we can't go far wrong; if we don't, we risk the fate of the sorcerer's apprentice.

This, the Know-Nothing AN, is hard to refute. Luckily, it refutes itself, for what we don't know can't take sides. And there is an important complication that it neglects: Among our (secondary) needs is the need to exercise our *capacities*. And like our needs, capacities can be primary or secondary, although here the basis for the distinction is a little different.

A *primary* potentiality or capacity is one that evolved because it conferred an adaptive advantage. Such is the capacity for running, jumping, or standing still. But most capacities are secondary, in a way best illustrated in terms of artifacts.

The bugging industry markets a small device that once installed in your correspondent's telephone set enables you to listen to any conversation within hearing range of the set. I gather you work it this way: You dial the number of the bugged set, and before it gets a chance to ring you blow a special whistle. This disconnects the bell and opens the line. This is a capacity of the phone system. But it wasn't built in. In the technical sense of "function" defined earlier, this isn't a function of the telephone, even though it can be made to function that way. Call it a *secondary capacity*.

It is likely that a great many of our capacities are biologically secondary. Take sleep again. Even if the fanciful Sagan–Webb–Meddis hypothesis is correct about the secondary need for sleep, it may be that sleep has since its "invention" developed important secondary capacities: such as some sort of neural programming in paradoxical sleep, for example (Jouvet, 1978). It wasn't developed for that, but that's what it does for us now. So it's no argument against Rotkin's view of female sexuality, even on the biological level, that "it wasn't developed for that," if indeed it wasn't. Sexual capacities, like most things social, are none the worse for being to the natural organism what the whistle-bug device is to the telephone.[11]

Unlike the distinction between primary and secondary needs, the difference between primary and secondary capacities has no biological significance beyond that of historical accident. Primary needs are "more real" in that if the psychological aspect of them could be painlessly suppressed they would not disappear, whereas secondary needs would. But capacities are no more and no less real for being primary. In biology, secondary capacities are called "preadaptations": But these are not a special sort of adaptation—they are just what, if conditions are favorable, will happen to be useful. So there is never any validity in the argument: "This is a biological potentiality (such as to have babies as opposed to writing sonnets). Therefore, you should develop it." These considerations also invalidate the Know-Nothing argument, for "Don't interfere with nature" presupposes that *nature* is what you would be interfering with. But throughout evolution the existence of preadaptations has meant that nature has never, as it were, left *itself* alone: there is no natural baseline that we could hope to remain at or return to.

9. NATURE AS A NORMATIVE CONCEPT: THE AESTHETIC ARGUMENT

I set out to consider evaluative ANs. I have been driven to conclude that insofar as these appeal to concepts of evolutionary biology the only valid argument is an uninteresting one: "It's impossible, so don't try." At root, it is with the *premise* that the gravest difficulties lie: with the concept of nature itself and arguments *to* the claim that something is "natural." For the concept of nature is, irreducibly, an evaluative one. *Nature is a utopia.*

What could be the biological meaning of Utopia? I suggest this: In biological jargon a Utopia is *a reconstructed niche to a reconstructed organism.* If our ecological niche were fixed, we could speculate about improvements to ourselves. If we could catalogue our capacities exhaustively, we might be able to devise a niche to which they would be perfectly adapted. But neither our niche nor our capacities are fixed. When we propose to make ourselves better adapted to our environment, we are pretending we can't change it. And when we think of changing our niche, we may be missing novel ways in which we might be preadapted to this one or any others. But among such a fluidity of possibilities as "nature" offers—as Utopia—we can make only a choice that is conditioned by our values.

Let me illustrate this with a familiar positive-naturalist argument for conservation. Here the evaluative element is particularly candid: "This species is endangered, so we should try to preserve it." There is no time for a proper discussion of this argument; but in light of the strategies we've considered it's easy to imagine how the discussion might go.

—You're just *sentimental*. You want the species preserved not because it's part of nature, but because it has such lovely soft eyes, or fur, or such quaint customs. Isn't the argument purely aesthetic?

—So let's avoid the distraction of sentimental appeal. Let's take the *smallpox virus*. It's probably endangered. Shouldn't we save it just because it is there?

—Well, *in the wild*, species are continually becoming extinct. So why should we interfere with the course of nature?

—But where we are is no longer the wild: the smallpox virus is becoming extinct precisely because we *have* interfered.

—On the contrary: We may seem to fight dirtier, but that's just anthropomorphic prejudice. What could be wilder and more natural than the fight for survival against smallpox?

—But we weren't threatened by it. Before we set out to exterminate it we were in ecological balance.

—So why shouldn't the balance alter? That's nature's way. Things change. And ours, too, for that matter. And aren't we part of nature?

And so on. I've met biologists who deplored the loss even of such a nasty bug; but maybe not in the wild, but in a jar somewhere. (But then is it really *it*, in its natural systemic identity, that we are preserving? Or are we creating another—*jarpox*, perhaps?) But then naturalists tend to be collectors, so it seems that even though the smallpox virus doesn't look as immediately attractive as the sperm whale, the argument in its favor is aesthetic after all. If so, it's a species of a genus that is very important, and to which I've paid too little attention: the genus of aesthetic arguments to and from nature.

The *genre* admits relatively trivial forms. Sometimes it is a prescription for the relief of anxiety. "Kinsey says 98 percent of males masturbate; so it's natural to masturbate; so I'm *normal*." In slightly loftier form, the books used to ask the anguished question: "Why are we the only species that kills its own kind?" Well, now it turns out that if you look at other species for more than a thousand hours you find out we aren't the only ones. What a relief: We're normal among species! (Wilson, 1975, p. 555).

We could also have said, How gloomy! So there is no redemption even in nature. Logically, both reactions are about equally silly. But they occur; and the popularity of theses about our relation to other animals is surely the result of the change they bring about in our vision of the human animal. To see ourselves as the outcome of evolution needn't change any beliefs that we have about human nature as it now is (although most likely it will); but it *looks* different in that light. And it is likely to foster attitudes that will have incalculable effects on how we think of science and of ourselves.

The whole argument of this paper can be seen as just such an aesthetic AN: a *meta-argument,* from the nature of biological Nature to a certain perspective on other ANs. Among the legitimate effects of this argument, if I am right, we may expect the following: an erosion of kind and stereotype thinking; a recognition of the multiplicity of levels of natural determination; a separation of the social structures favored by certain selective processes from the mechanisms of instinct that once served to foster them; a rejection of the search for some sort of *natural* concept of higher and lower forms of life, untainted by the values peculiar to our conceptions of consciousness and social life. Perhaps, in addition, we may have less respect for the average, not only because average doesn't entail *biologically normal,* but also because even if it did, the normal can lay no special claim to biological superiority. You should consider your freakier acquaintances all the more precious for being potentially pre-adapted to some possible stage in the directionless course of future evolution.

The change of vision that comes with thinking of ourselves as part of nature is an important one, and so is the repercussion that the change in our self-concept may have on the way we see nature. This, too, even as biology informs it, is fluid. For how we see what we see ourselves as, will in part depend on how we see ourselves. In the end, then, without quite siding with Oscar Wilde, we may find unexpected support in the contemplation of the biological concept of Nature, for the unpopular view that although a naturalistic ethics is not, after all, impossible, it may be possible just insofar as Ethics is a branch of Aesthetics.

NOTES

1. More variants could be obtained by applying a distinction between axiology, or judgments of worth, and deontology, judgments about what one must, may, or may not do. Axiology only partly constrains deontology. On some views *only what is good* may be done; on others *whatever is not bad* may be done. The number of variant arguments, both naturalist and antinaturalist, could be multiplied accordingly. But these refinements will not affect my discussion and I shall ignore them. Nor shall I offer to discriminate between

kinds of value, ethical and otherwise. In the sequel I shall require only the assumption that values, or ethics, provide rational reasons for acting.

2. Cf. Murdoch (1970), p. 8: "Reason deals in neutral descriptions. . . . Value terminology will be the prerogative of the will; . . . pure choice, pure movement, and not thought or vision."

3. For some criticisms of this approach, see Boorse (1976) and Woodfield (1976), p. 82, and further references given in the latter.

4. Cf. Wallace (1978). Wallace claims (p. 24) that adaptation is a "normative fact" for which natural selection provides an objective explanation in purely biological terms. But see de Sousa (1982).

5. A related difficulty is discussed in Lewontin (1978), p. 215: "If ecological niches can be specified only by the organisms that occupy them, evolution cannot be described as a process of adaptation because all organisms are already adapted." The solution Lewontin offers is the "Red Queen Hypothesis," attributed to Leigh van Valen: Species change in response to changing environments, and organisms have to "keep running to stay in the same place." This saves the notion of evolution by adaptation from its apparent absurdity, but it doesn't solve the philosophical problem in the text.

6. See, for example, the last chapters of Dawkins (1976) and Goudge (1967).

7. In *Philebus*, 45a–b, Plato describes the greatest and most intense pleasures as being those experienced in diseased conditions. Freud says that the pleasures of sublimation can never be as intense as those of direct instinctual satisfaction (1957–73, vol. 21, p. 103), and Mill insists that the "higher" pleasures are preferable even though they are not *greater* (1863).

8. Cf. King (1954) for the view that it can and Boorse (1975) for the contrary view.

9. On the importance of this distinction, see Vandenberghe (1980).

10. Dobzhansky (1973) makes essentially the same point with respect to the genetic effects of caste:

> Genetically conditioned adaptedness will be dissipated for at least two reasons. First, inept progeny will be pressed to follow their parents' careers despite the genetic incapacity. Second, whatever natural selection may have operated in the formation of the caste gene pool will probably be modified, abandoned, and perhaps even reversed. (p. 33)

In the text, I imagine that there may be conditions under which it continues but is very slight.

11. For some brilliant variations on this theme, see "Die Kultur als Fehler," in Lem (1979).

part two

Morality and Practical Reason

chapter eight

Rationality, Reason, and the Good

Kurt Baier

THE ALIENATION OF PRACTICAL REASON

It is generally agreed that the currently dominant conception of practical reason and practical rationality in disciplines that need to work with these concepts—such as welfare economics, decision theory, game theory, social choice theory, but also sociology and psychology—is that inspired, if not perhaps actually espoused, by Hume, according to which, in Nagel's words, "the only proper rational criticism of action is a criticism of the beliefs associated with it" (1970, p. 64). On this view, adopted also by many philosophers, such as Sidgwick, Falk, Stevenson, Rawls, and now also Brandt in his important book (1979), the aim of practical reason is to expose what is practical—feelings, desires, intentions, and dispositions to act—to as much as possible of the relevant, that is, difference-making, information. The ideal of practical rationality is that of the *fully* informed and logically impeccable person. A person is practically rational if and only if the practical in him, his feelings, desires, and so on, are as they would be if he actually had all the relevant information in principle available to him, and he made no logical mistake.

To me, and I suppose to others, the major attraction of this theory is its apparent ability to cope with a problem many other theories cannot handle. I mean the problem that Brandt calls the "alienation of practical reason"; that is, the danger that a theory of rationality and reason cannot

This essay is a revised version of a paper read at the Conference on Reason and Morality held at Simon Fraser University in February 1980. Research on this topic was made possible by a Fellowship at the National Humanities Center and a research grant from the Rockefeller Foundation. I am grateful for the opportunity provided by this release from other academic duties.

always answer the question "Why be rational?" By anchoring reason in desire, by making it the slave of the passions, this theory seems to be in an especially strong position to answer those who press that question.

However, this theory is also open to serious objections. Thus, in answer to the question, what it is for someone to *have* the relevant information, the theory must hold something like Brandt's view that a person has it if and only if "every item of *relevant available information* is present to awareness, vividly, at the focus of attention, or with an equal share of attention" (1979, p. 11). But it is extremely difficult to ascertain empirically whether a person has the information in this way, if indeed it is possible so to have it. Given the enormous amount of information that is relevant and available, it is hard to see how a person can, at the relevant time, whenever precisely that is, have, let alone know that he has, all that information vividly at the focus of attention or with an equal share of attention.

A second objection is that this account of practical rationality is counterintuitive. Some thinkers are indifferent to this objection, but I notice that Brandt is not, for he says, "We want to be sure that a proposal that looks promising does not overlook something important that is asked about in traditional ordinary-language normative questions" (p. 14). I think Brandt's proposal sets up an ideal of a different sort from that of rationality in ordinary language. To take one of Brandt's own examples: If I decide to go to Palo Alto rather than to Berkeley on my research leave, although Berkeley has something I need for my research that Palo Alto does not have and could not get, then that makes my decision irrational, because if I had known or properly attended to that fact, I would have chosen not Palo Alto, but Berkeley. Brandt's proposal overlooks the fact that ordinarily we should not call that decision irrational unless I knew about this inadequacy of Palo Alto or should and could have found out about it. For this reason, Brandt's ideal of rationality is both too tough and too lenient.

Brandt's proposal misconstrues rationality and irrationality as if these terms did the same job as "legality" and "illegality," as if they characterized a flaw of the *content* of the decision, of *what* was decided, instead of a flaw in *the way in which* the decision was arrived at. Brandt at times appears to sense that irrationality is concerned with the latter; for instance, in the beginning of his account of what he means by "all available information," where he rightly rejects the interpretation, "information available to an omniscient being," and even "the information an agent would have 'if his beliefs had been fixed by his total observational evidence and the principles of logic, both inductive and deductive' "(p. 13). He rightly rejects this because, although decisions made in light of such information would no doubt be *better*, this ideal of decision-making is hardly one that anybody can live up to, and so it cannot be used "as a tool of criticism" (p. 12) when a person does not live up to it. Unfortunately, he loses grip of this point when he goes on to say such things as "that it could be information it would be intolerably expensive to get, so that trying to get it might itself be irrational. But this will enable us to criticize the actions or desires of persons today, as being irrational, although they may not themselves be aware of the known facts which make them so" (p. 12). This is too tough because it returns to the criticism of the merit of the content of the decision rather than the merit of the agent's performance in arriving at it. The latter criticism must take into account how the agent was placed. If it would have been irrational for him to get the additional information, it could not also have been irrational for him to act as was perfectly rational on the basis of the information he already had. No doubt, if he had decided, irrationally, to get the additional information, the content of the decision based on it might well have been better and the making of it in that different context no less rational (but also not necessarily any more rational) than the content and the making of the decision when not so based. But the whole course of action aimed at enabling him to make the better decision with the help of the additional information would be irrational because, as Brandt himself argues, getting the additional information was irrational.

But Brandt's account of irrationality is also too lenient. It passes some things as rational that are not. A person who is hooked on drugs and does not cease to take them or fails to take steps he knows will enable him to shake the habit, although he knows that the addiction is ruining his life, acts contrary to reason, even if he does so in the full knowledge of the effects of drug-taking and attends fully to them. In fact, it is irrelevant whether he attends fully to these facts (whatever sense we can make of this requirement). What he does is contrary to reason (although possibly not sufficiently so to constitute an affront to reason as gross as irrationality) if he knows these facts and if (as is likely in the case envisaged) he should know that these facts about the consequences are sufficient reasons for him to give up the habit or, if he lacks the strength to do so, to take the steps he knows will enable him to shake it.

A third objection is that on this view, theoretical and practical rationality are not, as they appear to be, species of the same genus.

And finally, it should be noticed that even theories such as Brandt's cannot eliminate the *logical* problem of the alienation of reason, although they can perhaps alleviate the psychological difficulties associated with it. The reason is that the closer we come to solving the logical problem, the closer we are to depriving reason of its guiding function. If one holds, as Brandt does, that one is rationally motivated if and only if one is motivated the way one would be if one attended to all the relevant, that is, motivation-affecting facts, then reason is indeed not alienated in the case of a person who is already motivated by this *ideal* of the fully informed person. But what if someone is not so motivated? Would not reason then be just as alienated as it is in the case of other rival ideals of reason and rationality? If one were to tell a person who is indifferent to Brandt's ideal of reason that his motiviation (or the behavior resulting from it) is contrary to reason—that is, is other than it would be if he were fully informed about the "relevant" facts—this would not motivate him to behave differently. In his case, therefore, reason would be alienated. Once it is clear that the difference between Brandt's and other ideals of reason is not that Brandt's is not plagued by the logical problem of the alienation of reason, one can see that all Brandt has done is to select a relatively "low" ideal of reason, one that people are already by and large motivated by. But then an important new question emerges: Which of the competing ideals of reason is the best? For then the reach of an ideal's power to motivate can be seen to be only one among several points to be weighed.

In view of these weaknesses of this "thin" conception of practical reason and rationality, I want to examine the concept of rationality embedded in our culture and our language. I shall argue that, when once clearly understood, this ordinary conception of rationality and reason yields parallel accounts of theoretical and practical reason and rationality and is not exposed to the danger of alienating reason, which is the main support of its competitor, the thin theory, nor is it open to the already mentioned objections to that theory.

THE CONCEPT OF RATIONALITY

I begin with the concept of rationality. When we ascribe rationality to something, we usually ascribe one or other of four different but not unconnected things—a capacity, an ability, an appropriate standard of excellence in that ability, and a tendency.

When we say of a baby that it is a rational being, we ascribe a capacity, one which a puppy, for instance, lacks. The baby is "potentially rational," the puppy is not rational or is nonrational in that it lacks this capacity. Of course, a particular baby may be nonrational just like a puppy, for it may lack the capacity we ascribe to it. We can still say that it is a rational being, but only in an extended (fifth) sense, meaning that it is a member of a species whose normal young are potentially rational.

When we ascribe rationality to a normal adult, we ascribe a certain sort of ability. The child is not yet, the normal adult already is, in this sense rational, or "fully rational." Full rationality is an ability, acquired by every mentally normal human adult, to perform the various activities of reason; that is, those in which one employs reasons, such as explaining, arguing, proving, deliberating, choosing, and so on. One is *fully rational* when one has reached a certain minimal competence in these activities, just as one is a competent speaker of a language when one has completed the learning process and is able to understand and suitably respond to other speakers of the same language, when they speak to one.

In the third place, rationality refers to a certain standard of excellence in the evaluation of exercises of the ability involved in full rationality. Like other such evaluations or appraisals, this one also involves criteria and standards. The criteria are rather complex and themselves rest on a theory, at least an implicit one. For they are the extent to which a fully rational person has made use of the *relevant available guidelines* and the facts made relevant by these guidelines, facts that we ordinarily call the *reasons* that the person then had for solving the problem in hand as the reasons direct him. Rationality in this third, evaluative sense is the person's measuring up to some standard of acceptability in the way he complied with the reasons for the solution of the problem in hand. Ordinarily, the standard implied by "rationality" is *the minimal standard of acceptability*, a kind of "pass" in some activity of reason, "irrationality" the corresponding "fail." Irrationality thus is normally the falling below even this minimal standard of acceptability, a very gross or flagrant flying in the face of reason, as when a person, despite conclusive evidence to the contrary, maintains that her husband has been faithful to her, or continues to be terrified by a gun even when she knows it is not loaded, or for no reason whatever decides not to do something she had been greatly looking forward to doing.

Sometimes, however, the standard used, especially by philosophers such as Kant, is a much higher one. We may then want to speak of "perfect or ideal rationality"; Kant's holy will applied this high standard of perfect rationality. The expression "perfectly rational" is less clear than "perfect rationality." An army doctor may find a malingerer perfectly healthy without wishing to claim that he was in perfect or radiant health. Similarly, an action may be perfectly rational without displaying perfect rationality. A performance (what one does, believes, or feels) is perfectly or ideally rational if it is not just barely rational, that is, does not simply avoid irrationality, but is not in *any* way contrary to reason, as it would normally be contrary to reason, although not necessarily irrational, for someone to buy a typewriter he believed to be inferior as well as more expensive than another, simply because he liked the looks of the salesperson better than those of her competitor. I shall in these cases speak of the perfect or imperfect rationality of a performance. In this terminology, some performances are not irrational, yet they fall short of perfect rationality, and, though not irrational, are yet contrary to reason. Clarity about this distinction is of some importance because a strong case can be made for saying that immorality is not necessarily irrational, that it does not necessarily fail to come up to the minimal standard of rationality, but not that immorality does not necessarily fall short of perfect rationality, not that it is not necessarily contrary to reason. This is important because those who fail to note the difference between the two standards may then believe that *because* immorality is not irrational, it is therefore not contrary to reason. I believe this is a non sequitur.

Rationality in the evaluative sense is, as we have seen, a special case of conformity with reason. It marks a certain acceptable level of compliance with the guidelines of reason. But there is more to this case of conformity with reason, as we can see if we compare it with another term that also implies an acceptable level of compliance; namely, reasonability. Reasonability marks a higher degree of compliance with reason than does rationality. For me to demand of you that you get out of my house by the date on which your lease expires may be quite (that is, minimally) rational, but it is also quite unreasonable if you have just had a heart attack and it is dangerous for you to move. Conversely, it may be reasonable of me to expect you to pay the rent on time, but irrational of me to expect you (in a different sense) to pay the rent if I know your desperate financial situation.

Finally, rationality is a tendency. We can call it "dispositional rationality" or "the rational will"—the tendency to perform in accordance with the best reasons one has, to conform one's performance (what one believes, feels, or does) to what is in accordance with the best available reasons. We can call a person completely or unfailingly rational if her performance never falls below the *minimal* standard of rationality; if it is never irrational. And we can call her perfectly rational—although we perhaps are not likely to encounter such a person—if her performance is always in accordance with reason, never below that highest standard. A Kantian holy will would necessarily be such a perfectly (= ideally) rational being.

While, unfortunately, we have only one word, *rationality*, for these four different properties, we have a different word for the opposite of each of them: *nonrationality* for the lack of rationality in the capacity sense; *prerationality* for the lack of rationality in the ability sense; *irrationality* for the opposite of minimal rationality in the evaluative sense; and *a-rationality* for its opposite tendency sense, although it is doubtful whether anyone who is fully rational (and that is presupposed by a-rationality) could be entirely a-rational.

There would seem to be a core sense; namely, the ability sense (full rationality), in terms of which all the others can be explained and defined. The capacity sense can be defined in terms of the capacity to acquire full rationality. The evaluative uses, complete and perfect rationality, can be defined in terms of the appropriate standards by which the evaluatively rational person judges the exercise, whether his own or other people's, of the ability involved in full rationality. And the tendency sense can be defined as the tendency of a rational person in the ability sense to exercise that ability in conformity with at least the minimal standard of evaluative rationality.[1]

THE CONCEPT OF REASON

We can now elucidate the concept of reason. It involves more than is usually thought, more than an individual talent, skill, or power, such as intelligence or the eye of the soul. It is more like the individual power of speech, whose full development and flowering requires the existence of a social environment in which others already have and use that power and from whom novices can learn how to use their own as-yet-unformed power.

It is for this reason that even very intelligent animals, such as the primates, do not possess reason, even to a low degree of excellence. For, lacking a language and a culture, they also lack the ability to accumulate and transmit to future generations the fruits of individual experience. But reason presupposes the accumulation of individual knowledge and wisdom made possible by language and culture. Those endowed with reason—that is, the capacity to solve their problems *with the aid of the guidelines provided by their culture*—have the enormous advantage that, unlike the other animals, they need not start their individual learning careers from scratch. But as with language, individuals cannot use that power unless society provides the necessary aids for its use.

There is, however, a special feature of the enterprise of reason that transcends the social elements even of language. Insofar as reason is an individual power, like the power of speech, it is the same as rationality in the capacity and ability senses. But as we have seen, the exercise of the ability to perform the various activities of reason, which itself presupposes the power of speech, depends on the public availability of general guidelines for use by individuals in the solution of their particular problems. These general guidelines must not, however, be thought exactly analogous to the rules of grammar. For in the case of the former, but not those of the latter, the excellence of individual solutions to individual problems hinges directly on the excellence of these guidelines. The currently available guidelines are no more than what, at this time, the society has come up with as the best guidelines for its members to use in handling the particular problems they are likely to encounter. Every member of a society, in using its guidelines, is at the same time *testing* them, and so may be able to make suggestions for their improvement. This is the great advantage of *their generality* and *their public availability*. By contrast, in using language and so following the inherent rules of grammar, the users are not at the same time testing these rules; for there is nothing to test. The rules are conventional. Unlike the power of reason, the power of language is not in the same way self-critical and self-correcting. No doubt individual speakers may enrich and change the language, and although its grammar can perhaps be improved in some ways (for example, simplified), it is hard to see how it could be corrected.

If, unlike intelligence, reason is more than an individual power, if it is an individual power whose exercise, like that of speech, depends on the existence of a social practice such as a language, can we say what that social practice or enterprise is, what its function is, what constitutes an improvement of its guidelines, and so on? As I said, the social practice of reason comprises the activities of reason, those in which we employ reasons. A quick glance at the activities of reason will reveal the *aim* of the enterprise of reason. Admittedly, these activities are a mixed bunch, including things as diverse as proving, reasoning, arguing, excogitating, concluding, predicting, explaining, deliberating, choosing, justifying, and more. Nevertheless, we can say in general what is the aim of all these activities and of the various different general guidelines associated with them. It is to enable individuals to achieve better solutions to their problems than would be possible for them without the help of these publicly available guidelines. Of course, within this general objective, each of these activities has its own peculiar end, which an individual may be accomplishing more or less fully or not at all. In proving something, the end is to *raise certainty* to the highest possible level; in explanation, the aim is to raise the extent of *understanding*; in belief-formation, it is to increase our fund of reliable beliefs; in intention-formation or action, it is to increase the efficiency of our means as well as the goodness of our ends.

This sketch of the enterprise of reason enables us to distinguish sharply between, on the one hand, the purpose or function of the enterprise of reason and, on the other hand, the ideal of conformity with reason, which comprises more specific ideals, such as consistency, logicality, rationality, and reasonability. The enterprise of reason comprises many activities, each of which has its own characteristic goal, the attainment of which would help individuals to raise their standards of performance in finding certainty, truth, clarity, understanding, the good, and so on. Hence, to repeat, the generalized purpose or function of the enterprise of reason is to enable individuals to perform certain important activities better than they could in the absence of such guidelines. The ideal of conformity with reason, and so of rationality, is concerned with individuals' adequately taking advantage of them. When we say of someone that it would be irrational for him to do or believe or feel something, we do not necessarily *recommend* that he not do or believe or feel this—for we may say it behind his back—but we imply that we would be critical of him if he performed in this way. Indeed, in the case of some guidelines, we think that contrariety to reason is properly met not merely with criticism, but with suitable sanctions.

Thus, whereas the function of the enterprise of reason implies that the continuous improvement of the guidelines is allowed, indeed wanted, the critical appraisal of individuals' conformity with reason must take into account what facts and what guidelines were actually available to a given person, and how far what he was actually aware of fell short of what could in reason be expected or demanded of him in that respect. If it were irrational for a person to make the effort to acquire additional information, then it would be unreasonable for others to expect that effort of him, and so it would be unreasonable to criticize his performance as irrational if he could have done better only if he had had the additional information that it would have been irrational for him to acquire.

Let me note that my account is not open to the Humean taunt that reason cannot move to action. I once argued that since conformity with reason implies conformity with (good or the best) reasons available to one, the question "Why follow reason?" can simply not arise and so does not stand in need of an answer. For if one fully understands the question "Why?", one also knows that it amounts to a request to be given a reason, but this shows that the request to be given a reason why one should follow the (good or best) available reasons simply does not make sense. Raising the question "Why?" implies that one has entered the "game" of justification by reasons; hence, one is committed to rejecting this particular Why-question. The radical skeptic may, however, reject the whole enterprise of giving reasons, which precludes him from raising this Why-question. His Why-question could then be read as a request for facts that actually weigh with him. To such a radical skeptic, that earlier response of mine must seem an evasion of the basic problem.

Fortunately, the account of reason I have just sketched can provide a better answer to the skeptic. If it is granted that the ends of the various activities of reason are good ends and if, with the help of the enterprise of reason, people can attain these ends at a higher aspiration level than without such help, then surely this is a good, *prima facie,* means-end reason (a type even skeptics usually accept as providing a motive) to act in accordance with rather than contrary to reason. In this way, then, the whole enterprise of reason is hooked to the good, and so its dictates, recommendations, and permissions are justified by their contribution to the good.

To illustrate: What I call "cognitive" reasons are employed in the activity of examining what to believe, and "practical" ones are employed in the activity of examining what to do. The specific aim of the first is beliefs that are true; the second is intentions or acts that are good. We could say that the aim in the case of the first is the true and in the case of the second the good. For the enterprise of reason to be justified, then, the guidelines must be worked out (and continually corrected) in such a way that they constitute better evidence (in the case of cognitive reasons) and principles conducive to the adoption of better ends and better means (in the case of practical reasons) than would be possible if people did not have these guidelines available to them, or if they failed to make use of them. It should also be clear that universal applicability, universal easy availability, widespread use, and continual revision of the guidelines in light of the results obtained by using them must tend to make them increasingly superior, as time goes on, to what an individual could come up with on his own.

PRACTICAL REASON AND THE GOOD

I can now turn to my main question, the sense of "the good" in terms of which the enterprise of Practical Reason must be justified. It is not difficult to develop methods for answering the question of what are good means, but the question of what are good ends is notoriously troublesome. In fact, it is so troublesome that many philosophers have come to the conclusion that no objective answer to that question is possible. The problem is this. It is not enough to say, as I just did in the preceding section, that the enterprise of reason as a whole is hooked to the good on account of its being designed to enable members of a social order to attain, with the help of the guidelines enshrined in its culture, their individual ends at a higher aspiration level than would be possible without their help. It is not enough because, although the attainment of his ends, considered by itself, may be a good thing from each person's point of view, it may not be a good thing, *objectively speaking*, that each person should attain his ends. The sadist's attainment of his end, although probably a good thing from his point of view, may well not be a good thing absolutely.

This problem arises in whatever way we construe the claim that a good end is one that it is a good thing the person in question should have, pursue, and attain. There are two main ways of construing this claim: an easier way and a more difficult one. The easier way is to read it as the claim that it is a good thing from some person's point of view that someone (himself or another) should adopt, pursue, and attain it. The drawback of this solution is that it is then possible, and under normal conditions likely, that what is a good end from one person's point of view will not be a good one from that of another. This is a troublesome consequence, especially if, as seems likely, this will often be the case. For then there often will be no end that is even a good one, let alone the best one, from everybody's point of view. There would, then, often appear to be no intersubjectively rational answer to the question of what end that person should adopt, since there may be no end such that everyone could in reason agree that it is a good thing that he should adopt it.

The second, more difficult way is to construe a "good thing" to mean "an independently good thing"; that is, a good thing irrespective of whether it is a good thing from the point of view of anyone and even everyone, as Moore and Nagel have done.[2] But then it becomes difficult, if not impossible, to answer the question how anyone can ever *know* that something is independently good in this sense.

My solution to this problem follows the lead given by Hobbes. The solution is possible if and only if what are often plausibly portrayed as facts about the world we live in really are such facts. The first assumption is that, among the factors that determine what is a good thing from the point of view of a person, that is, what favorably affects his life, we must include not only his innate endowment, the favorableness of his environment, and his luck, but also and especially what other people will do for and to him. If this last factor is especially important, then it will be rational to hope for, ask for, demand, and where possible try to promote a favorable contribution from others. The second plausible assumption is that there are two obvious ways of ensuring such favorable attitudes and responses by others, and that the first is ineffective without the second. The first is simply to try, by one's own efforts, to build relations of cooperation and trust with other individuals, whereas the second is the creation of a favorable interpersonal climate affecting not only personal acquaintances, family, and friends but also strangers within the framework of a social order that coordinates people's activities. One further plausible belief that supports this assumption is that the favorable contributions people can make to one another's lives are greatly enhanced when their activities are coordinated in large-scale cooperative enterprises, and that these can be created only if there already is the friendly interpersonal climate extending beyond acquaintances also to strangers.

Hobbes noticed one peculiar and most troublesome type of situation, which appears to be common in large-scale interaction and in which coordination on a voluntary basis seems not enough to ensure the greatest benefits of interaction. I mean the type of situation, now often called Prisoners' Dilemma, in which the payoffs, to all affected, of a certain coordinated strategy among the interacting parties are greater than the payoffs to them of the best noncoordinated or independent strategy. By the best independent or noncoordinated strategy, I mean one of which a person can say that it is his best reply, *whatever the other parties may be doing*. In such situations, a group of Rationalist Egoists—persons determined to reap the greatest benefits for themselves in whatever way that affects others, that is, persons unwilling to forego the chance of the greatest gain for themselves even when that involves inflicting the greatest loss on the others—must of necessity reap suboptimal results; that is, outcomes in which their payoffs are smaller than they would be if they adopted a coordinated strategy and so departed from that independent pursuit of their own good. The problem is that, as Rational Egoists, they are incapable of adopting such a coordinated strategy because it would involve both foregoing the chance of the best outcome and risking the worst.

Two things are needed for people in such situations to be able to achieve results as close to optimal as the situation will allow. The first is that they must be willing to adopt an attitude of conditional "goodwill." That is, they must, on condition that the others are doing the same, be willing to forego the chance of getting the highest payoffs when that can be achieved only at the expense of those with whom they interact. This attitude is not one of altruism in the sense that it is motivated by a "direct" concern for the well-being of others. The person of conditional goodwill may be indifferent about the well-being of others (except where he stands in special relations to them), but he is willing to restrain his pursuit of his own good where that is necessary for the well-being of others, provided these others impose comparable restraints upon themselves. The motivation and the justification are self-interested, even though the effect of the constraints is much the same as that of altruistic motivation. Of course, the same favorable results may be achieved, perhaps more reliably and cheaply, if the motivation of all or at least a significant number were genuinely altruistic. Even in such a case, the *justification* of endowing others with such altruistic motivation must remain self-interested. If we were designing the motivation or an educational system shaping the motivation of those dear to us, we should need to know whether they will be thrust into a world of egoists or altruists. We should not feel justified in subjecting those dear to us (or those for whose fate we feel some responsibility) to the handicaps to which altruists are exposed in a world of unrestrained self-seekers. But if we can be sure that all or most will have the same or similar motivation, we shall opt for moderate altruism rather than rigid egoism. If we must assume that they will live in a world of people with a wide range of motives, conditional goodwill would seem to be the best bet.

The second is that they must have reasonable assurance that others will in fact adopt that attitude of conditional goodwill, for otherwise, instead of doing better, they may well do worse by adopting an attitude of conditional goodwill than they would if they followed the best noncoordinated (self-interested) strategy.

Hobbes believed that human reason enables us to grasp and satisfy the first condition, and that the existence of an absolutist state would satisfy the second. He thought that it would therefore be rational for a Rational Egoist to want an absolutist state and that in such a state it would always be rational for him to obey its coercive rules. Hobbes believed, in other words, that the supreme principle of Practical Reason is the principle of Rational Egoism. That is:

(i) Only facts showing that X's doing A would be in X's best interest, constitute reasons for X to do A.

or

(i') Facts showing that X's doing A would be in X's best interest are the supreme (overriding) reasons for X to do A.

And he believed, furthermore, that reasons based on that principle dictate the creation of an absolutist state, and that in an absolutist state and only in such a state are people able, by following reason, to come as close as possible to the lives optimal for them.

It is important to see that and why Hobbes is mistaken. Hobbes saw that if his argument was to succeed, everyone would have to have sufficient self-interested reason always to obey the law; that is, the coordinating coercive rules laid down by the absolutist state. He is probably right in thinking that the sanctions attached to the law tend to provide the assurance the person of conditional goodwill needs that others will not take advantage of his law-abidingness to reap additional benefits for themselves by breaking the law and harming the law-abiding ones. Hobbes also noticed that he had not shown that Rational Egoists could be persons of conditional goodwill. For he had not shown that, as Rational Egoists, they could consistently ignore opportunities to take advantage of others who obeyed the law. He had not, in other words, shown that Rational Egoists always have adequate reason to obey the law. All he had shown was that under the principle of Rational Egoism everyone had adequate self-interested reason to strengthen his own position so as to be able to break the law with impunity while at the same time ensuring that others would never be in that position.

Every Rational Egoist has self-interested reasons to ensure by stringent policies of "law and order" that crime does not pay *other* people. But if everyone consistently follows this principle, this gives rise to important conflicts within the system. For such Rational Egoists also have self-interested reason to attempt, perhaps by bribes, threats, and other methods, to bend the law itself to their own advantage, whatever the cost to others. And their officials, whose task it is to ensure that the rules are properly enforced, have self-interested reasons to enrich themselves by bending the law in their own favor or in favor of those who are paying them so to bend it. Given the unequal abilities of different people to promote their advantage, such a social order of Rational Egoists will tend toward an increasingly unjust absolutism. But as such a society moves more and more in that direction, more and more of its members will find it contrary to their interests to keep, and therefore in accordance with self-interested reason to try and break the law or overthrow the government, even at some risk to themselves. Such societies of Rational Egoists will thus tend to be unstable, with periodic revolutions and many of the very drawbacks of the Hobbesian state of nature.

Hobbes's argument to rebut this is, notoriously, feeble. His claim is that it is never in accordance with reason for a Rational Egoist in an absolutist society to break the law. He admits that it may turn out to have been in one's interest to have broken the law, but he claims that it could never be in accordance with reason to think so in advance. This argument rests on two claims, only one of which is sound. The sound one is that anyone violating the law can gain from his violation only by "the errors of other men." We can accept that in an absolutist society punishments are so tailored that crime never pays when the criminal is caught. However, the second—namely, that one "could not foresee nor reckon upon" such errors, and that therefore in breaking the law one is necessarily always acting contrary to reason—is unsound. Hobbes here faces a fatal dilemma: Either the absolutist society spends an inordinate amount of its resources on penal machinery and imposes savagely severe penalties on the culprits caught, or it does not. In the latter case, potential law-breakers will often be sufficiently sure of not being caught to make it irrational for them not to risk breaking the law if that promises great gains. In the former case, the more the absolutist state approximates this penal ideal, the weaker the case for such a state, and the stronger the case, on other, self-interested grounds, for a more limited, less savage, and economically more productive state.

The main flaw in Hobbes's position clearly is his failure to provide a conceptual framework in which the members of a legal order have adequate (*prima facie*) reason always to obey the law. An egoistic member of Hobbes's absolutist state must regard the social mores, custom, and law as hurdles intended to hold back others. He will support their existence only to ensure that *others* will abide by the law. He has no adequate reason to abide by it himself. The Rational Egoist's attitude toward law will therefore be one of cautious evasion wherever possible, supplemented by whatever efforts he can make to secure laws that will promote his personal or sectional or class advantage.

If this is the crucial flaw in Hobbes's position, then the solution must lie in getting law and custom regarded in the society as reasons that override the individual's reasons of self-interest. But this solution requires the abandonment of Rational Egoism. One popular theory, which one might call Rational Conventionalism, does just this. Its theory of what constitutes practical reasons runs as follows:

(ii) The requirements of the social order are to be regarded by its members as reasons for acting accordingly and, where they come into conflict with independent self-interested reasons, as overriding them.

Rational Conventionalism has certain strengths which Hobbes's Rational Egoism lacks. It makes the important move of dividing practical reasons into those that any person has, whether or not he lives in a given society, which I call "independent reasons," and those that he has only as a member of the society, which I shall call "conventional reasons." Furthermore, it gives different weights to these types of reasons, irrespective of their content. It is clear that a society of strict Rational Conventionalists would not be plagued by the instability and conflict to which Rational Egoism is subject. Nevertheless, this view is plainly unsatisfactory. For it may not be able to give to all the members of a society any good independent reason why they should regard the requirements of the social order *as reasons*, let alone overriding reasons, for them to act accordingly. After all, those requirements may be damaging to the interest of given members or whole classes of them. Rational Conventionalism is therefore particularly prone to the weakness Brandt calls the alienation of reason. For instance, a slave will, if rational, find it hard to understand why he should regard the provisions of the Runaway Slave Act as *reasons* for him to act accordingly.

The mistake is plain enough. If these social requirements are to constitute *genuine* overriding reasons for everyone, then everyone must have independent reasons to want there to be such social requirements and to have them regarded as overriding reasons. Now, it may well be true that people by and large would be better off in a society of Rational Conventionalists than in a Hobbesian absolute state, simply because there is less oppression and instability under such an order. Nevertheless, this would show only that everyone has *some* reason to want the social requirements regarded as overriding reasons, but not that everyone has *adequate* reasons. The question, then, is what social requirements must be like if *everyone* is to have adequate reason so to regard them. This question is important because, as our analysis of Hobbes's argument has shown, every member of a social order has adequate reason to *want* its requirements to be such that everyone governed by them has adequate reason to regard them as overriding. For only then can the advantages of Rational Conventionalism (such as social stability) be combined with those Hobbes was hoping for; namely, the backing of reason for such a social order. For in such a social order the social requirements really would *be* reasons overriding those of self-interest. And that would of course justify one's so regarding them as well as expecting others to do likewise.

What, then, would bring it about that everyone has adequate independent reasons for so regarding them? Plainly, it must be a condition on their content. Not any and every social order provides everyone with adequate independent reason to regard its requirements as overriding reasons. Only those social orders do that meet a certain standard of excellence. It is not difficult to find a standard sufficiently high to provide adequate reasons: The society must be such that everyone has the best possible reasons *anyone* could in reason demand; namely, the best possible reasons *everyone* could have. Obviously, one could not in reason demand the best possible independent reasons *he* could have, for that would involve society giving him all he wants for himself and his favorites, irrespective of how that affects others. If we bear in mind the nature of the enterprise of reason and the role reasons play in it, then it is clear that the best reasons *anyone can in reason demand* are those that *everyone can have*. For from the point of view of reason, no one has a position of special privilege until there are special reasons why he should be granted it.

What, then, is the *best* independent reason everyone can ask for? It would have to be a better reason than the best provided by either Hobbes's Rational Egoism or Rational Conventionalism. For the most that can be claimed by these systems is that in their type of social order everyone would be better off than in a state of nature. But this only gives everyone adequate reason not to want to return to the state of nature. It does not (necessarily) give him adequate reason to be satisfied with or even merely to acquiesce in such a social order. But suppose the social order were to provide everyone with equally good reason to regard its requirements as constituting reasons overriding those of self-interest, and suppose these reasons are so good that no single person's reasons can be strengthened without *ipso facto* someone else's being weakened; then everyone has reasons as good as everyone can demand,

and that surely is adequate reason, since there could be no better reason for everyone.

Of course, to say only this is to leave unanswered two difficult questions. The first arises out of the reflection that few, if any, societies can be expected to live up to this ideal standard. The question then is how far below such "perfect equitability" a society may fall before its coercive rules cease to provide adequate reason for conformity. This is a problem all those face who provide initial justification for conditions that Rawls calls "ideal compliance" (1971, pp. 8, 245, 351).

The second unanswered question is how "equally good reason" and "strengthening a reason" or "weakening a reason" are to be interpreted. One plausible method would be Rawls's powerful device of an "original position behind a veil of ignorance." But this is not the place to take up either of these two large problems.

I want to conclude by returning to the question that led me into this last discussion: the sense of "the good" in terms of which the enterprise of Practical Reason must in my opinion be justified. The problem was how to interpret the expression "the goodness of ends." The interpretation I regarded as the most persuasive was this. A given person's end is a good one for him to adopt, pursue, and attain if and only if it is a good thing, from everyone's point of view, that he should do so. The problem was that given a plausible construal of the way the world is, there will be few ends that are intersubjectively good in this way. Practical Reason thus would be of only very limited use.

The solution I am arguing for should by now be clear. I have assumed that many of those ends, which, though good from some points of view, are not intersubjectively good, fail to be so because they are adopted and pursued in Hobbesian or similar situations. But even in these cases it is in principle possible for people to be so organized in coercive social orders that it is perfectly rational for every member to recognize its coercive rules as providing reasons to comply with them that override whatever independent reasons a member may have for acting differently. This is so because of the especially important role that other people's behavior plays in making one's own life as good as possible. A social order may therefore simply lay down those requirements that demand of each member those favorable contributions to other people's lives— whether by refraining from pursuing those of his ends whose pursuit and attainment would unfavorably affect others or by positively aiding them along Good Samaritan lines—which, when generally complied with, generate for each member a better life than he could hope for in an inequitable social order. It is then perfectly rational for every person who lives in a state of nature or in an inequitable society to want to live in an equitable society. And it is perfectly rational for every member of such an equitable society to want its demands complied with by every member and to comply with them himself. For this reason, it is also perfectly rational and reasonable for people to make such demands on one another and, because of the inevitable temptation not to comply with them, also perfectly rational and perfectly reasonable to insist that these demands be generally sanctioned in a suitable way.

It may now be thought that the fact that some could hope for even better lives in inequitable societies that favored them over others constituted an adequate reason for them to want to work for such an inequitable order. Now, clearly, this could be rational, given certain specific information about the intelligence, rationality, and information of others, for such a hope and such an enterprise need not involve so gross a departure from the ideal of rationality as to involve irrationality. But it would not be in accordance with the idea of perfect rationality, that of flawless accordance with reason. For the fulfillment of such a hope would involve the making of certain demands by the socially favored on the socially disfavored, which it would not be reasonable for them to make, because it certainly would not be ideally rational for those on whom the demands are made to want to comply with them. But the ideal of perfect rationality requires not merely that a person not do anything himself that is contrary to reason but also that he not make any unreasonable demands; that is, demands it would not be in accordance with reason to comply with. For demands are reasonable not simply whenever it is rational to *make* them, or rational to hope or expect that they will be met, but only if it is also in accordance with reasons for those on whom they are made to comply with them.

NOTES

1. These distinctions, simple as they are, are nevertheless often neglected. Even writers as sophisticated as Anatol Rapoport are led into errors by their failure to note them. Thus Rapoport writes:

> A controversy is still carried on here and there about whether the one or the other choice is 'really' rational. What is 'really' rational is, of course, a matter of definition and so not something that deserves a serious controversy. Much more interesting is the question of what people actually do when confronted with a Prisoner's Dilemma situation. In fact, if we could get an independent assessment of what constitutes a 'rational actor', the question of which choice is rational in Prisoner's Dilemma could be put to an experimental test. Then what a 'rational actor' does will provide the answer to the question. (1974, pp. 17–34)

However, the question of which choice is rational cannot, without additional assumptions, be put to an empirical test. For in that question, "rational" is used in the evaluative sense, while in the expression "rational actor", it is used in the ability sense. Hence, even if we can determine empirically, as we probably can, that a given person is a rational actor, that is, a fully rational person, this still leaves completely open the question of whether what he chooses will be rational or irrational, in the evaluative sense, for having the ability and knowing when to exercise it does not imply that one will exercise it up to even a minimal let alone the highest standard. But what is wanted here is the highest standard. We want a solution to prisoners'-dilemma situations that will guide the merely indifferent practitioners. Finding out what practitioners, from indifferent to ideal, actually do, will not tell me what is ideal. We cannot assume that the majority defines the ideal. To hope for an empirical settlement of the question of what choice is rational in the evaluative sense is particularly misguided in such cases as prisoner's-dilemma situations, where many rational actors are geniunely puzzled about what is really (that is, evaluatively) rational.

Rapoport is also in error when he implies that, because whether the choice is "really rational" depends on the definition of "rational", such a definition is arbitrary and so the disagreement a merely verbal one. The fact is, rather, that because of the evaluative content of "rational" in the evaluative sense, how "rational" in that sense is defined, is of considerable practical importance. For the definition purports to guide practitioners in the performance of the activities of reason. Since, if I am right, it is to be defined in terms of conformity with the best available reasons, its definition is tied to a theory of reasons.

2. Cf. Thomas Nagel (1970), p. 20, fn. 1:

An objective principle provides reasons for everyone to desire a common goal in a different way from a subjective reason which happens to yield a common goal for everyone. The latter depends on some appropriate relation between each of the individuals and the end in question, whereas the former does not. Thus what has objective value is not thereby of value *to* anyone, not even to everyone.

chapter nine

Must the Immoralist Act Contrary to Reason?

Kai Nielsen

Treating vice with the greatest candour, . . . there is not, in any instance, the smallest pretext for giving it the preference above virtue, with a view of self-interest; except, perhaps, in the case of justice, where a man, taking things in a certain light, may often seem to be a loser by his integrity. . . . A sensible knave, in particular incidents, may think that an act of iniquity or infidelity will make a considerable addition to his fortune, without causing any considerable breach in the social union and confederacy. That *honesty is the best policy*, may be a good general rule, but is liable to many exceptions; and he, it may perhaps be thought, conducts himself with most wisdom, who observes the general rule, and takes advantage of all the exceptions.

—David Hume

I

Kurt Baier argues that the relation between the moral and the rational is such that it is necessarily contrary to reason to be immoral.[1] I shall argue that while being moral can be *consistent* with reason it is not *required* by it and that in certain circumstances it can be the case than an immoralist need not be irrational or even less rational than even a well-informed person of moral principle.

Baier contends that we can establish a correct moral method: a method that will show that reason requires us to commit ourselves to the principle that, where there is a conflict, moral considerations *always* override nonmoral considerations. We can do this, he believes, "without laying ourselves open to the objection that we are imparting substantive conclusions into our deliberations under the pretense of having found them by a neutral (meta-ethical) inquiry." While Baier concedes that the nature of the moral point of view is indeed currently contested, he denies that it is essentially contested. Rather, the "moral point of view" can be "properly identified in terms of a set of demands on a method for determining what to do." We need not talk tendentiously of the function of morality. Instead, we can show that these demands are demands that this method "must satisfy if the resulting moralities are rightly to be regarded as constituting paramount practical reasons." The correct moral method is the "one that can best satisfy these demands."

The various conceptualizations of a correct moral method can be construed as rival hypotheses about which method best satisfies the crucial constraint: that the moralities that would result from its correct application are rightly to be regarded "as constituting paramount practical reasons."

Baier articulates five demands that a correct moral method must satisfy. The first demand is what he calls, somewhat misleadingly, the demand for *soundness.*[2] A system of coordinative guidelines is sound, according to Baier, if "everybody has *equally good* reason to regard its precepts as paramount practical reasons." A morality is something that by definition makes a claim to soundness. It makes no sense for me to assert that these are my moral views but I know they are unsound. If I believe at t_1 that p is morally required of me and I come to believe at t_2 that my believing p is unsound, I must at t_2 change my morality—change in that respect at least what I think is morally required of me. Furthermore, for a morality to be sound, Baier argues, it must be established within that conception that it is a good thing if people are moral and a bad thing if they are not. ("Good" and "bad" here are of course used in a nonmoral sense.) The second demand of practical reason captures that. It is the demand that it is a good thing if people have a morality because it is a good thing if people are moral and a bad thing if they are not. Without a morality, Baier argues, they cannot perform the cognitive and executive tasks that are essential if they are to act reasonably. The morality that this demand requires is one in which people act in accord with not only a morality that *purports* to be sound, but one that *actually is sound*.

The third demand of practical reason is "for everyone to be moral and for social pressures to be applied in support of the precepts of morality." The fourth demand, closely related to the third, is that *the precepts of morality are to be taken as overriding* all other guidelines, including the guidelines of self-interest. The demand is that "people treat moral precepts as supreme guidelines." That everyone must always be moral is, on Baier's account, taken to be a demand of practical reason.

Baier's fifth demand of practical reason is that "morality be in accordance with reason and immorality contrary to reason." If it is not, then we need not, Baier would have it, take much notice of the dictates of morality. Moreover, we could not have the fourth demand without also having the fifth. Baier does not say this explicitly, but it is natural to take him to be claiming here that the fourth demand implies the fifth. If the precepts of morality (a genuine sound morality) are overriding, then "these precepts must themselves be treated as *reasons* outranking all other types of reason." Since the moral point of view is the highest point of view of all the guidelines for action, when viewed from what he calls "the point of view of reason," it must also "be the case that being moral *really is* in accordance with reason, being immoral contrary to it."

II

However, we need to ask for the justification for taking these five demands to be the paramount demands of practical reason. How can it be shown—or can it be shown—that these demands "correctly express crucial requirements of practical reason itself?" Why are these demands the crucial requirements of practical reason? Indeed, do they really have such a status? To show that they do, Baier needs to articulate and defend a distinctive conception of practical reason and, as well, to bring into the foreground "two important facts about interaction between people." And this is precisely what he does do in both "The Conceptual Link Between Morality and Rationality" (1982) and in "Rationality, Reason, and the Good."

Baier distinguishes reason from "mere intelligence." He takes reason to be the name "of several interrelated powers." The powers Baier has in mind are (1) the ability to apply suitably "certain general guidelines of a culture to particular problem cases"; (2) the ability to assess the merits "of the currently prevalent guidelines and of improving them in light of the relevant ideal"; (3) the ability (in some approximation) to ascertain theoretical truths (including knowledge of what is the case) for "problems of what to believe"; and (4) the ability to ascertain or appreciate "the good in the case of practical reason for problems of what to do." Rationality "is the possession of the power of reason, the skill of using it, the tendency to use it, and success in its use up to a certain standard of excellence." Guidelines of practical reason in a particular society function "to enable members of a culture, by suitably applying them to particular problem cases," to improve their lives over what their lives would be if they simply followed their own inclinations or without these guidelines tried to solve their own practical problems. They are guidelines that tell us what to do in certain circumstances.

Baier believes that there are facts about the *interaction* of people such that when they are thought through and considered in relation to the above conception of practical reason it will be evident that we should accept these five demands (putative demands) of practical reason and that a sound morality is necessarily in accordance with reason and immorality is necessarily contrary to it. Baier lists two such facts:

1. The best life for human beings is one in which they interact with one another and cooperate in common enterprises and pursuits.
2. In common cooperative enterprises, sometimes a certain outcome pattern results which fits the pattern of the Prisoner's Dilemma. That is to say, if each person in such a situation does what will answer best to his own interests, given what others are or may be doing, then everyone will achieve only their third best results. Alternatively, if others follow a certain coordinative guideline, everyone will achieve their second best results. Thirdly, if some take the first alternative and some the second, the first group will achieve their best results and the latter their worst.

Baier's claim is that if we take into consideration these facts about interaction—genuine social facts about our lives together—and if we are clear about what practical rationality is, then we will in such circumstances come to see, if we are rational, that the five demands on moral method do express crucial requirements of practical reason. In reasoning about what to do, a rational and well-informed person will reason in accordance with them.

He claims that this holds even of those people who take rational egoism as the supreme general principle of practical rationality for individuals, namely the principle: "Always do what is in your own best interest." In situations of human interaction, such egoists will always translate this into the corollary principle: "Always do what, considering what others are or may be doing, best answers to your interests." Even such rational egoists will come to see, if they are tolerably intelligent and well informed, that in prisoners'-dilemma situations, situations that are pervasive in our lives, that it is more rational for them to opt for living in a social order that has coordinative guidelines, generally understood and generally accepted, than to opt for a society in which everyone tried to do what best answered to their own interests, given their understanding of what others are or may be doing. A rational agent will recognize that the prospect of stern penalties indeed is great if people one-sidedly follow a policy of trying to further their own interests in the light of what others predictably will do, hoping thereby to gain greater rewards than they would gain by sticking with the general adherence to coordinative guidelines. Being a free-rider in such a circumstance is very risky indeed. Rational agents will design social policies to detect and discourage such otherwise attractive behavior (attractive at least to rational egoists). In short, such rational egoists are not likely to get away with such directly self-serving behavior, and the penalties for so acting are great. This being so, it is rational for everyone to have a set of coordinative guidelines in place, spelled out, promulgated, and backed up with sanctions sufficient to deter rational egoists who will not act in accordance with the dictates of morality.

To reason in such a way is to support the second and third demands; namely (a) that it is a good thing that people be moral and a bad thing for them to be immoral, and (b) to support the recognition that social pressures are to be applied to ensure that everyone act in accordance with the moral point of view. Even when they are inclined to be immoralists (inclined, that is, to take as the supreme principle for their own actions the principle that they always do what would "constitute their best reply to whatever others are or may be doing"), rational and informed people will recognize that immoralism will not pay. Indeed, they will see, Baier claims, that it will never pay. They will see, if they carefully reflect, the desirability of making social sanctions supporting morality so effective, so stringent both in terms of severity and certainty, and thus very costly for themselves, that immoralism (or amoralism, if you will) would not pay. If *people* take as their supreme principle of action "Always do what constitutes your best reply to whatever others are or may be doing" and act on that principle, they could not lead as good a life, *as a group of people,* as they would if they would accept instead as supreme principles of practical reason certain coordinative guidelines, even purely conventional coordinative guidelines, which would be in accordance with the moral point of view. But this shows that such a principle of self-anchored egoism, as Baier calls it, could not be the correct formulation of the supreme principle of practical reason. It would have suboptimal results.

III

Baier next introduces a very controversial thesis. He argues not only that rational agents would in prisoners'-dilemma situations want a social order utilizing coordinative guidelines, but he also argues for the controversial thesis that a person starting from rational egoism would want, or would come to want if he deliberated carefully, to follow those guidelines himself even in circumstances in which following them did not constitute his best reply to whatever others are or may be doing. Any egoist, if he were rational, would come to regard such nonegoistic principles to be the supreme principles of practical reason. This surprising claim is a crucial point for Baier because only if it is so will it be the case that rational agents will follow—or so he claims—such coordinative guidelines *voluntarily*. They see, for the reasons already given, that general adherence to such guidelines is plainly desirable. But if they, as individuals, stick with rational egoism as their supreme principle of rationality, they will then still not follow these coordinative guidelines voluntarily, but only when the sanctions were so certain and so severe that not following these coordinative guidelines will be counterproductive. This shows, if correct, that Baier's fourth demand—that the precepts of morality are overriding—is also a crucial requirement of practical reason. People will want such a system of coordinative guidelines for *its own sake* and not simply as a means to an end.

IV

Baier concludes his case by arguing that rational people will want not only some system of coordinative guidelines or other rather than none, but they will want a distinctive set of coordinative guidelines. Baier, unlike David Gauthier, is not settling for a conventional morality.³ This comes out with particular clarity in "Rationality, Reason, and the Good." Some systems will afford people significantly better chances of leading a worthwhile life than others; for example, a set of coordinative guidelines favoring ruling class interests will not do this as well as a set of guidelines answering to the interests of everyone alike. In finding the crucial requirements of practical reason, we will want not just some set of coordinative guidelines, but *sound* coordinative guidelines. We will want, that is, coordinative guidelines where everyone has equally good reason to regard its precepts as paramount practical reasons. This shows, Baier claims, that rational people will accept the first demand as a crucial requirement of practical reason. A satisfactory system of coordinative guidelines must be such that "everybody subject to these guidelines have adequate reason to regard them as paramount practical reasons." *Everybody* must have as good reason so to regard them as *anybody* can in reason demand to have. This will be so if *everybody* has as good reason as *everybody* can *have* for so regarding a distinctive system of coordinative guidelines. "No one," Baier maintains, "can in reason demand a better reason that that, since from the point of view of reason no one is *ab initio* in a privileged position to ask for a better reason than anyone else."⁴

Baier's talk of soundness is rather peculiar. In showing a system of coordinative guidelines to be sound, he is not claiming that they can be reduced to a set of valid arguments with true premises. Rather, for

Baier, when we are trying to articulate a method for determining what to do, a criterion of soundness will tell us how the relevant properties of the various actions open to us are to be evaluated. The requirement of soundness, Baier avers, is very likely the most important demand on a method for determining what to do. It is a demand we make on anything we would accept as a legitimate morality. But in spite of the importance he attaches to it, what he means by "soundness" is not explicated, though, as we have seen, he does tell us that a system of coordinative guidelines is sound if "everybody has equally good reason to regard the precepts as paramount practical reasons." So we, on his conception, have a sound morality where all rational agents have equally good grounds to regard its moral principles as having overriding rational authority in situations where questions of the guidance of conduct arise. A fair number of questions arise about this conception of soundness, but since the critique that follows does not turn on the details of this conception, I shall not pursue them here.

Baier also believes that he has shown that "to be sound, a morality must be such that it is a good thing if all people are moral and a bad thing if they are not," and he also concludes that the five demands have the backing of practical reason and can thus be "used to define or delineate the correct method for arriving at normative moral conclusions." This, in turn, Baier would have it, means that morality is *necessarily* in accordance with reason and immorality *necessarily* contrary to it.

V

I want now to turn to an assessment of Baier's account, an assessment that will also involve some further explication of his complicated and nuanced view. (I will not, however, try to sort out everything that needs to be sorted out in his account, but only those things that are germane to the points that I wish to criticize.)

Baier maintains that a group of rational people, starting out with a subscription to rational egoism, would not just want a sound system of coordinative guidelines taught as something for others to follow but not for themselves to follow, except where following such a system would also coincide with the principle of self-anchored egoism—that is, "Always do what constitutes your best reply to whatever others are or may be doing"—but they would also want those principles taught in such a way that they themselves would be socialized into reasoning and acting in accordance with them even when so reasoning and acting would not for themselves (as individuals) be justified in terms of the principle of self-anchored egoism. Even as an individual member of such a group, he will, if rational, will to be so socialized. He will see this, Baier maintains, as a requirement for his own rational action. He would accept, according to Baier, as his supreme principle of practical reason, what he, at least, believes to be a sound system of coordinative guidelines and would thus be led to abandon his rational egoism. He would so act even in individual situations where so acting did not serve his own interests. He would strive to be not just a man of good morals but also to be a morally good man.

Baier is not just saying that rational egoists would want each other so to act, but that each such egoist would will that he would himself be so socialized that he would come to embrace the moral principles of a system of sound coordinative guidelines as ends in themselves. He would want, if he had perfect rationality, to so order his life that he would always act as these coordinative guidelines dictate. He would, like a good Hobbesian, see the danger of not doing so—that is, the desta-bilizing effects on the social order and thus the disadvantage to himself—but beyond such instrumental considerations, he would also believe that any other way of orienting his life would offend against rationality.

Baier has not shown anything that strong. A rational individual could without error reason as follows: I, for roughly the reasons that Baier gives, want a sound system of coordinative guidelines to be firmly entrenched in my society. This requires a certain socialization of the people in the society and I cannot in reason desire that such socialization be withheld from me, for others are not going to accept such an exemption. And, even if they did, I do not want to see the practice started, for if this became a practice, it would be applicable to others as well and that would hardly be in my interest. But I still rationally can and do wish that such socialization not be successful in my own case. I wish, speaking for myself alone, that socialization to stick only to the extent that I am able successfully to simulate acting on sound coordinative guidelines, to have the ability actually to act on them when it is my interest to do so and clairvoyantly to recognize situations in which this is so and situations in which this is not so. I indeed recognize the value of the existence of social arrangements in which everyone, including myself, is taught to adhere to these coordinative guidelines, but I hope that such teaching will not be successful in my case because what I want to be able to do, in every case where I prudently can, is to give my interests pride of place and do what I have the best reason to believe, everything considered, furthers my own interests. I hope that I will always be able to take the interests of others to be subordinate to what I have the best reasons for believing will, everything considered, best further my own interests. This may not show a lot about what I actually will do, but it does show something important about the order of my commitments.

Such a person is an immoralist, but Baier has not established that such an immoralist in thinking as he does and in hoping that he can act in such an unprincipled way, where it suits his advantage, is being irrational or even less rational than a person of sound moral principle. What Baier has at most shown is that such an immoralist would want a sound system of moral guidelines in place in society and would recognize the value of devices in the society that successfully socialize everyone into that morality. But Baier has not shown that reason requires that such a person desire that such socialization stick in his own case beyond giving him the ability successfully to simulate acting on principle, and to act, if he so chooses, to counteract the effects of such socialization where it plausibly threatens to become catching and thus to make his society unstable. And he has not shown that such a person must be less rational than reasonable persons of sound moral principle. Baier may have established that it is rational to have a sound system of moral practices and irrational not to have one, but he has not shown that a person who acts immorally necessarily acts irrationally or indeed in any way acts with diminished rationality or makes any intellectual mistake at all. He has not shown that immoral behavior must be contrary to reason. We still have the problem of Hume's sensible knave.

VI

Such a person could not give a public defense of his position, and he would probably be ill-advised even to defend it privately to his friends (if indeed he could have "friends"), but everyone when they hear such a description of a possible scenario for how a person might act can come to recognize that such immoral behavior need not necessarily be either irrational or even contrary to reason where it is tolerably plain that it will not be copied. Thus Baier fails to establish a necessary connection between being immoral and being less than fully rational. He has not shown that the immoralist must suffer from some defect of reason.

It might *in fact* always turn out to be the case that the social sanctions might be sufficiently stringent and efficient such that it would always transpire that it never was in his interests not to act in accordance with them. But that turn of events would not make them his supreme principles of practical reason or make his acting immorally *necessarily* irrational or even contrary to reason.

Baier might try to rebut this, arguing that a rational immoralist would recognize that if this is the way he rationally responds, then this is also the way others would too, and if people generally acted like that, then the commonly recognized public good of achieving conformity to coordinative guidelines would then require a very effective and very certain system of social sanctions. If he were thoroughly rational, he would also have to recognize that the achieving of *such* a system of sanctions would have to require an extensive amount of coercion in society, a coercion sufficient to get chaps like himself to act morally. He would further recognize, if he were through and through rational, that he could not rationally wish for so much coercion in society, including coercion directed against himself, so he must, to be consistently rational, opt for a society in which he would, and others would as well, *voluntarily* accept such guidelines. He would not want a Hobbesian sovereign.

In reply to this attempt at a rebuttal we should recognize what Baier seems at least to miss; namely, that this is just another situation in which our putatively rational immoralist (Hume's sensible knave) accepts these guidelines because he sees it is in his long-range self-interest to do so. If others could be so conditioned to adhere to coordinative guidelines, even when adhering to them is not rooted in the principle of self-anchored egoism, and if our putative immoralist could escape such a conditioning (without others emulating him), then he could still rationally wish that such a state of affairs obtain. He could rationally want it to be the case that he *not* be so successfully socialized that he would become a person of moral principle. He could rationally wish to be a man of good morals without wishing to become a morally good man. What he would not of course want is for this to be publicly noticed.

That this is so unlikely a possibility that it is desert islandish is not here to the point. After all, it is Baier who is maintaining that there is a conceptual (logical) connection between being immoral and having a defect of reason. It should also be noted that it is not so evident that each person's rationale for action is so transparent to others that such situations would not in fact obtain, but even if they did not, this would not establish the necessary connection that Baier seeks. Whether immorality is irrational or contrary to reason would be very much dependent on what in fact people can get away with. The choice for *an individual* may not be between accepting coordinative guidelines voluntarily or by coercion, but between accepting them voluntarily as his supreme principles of practical reason and accepting them voluntarily, but still conditionally on their best answering to his own interests.

I agree with Baier that if the *social* choice (a choice that involves considering everyone in the society) is between a system governed by the principle of self-anchored egoism and a *system* governed by coordinative guidelines, the latter *system* is clearly preferable, that is, the better social alternative, the better system to see instantiated in society, for such a social acceptance of the former would have suboptimal results.

But this does not establish that an individual's acting immorally in certain determinate situations must be, or even is, contrary to reason.

VII

I think Baier makes a well-taken and important point when he argues that rational persons, when considering the interests of everyone alike, would opt for the acceptance of what they at least believe to be a sound system of coordinative guidelines and that they would take such a system as overriding systems not so constituted. Moreover, a sound system of coordinative guidelines, and thus a sound moral system, must be such, when viewed from an agent-neutral perspective—that "*everybody* subject to these guidelines have adequate reason to regard them as paramount practical reasons." For this condition to be satisfied it must be the case that "*everybody* has as good reason so to regard them as *anybody* can in reason demand to have." This in turn is satisfied if "everybody has as good reason as *everybody* (not *anybody*) can have for so regarding a system of coordinative guidelines." Baier, again trying to block the immoralist's option, remarks that "no one can in reason demand a better reason that that, since from the point of view of reason no one is *ab initio* in a privileged position to ask for a better reason than anyone else."

The immoralist can respond in at least two ways. First, he can perfectly coherently reject the idea Baier tries to defend in "Rationality, Reason, and the Good" that there is anything properly called 'the point of view of reason'. Instead, we can only properly speak of what it is rational to do from a particular point of view, such as a technical point of view, a prudential point of view, a self-interested point of view, a moral point of view, an aesthetic point of view, and the like. The unity of practical reason that Baier speaks of is a myth. What we have seen is that it is at least conceivable that what it is rational for an individual to do on a given occasion from a self-interested point of view may conflict with what it is rational to do from a moral point of view. There is no coherent sense of what it is rational to do *sans phrase* enabling us to show that an individual always acts irrationally or less than perfectly rationally, if he does not in all situations act from the moral point of view. Where he views the matter disinterestedly, treating his own interests as having no privileged place, trivially, the moral point of view wins out over the self-interested point of view.

Where, alternatively, he sees things from the point of view of his own interests, always giving his own interests pride of place, again, trivially, the self-interested point of view wins out. But there is nothing in "pure reason", including "pure practical rationality", driving him to accept one point of view rather than the other. Whether certain sentiments would so drive him is another matter. Learning to be moral may essentially involve learning to come to *care* in a certain distinctive way. Still he can intelligibly ask why he should (nonmoral "should") cultivate such caring. He can perfectly intelligibly ask why he should take the disinterested point of view required by morality. (The kind of caring needed involves being disinterested in a certain way.) In determinate but partially different ways, both points of view, and other points of view as well, say, an aesthetic point of view, can be objective. (However, it is the case that the concept of objectivity is sufficiently ambiguous and many faceted so as to be of little use here.)[5]

Thomas Nagel has given us a useful way of generalizing such a rejection of the claimed unity of practical reason. Nagel believes that there is a "distinction between reasons that are relative to the agent and reasons that are not," and that this distinction is an "extremely important one" (1980, pp. 102–3). He calls them (following Derek Parfit) "agent-relative reasons" and "agent-neutral reasons." An agent-neutral reason is a reason that "can be given a general form which does not include an essential reference to the person to whom it applies" (p. 102). Agent-relative reasons, by contrast, "include an essential reference to the person to whom it applies" (p. 102). Nagel's paradigm case of an agent-neutral reason for action is that it would reduce the amount of wretchedness in the world. It is, he maintains, a reason for anyone to do or want something that doing it would reduce the amount of wretchedness in the world. Such a reason, if there are any such, is an agent-neutral reason. His paradigm of an agent-relative reason is that it is in a person's interest: "If it is a reason for anyone to do or want something that it would be in *his* interest, then that is an agent-relative reason" (p. 102). In such a case, if something were in Sven's interest but contrary to Axel's, Sven would have reason to want it to happen and Axel would have the same reason to want it not to happen. Agent-neutral reasons are reasons for doing things or wanting something to happen that anyone would have even if he were "considering the world in detachment from the perspective of any particular person within it" (p. 103).

Agent-relative reasons, by contrast, although they can be just as objective as agent-neutral reasons (anyone can come to appreciate their force), only commit us to believing that someone has reason to act in accordance with those reasons if they are related to a particular agent in the right way. That it would improve his talents is an objective reason, but it is still an agent-relative reason for that person to do it. But, as Nagel puts it, "someone who accepts this judgement is not committed to wanting it *to be the case* that people in general are influenced by such reasons" (p. 103). Her judgment commits her to wanting something only when its implications are drawn for the individual person she happens to be. So far as others are concerned, "the content of the objective judgement concerns only what they should do or want" (p. 104). It says nothing vis-à-vis that particular action or state of affairs, about what they should want to be done or to be the case for that particular person in that particular case. That it would develop her talents, if it is a genuine agent-relative reason, is an objective reason (if that isn't a pleonasm) for her to do it, but not a reason for me to want her to do it.

There is nothing in what I have said that entails or even suggests that there are no genuine agent-neutral reasons or that, where agent-neutral reasons and agent-relative reasons clash, agent-relative reasons always or even ever override agent-neutral reasons or vice versa. What I have argued is that where agent-neutral and agent-relative reasons clash, there is no point of view of reason that shows that agent-neutral reasons must always, for any thoroughly rational agent, override the agent-relative reasons.

I do not deny that both agent-relative reasons and agent-neutral reasons can be objective, "since both can be understood from outside the viewpoint of the individual who has them" (p. 102). What I am claiming is that there just are these different kinds of reason with no further court of reason to appeal to to tell an agent what she is to do when, on a given occasion, they dictate different courses of action. Baier's ethical rationalism commits him to the view that agent-neutral reasons are overriding or superior reasons, but he has given us no adequate grounds for believing that they are. They of course are *if* an agent is considering the world in detachment from the perspective of any particular agent within it. But Baier has not shown why or even that a clear understanding of her world (including her own situation) always requires *an agent* to adopt that perspective. Even a person who has what Baier calls "perfect rationality" need not always, or perhaps even ever, give such pride of place to agent-neutral reasons. When the immoralist deliberately lets certain agent-relative reasons override agent-neutral reasons, she need not in any way be acting contrary to reason.

Indeed, the best agent-neutral reason that *anyone* could in reason demand are the best possible reasons *everyone* could have. Where we are thinking of agent-neutral reasons and about the role they play in society, it is clear enough, as Baier puts it in "Rationality, Reason, and the Good," "that the best reasons *anyone can in reason demand* are those *that everyone* can have." But that does not obtain for agent-relative reasons, and there is no sound argument in Baier's account to show that agent-neutral reasons are superior reasons to agent-relative ones such that the individual who does not treat them as overriding must somehow be flaunting the "enterprise of Reason."

There is a second way the immoralist can respond to Baier. Even accepting, for the sake of discussion, that there is something legitimately called "the point of view of reason" and even accepting that from that vantage point no one individual is "*ab initio* in a privileged position to ask for a better reason than anyone else," it still does not follow that the immoralist acts irrationally or with less than perfect rationality in not, on a given occasion, accepting "the point of view of reason." This sounds paradoxical, but consider the fact that the immoralist need not in acting immorally be acting against his own interests (even long-term interests); he need make no mistake in deductive or inductive reasoning; he can have a clear picture of what the facts are, including the various outcomes portrayed in prisoners'-dilemma situations; and he can, as well, Plato to the contrary notwithstanding, be quite thoroughly in control of his passions. All these are plain and paradigmatic marks of rationality. In these ways, it need not at all be the case that the immoralist is defective rationally.

Baier, in spelling out the several interrelated powers that he takes to be constitutive of rationality, provides some additional characteristics or features of rationality. But there is nothing here that the immoralist could not consistently possess. He could readily apply "certain general guidelines of a culture to particular cases," although he would sometimes do it for ends different from those of the person of moral principle, including ends that might be manipulative. He could, without compromising his immoralism, also assess the merits of these guidelines and indeed know how to improve them in the light of moral ideals. One can understand the moral point of view without being moral just as one can drive fat oxen without being fat. No reason has been given for thinking the immoralist's power of reason need be weaker than that of the person of sound moral principle.

Baier might argue that since the immoralist does not use his power of reason to improve coordinative guidelines, he is, to that degree, defective rationally. But it should in turn be replied that the immoralist very well could use his powers of reason to improve the prevalent coordinative guidelines in the light of the very conception of morality Baier defends. He could, just as much as Baier's persons of moral principle, regard morality (even a sound morality) as consisting "in following what one has adequate reason to think is required by guidelines for interaction among members of a moral community" and even strive, quite consistently with his immoralism, to improve the extant morality in the society in which he lives along these very lines, while still, consistently and rationally, as an individual, although not as a moral person, refusing to act on what he acknowledges is *publicly* required. Doing this need not be at all Dostoevskian perversity. The rational immoralist (Hume's sensible knave) just wants to be a prudent free-rider with stable and sound moral institutions in place. Even with the acceptance of that vague rationalist something called the "point of view of reason", we need not believe that the immoralist need be at all irrational or even defective in his rationality. Whether such a person is someone we are likely to meet up with is not to the point, for Baier's claim about the connection between immorality and rationality is a conceptual one. His claim is that immorality is always *necessarily* contrary to reason.

VIII

"Morality is necessarily in accordance with reason and immorality necessarily contrary to it" needs disambiguation. There are at least two ways it may be taken. (1) "It is rational for everybody in a society to have a sound system of moral practices and irrational not to have them," and (2) "A person who acts morally necessarily acts rationally and the person who acts immorally necessarily acts in a way that is contrary to reason." Baier may well have established, given his reading of "rational", the truth of (1), if it indeed needs establishing. I have not disputed that, but I have argued that he has not established the truth of (2), and that there are indeed very good grounds for doubting that (2) is true.

This is, some might have noticed, in effect a replay with new arguments and in new terminology of an old dispute between Baier and myself.[6] Some decades ago we both argued, running against what was then orthodoxy, that "Why be moral?" need not be a pseudo-question. But Baier thought that he had given a satisfactory argument establishing both that we (that is, people generally) should be moral and that, when an individual asks on a given occasion "Why should I be moral?" he had shown that we have a sound argument for saying that he should; that is, to correct a possible ambiguity, if he is rational he should, even when viewing things strictly from his own point of view, conclude that he should. I argued in that early exchange that Baier had successfully answered the question "Why should we be moral?" but not the question "Why should I be moral?" In this respect our positions have remained unchanged. Whether this reflects a hardening of the intellectual arteries on the part of one or another or both of us is better left for others to judge.

NOTES

1. I am principally concerned here with Kurt Baier's "The Conceptual Link Between Morality and Rationality" (1982) and his "Rationality, Reason, and the Good" in this

volume. The quotations given in the text, unless otherwise specified, are from these two essays. But the following essays of Baier's are also plainly relevant: (1963; 1977; 1978a; 1978b; 1978c; and 1981).

2. Baier never defines "demand" or explains what he means by it or indicates that he is using the term in any special way. I would surmise, looking at his employment of the term, that he means by "a demand" something it sometimes means in ordinary use; namely, something that is strongly required or claimed as being necessary. Baier introduces his talk of demands as follows: "My thesis is that the moral point of view is properly identified in terms of a set of demands on a method for determining what to do, demands which this method must satisfy if the resulting moralities are rightly to be regarded as constituting paramount practical reasons." I take it that Baier means by "demands" here "authoritative requirements" for a proper method for determining what to do. These demands (authoritative requirements) are demands that Baier seeks to show are demands that thoroughly rational people would regard as central constitutive elements of the moral point of view.

3. David Gauthier (1978a; 1980; and 1979). It is instructive to contrast Gauthier's views and Baier's with those of Derek Parfit. See Parfit (1979).

4. It is important to keep in mind here what Baier has said about universalizability. See, for example, (1978a), pp. 68–69.

5. Thomas Nagel (1980).

6. The previous stating of these issues occurred in Kurt Baier (1958), pp. 257–320, and in Kai Nielsen (1974), pp. 473–492.

chapter ten

Reason in Ethics—or Reason Versus Ethics?

Jan Narveson

1. MAXIMIZATION AND INDIVIDUALISM

The dominant conception of rational action in recent years has been that the rational individual "maximizes his utility," his utility being measured by his own assessments of what is valuable, desirable, worth pursuing. It is usually supposed that this conception is individualistic, and those who so characterize it also have a tendency to say that that's just the trouble with it: People are not (it will be said) egoists or isolated, atomic units or centers of action, paying no heed to their fellows and freed of any binding relations to them. There is ample room for confusion here, and the matter is important. Let us begin by attempting to clear it up.

Philosophers—and in practice, nearly every person in daily life—must confront the specter of Egoism, according to which people act, or on an alternative version ought to act, only on the basis of "their own interests." But ever since the time of Bishop Butler (at least) we have known that there lurks in this phrase a crucial ambiguity. People have all sorts of interests. Some of these are straightforwardly identifiable as interests *in* themselves, interests in their *own* good rather than that of others. But others of their interests at least seem to be equally straightforwardly identifiable as interests *in* the good of others; and still other of their interests do not seem readily characterizable as interests in anybody, self or other, but rather *in* states of affairs in the nonhuman (or even nonanimate) world. Still, all of these are interests *of* the agent in question. Now, the thesis that rationality in action consists in "maximizing one's utility" would be plausible as a sweeping characterization only if, at best, we take it to imply that the interests *of* the self, rather than that presumably much narrower subset of those interests that are interests "in" oneself, are what utility is a function of. If Smith loves Jones, then Smith's utility is increased if a good thing happens to Jones (or at least certain sorts of good things). But then, if Smith hates Jones, Smith's utility may be increased if bad things happen to Jones. So the maximizing theory of rationality apparently allows the possibilities (a) that persons are rational to promote their own self-interest, conceived as narrowly as you like, (b) that persons are rational to pursue the good of (some or all) others, *and* (c) that persons are rational to pursue evil for (some or all) others, *as well as* (d) that persons are rational to attempt to realize states of affairs having no *logical* connection with anyone's good or evil.

This last possibility may strike us as unintuitive, even absurd. If it does, I suspect that this is because we have fallen afoul of the same ambiguity. If one's interest is of type (d), then we should certainly expect the agent to be glad if he should become aware that his action has been successful and sad if it has, as we say, come to grief. I am attempting to fly a kite. If it soars, so do I; if it refuses to ascend or comes crashing among the trees, I am annoyed. We can hardly say that persons may be rational to attempt to realize states of affairs having *nothing to do with* anyone's well-being or the reverse; but still, the states of affairs they are attempting to bring about may well be states whose descriptions would not logically require any reference to anyone's good or evil. We know what the flyer of kites is attempting to bring about, and we can assess his actions in the light of their bearing on the matter. Is this *sufficient* to identify him or her as a rational agent?

Suppose that *A* professes to be interested in flying a kite, but when things go badly, *A* shows no sign of caring one way or the other: She seems perfectly indifferent whether the kite flies or comes down. This strikes us as inconsistent. Either she isn't really interested in kite-flying after all, or she is suppressing outward signs of interest. We need more information to discern whether we have a case of rational action at all. And if that is so, then we may be on the way to the conclusion that utility is really some state, or class of states, of the soul of the agent after all. And then, misleadingly, we might be driven to conclude that people are really, at a deeper level, "self-interested" after all. But this *would* be misleading, since we now lose all hold on the differences we are attempting to capture when we marshal such characterizations as "egoistic", "altruistic", and the like.

In what sense, now, is the utility-maximizing theory "individualistic?" So far as I can see, it is so only in the sense that people's interests are logically independent: It is not necessarily true that when *A*'s utility increases, *B*'s increases, decreases, or remains the same. These are matters of fact. Is it *possible* for someone to be supremely happy when his fellows are suffering all round him? Does "material wealth" increase utility even if it is gained by the impoverishment of others? These are questions of fact, according to this theory. It does not assume answers to them, or, more especially, that the answers are the same for everyone. It leaves open what the effect of cultural factors may be on them. And it leaves open the question whether we may be responsive to the needs of our fellows. In an important sense, therefore, it leaves the question of "individualism" quite open.

In another sense, however, it does not. The maximizing theory is a theory about the rationality of *agents*. Once we know what an agent's utility function is, together with relevant information about his options, then we know what it is rational for him to do. Should there be utilities of other agents that do not figure in his utility function, then we also know that those other utilities are so far *irrelevant* for purposes of assessing rationality. Now suppose that we have an idea of "collective" rationality, according to which the agent's *society* would be "rational" to do something or other. There is, to be sure, a question about the meaning of attributions of rationality or the reverse to a society. But unless we have an analysis of social rationality which includes the feature that "It is rational for society S to do x" *entails* "If A is a member of S, then it is rational for A to do y", and x and y are identifiable actions, then the maximizing theory implies that there is no necessary connection between social and individual rationality. To repeat: the individual may very well be such that his utility *is* related to various features of his society, possibly including its "rationality." But whether he is is an open question so far as rationality itself is concerned.

Recently we have been exposed to Professor Brandt's interesting ideas about rationality, which have it that not only actions but also desires may be assessed for rationality: A desire is rational if its agent would continue to have it even in the face of very full information about its effects, causes, and so forth. On Brandt's theory, it would clearly be very difficult to establish whether a desire was rational, and since on his view the full rationality of actions is not only a matter of whether they are well calculated to achieve the agent's end for that action, but also of whether the desire for that end is rational, it is therefore difficult to determine whether any act is fully rational.

Brandt's theory is obviously important and, in a sense, plausible. But it raises the question of where the notion of rationality fits into *moral* theory. It is plausible to say that we really can't be sure, or at least it is by no means an easy thing to determine, whether our actions are *ultimately* rational. Perhaps if I really knew everything possibly relevant, I should be living an utterly different life from the one I am living now. But is this the sort of thing we have to know in order to determine whether what I am doing is morally right? I should think not. For purposes of moral theory, it may well be that assessments of rationality need not be "ultimate". But this brings us to the question of what moral theory is a theory *of* and to the related question of just where questions of rationality come into it. Meanwhile, it should be noted that Brandt's theory can hardly be taken to imply that rational action has nothing to do with maximizing the agent's utility. That theory is far too noncommittal for that for one thing. And for another, it really presupposes the maximizing theory: For if the point of action were not to satisfy desires, why should we bother to try to find out what we would desire if our information were better?

2. REASON IN ETHICS

What are we asking when we ask whether ethics is rational and when we look for a "rational theory" of ethics? It seems to me that the only reasonable answer is that we are looking for an ethical theory that it would be rational *to accept*. But rational for *whom* to accept? Couldn't it be that it might be rational for individual A to accept T_1, for individual B to accept T_2, and perhaps for individual C to accept none at all?

At this point, we had better make some distinctions. Being old-fashioned, I continue to accept that there is a difference between two parts of ethical theory—granted that one shades into the other, no doubt—viz., between what used to be termed *meta-ethics* and *normative ethics*. A *normative* theory is one that includes statements to the effect that certain kinds of actions are right or wrong, or that they are right for certain kinds of people in certain kinds of circumstances. (In the latter sentence, the word "for" does not mean "according to"; rather, "x is right for A to do to C" means that A morally ought to do x.) A *meta-ethical* theory is one that gives an answer to the question "What is morality?", to questions about the logical relationship among ethical statements, between ethical statements and various others, and so on. And, again being old-fashioned, it is hard to see where questions of individual acceptance or nonacceptance come into it regarding meta-ethical theory. For theories of a broadly logical character, I assume that the goal of rationality is simply truth. Either one normative statement implies another or it does not; rational choice, the promotion of one's interests, has, one would think, little to do with it. At the risk of naïveté, I am still inclined to say some such thing. And if it were obvious that normative statements in ethics were also simply true or false, then we could cheerfully, or at least equally cheerfully, say the same thing in their case. But this is widely disputed, and the disputation is clearly not without point. For to accept a normative ethical statement is, it seems, to make some kind of practical commitment (just what kind will be considered below). And if practical reason consists in maximizing one's utility, then whether one ought to accept an ethical statement, given that it imposes a practical commitment of some kind, is evidently a practical question itself and therefore one to which considerations of utility are relevant. And why couldn't it be true that A's utility is promoted by A's acceptance of T_1, B's by B's acceptance of T_2, and so on, where T_1, T_2, and so on, are different and incompatible?

The answer to this last must lie in the nature of moral statements and of what constitutes "accepting" such statements. In "accepting" a moral statement, what is one committed *to*? Indeed, what constitutes "commitment" for such purposes? What makes it plausible to suppose that the kind of variability contemplated above is a live option is, I think, this: that A's utility might certainly be promoted to a greater degree by A's performing the set of actions called for by a certain general rule than were he instead to perform those called for by another, whereas with B the reverse might be the case. And one aspect of the kind of "commitment" that acceptance of a moral principle involves is *some* sort of commitment to doing the things that the principle calls upon people to do: one aspect, but *only* one. For although that sort of commitment, whatever it is, is necessary for saying of someone that he has accepted a moral principle, it is not sufficient. One who simply performs certain kinds of acts regularly on certain occasions does not thereby manifest moral commitment: that behavioral regularity might have nothing whatever to do with morality. Nor is one who regularly performs such acts *as* conforming to a rule of action necessarily doing so either. One might on principle do such things as jog two miles a day or listen to the next Haydn symphony in order during one's lunch break, but this doesn't make them moral principles. What does? A major part of the answer at least surely lies in the direction of society. A moral principle is "prescribed" not only to oneself but also to others in some way. The questions to consider are: Which others? And which way?

The range of plausible answers to the first question extend from "everybody" to "one's society". Philosophers have been inclined toward the first, and there is much to be said for that. But we should not dismiss out of hand the more "relativistic" option that the range of morality extends to members of a particular society rather than mankind in general. In fact, the two answers have more in common than may at first appear. To see this, let us consider a yet narrower answer. What about an ethics of one's profession, for instance? Or perhaps of one's club?

Notice the naturalness of using the term "ethics" in the last several sentences. Had we said "Why not a *morality* of one's profession?", it would have sounded odd. Or it would bring up a rather different idea: that of the degree to which a particular profession lived up to the general requirements of morality ("the morals of a tomcat", "the morals of a used-car salesman"), rather than the idea of a specific set of requirements holding for that profession or group as distinct from any other or of society at large. Roughly, the reason why more specialized groups have "ethics" rather than "moralities" is that there are relatively specific modes of interaction that the members of a more specialized group have with each other, or with society at large, which form the basis for quite specific expectations on each other's behavior, whereas morality is to apply to our interactions with others in point of the miscellaneous constellation of life activities in general. In particular, morality applies to our interactions with people we don't know personally and with whom we have no antecedent arrangements, as well as to our interactions with those we do know and those with whom we have special connections and arrangements. Now a society, unlike a club, profession, or association, is what we might call an "existential" unit: Its members just happen upon each other, rather than having *joined*. Like as not, a typical member will be one by virtue of having been born into it; and even those who "join" it by moving into it don't generally sign up or work out the terms of their association with the rest. Morality is to govern the interactions among such persons. We may conceive it as a sort of ideal of morality that it is *as if* we had "joined" an association whose membership rules are the principles of morality, but the *as if* is essential; it cannot literally be so.

Now the maximal group with whom one can possibly interact is everybody there is at a particular time (Regarding future people, there cannot be interaction, but there can be one-way interaction. We can affect them, but not vice versa. We leave aside this important special case.[1]) But of course this is only an "in principle" possibility: Likely, we shall not interact with the vast majority. And if we consider what we mean by a "particular" society as distinct from mankind in general, it is that both geographical and cultural factors conspire to draw a boundary around the group in question, which has the effect of making those within it think of the members of that group as, in effect, "everyone". Why so? Well, for one thing the cultural factor of language is such that their communication with anyone beyond would be extremely rudimentary, and so the grip of a general canon of interaction extending to their miscellaneous life relations will be very restricted; and both geographical and cultural factors will bring it about that typical members are most unlikely to come into contact with nonmembers. Or rather, this was generally so and of course is becoming less and less so with the advance of modern communications and so forth. Thus the possibility of and the need for a universal morality, extending beyond the reach of particular societies, is strong upon us as a practical matter.

We need not pursue the question of morality's being "relative" any further at this point, for what matters is that by a 'morality' is meant a set of rules or principles to govern the general interactions of persons. This brings us to the subject of the kind of "governing" in question. Obviously we do not mean governing in the literal sense, in which a government can "govern" the behavior of its subjects. It is another part of the essence of morality that it be anarchic in that sense, or informal in that there are no specific persons, no established or establishable agencies, whose office it is to enforce the rules, any more than there can be such persons or agencies to *make* the rules. There are no particular rule makers or enforcers: rather, *everyone* does *both*. Morality is "enforced" by the informal deployment of a great variety of interpersonal control mechanisms, ranging from smiles and frowns to group therapy to executions.

What is the object of this reinforcing activity? It is to get individuals to conform to the principles in question voluntarily and habitually. We aim at "internalization": If successful, these activities will result in the persons at whom they are aimed intentionally conforming their behavior to the principles in question. Morality, then, is both external and internal. It is external in that it is to govern our interactions and is to be inculcated generally (and that it is of general concern, but more about that below); it is internal in that the primary "enforcement" is by the individual upon himself at the moment of choice and action. Here again we see that morality cannot be centrally administered and enforced, as well as why full moral agents are said to be "autonomous" *and* why moral principles must somehow be self-legislated. For the only certainty of conformity to be had when disobedience is a clearly available option is when the individual genuinely identifies with the principle—when he values conformity to it or the state of affairs it is designed to promote.

At this point, let us invoke the customary distinction between the *de facto* and *de jure* senses of "morality", or what we may equally call the anthropologist's sense and the moralist's sense (or, somewhat misleadingly, the 'ideal' sense). When we speak, in the former way, of "the morality" of a particular society, what we refer to is a certain set of principles that *are* widely reinforced in that society: but when we speak, in the latter way, simply of "morality," what do we mean? Surely the set of principles that *ought* to be thus reinforced in that society, if it is a particular society we have in mind, or perhaps in the whole group of moral agents generally.

Now, the *ought* in this last sentence might, understandably, be thought to be a moral term, or the term used in a moral sense. But wrongly.

Or rather, it of course can be said as a moral criticism that someone ought to have criticized someone for something, thus invoking principles assumed antecedently to be pertinent, but the point is that it need not. When we address ourselves to the question what the morality of a certain group or of people in general ought to be, we face a question of rational choice: What principles *is there good reason* to have generally reinforced in the ways in question?

A rational morality, then, is one which there is good reason to generally reinforce. Now, there could not be good reason for that unless there were good reason to want everyone to conform to the principles thus reinforced. But people cannot be expected to conform just because somebody else wants them to; and although we can expect to do better if in addition to our wanting them to, there is reinforcement of the above kinds inducing them to so conform, we can still hardly expect everyone to conform on that basis. Certainly we shall do best of all if those being induced are not just "brainwashed" or prodded but in fact agree that the kind of behavior their society is trying to get them to conform to is behavior that they, too, want everyone to manifest. In short, a rational morality, one that there is good reason to generally reinforce, is a set of principles that everyone has good reason to want generally practiced.

It is no good saying that a rational morality is simply one that it would be rational for a society in question to adopt. Morality is social, but reason (as argued above) is individual. Each individual addresses himself to the question whether to go along with the requirements his society seeks to impose on him. If he sees no reason to accept those requirements, we can hardly expect reliable conformity. And it is not obvious that "it would be good for society" provides such a reason. Many philosophers insist at this juncture that the individual "cannot dissociate himself" from society, that he is at one with society, that his society has shaped him and made him what he is, and so forth. But these arguments have the singular demerit that if they were correct, the problem of individual alienation from social standards would not have arisen in the first place! For if I "cannot dissociate" myself from society, how could I intelligently raise the question whether to follow "society's" dictates? (Note that there would also be no independent possibility of *examining* the particular program of principles one's society is trying to induce one to conform to. Questioning those principles automatically implies that one is to some extent distinct from the agency whose principles they are.) Better arguments are not far to seek, however. A good deal of mileage can be made from considerations of interdependence: For instance, a rule against doing violence to others gains a good deal of support from the consideration that one is dependent on others in multifarious ways. But this breaks down at the crucial microlevel: I may well not be dependent in any appreciable way on the particular person I am now bent on doing mayhem to. What then?

We are now in a position to answer the question about variability. Different people may indeed "accept" different moral theories in the sense that each may think that a particular theory will do the job that morality is to do; but they can't all be right. We have not ruled out the possibility that no theory will do the job because the job itself can't be done: *No* uniform rule for all of society (or all of mankind) could secure the rational acceptance of all. They could all be wrong. But a multiplicity of mutually inconsistent ones is what is in question, and that is what we can decisively rule out. A uniform rule can be adopted that allows individual variability on a certain matter or range of matters. Indeed, that is the proper rule (I think) regarding most matters of individual behavior. But that is itself a uniform rule, and is to be reinforced as such: Those who insist on disallowing some practices within the range in question would have to be judged in error, *or* the rule in question would be in error. It is not rational for an individual to judge a proposed morality simply in terms of the benefits to himself were everyone to act in accordance with it; for we are proposing rules that will ultimately be self-enforced and voluntarily adopted. If a proposed moral rule, however advantageous to myself were everyone else to buy it, is such that it would be irrational for others to accept it, then that rule is a nonstarter and it is irrational for me to insist that it be adopted. Or rather, it is irrational for me to insist that my fellow rational beings adopt it. The Ayatollah Khomeini may be able to dispense with such scruples when dealing with like-minded fanatics—although even here it may be only that their behavior is rational in the light of the (very different) values he may be sure that his followers hold, rather than that their behavior is irrational. The point remains that if rationality is the rule, then it is irrational to expect others to comply with a rule that it would be irrational for them to adopt: irrational in the simple sense that it is known in advance that what one is attempting to do cannot succeed given the means in question (see Baier, this volume).

3. CONTRACTARIAN MORALITY AND GAUTHIER'S GAMBIT

The foregoing considerations naturally suggest the idea that an acceptable moral principle, from the rational point of view, would be one calling for actions (or refrainings) that are mutually advantageous. If each person judges from his or her own point of view, and if we can expect that point of view to be different from person to person, then if we are to get uniform rules of behavior for all, those rules will have to be recommended from each of the several distinct points of view in question. Mutual advantage is a sine qua non.

But reflection along this line soon carries us onto a formidable snag. When we talk of "mutual advantage", we are obviously using a notion variable in degree. How much or how great an advantage is meant? The obvious answer is, of course, *maximum* advantage. Each is out to do the best he can by the program of values he has—to "maximize" his utility, as we say. And then we encounter the snag in question. It may well be mutually advantageous for two or more persons to adopt a particular constraint, in the sense that each is better off given that both act within the constraint in question than they would be if both act without it. But in turn, it may be that either one of them would be still better off disregarding the constraint if the other person observes it. This is the situation of the Prisoner's Dilemma. In it, self-interest seems to be self-defeating. If each knows that the other will ignore the constraint as soon as self-interest dictates that he do so, then the mutual constraint will not be adopted at all. Yet if it is not adopted, both parties are worse off than each would have been had they both acted within the constraint. If rationality bids us maximize, and if maximizing behavior falls afoul of Prisoner's Dilemma, then something puzzling is going on, for rational persons will pursue courses of action that leave them worse off than they might have been. (If Hobbes is right, it leaves them not only worse off, but very badly off indeed!)

Given independent agents who make their own decisions in the light of their own interests or values, morality, given the picture of it sketched above, *must*, if it is to lay any claim to rationality, have the status of a kind of *agreement*. Why an "agreement"? An agreement is a voluntarily adopted mutual program of behavior that includes a constraint. The behavior agreed to would not be voluntarily engaged in for its own sake. This much follows from its involving a constraint. And if it is to be engaged in, it will be rational to do so only if other persons, similarly free agents, adopt similar constraints. Morality involves precisely such constraints. And there are no external authorities, no governments or gods, to whip us into shape; we have only our various values to guide us. Either, then, we constrain our behavior by a voluntary, internal process or we do without constraints altogether. But that is the essence of the interpersonal activities we refer to as "agreements". If our picture of rationality is correct, therefore, morality must be an agreement.[2] Now, rationality tells us to maximize, and maximization evidently tells us to throw over any constraints when it serves our interests. Yet mutual constraints are advantageous. Where, then, do we go from here? Do we conclude that morality is hopeless from the rational point of view?

There have been many reactions to this problem. Some have professed to find it hopelessly artificial and abstract. Such people, it seems to me, have either missed the point or are whistling in the dark. People *do* break promises, do cheat, and do take advantage of the restraints of others. Their behavior cannot straightforwardly be dismissed as irrational, and testifies eloquently, so far as I can see, to the real-world character of the Prisoner's Dilemma. Others have cheerfully (or not so cheerfully— cf. Nielsen's essay) accepted that morality is irrational, or at least, more guardedly, is nonrational or underdetermined by rationality. And still others hold that Prisoner's Dilemma simply exposes the inadequacy of the maximizing theory of rationality. But among the many treatments, one in particular is eminently worthy of our attention: that of David Gauthier. It is he who has most clearly perceived the inevitability of the contractarian approach on ethical matters, and it is he also who is most keenly aware of the need for a satisfactory solution to the apparent paradox posed by Prisoner's Dilemma. It behooves us to look at his position on this matter and to see whether we can impove on (or, as we shall see, perhaps clarify) his account.

Gauthier formulates the general condition of rational action as follows: "A person acts rationally only if the expected outcome of his action affords him a utility at least as great as that of the expected outcome of any action possible for him in the situation" (p. 418).[3] But this conception, he shows, leads to Prisoner's Dilemma. In such situations the rational action for each agent leads to a situation in which each could have done better for himself. Since this is so, it seems that the conception is in some interesting sense inadequate. The trouble is due to interdependency. When we act independently, the above maxim maximizes one's utility. But when there is interdependency, it does not. For such situations, Gauthier formulates a different condition:

> The condition would be: A person acting interdependently acts rationally only if the expected outcome of his action affords each person with whom his action is interdependent a utility such that there is no combination of possible actions, one for each person acting interdependently, with an expected outcome which affords each person other than himself at least as great a utility, and himself a greater utility. (p. 427)

This new condition he calls the condition of *constrained maximization*. It is constrained in that it bids one to perform actions in some situations that do not maximize: Given the actions of others in the situation as required by the condition, one would be able to do better, but the condition requires that one forego these opportunities. The question is, is the adoption of the condition compatible with the general conception of rationality as maximization of utility?

Gauthier argues that it is so compatible. The argument is most ingenious:

> Suppose a person is to choose his conception of rationality. In such a situation of choice, the several possible actions have, as their outcomes, different possible conceptions of rationality. . . . What conception of rationality is it rational for him to choose? . . .

> Our previous arguments make the answers to these questions evident. If we compare the effects of holding the condition of straightforward maximization with the effects of holding the condition of constrained maximization, we find that in all those situations in which individual utility-maximization leads to an optimal outcome, the expected utility of each is the same, but in those situations in which individual utility-maximization does not lead to an optimal outcome, the expected utility of straightforward maximization is less. In these latter situations, a constrained maximizer, but not a straightforward maximizer, can enter rationally into an agreement to act to bring about an optimal outcome which affords each party to the agreement a utility greater than he would attain acting independently. (p. 429)

There is an important caveat:

> Now it does not follow from this that such an agreement will come about, for at the very least the status of the other persons in the situation—whether they are straightforward or constrained maximizers, or neither—will be relevant to what happens. And even if an agreement is reached, a constrained maximizer is committed to carry it out only in the context of mutual expectations on the part of all parties to the agreement that it will be carried out. It would not be rational to carry out an agreement if one supposed that, because of the defections of others, the expected outcome would afford one less utility than the outcome one would have expected had no agreement been made. Nevertheless, since the constrained maximizer has in some circumstances some probability of being able to enter into, and carry out, an agreement, whereas the straightforward maximizer has no such probability, the expected utility of the constrained maximizer is greater. Therefore straightforward maximization is not self-supporting: it is not rational for economic man to choose to be a straightforward maximizer. (pp. 429–30)

The argument, in short, is that a straight maximizer would choose to become a constrained maximizer *if he could.*

There are deep and troubling questions to raise about this. One is whether it is really possible to identify the notion of a constrained maximizer given the last condition. A constrained maximizer is one who performs the optimal action when he is dealing with another constrained maximizer. But how do we eliminate the apparent circularity threatening this characterization? The qualification, after all, is essential. A rational person cannot, on the view in question, hew to a policy of performing the optimal action *regardless* of what the other agents do. That would be suicidal. But what, then, are we to do? Supposing this problem is soluble, we have the still deeper question whether it is *possible* to *become* a constrained maximizer if you aren't already. Gauthier has posed an intriguing hypothetical question: Would a straightforward maximizer choose to become a constrained maximizer if he could? But is it possible for him to *make* any such choice? Why are we not all foredoomed to remain straightforward maximizers, if there is a *conceptual* connection between rationality and maximization?

These questions are deep indeed. But perhaps they are too deep. Perhaps we should see what can be done without running afoul of them. Supposing that we accept the general conception of rationality as maximization, how might we make progress toward the idea that morality— now more or less identified with the rules constraining individual behavior in the direction of optimality as understood by Gauthier—is nevertheless rational?

4. GAUTHIER'S GAMBIT DECLINED

The thesis we are attributing to Gauthier is that it is (simpliciter) rational to do *x* if (1) everyone's doing *x* (among the relevant persons) would be advantageous for all as compared with no one's doing *x*; (2) there is some reason (never mind how we got it) to expect others to do *x*; and yet (3) in the case at hand (at least), it would be still more advantageous—in the respects in which "advantage" was reckoned in clause (1)—to perform some act alternative to *x*. If we accept the idea that rationality is maximization, it is not obvious that this view is correct. It is not perfectly clear to me that it is false either, but it must at least be admitted that it is not obviously true. We shall therefore decline to accept it. We shall, if grudgingly, admit that one who fails to do *x* in the circumstances in question may be acting rationally. So we must now face the question: Assuming that morality would call upon the agent to do *x* in those circumstances, is morality thus shown to be irrational?

In order to see that an affirmative answer to this question would be overhasty, even given this concession, let us recall our earlier discussion of the meaning of "acceptance" in reference to moral principles. On the one hand, I suggested, accepting a moral principle is acting on it, or more precisely, forming a general intention (at some degree of firmness) to act on it. The more solidly one accepts it in this sense, the less likely is it that one will do other than what it requires, so long as one believes that the principle *does* require a given act in the circumstances in question.

This we may call the "inner" aspect: It's the internalization of the behavioral tendency which the principle in question calls upon one to have. But on the other hand, there is an "outer" aspect as well. This consists in one's participation in the social reinforcement of the behavioral tendencies in question: praising and blaming in such a way as to stimulate the relevant behavior in the persons at whom these activites are aimed, for instance, and urging people to do the things in question.

These two aspects of acceptance of moral principles are evidently not identical. We needn't have powerful imaginations to conjure up the possibility that someone might advocate the doing of x, praising those who do and blaming those who do not, while quietly doing y for his own part when it came to the crunch. Similarly, though less probably, it is quite possible to have a firmly internalized principle that one refuses to promulgate and reinforce. What reason will say about seriously separating these two aspects in one's own life is another matter, to which we shall come shortly. But meanwhile, since they are distinguishable, the question arises whether reason will say anything different about them insofar as they are. And here the force of the contractarian conception comes through very clearly. For whatever may be the case with acting on such principles oneself, reason speaks strongly and unequivocally in favor of participation in the activities that are aimed at getting *others* to do so. If we can establish this, we shall be in a position to put the "rationality of morality" in an interesting and, I believe, plausible perspective.

We begin by reviewing the possibilities of a prisoner's-dilemma situation. There are two possibilities of what we may call uniform action: (1) both performing and (2) neither performing that act which we for the present assume is optimal. As between these two options, both performing is agreed by all to be much preferable: For example, both keeping their exchanged promises is better from the point of view of each than both breaking them. But as between the two nonuniform possibilities, things are different. From the point of view of each party, himself not performing and the other person performing is preferable. These pairs of actions are, then, rated differently by the two parties, whereas the uniform ones are rated the same. But also, *prima facie* at any rate, the nonuniform options respectively preferred by the two parties are also preferred by each to the uniform options. Of the four possibilities, A ranks the option [B performs, A doesn't perform] above all others, while B ranks the option [A performs, B doesn't perform] above all the others. We can schematize this for convenience, letting 'A' in the possibilities list signify the event of A's performing, and 'a' signify the event of his not performing, and similarly for B. Then we have:

	A's Preferences	B's Preferences
1.	aB	Ab
2.	AB	AB
3.	ab	ab
4.	Ab	aB

What is noteworthy about this schedule of preferences is that each party prefers the other party's performance to his nonperformance no matter which option he himself contemplates taking. If I intend to be faithful to the rule of promise-keeping, it is much better for me if you are too; and if I intend to be a blackguard and break the bargain, it is also better for me—better in terms of the particular goods at stake in the particular promising activity in question, that is—if you are faithful to it as well. It may then be foolish for you to be, but at any rate that is still my preference. Thus it seems that every party in such a situation has *an* interest in upholding the practice of adhering to one's agreements and, more generally, in taking the cooperative option in situations where general cooperation is better for everyone than general noncooperation.

The only question that remains, therefore, is whether this interest is sufficient to ensure the rationality of engaging in the public activities of advocating and professing support of the relevant rules. Were these activities particularly onerous, we could not, of course, be sure of this. In fact, however, the public "system" in question is so loose and unstructured that we really require very little more than that one refrain from positively dissenting from those rules. And it is surely clear that active public dissent would be irrational, *prima facie*. For one who publicly advocates that promises be ignored, that the personal safety of persons not be respected, and that people should refrain generally from activities that are of use to everyone *including* the speaker (which, by hypothesis, we are confining ourselves to here) is, as the expression has it, Asking For It! He is advocating his own disadvantage. Naturally, he is also inviting public doubts about his sanity, or at least his sincerity, and these, too, are things it cannot normally be rational to desire.

Two supplementary points need to be made here. First, we must bear firmly in mind that when such matters as promising and personal safety are said to constitute prisoner's dilemmas, they are so only with respect to the particular values involved: the particular goods promised, the particular (if very central) value of personal safety, and so on. They are dilemmas *if* these are the only values that make the difference in that case—dilemmas "other things being equal." But obviously other things might not be equal, particularly when we make no restrictions on the range of values that might move people. The aim of the present construction is to show how morality can be rational even though we do not assume anything other than maximization. To do that, we must show how the Other Things involved will typically not be equal, but instead will favor morality. Second, the reference to "things it cannot normally be rational to desire" in the foregoing paragraph must be viewed with alarm. We cannot make this project depend on some question-begging notion of "normalcy" if, as said above, we make *no* restrictions on the range of values that might move people. Just how considerations of "normalcy" affect matters is an important, though I think manageable, issue to which we will return below.

The most worrisome problem about establishing the rationality of (at least passive) support of morality is surely this. If we supposed there were *genuine* prisoner's dilemmas involved in adhering to the standard moral rules, and if those to whom we are supposed to be advocating such adherence are themselves rational, then how can we stand any chance of *success* in such advocacy? Why won't our audience think that we are merely wasting our breath in advocating confessedly irrational action?

To this, it seems to me, we require two answers, neither of which would be sufficient taken by itself. One of the answers is that the methods of advocacy we are contemplating do not leave the utilities involved unaffected. The information that one's fellows have a disposition to make life in various respects unpleasant for you if you do not comply with the rules in question is of interest to most people because most people care about what others think of them. We are not, as the poem goes, islands. Now some will want to represent this as a concession to the insufficiency of "rationality, taken by itself". But *is* it? It is rational to maximize our utility, from whatever sources it may stem. If it stems in part from our sensitivity to our fellows, that does not make it any the less rational to maximize it. But I agree that this answer is not sufficient by itself. If it were, for one thing, it would establish the rationality of *any* rules that were socially reinforced by the sort of informal methods (praise, blame, and so forth) we are considering, and this we assuredly do not wish to allow. We want to recognize the possibility that the *de facto* rules of a given society are unsatisfactory or even evil, and we wish the claim that they are so to be supportable by reason, in principle. It can still be rational to *act* on a rule that is irrational. One might conclude that it is not worth it to protest and attempt to get a different rule accepted; but the rule is shown to *be* rational by showing that it would be rational to *advocate*, because rational to have generally followed.

This brings us to the other argument, which is due to Gauthier himself. When we point out to someone that all of us, including him, will be better off if all adhere to rule *R* than if none do, we bring up the question of how likely it is that most people will comply—since if

most do not, the case for him in particular complying is clearly weakened—
and also the question of how likely it is that he in particular will be
able to reap the benefit of his own noncompliance in the face of general
compliance. We have tentatively rejected the claim (which *appears* to be
made by Gauthier) that it *simply is* rational to act in conformity to *R*
under this condition. But we can hardly overlook the point that it must
be generally unrealistic to expect to be able to follow a *policy* of being
noncompliant whenever possible. This is obvious, of course, when one
acts under detection. Others will be motivated to take preventive and/
or punitive measures for noncompliers, and our foregoing arguments
establish that they are rationally motivated to do so. The more interesting
case, therefore, is that in which you can "get away with" noncompliance.
Let us consider that case especially.

The expression "getting away with" is slightly ambiguous. In the
main, it conveys the sense that other people will not know who did the
thing in question. But there is a different idea one can associate with
it as well: This is the sense that other people will not even know that
the thing has been done *at all*, whether by you or anyone else. Thus
one drives up to a red light at two in the morning, looks all around
and sees no other vehicle anywhere on the relevant streets, and one
drives right on. Nobody sees you doing it, but also there are no effects
at all that anyone will become aware of. This second and rarer type of
"getting away with" noncompliance is not what we are here considering.
It is reasonable to take the view that there are no *rational* rules that can
be violated in this way, because there is literally no reason at all for
anyone to comply with them. On our view, possibly, there will be no
moral rules, in the preferred sense of rational rules, that are susceptible
to this sort of violation. If so, however, then we must bear in mind
that the rational rules of morality will be such that violation of them
does have effects on others. They will know that someone violated them,
even if they don't know *who*. But the rational reaction to this is to take
preventive measures, if possible: put more policemen on the beat, for
instance, which means increasing the taxes that enable those policemen
to function; and you, the noncomplier, will likely be among those who
pay. It also increases the danger of false arrest (as well as true arrest,
in the case of malefactors) and so on. The point is that there are indirect
costs of noncompliance—costs to the violator as well as to others—to
consider. We may perhaps summarize these under the heading of making
one's community a worse place to live in. Whenever one violates a
rational moral rule, one causes such a worsening to some degree or
other, and this will be something for the rational person to consider.
The net effect of all this is that it is *not* plausible for rational individuals
to complain that the public advocacy of cooperation rather than individual

"maximization" is irrational because it is an advocacy of irrational activity. On the contrary. The argument that we ought all to try to bring about a disposition to comply on the part of everyone because we would all be better off if we succeeded is strong because we all have an interest in its general success. And it will succeed on the following occasions: (1) cases where the audience is at least mildly public-spirited anyway, and (2) cases where the attractions of living in a community of the type there would be, given general compliance, plus the information that one's own noncomplying activity tends to inhibit the realization of that kind of community and thus tends to bring about a worsening of one's situation in at least those respects, tilt the balance of utility in favor of compliance. If it is possible for it to succeed and we have an interest in success, then how can it be denied that it is rational to try? (Note that I have left out what is in fact by far the most important set of cases; namely, the training of children. Let us agree that this is not to be straightforwardly accounted a case of "persuasion" by "argument". But it is hardly to be overlooked that the foregoing arguments show (a) that it is obviously rational to implant these dispositions in children, *and* (b) that no rational adult can regret having been brought up that way, since the overwhelming probability is that he is better off for having been so, unless the community in which he has developed them was a singularly unfortunate case.) Here, then, the cases made by Baier and Kavka are, I submit, overpowering.

5. RATIONAL MORALITY AND TEMPTATION

What do I suppose myself to have demonstrated by the foregoing arguments? In this section, I shall argue that it may be a good deal more than one might have thought. Or at least, it may be something that is reasonably taken to be one of the time-honored goals of moral philosophy; namely, the goal of rationally demonstrating that some sorts of actions are right and others wrong. It seems to me that the picture of morality we have been considering does yield that result. The essence of morality is that it is a body of principles such that any rational person would want to have them generally observed and would accept that he should participate, at least very weakly, in a social system designed to bring about that general compliance. Now there are some principles that do have that property. These are principles calling upon all to refrain from inflicting nontrivial harms on others so long as those others have violated none of the set of principles that has this property (e.g., they have harmed nobody); principles requiring people to do whatever they have deliberately conveyed to others that they will do, so long as the conditions under which expectation of performance is rational obtain;

and, I think, principles calling upon us to be willing to render needed services to others when the cost of doing so is comparatively minor. If these do indeed have the property in question, then it follows, if the conception of morality laid down above is correct, that the acts forbidden by those principles are in truth wrong. Their wrongness consists in the fact that reason calls upon us to strongly advocate and support the habit of refraining from them; and it does. *Consequently,* these arguments also prove that one *morally ought* to refrain from them. For *there isn't anything else for "moral oughtness" to be,* other than the deontic modality applying to the acts specified in the principles that have the above property.

My claim, in short, is that to *prove* that a certain action morally ought to be done is and can be no more than to prove that it is rational to accept that the principles of morality should include ones which, given the facts of the situation, yield the output that that act ought to be done. A principle of "de facto" morality is one that is widely informally reinforced over the group whose morality it is and reinforced *as* overriding individual inclinations to the contrary. To be a principle of "ideal" morality is to be a principle which it would be (1) strongly rational to want to have thus reinforced (a principle which it would be irrational not to want thus reinforced), and (2) strongly rational to advocate for that role, the rationality of advocacy being determined not only by the strong rationality of wanting the rule to be thus reinforced but also by the essentially universal appeal of the rule in question.

The expression "essentially universal" in the foregoing sentence brings up a matter that I have been shelving thus far: What about the possibility of persons so different in their psychologies that they would not, for their part, find it rational even to want the above sort of universal reinforcement? Might not there be monsters, people who take such delight in harming others that they would be miserable in any moderately moral community? Shouldn't we follow Kavka at this point, simply accepting that the task of "converting to a virtue a hardened cynic or immoralist" is "too much to ask", and adopting instead the "more modest aim" of convincing the "puzzled ordinary person"? (Cf. Kavka's essay, this volume.) But is it a *question* of converting them *to virtue?* My point is that it is not. It is a question of getting them to accept no more and no less than what is specified in the preceding paragraph: viz., that it is irrational not to support and advocate that certain types of behavior, specifically ones that are harmful, be publicly proscribed. Now a primary type of such behavior is the lethal type. And anyone who seriously dissents from the (actually very modest) project identified here must realize that he is, in effect, inviting others to kill him. I am prepared to conceded that there may be a few to whom life itself is indifferent. With regard to them, I accept Kavka's restrictions: They can safely be left out of the scope of our argument. But notice that these people are *not* "hardened cynics". Nor are they examples of "rational egoism" at work. They are, instead, suicidal psychopaths—not exactly Thrasymachus's type! I submit that these are persons with whom the argument is won by default, rather than persons who should make us worry that perhaps the argument is lost.

Some philosophers have supposed that there is more to it than that. But it is not easy to identify this "more" in a satisfactorily non-question-begging way. For instance, one might express it as the demand to prove that we "ought to be moral". But a modest amount of reflection on the foregoing suggests that that *has* been proven. For it *is* part of the idea of those principles that they are to override individual inclination to the contrary. (More accurately, the principles, properly stated, will explain how much and what sort of individual inclinations do not constitute acceptable excuses from the required acts or omissions, and what morality is to override will then be inclinations that fall within those specifications; but that is a matter of detail in the present context.) If so, then we cannot suppose that some agent, *A*, *morally* ought to do *x*, but *otherwise* ought *not* to; or that it is *only* true that he "morally" ought to do it, but still an open question whether he *really* ought to. If one has established that it is rational to believe that *A* ought to do this, how can that be open? And if it is open, then should we still be concerned about Nielsen's objection to this? (Cf. Nielsen's essay, this volume.)

However, perhaps we can simply settle for the formula "rational to do it". What has been proven is that it is rational to *advocate* to everyone that they do it; but what has not been proven is, simply, that it is rational to *do* it. If we accept maximization as our guide, and if we allow that prisoner's-dilemma problems form the substrate of morality, then we must surely accept the possibility of its not being rational to *be* moral in the sense of always doing the moral thing. And daily discourse seems to reflect this. When people perform particularly vile or villainous actions, the epithet that first comes to mind is not "irrational", but rather "evil", "odious", and the like.

But the question is *whether we should be trying* to "prove" that it is rational to be moral; that is, always rational to do what morality, quite reasonably, requires. For consider the consequence if such a thing were provable. How, then, could we make any *sense* of immorality? Suppose that those who do wrong are somehow engaged in the practical equivalent of denying the principle of noncontradiction, whatever that might mean. Surely it must then be extremely puzzling how anyone can do such things. Outrightly irrational actions are unintelligible, baffling: How could a person do such things? we ask ourselves. But we do not have such a reaction to news of immoral behavior. Why not?

I suggest, in fact, that it is an advantage of the present view that it does make sense of wrongdoing, and more especially of the phenomenon of *temptation*. On the present view, there is an entirely understandable potential for conflict within the soul of any rational being. The things that morality is concerned to restrict are, after all, at least apparently profitable to the agent. In fact, that's why they need to be restricted by this particular set of methods. Were they outrightly and obviously unprofitable, only fools would be immoral; but while we may wish this were so or even sincerely believe it, we can hardly claim it to be demonstrable truth. The immoral person may well be acting rationally; it is therefore no surprise that people sometimes are immoral, sometimes succumb to temptation. The situation of the person who is strongly tempted is not properly characterized as one of Reason versus Inclination, as Kant would have it. It is, rather, a conflict between two assessments of what it is reasonable to do. We shall endeavor to persuade the agent, if we have the chance, to follow the straight and narrow, and our argument will be plausible—in part because we are to some degree in a position to *make* it rational for him to do the right thing. But if we fail, we cannot be certain that it was because our agent was irrational: He may well not have been.

6. WHY BE MORAL? A CONCLUDING NOTE ABOUT THE HARMONY OF THE SOUL

It is rational to support and promote morality; but, we allow, it may not always be rational to practice it. It is rational, too, to be moral in the sense of cultivating a general disposition to cooperation. For morality will generally pay. As successful businessmen will usually attest, honesty is quite literally the best policy. Moreover, being moral will promote community wellbeing, and to live in a good community is surely an important desideratum in nearly anyone's life. It is not difficult to accept the conclusions of such thinkers as Bishop Butler and Henry Sidgwick: Morality will, for nearly anyone, very nearly coincide with self-interest. In this, Kavka's argument is surely irresistible.

It has long been felt in some quarters, however, that this conclusion is unsatisfactory. In their somewhat different ways, both Plato and Kant have claimed that morality is to be reckoned as something good in itself, rather than in its effects, however plausibly we may appeal to the latter. And no doubt it will seem obvious from the foregoing that the contractarian project is, in this respect, simply doomed. Did not Plato himself put such an argument into the mouth of Glaucon, specifically for the purpose of rejection by Socrates?

But let us not be too hasty. We have all along been careful to distinguish between the particular utilities at stake in any particular situation in which a prisoner's dilemma problem faces us, those in virtue of which it is (or anyway seems to be) a dilemma, and the *total* utility of the individual's action in the situation. As I have noted above, when we characterize some hypothetical situation as a prisoner's dilemma, we must make some such stipulation as that the particular utilities in question are the only ones that matter, that all other things are equal, or some such thing. But again, at the risk of becoming tiresome, one must point out that other things rarely are equal in real life. The question is whether the approach we have been pursuing in this essay enables us to appeal *systematically* to any "other things" that might bear significantly on the moral situation. I suggest that there is. This relevant factor may in fact be what is needed to understand Plato's claim that immorality disrupts the "harmony of the soul". Let us see.

According to our arguments, the rational individual accepts the conclusion that there are certain principles which he ought, as a rational being, to advocate and inculcate in the community at large. He ought to share in what we may call the "administration" of morality, praising those who do well by standards implied by those principles, blaming those who do badly, and generally attempting to bring it about that everyone—or at any rate, everyone apart from himself—internalizes those principles as bases for action. And as for the exception noted in the last sentence, he likewise realizes that he cannot rationally *advocate* that he himself be considered an exception to the proposed rules, since he realizes that no one else could have reason to allow the exception. Likewise, he realizes that failure to conform on the part of anyone, himself included, has a destabilizing effect on the whole project. Moreover, he is aware that the internalization necessary for the success of morality as an ongoing social project involves commitment. Specifically, it involves recognition that deviation in act from professed principle is inconsistent. To agree that x ought to be done, yet to refrain from doing x, is to cast doubt on one's acceptance of its moral status. Given all this, is it any surprise if the immoral person suffers from a sense of tension among the various "parts of his soul"? If one agrees that one ought to promulgate and inculcate the principle that certain things ought to be done, and one agrees that the principle in question in fact meets the truth-conditions for moral principles, then one is agreeing that those things ought to be done. And one agrees that to say that they ought to be done is to commit oneself publicly to doing them. Yet, we are supposing, it might not be rational to *do* them as well. But how so? For one is accepting an argument the conclusion of which is that one ought to do them. Not to do them after all that is surely to invite tension and disruption. Those who adhere to their principles may be viewed with envy in this respect; the price of immorality will at least be a substantial one in psychological terms. The price is a "bad conscience", as we say.

Whether this consideration is sufficient to retrieve the full burden of Plato's argument is another matter: It does not obviously prove that it is better to suffer wrong than to do it, no matter how great the suffering might be. But it is doubtful that the latter is a requirement of rational morality anyway. It is enough if we need not admit that persons who adhere to the principles of morals are irrational, and if we can point to considerations that (1) make it generally rational to be moral, and (2) show that there is always a price to pay for being immoral. This is "enough" if we are trying to explain why the moral life is the way it is. Perhaps it is not enough if we are trying to talk every rational being into becoming a saint.[4]

NOTES

1. The case is dealt with, along lines I would in general accept, by Kavka in the present volume. I have also addressed myself to it in "Future People and Us" (1978).

2. Cf. also my treatment in "Human Rights: Which, If Any, There Are" (1981).

3. My references are to Gauthier (1975a). Gauthier's essay in the present volume is along similar lines.

4. It will be evident to readers familiar with the work of Bernard Gert that I have learned—or possibly borrowed?—much from him. See *The Moral Rules* (1966).

chapter eleven

Justice as Social Choice

David Gauthier

I

What the good is to an individual, the just is to society. The parallel is aptly formulated by John Rawls: "Just as each person must decide by rational reflection what constitutes his good, that is, the system of ends which it is rational for him to pursue, so a group of persons must decide once and for all what is to count among them as just and unjust" (1971, pp. 11–12). It may seem that we can extend the parallel by adding at the end of Rawls's statement, "that is, the system of ends which it is rational for them to pursue." But this may mislead; an individual's good may perspicuously be characterized as a system of ends, but it is an open and controverted question whether the justice of a society is also a system of ends.

The rational individual pursues his or her good; the rational society pursues (its) justice. The principles in accordance with which the rational individual pursues his good are the subject of decision theory, the theory of individual choice. The most widely accepted view at present is that these are principles of expected-utility maximization. The underlying idea is quite simple. An individual's good is determined by his considered preferences over the possible outcomes of the courses of action, or more generally ways of life, available to him. We introduce a numerical measure of these preferences, *utility*, so that we may replace the idea of pursuing a system of ends with the more precise one of maximizing a single quantity. The rational individual, in pursuing his good, may be represented as seeking to maximize his utility. The further complications of *expected* utility I here leave to one side.

Given our parallel between individual good and social justice, we should be able to determine the principles in accordance with which the rational society pursues justice. These then would be the subject of the theory of collective decision, or social choice. In this way the theory of justice would be part of the theory of rational choice.

Once again we echo a position advanced by Rawls (1971, pp. 16–18). But his account of the connection between justice and rational choice differs from ours. Rawls treats the principles of justice as the *solution* to a problem of individual decision. Put any person behind the veil of ignorance; confront him with the problem of selecting principles for the basic structure of society; the principles he chooses are the principles of justice. But if this were the sole connection, the theory of justice would not be part of the theory of rational choice. Rawls's theory of justice, like a theory of investment, makes use of rational-choice procedures. Arriving at the principles of justice, as arriving at investment strategies, requires solving certain decision problems. The principles used to solve these problems are of course themselves part of the subject of the theory of rational choice. But their application is no part of that theory.

In claiming that the theory of justice is part of the theory of rational choice, I am not claiming that the principles of justice are arrived at by a procedure that requires us to solve a problem or problems of rational decision. It may be that the principles of justice are arrived at in this way; indeed, I shall go on to argue that they are. But this is not the present claim, which is rather that the principles of justice are principles for *making* rational choices. They are not principles for rational choice by an individual seeking his or her good, but principles for rational choice by a society—a group of individuals—seeking justice, and so derivatively principles for choice by each person as a justice-seeking member of the society. It is the role of the principles of justice in the making of decisions or choices, not their role as the outcome of a choice, that makes the theory of justice part of the theory of rational choice.

On the view that we are advancing, meta-ethical questions, at least in the domain of justice, reduce to meta-choice questions. The principles of justice have the same status as the principles of rational choice, whatever that status may be. 'Ought'-judgments, in the domain of justice, are simply judgments about what is rational for individuals as members of a society to do or to choose. Of course, I do not claim that this captures all of our ordinary thinking about ethical judgments. Rather, it salvages what is rational in the ragbag of our everyday ethical attitudes. Incorporating the theory of justice into the theory of rational choice is an exercise in rational reconstruction, and questions of meta-ethics or meta-justice must be suspended until the reconstruction is completed.

II

As justice is to good, so social choice is to individual choice. If we think of the pursuit of justice as the pursuit of a system of ends, then we may suppose that the theory of social choice should be modeled on that of individual decision. We may suppose that, just as the individual may be represented as seeking to maximize some quantity, usually termed utility, so society may be represented as seeking to maximize a quantity, usually termed *welfare*. An individual attains her good, to the extent possible for her to do so, by maximizing utility; a society attains justice, to the extent possible for it to do so, by maximizing welfare. This easy identification of justice with welfare should arouse suspicion; we shall indeed reject it. But let us pursue this supposed parallel between individual and social choice—a parallel well entrenched in the literature—in somewhat more detail.

Extending the parallel between individual good and social justice, we suppose that the latter is determined by society's preferences over the possible outcomes of the available alternative social policies. We introduce welfare as a numerical measure of these preferences. The principles of social choice, and so of justice, will then be principles of expected-welfare maximization. But we shall of course want the preferences of society to be positively related to the preferences of the individuals who compose it. Social-choice theorists then face two alternatives.

First, the social preference ordering may be based on, and only on, the information provided by the individual preference orderings. This excludes the introduction of any interpersonal measure of preference, since such a measure is not recoverable from the individual orderings. And it raises the dread specter of Kenneth Arrow with his impossibility theorem (Arrow, 1951, 1967). Given weak conditions—conditions that require a positive connection between social and individual preference, that exclude a dictator, and that require that the social ordering over every subset of alternatives be recoverable from the individual orderings over those alternatives—Arrow demonstrates that no social choice rule will yield a social-preference ordering for each set of individual preference orderings.

The impact of this devastating result may be weakened by allowing social choice to bypass a social-preference ordering, so that the rule for social choice must yield a nonempty set of socially best alternatives for each set of individual preference orderings. But the rules that pass suitably modified versions of Arrow's conditions and yield a social-choice set are disappointingly few. Indeed, for plausible conditions, the only admissible rule identifies the choice set with the set of efficient or Pareto-optimal outcomes—those to which there is no alternative preferred by some person and dispreferred by none.[1] This rule assigns equal social welfare to all those outcomes among which any serious question of selection arises. Interpreted in terms of justice, it endorses as just any outcome so long as each alternative to it would make some person worse off. Slavery is just in any society in which the slave owners could not be fully compensated for its abolition. It seems evident that the Pareto-extension rule is inadequate.

Second, the social-preference orderings may be based on information afforded by an interpersonal measure of individual preferences. The existence of any measure enables us to represent each person's preferences by a real-valued utility function. Now, even without the assumption of interpersonal comparability, if we suppose that social preference must also be represented by a real-valued welfare function, and that social indifference between two possible outcomes follows from the indifference of all individuals between the two outcomes, then welfare must be a weighted sum of individual utilities. If we then suppose that preferences are interpersonally comparable, we may treat the weights as reducing the utilities of different individuals to the common measure that comparability affords, and social welfare is simply the sum of comparable individual utilities. These results, demonstrated by J. C. Harsanyi, constitute a proof that if social choice is to be based on social preferences derived from interpersonally-comparable individual preferences, then rational social choice must be *utilitarian* (see Harsanyi, 1955, and 1977, chap. 4).

Unlike the Pareto-extension rule, the utilitarian rule enables us to distinguish, in terms of social welfare, among those possible outcomes that are serious candidates for selection. It offers, at least in principle, a workable social-decision procedure. The procedure is naturally associated with welfare rather than with justice, since it focuses entirely on the production and not the distribution of social goods. The utilitarian rule, and indeed any rule that models social choice on individual choice, or that models social preference on individual preference, must have this productive focus. Although the utilitarian does not treat society as having a good of its own independent of the goods of the individuals who compose it, yet she does treat society as having a good comparable to individual goods with respect to its role in rational choice. She treats society as pursuing a system of ends, although a system determined by the systems of ends of its component individuals, and supposes that it is possible to substitute maximization of a single quantity for pursuit of this system of ends.

I cannot embark here on a full-scale critique of the utilitarian view, or of the deeper, underlying view that social choice and social preferences parallel individual choice and preference. But I will propose, and endeavor to make plausible, an alternative account. Once again, I appeal to Rawls for a formulation of the idea at the root of this alternative—that society is a "cooperative venture for mutual advantage" (1971, p. 4). Social choice must be rational from the perspective of each individual within society. If an individual is to act on, or in accordance with, the principles of social choice or of justice, then she must find that membership in society enables her to pursue her own system of ends more effectively than were she to act on her own, independently of others, in a "state of nature." We do not claim that all actual societies may correctly be characterized as cooperative ventures for mutual advantage. We do claim that societies that command the rational support of their members must be so characterized.

Society, then, does not pursue its own system of ends, even a system derived from the ends of its member individuals. Rather, social decisions, insofar as they are rational, are directed to the promotion of the several individual goods in such a way that mutual advantage is assured. Although these decisions relate to the production of benefits, yet they are also, and not merely derivatively, concerned with the appropriate distribution of the benefits that society makes possible, and the criteria for appropriateness here reflect the underlying ideas of cooperation and mutuality. Society thus aims not simply or straightforwardly at maximum welfare, but rather at fairness, and so at justice. The idea of society as a cooperative venture for mutual advantage links rational social choice with justice. And this aim of justice is to be achieved not by decision-making that embodies a single, social, maximizing procedure, but rather by decision-making through agreement among the individual participants in the cooperative venture. Put differently, the principles of justice are those principles for making social decisions or choices to which rational individuals, each seeking to cooperate with her fellows in order to maximize her own utility, would agree.

III

Beginning with the idea that the theory of justice is part of the theory of rational choice, we have now come to the view that the theory of justice makes use of rational-choice procedures. For we are now supposing that the principles of justice, of rational social choice, are themselves to be treated as the solution to a problem of rational decision, or more accurately, of rational agreement among individuals. Thus, on the one hand, these principles characterize rational social activity, conceived as cooperative and mutually advantageous, in the way in which principles of expected-utility maximization characterize rational individual activity.

But on the other hand, we now claim that these principles are themselves the object of a particular rational activity—that of agreeing to principles for cooperation.

Rawls poses the problem of rational agreement on principles of justice as one of individual choice. He insists that "the parties have no basis for bargaining in the usual sense" (1971, p. 139). The idea of agreement is idle in Rawls's theory because the individuals who are to agree on principles of justice are placed behind a veil of ignorance so thick that the differences among them are obliterated. Each person simply asks himself which principles it would be rational to accept in ignorance of all particular facts about his talents and aptitudes, traits of character, and circumstances. Each knows that since all persons are similarly ignorant, the reasoning that will convince one must convince all. Thus each may represent himself as deciding on or choosing the principles of justice from behind the veil of ignorance; the principles that anyone chooses must be those that everyone chooses.

Here we do not follow Rawls. His use of the veil of ignorance is ultimately motivated by his insistence that the parties are to seek a conception of justice appropriate to "free and equal moral persons" (1980, p. 521). The real differences and inequalities that characterize them are to be dismissed as morally irrelevant. Thus the principles of justice, in Rawls's view, must be related to a prior moral conception of the person. But if we insist strictly on the parallel between individual good and social justice with which we began (and with which Rawls may, to the unwary reader, have seemed to begin), then we may not appeal to this moral conception. Rather, the human person must be viewed in the same way from the standpoint of justice as from the standpoint of good. If the individual is represented as a maximizer of expected utility, so that his good is what he chooses on the basis of overall considered preferences, then justice among several individuals must be that to which they would agree on the basis of, and only of, their overall considered preferences. Whether our concern be with individual good or with social justice, a prior moral conception of the person has no place except insofar as it may happen to enter into and to inform considered preference.

In rejecting the view that the principles of justice are to be the object of choice behind a veil of ignorance, we do not remove all constraints on the circumstances in which they are to be selected. We suppose that the principles are to provide a basis not only for making future social decisions but also for evaluating past decisions and existing institutions and practices. We shall therefore not want the selection to be influenced by actual social circumstances; we cannot allow those factors that we seek to evaluate in terms of the principles of justice to be assumed in the process of agreeing to those principles. If we were to consider an agreement in which each person assumes his existing social position, then we should in effect allow the status quo to constrain the choice of principles of justice, although we should have no reason to suppose the status quo to be itself mutually advantageous or just.

Furthermore, we shall not want the selection of principles of justice to be affected by the actual capacities of individual persons as bargainers, or by the ability each person has to advance his interests in the context of making agreements with others. The principles of rational choice are defined for an ideal decision-maker; if their use must be tailored to the capacities of particular agents, yet we do not suppose that the principles themselves should be related to the imperfect rationality of real persons. Similarly, the principles of justice are defined for an ideal society, even though their application must be tailored to the capacities and circumstances of the actual members of an imperfect society. We must therefore suppose that the process of agreement leading to the choice of principles must be itself ideal, so that the parties to the agreement, whatever their actual capacities, are to be thought of as bargainers able to advance their interests equally with their fellows, and as fully and effectively as possible. We achieve this ideal conception not by placing the bargainers behind a veil of ignorance, but rather by taking each to be adequately informed not only about his own good but also about that of his fellows. Communication among the persons must be full and free; no one is able to deceive another about anyone's interests or bluff successfully about what anyone is willing to do. The process of bargaining must be thought of as effectively cost-free, so that the participants are not under pressure, and especially not under differential pressure, to reach agreement. No one is in a position to benefit by his superior ability to outwait the others. Threats are useless to ideally rational bargainers, for insofar as a threat involves the claim that one will act in a non-utility-maximizing way unless some other person accedes to one's wishes, everyone knows that no one would carry out such a threat, so that the attempt to threaten would be idle. In these several ways, then, we require that the process of bargaining exhibit procedural equality and maximum competence among the persons who are to agree on the principles of justice.

It does not follow, either from the insistence that social contingencies shall not affect the process of bargaining, or from the requirement that as bargainers individuals be ideally competent, informed, and rational, that the natural capacities of the actual members of society are also irrelevant to the agreement. Just as each person in determining his own good takes his particular capacities and interests into account, so each person in agreeing on social justice must be expected to take his capacities and interests into account. But no one is thereby able to tailor principles to his own differential advantage, since each is equally able to demand that his capacities and interests be recognized in the content of agreement. Each bargainer thus serves as an ideal representative of the particular person he will be in the social world to be shaped by the agreed principles of justice; thus fairness is assured at the procedural level.

Before I offer an account of bargaining that will enable us to characterize the particular agreement leading to principles of justice, let us note that in that agreement there must be a fundamental parallel between the bargaining process and the bargaining outcome. If society is a cooperative venture, then the principles of social choice must be principles for making cooperative or agreed decisions. If these principles are selected by agreement, then they must implicitly characterize the process by which they are selected. We may illustrate this by reference to Rawls's argument. The principles that rational persons would choose behind a veil of ignorance must parallel the principles that guide the reasoning of such persons in making their choice. Rawls supposes that the two principles of justice central to his theory are themselves a special case of a more general principle, the lexical difference principle, which expresses a *maximin* requirement; the minimum level of welfare received by any party to the agreement is to be maximized (1971, pp. 83, 152–153). Now the reasoning that, according to Rawls, leads to the choice of the principles of justice is *maximin* reasoning: choose the outcome that maximizes one's minimum benefit. It is hardly surprising that persons who reason in this way would choose maximin principles. The principles of rational social choice thus reflect the principles of rational individual choice by which they are selected. In our account, the principles of rational social choice will instead reflect the principles of rational bargaining—the principles that each individual rationally follows in entering into agreements with his fellows.

IV

The general theory of rational bargaining is underdeveloped territory. We may indeed ask whether a pure bargaining theory is possible, whether there are principles of rational bargaining with the same context-independent universality of application as the principle of expected-utility maximization. John C. Harsanyi has insisted that there is such a theory, claiming to have built it on the work of Frederik Zeuthen and John F. Nash (Harsanyi, 1977, pp. 11–13). Alvin E. Roth would insist that bargaining is context-dependent (Roth et al., 1981, pp. 174–177). Although the Zeuthen–Nash–Harsanyi approach has commanded widest support among those who believe in the possibility of a pure theory, it is by no means without competitors. Undaunted both by Roth's skepticism and by Harsanyi's dogmatism, I would recapitulate here a position developed in a series of papers since 1974.[2]

In bargaining, it is natural and seemingly necessary to think of each person as beginning from a base point—a prebargaining payoff that is not called into question by the bargaining situation and that must be realized for the particular individual to be willing to accept any bargain. In our problem the prebargaining payoff may be associated with what each person could expect to gain from his or her own efforts in the absence of any agreed or cooperative interaction. Or more precisely, the prebargaining payoff may tentatively be so identified; we shall have to ask whether there are other constraints that must be imposed on it. For the present we simply assume that the base point is fixed in some way for each person.

It is then natural to think of each bargainer as advancing a claim, reflecting his or her desire to gain as much as possible from agreement, but constrained by the recognition that others must not be driven away from the bargaining table. Since those others must expect to benefit from any bargain into which they willingly enter, they could not be expected to entertain a claim acceptance of which would leave them with a payoff less than they would expect from no agreement, and so less than that afforded by their base point. The desire to benefit maximally, and the need to reach agreement, thus fix each person's claim as the most that she could receive from any possible outcome that affords every other person at least as much as her base-point payoff. Individual expected-utility maximization and mutual advantage prove to be not only necessary but also sufficient to determine all claims.

However, we must beware lest we understand the fixing of claims in an overly simple way. In a situation involving more than two persons, each person's claim must be restricted to those parts of the overall cooperative venture to which she contributes. Otherwise, even if all others were better off than in the absence of any venture, yet some would be worse off than with a modified cooperative venture that would exclude the particular person whose claim is in question. One's claim must not be so great that it would be advantageous for others to exclude one from the bargaining table; one must avoid driving them away and one must also avoid being driven away or excluded oneself. Although this is implicit in the idea of mutual advantage, exclusive attention to two-person agreements might lead us to overlook the full extent of the constraint that mutuality entails.

Claims, even though they are compatible with mutual benefit, will in general be incompatible one with another; each will demand the most that would be compatible with her participation in a mutually advantageous venture. Thus to reach agreement bargainers must offer concessions. Given that no one wishes to concede—given that any concession represents acceptance of a diminished payoff—then rational bargainers will endeavor to minimize their concessions. Now the magnitude of a concession is established not with reference to some absolute scale of utility, but rather with reference to the particular bargaining situation; concession is a measure of the *proportion* between the part of one's claim that one abandons, and the entire claim, or gain over one's base-point payoff, that one originally advances. Since the bargainers are equally and fully rational, the maximum concession—the greatest proportion of his or her original claim that any bargainer gives up—must be minimized. Since all benefit from reaching agreement, some set of concessions is rational for all to accept, but a particular set is rational for all only if any alternative would require a concession at least as great as the maximum in the given set.

In bargaining, therefore, rational persons will act on a principle of *minimax concession*—the greatest or maximum concession must be a minimum. This principle may be formulated equivalently as a principle of *maximin relative benefit*.[3] We may measure the relative benefit of an agreement to an individual as the proportion her actual gain over the base point payoff bears to the potential gain represented by her claim. Relative benefit is thus the proportion of potential benefit that one actually receives. And we may now relate rationality, as expressed by minimax concession, to fairness or justice, which we claim is captured by maximin relative benefit. If an agreement is to be considered fair by those party to it, then no one may receive a relative benefit smaller than necessary—smaller than the minimum relative benefit of that outcome which, in relation to the other possible outcomes, has the greatest or maximum minimum relative benefit. Given that all persons benefit from reaching agreement, some set of relative benefits must be fair, but a set is fair only if any alternative would afford some person a relative benefit no greater than the minimum in the given set. Maximin relative benefit ensures that no one's advantage is sacrificed to benefit someone who, relative to the context of agreement, is better placed.

The principle of minimax concession, or maximin relative benefit, is uniquely acceptable to every party in the bargaining situation. Developing a contrast suggested by T. M. Scanlon, we may ask whether a principle is acceptable because any individual "judges that it is one he could not reasonably reject whatever position he turns out to occupy," or whether it is acceptable because "it would be the rational choice for [any individual] behind the veil of ignorance," or in ignorance of the position he is to occupy (1982). In our view the latter, which is of course what Rawls supposes, is insufficient to establish the impartiality requisite for justice. Impartiality requires acceptability in every position rather than acceptability in ignorance of one's position. The former does and the latter "does not take seriously the distinction between persons," to turn against Rawls the criticism that he levels at the utilitarians (Rawls, 1971, p. 27). There is no reason to suppose that a principle that would be acceptable to any person in a hypothetical state of ignorance of all particulars would be acceptable to every person in every possible position that the principle would license. And so there is no reason to suppose that such a principle is truly impartial. Only acceptability from every standpoint that satisfies the principle can meet the demand—both rational and moral—that we make on justice. The idea of rational agreement by all persons on a principle demanding that the greatest concession anyone makes be minimized, or ensuring that the smallest relative benefit anyone receives be maximized, addresses the demand for acceptability from every standpoint.

At this point some examples may be illuminating. These will illustrate the application of the principle of minimax concession to particular situations; they will not relate to the agreement on the principle itself.

Suppose that, in order to take advantage of linearly increasing returns to scale, Mabel and Abel decide to pool their investment funds. Mabel has $600, on which she could expect to gain $180, and Abel has $400, on which he could expect to gain $80. Together they have $1,000, on which they can expect to gain $500. Clearly, Mabel insists on a gain of $180 as her base-point return, since she could achieve that without cooperating with Abel; she claims $420, the total gain ($500) less what Abel could achieve without her ($80). Abel of course insists on $80 as his base-point return and claims $320 ($500 less the $180 Mabel could achieve without him). If Mabel receives $x from their agreement, then her concession is the proportion between the part of her claim that she abandons, or $420 less $x, and her entire claim over her base-point payoff, or $420 less $180.

If Abel then receives $(500 − x) from their agreement, then his concession is the proportion between $320 less $(500 − x,) and $320 less $80. It is evident that the maximum concession is minimized when their two concessions are equal or, in other words, when:

$$\frac{\$420 - \$x}{\$420 - \$180} = \frac{\$320 - \$(500-x)}{\$320 - \$80}$$

Solving for x, we find that $x = $300; Mabel receives a gain of $300, and Abel receives a gain of $200. This is of course what we should intuitively expect; each receives the same proportion of his and her investment. (The astute reader will have noticed that in this example we tacitly assumed that each person's utility is linear with his and her monetary return. If this were not so, the conclusion would be that each should gain the same proportion of his and her investment when both gain and investment are measured in terms of utility.)

Consider a second example. Adelaide and Ernest also plan to pool their resources in a joint venture, but here neither can gain independently. Furthermore, circumstances are such that Adelaide may achieve a net benefit of $500, if she receives all of the gains from their joint venture after Ernest's costs are covered. Ernest, however, may achieve a net gain of only $50, if he receives everything after Adelaide's costs are covered. Suppose, further, that for every dollar increase in Ernest's gain, Adelaide must lose $10. Thus if Adelaide receives x and Ernest y, $x = 500 - 10y$.

In this case the base-point payoff for each is $0; Adelaide claims $500 and Ernest clams $50. Adelaide's concession, if she receives x, is $(500 - x)/500$, and Ernest's concession, if he receives y, is $(50 - y)/50$. Again it is evident that the maximum concession is minimized when their two concessions are equal, or, substituting $(500 - 10y)$ for x, when:

$$\frac{10y}{500} = \frac{50 - y}{50}$$

Solving for y, we find $y = \$25$; Ernest receives a gain of $25, and so Mabel receives a gain of $250.

Suppose now that Ernest complains that Adelaide is getting far more than he—$250 as opposed to a mere $25. Adelaide will reply that Ernest is conceding far less than she—$25 as opposed to $250. If Ernest were to argue that he should receive a larger relative gain since his absolute gain is so much smaller, Adelaide would reply that he should make a larger concession since its dollar amount is so much smaller. If Adelaide were to argue that Ernest should care relatively little about how much he concedes, Ernest would reply that he cares equally little about reaching agreement. His smaller stake reduces the pressure on him to refuse a concession, but equally it reduces the pressure on him to reach agreement, and so to make a concession. Her larger stake increases the pressure on her to reach agreement, but equally it increases the pressure on her to hold out against a concession of comparable magnitude.

The fundamental rationale for minimax concession and its twin, maximin relative benefit, does not require the introduction of any interpersonal measure of preference. Rather, the rationale turns on an interpersonal comparison of the proportion of each person's stake in the bargaining situation that is afforded him or her by each of the possible outcomes. However, were we to assume an interpersonal utility (as the use of money may encourage), and were we then to be tempted by some principle requiring maximum equal gain, or, with Rawls, maximin overall return, then we should remind ourselves that the present approach prescribes agreement on that outcome at which pressures toward equality of gain, as measured from each person's base point, are counterbalanced by pressures toward equality of loss, as measured from each person's claim. The unique acceptability of minimax concession, at least in those situations in which agreement depends only on the formal structure of the situation and the payoffs of the possible outcomes, is made evident when we balance gain in relation to noncooperation with loss in relation to potential benefit.

V

We may give this part of our argument greater precision by deriving the principle of minimax concession from a set of conditions on rational bargaining. To prepare for the derivation, we first define a set C of concessions as *feasible* relative to a situation S if and only if there is a *1-1* correspondence between the persons in S and the members of C such that, if each person makes the concession correlated with him or her, a possible outcome of S is realized. Next, we define the *magnitude* of a concession c relative to a feasible set C of which it is a member: Let the outcome realized by C have utility u for the person with whom c is correlated; let that person claim a utility $u\#$ and let his or her basepoint utility be u^*; then the magnitude of c is $[(u\# - u)/(u\# - u^*)]$. It is evident by inspection that this captures our previous account; the magnitude of a concession is the proportion between that part of one's claim that one abandons and one's total possible gain over one's basepoint payoff. We may note that the *relative benefit* of the outcome realized by C to this person is $[(u - u^*)/(u\# - u^*)]$, although this is not required for our derivation.

We define a *maximum* concession in any feasible set C as one with a magnitude at least as great as that of any member of C. A *minimax* concession in any situation S is then one that is maximum in its set and no greater in magnitude than a maximum concession in each feasible set in S. Thus for any situation S, every feasible set of concessions in S must have a member with a magnitude at least as great as that of the minimax concession in S.

The conditions on rational bargaining then are:

1. Each person A must claim an outcome that affords him or her maximum expected utility, compatibly with affording no person

less expected utility than in the absence of an agreement to which *A* is party.

2. Given claims satisfying condition 1, each person must suppose that there is a feasible set of concessions such that *every* rational person is willing to entertain it; that is, willing to make the concession required of him or her provided the others make the concessions required of them.

3. Each person must be willing to entertain a concession as part of a feasible set of concessions if its magnitude is no greater than that of the greatest concession that he or she supposes some rational person willing to entertain.

4. No person is willing to entertain a concession if it is not required by 2 and 3.

We justify condition 1 by appealing to each person's concern to be included in an agreement and yet to maximize his utility. We justify condition 2 by appealing to the mutual advantageousness of cooperation, and so of agreement on an outcome that can be realized only if all make the concessions required of them by a feasible set. It is not enough for each person to be prepared to make a concession required by some feasible set, since this would not ensure that all were prepared to accept the *same* feasible set.

We justify condition 3 by an appeal to the *equal* rationality of all parties to the agreement. Since each person wants to minimize the concession he makes, I cannot suppose it rational for you to entertain a concession if I would not entertain a concession of equal magnitude. And condition 4 is justified by noting the unwillingness of rational persons to make concessions except where necessary to gain some benefit.

By condition 2 each person must suppose that there is a feasible set of concessions that every rational person is willing to entertain. But every feasible set of concessions contains a concession with a magnitude at least as great as that of the minimax concession. Therefore, each person must suppose that there is a set of concessions that every rational person is willing to entertain, and that requires some person to entertain a concession at least as great as the minimax concession. So each person must suppose that some rational person is willing to entertain a concession at least as great as the minimax concession. Then by condition 3 each person must be willing to entertain a concession at least as great as the minimax concession.

In every situation there is a feasible set of concessions containing no member greater in magnitude than the minimax concession. Thus condition 2 cannot require any person to suppose that there is a feasible set of concessions that every person is willing to entertain and that contains a concession greater in magnitude than the minimax concession. And so condition 3 does not require that any person be willing to entertain a concession greater in magnitude than the minimax concession. Hence, by condition 4, no person is willing to entertain a concession greater in magnitude than the minimax concession. And so each person must be willing to entertain those and only those feasible sets of concessions in which there are concessions with magnitudes as great as, but no greater than, the minimax concession. But this is the principle of minimax concession. Our derivation is accomplished.

VI

Several problems remain. First, I have left to one side the question of what constraints, if any, are to be imposed in determining the base point for rational agreement on the principles of justice. Is the base point to be identified simply with the outcome if each seeks to maximize his or her own utility in the absence of agreement? Second, I have not considered the problem of compliance with the decisions reached in accordance with the principle of minimax concession. From the standpoint of a particular individual, those actions required of him as part of a cooperative scheme to realize maximin relative benefit need not be those supported by expected-utility maximization. Why then should he comply with the requirements of the scheme? Individuals may have to forgo what we have accepted as individually rational if they are to do what we have claimed is collectively rational. And third, I have not determined the scope of the principles of justice. I have not considered what types of issues are to be decided by an appeal to minimax concession. Here I can only sketch an approach to these difficult questions.

The first two issues are connected. The rationale for compliance with principles of justice is related to the selection of the base point from which concession, or relative benefit, is calculated. As an initial approximation, the base point may be associated with the payoff each person could expect in the absence of cooperation. Society would then be viewed as a venture beneficial to each person, not in comparison with no interaction, but in comparison with noncooperative interaction, with others. But will such a venture be welcomed by each participant? Suppose that there are some persons who prefer cooperation to noncooperation, but who also prefer no interaction to noncooperation, and perhaps even to cooperation. From their standpoint society is a venture entered into primarily to reduce the costs imposed on them by state-of-nature interaction of a noncooperative kind. But their willingness to participate in such a venture, and in a particular distribution of benefits from it, may then be dependent on the presence of whatever factors forced them to acquiesce in the disadvantageous interactions of the state of nature. They may insist that they have no reason to participate *voluntarily* in social cooperation unless the benefits they receive are related to an agreement they would make either from a base point of *no* interaction or from a base point determined by noncooperative interaction that they would consider advantageous in relation to no interaction. Although we cannot argue this point here, we should maintain that voluntary compliance with the terms of cooperation—and so compliance with the principles of justice or social choice—is rational in general only if the base point is not itself considered disadvantageous in relation to no interaction. And this is in effect to say that the state of nature, as determining the base point for social agreement, is to be conceived in Lockean rather than in Hobbesian terms.

An example may suggest the rationale for this position. Consider the present situation in South Africa. We may suppose that interaction between blacks and whites is largely noncooperative and imposed by the power of the whites. Suppose that a sophisticated defender of the South African system were to point out that everyone, black and white alike, could benefit were the repressive apparatus required to maintain the present system of apartheid to be dismantled and replaced by genuine interracial cooperation. Of course, our defender would insist, the present distribution of goods and services must be taken as the base point; each person is to get what he now has, plus the cooperative payoff resulting from dismantling the repressive apparatus.

Black South Africans would be unlikely to give such a proposal serious consideration. Were the present coercive framework of interaction to be dismantled, they would not find it rational voluntarily to maintain a system resting on the distribution of benefits and costs that apartheid upholds. They would not agree to a cooperative venture taking the present noncooperative state of affairs as the base point.

A second example is suggested by the rise and suppression of the Solidarity trade union in Poland. As the repressive apparatus maintaining the power of the Communist minority was relaxed, it became evident that the members of Solidarity were not prepared to accept the existing distribution of power as the base point from which future social cooperation would proceed. Hence, martial law brought the radical innovation of free workers in a workers' state to an end.

Introduction of the Lockean state of nature moralizes the base point for social cooperation. Thus moral factors enter into the derivation of the principles of justice. But the manner of their entry must be carefully noted. Only those moral considerations are introduced that are necessary to attain rational compliance with the principles. In effect, the principles of justice have moral force; they require each person to refrain from seeking his or her greatest expected utility if and insofar as this would conflict with carrying out decisions based on the principles. For this to be rational, a further moral factor must be introduced—the requirement that no one benefit at the expense of others in any interaction taken for granted in determining the base point. But this moral factor is introduced only to ensure the rationality of compliance with the principles of justice. Thus it, like the principles themselves, are ultimately derived from purely rational considerations. It is not introduced as an independent moral element in the argument in the way in which Rawls introduces the conception of moral persons or in which Nozick introduces natural right. It is not an a priori constraint on what each person may do, unmotivated by the idea of a cooperative venture for mutual advantage.[4]

I have offered no demonstration that, to be rational, compliance requires the Lockean constraint on the base point for agreement. I have not demonstrated that compliance, insofar as it overrides individual expected-utility maximization, is *ever* rational. The arguments needed to establish the position sketched here must be reserved for another occasion.

VII

What is the *scope* of social choice? In conceiving of society as a cooperative venture for mutual advantage, we immediately limit *social* choice, and so the principles of justice, to those contexts in which each person rationally forgoes *individual* choice based on principles of expected-utility maximization. Each must expect to benefit from cooperation. Thus pure redistribution—redistribution from the base point established in a Lockean state of nature—cannot be a matter of rational social concern, and it cannot be justified by an appeal to rational principles of justice or social choice. Pure redistribution must be the effect of private charity, not public justice.

There are two primary aims that afford persons reason to agree to and comply with principles of social choice: to ensure protection and to increase production.[5] *Protection* is to be understood not primarily in reference to external threats, but internally; society protects each of its members against the force and fraud that characterize the interaction of persons in a Hobbesian state of nature. In effect, the protective role of society is to guarantee a Lockean framework for interaction. But in providing this guarantee there are, strictly speaking, no alternatives among which society may choose, no goods whose distribution raises a problem of social choice. Justice requires that each individual's fair base point be maintained. Insofar as there are ways of accomplishing this that differ significantly for the individuals protected, we must suppose that in affording protection society also provides further goods the distribution of which does give rise to a genuine problem of social choice. But then this further distribution is not itself part of the strict assurance of protection, and it must be assessed rather by the standards appropriate to production. The protective role of society may best be conceived as the guarantee of *rights*.

The goods of *production* fall along a continuum whose end points are those familiar categories distinguished by the economist—private and public. Given that protection is assured, so that force and fraud are eliminated from the interactions of the members of society, then purely private goods are efficiently produced through invisible hand processes in which each seeks his or her private gain—or, in other words, through interaction in which each seeks to maximize his or her expected utility. But there is then no place for social choice in determining the production and/or distribution of these goods. Given the efficiency of the market in which only individual decisions are required or permitted, it is not possible that each should expect to benefit from superseding individual decision by social decision. The market ensures mutual advantage—that is, a Pareto-optimal outcome—without any need for cooperation, and it does so in a manner that, being dependent only on the voluntary choices of individuals, transmits the moral characteristics of its starting point to its outcome. If each individual's base point satisfies the Lockean constraints, then no question of justice arises with respect to efficient market interaction.

Public goods, however, raise different problems. If each person acts privately to maximize his or her expected utility, then the possibilities of free-riders and parasites lead characteristically to the underproduction of public goods and overproduction of public bads. There will be too few lighthouses and too much air pollution. Here, then, is a further role for social choice, and here the principles of justice come into their own. In deciding how public goods are to be produced and distributed in excess of the quantities that individuals would voluntarily supply if each were to maximize his or her expected utility in the absence of cooperative arrangements, we must appeal to the principle of minimax concession.

In a recent book Andrew Levine attacks the coherence of liberal democracy, basing part of his argument on the claim that liberalism constrains the scope of democratic choice.[6] But of course the core idea of liberal democracy is to combine the requirement that social choice equally reflect each person's concerns and interests with a clear limitation on the sphere appropriate to such choice. This limitation is effected by an appeal to the idea of individual liberty. We make it more precise by replacing the idea of liberty with that of voluntary *ex ante* acceptance of social-choice, rather than individual-choice, procedures. An individual's liberty is guaranteed insofar as the scope of social choice is determined by an appeal to what she would rationally accept as an improvement on the Lockean state of nature. We have argued that an individual—any individual—would rationally accept the social provision of public goods, on the basis of minimax concession or maximin relative benefit, but reject the social provision of purely private goods. In the nineteenth century the workings of liberal democracy were clearly flawed by a failure to accept fully the role of society in the provision and distribution of public goods. This failure continues to infect libertarian theory. In the twentieth century the flaw has increasingly been a failure to accept fully the role of the market in the provision of private goods, which infects socialist and welfare-state theory. But the liberal democratic project is in essence the political embodiment of the conception of society as a cooperative venture for mutual advantage, which is itself the key to understanding the theory of justice as part of the theory of rational choice. What remains is to find a battle cry more inspiring than "To each so that the minimum proportion of potential benefit is maximized."

NOTES

1. See Amartya K. Sen (1970), especially pp. 74–77, for a discussion of some of the issues involved in the determination of a choice set.

2. The principal previous accounts are in Gauthier (1974c), pp. 55–58, and (1978e), pp. 54–60. An informal exposition may be found in (1978a), pp. 19–22. A brief but more formal account is in (1978c), pp. 92–93. The approach is applied critically in discussions of Rawls, Arrow, and Harsanyi in Gauthier (1974b), (1978d), and (1978b), respectively.

3. I have also spoken of maximin relative advantage and maximin relative utility in earlier accounts; let me now fix on relative benefit. The argument in (1974c), pp. 56–57, and (1978e), p. 58, to move from maximin relative benefit to maximum equal relative benefit is fallacious; see Roth (1979), pp.105–7.

4. See Rawls (1980), especially p. 520; Robert Nozick (1974), especially chap. 3.

5. The protective/productive distinction is taken from James M. Buchanan (1974), pp. 68–70.

6. Andrew Levine (1981); see, for example, p. 152: "The liberal democratic project is feasible only at the tremendous cost, indeed the impossible cost for any democrat, of abandoning the substance of the democratic component."

chapter twelve

Sociobiology and the Possibility of Ethical Naturalism

Richmond Campbell

Ethical Naturalism, as the term will be used here, is the thesis that some moral judgments can be justified and others discredited on the basis of purely factual premises that can be verified by empirical investigation or at least confirmed through scientific methods.[1] This point of view is represented recently in the work of the sociobiologist Edward O. Wilson, *Sociobiology: The New Synthesis* (1975a) and *On Human Nature* (1978). It is of course deeply controversial. Some critics[2] charge that Wilson's position embodies the notorious Naturalistic Fallacy. Others[3] claim that his position depends on the false assumption of genetic determinism. Both sides are mistaken. Wilson does appear to commit a number of philosophical howlers. He simply ignores, for example, the question whether moral judgments can be logically deduced from purely factual ones. This and other embarrassments are noted. But I shall argue that Wilson is not committed to deducing an "ought" from an "is", whether or not that would be a fallacy, and what is more important, the possibility of ethical naturalism does not depend on such a deduction. The issue of genetic determinism is another red herring. The sociobiological approach to human behavior and thought implies a biological conception of mind, which in turn may suggest—though it does not entail—the view that human behavior and thought are biologically fixed and un-alterable. I shall argue that the latter is not Wilson's view and in any case is not plausible on empirical grounds and hence cannot provide an empirical foundation for moral values. What *could* provide such a foundation, I will argue, is a conception of justification based on rational choice and a biologically informed conception of rational choice.

1. FIVE PROBLEMS FOR WILSON'S PROGRAM

Many of Wilson's statements seem calculated to offend moral philosophers. Perhaps the most quoted is: "Scientists and humanists should consider together the possibility that the time has come for ethics to be removed temporarily from the hands of philosophers and biologicized" (1975a, p. 562). Wilson does not offer a definition of his new term, but one can easily infer what he has in mind from other statements. To biologicize ethics is among other things to discover the biological significance of moral principles through understanding their biological basis in the emotive centers of the human brain: "Ethical philosophers intuit the deontological canons of morality by consulting the emotive centers of their own hypothalomic-limbic system. . . . Only by interpreting the activity of the emotive centers as a biological adaptation can the meaning of the canons be deciphered" (1975a, p. 563). When we come eventually to understand fully the biological significance of moral principles, we will have, Wilson believes, a sound basis for selecting a more intelligible and reliable code of moral values.

> The principal task of human biology is to identify and to measure the constraints that influence the decisions of ethical philosophers and everyone else, and to infer their significance through neurophysiological and phylogenetic reconstuctions of the mind. This enterprise is a necessary complement to the continued study of cultural evolution. It will alter the foundation of the social sciences but in no way diminish their richness and importance. In the process it will fashion a biology of ethics, which will make possible the selection of a more deeply understood and enduring code of moral values. (Wilson, 1978, p. 203)

It is hardly surprising that philosophers should find these pronouncements presumptuous and indeed naive. Passages like the last raise five basic issues about the possibility of providing a biological foundation for morals.[4]

(1) *The Genetic Fallacy.* It is a fallacy to suppose that a correct explanation of the genesis of a belief necessarily indicates whether it is justified. Suppose that Harry believes that he will flunk tomorrow's test. The correct explanation of Harry's belief could both explain and justify it; such as if Harry's awareness of his poor past performance and lack of study caused him to believe that he will fail. But the correct explanation for his belief need not justify it. The correct explanation may be that Harry believes that a certain fortune teller who predicted his failure tomorrow can foresee the future by looking into a crystal ball. Although Harry's belief that he will fail is justified, given his past performance

and lack of study, the correct explanation of why he has this belief does not indicate whether it is justified. Similarly, although the correct explanation of why people have the moral beliefs that they do might sometimes also indicate whether they are justified, certainly it need not in general. To avoid the fallacy of assuming that a correct explanation of the origin of moral beliefs will lead necessarily to correct conclusions about their possible justification, Wilson needs to offer a theory of justification that would show the special relevance of biological explanation to justification. No such theory is explicitly provided.

(2) *The Gap Between Natural Selection and Justification.* Is there a way for Wilson to avoid commiting the genetic fallacy? Perhaps not. It would appear that the only way that evolutionary biology can explain the origin of moral beliefs would be to argue that the beliefs, understood as behavioral dispositions, would have a biological advantage from the standpoint of natural selection. This kind of argument has been made using the biological theories of kin-selection and reciprocal altruism.[5] But why should such an account be considered relevant to the *justification* of the moral beliefs? Suppose that some people believe sexual reproduction of any kind is morally wrong and behave accordingly. On the assumption that dispositions to behave are transmitted biologically, their moral belief, understood as a disposition not to reproduce, will be selected against. Yet it hardly follows that the moral belief is unjustified. Imagine that the antireproductive moral belief is based on a concern for future generations coupled with sound evidence that certain cosmic events beyond human control will cause future generations to die slowly and painfully from radiation sickness.[6]

(3) *The Naturalistic Fallacy.* Some philosophers regard the above troubles as mere symptoms of a deeper malady—the assumption that moral principles can be deduced from facts of science alone. The paradigm of this fallacy is Moore's example of Herbert Spencer's Social Darwinism, which identified moral progress with evolutionary change and thus permitted a deduction of morals from biology.[7] It is clear, though, that Wilson's position is not Social Darwinism. Moreover, Wilson makes no explicit claim that a moral judgment can be logically *deduced* from premises of pure biological facts. Nor does he anywhere claim that the linguistic meaning of an ordinary moral statement can be rendered by a statement of some combination of biological facts.[8] Nevertheless, Wilson owes his philosophical audience some theoretical account of how biology alone can justify moral values. There are two possibilities for solution. One is that the justification relation is one of deduction. Then we are back to the Naturalistic Fallacy, and Wilson needs to explain why this mode of justification is not a fallacy. Or some other kind of justification

is possible, consistent with his scientific conception of the world. But what is that? Either way there is a serious gap in Wilson's reasoning.

(4) *Wilson's Emotivism*. Perhaps there is some way to meet the last objection by showing how to deduce a moral "ought" from a biological "is", but it is not clear that this achievement would vindicate a thorough-going ethical naturalism. A number of philosophers[9] have argued that such a deduction would succeed only in revealing something interesting about how our language functions. There would still remain the meta-physical question whether moral properties of human behavior really exist and whether these are physical properties of the natural world. Ironically, the passages quoted earlier suggest that Wilson thinks that moral judgments at every level can be explained within a scientific conception of the world *without* postulating any moral properties at all. This is not a linguistic theory, but a theory of mind.[10] Moral thinking is, Wilson implies, nothing more than a certain kind of emotive brain activity that can be accounted for without any implication that this activity is a response to moral properties in nature. It would seem therefore, that quite apart from the question whether our linguistic and logical conventions support a deduction of a moral principle from statements of biological fact, Wilson cannot easily endorse the existence of moral properties in the natural order. From the standpoint of his understanding of moral thinking, that endorsement would be entirely gratuitous.

(5) *The Fallacy of Genetic Determinism*. How, then, can Wilson possibly succeed in justifying any moral judgments given his understanding of their nature? Some passages suggest that he would argue from the biological inevitability of certain forms of behavior[11] to their moral permissibility. The following passage may seem to suggest, for example, that many aspects of attitude and behavior that feminists oppose are morally permissible, since they are really a product of our genes and cannot be altered in any significant way through environmental changes.

> In Hunter-gatherer societies, men hunt and women stay at home. This strong bias persists in most agricultural and industrial societies and, on that ground alone, appears to have a genetic origin. . . . My own guess is that the genetic bias is intense enough to cause a substantial division of labor even in the most free and equalitarian of future societies. . . . Even with identical education and equal access to all professions, men are likely to continue to play a disproportionate role in political life, business and science.[12]

In order to justify the unstated suggestion that a sex bias in politics, business, and science is morally permissible, all that is required is a weakly formulated assumption that "ought" implies "can". Perhaps it will be granted that if a certain kind of behavior pattern cannot be altered because it is at all times beyond human control, then it must not be that it ought to be altered and hence it must be permissible.

It may be objected that the permissibility claim is not really justified by this argument, since on Wilson's view the "ought" implies "can" assumption is normative and thus would have no cognitive status. But this objection seems lame in the present context. Wilson could concede that the assumption is normative but plausibly argue that it is presupposed in every serious moral point of view, including feminism.

The real difficulty with this way of making the connection between biology and morals is that genetic determinism itself is singularly implausible. Indeed, most sociobiologists reject this doctrine for fairly obvious reasons. Since much has already been written on this point,[13] I shall state the two main objections in summary form. First, even if there were a rigid causal connection between genes and behavior involving no other factors, the DNA material itself is not immutable. Techniques in genetic engineering are beginning to make it possible to alter DNA for specific purposes. There is in genetics no theoretical limit on the discovery of new techniques for accomplishing these alterations. Hence, even if humans can select only certain future patterns of behavior through manipulation of the genes, nothing in biology would limit the moral choice between these possible behaviors. The second objection, which is perhaps more obvious still, is that if there is a causal connection between genes and specific types of human behavior, genes constitute only one causal factor among many. A genotype is, to use Mackie's term, an INUS condition for its phenotypic effect.[14] It is just false that the genome of an organism is sufficient by itself for its phenome.

The Mexican salamander provides a dramatic illustration of the second point (Harsanyi and Hutton, 1981, p. 168ff). One form has gills, a ponderous body, and a tail designed for swimming; another, living on land, breathes air and has a smaller, lighter body. In each case the form has a genetic basis (is causally related to the organism's genes), yet surprisingly the genetic basis resides in identical DNA. These two forms can be produced from *monozygotic* twins just by allowing the embryos to develop in appropriately different environments. There is no paradox so long as we do not assume that genes are the *only* causal agent responsible for the resulting phenotype. This point is no less valid applied to the role that genes may play in producing sexism, aggression, xenophobia, deceitfulness, or any of the other traits whose origins have been given a sociobiological explanation.

Actually sociobiologists do not themselves endorse genetic determinism. Richard Dawkins says: "It is a fallacy—incidentally a very common one—to suppose that genetically inherited traits are by definition fixed and unmodifiable."[15] Wilson, too, despite the remarks on sexual inequality quoted above, is in basic agreement. Although in his fullest discussion of behavioral differences between men and women he says that "sexual division of labour is not entirely an accident of cultural evolution" (1978, p. 137), he also implies that these differences can be exaggerated or diminished depending on the choices that society wishes to make. One choice open to society is:

> *Train its members so as to eliminate all sexual differences in behavior.* By the use of quotas and sex-biased education it should be possible to create a society in which men and women *as groups* share equally in all professions, cultural activities, and even, to take the absurd extreme, athletic competition. Although the early predispositions that characterize sex would have to be blunted, the biological differences are not so large as to make the undertaking impossible. Such control would offer the great advantage of eliminating even the hint of group prejudice based on sex. It could result in a more harmonious and productive society. (1978, p. 138)

Wilson makes similar comments for the other aspects of behavior for which sociobiologists have claimed there is a stong genetic basis.[16]

By now the puzzle about how Wilson proposes to get morals from biology can only seem deeper. If Wilson had believed in genetic determinism, he might have argued that the pursuit of certain values, such as sexual equality, is hopeless in the face of genetic influences and hence cannot be justified. Instead, he rejects genetic determinism, and his reasons seem to imply that biology is fully consistent with the pursuit of *any* values and that at best biology can help us figure out efficient means to our antecedently chosen ends. From this standpoint the justification of these antecedently chosen ends would be a matter completely beyond the proper sphere of biological science.

2. JUSTIFICATION AND RATIONAL MOTIVATION

How then do we get from sociobiology to the possibility of ethical naturalism? To answer this question we need first to understand what we would be willing to count as justifying a system of moral values. This problem is the focus of the present section. In the next we will turn to the relevance of biology for such a justification.

In this century the matter of justifying moral values has been taken to pivot on the answer to another question: What are moral values?[17] If we know that someone believes that hunting for sport is morally wrong, we know something about that person's moral values. For that person, sport hunting is morally wrong. But what is meant in saying this? On one kind of view what is being ascribed to the person is a belief about whether sport hunting has the *property* of being morally wrong. The existence of this property is understood on this view to be independent of whether anyone believes the property to exist. From this "objectivist" perspective, there seems to be no alternative but to conclude that moral values are justified—to the extent that they can be justified at all—by justifying the relevant beliefs about the existence of moral properties.

Once we adopt this conception of moral values and their justification, ethical naturalism is forced into a familiar mold. Ethical naturalism (as the term is used here) says that moral values can be justified by empirical facts alone and justified in a manner that would fit into a naturalistic or scientific understanding of the world.[18] On the present conception this means that empirical facts alone can provide evidence that is scientifically adequate to establish the presence of certain moral properties. It is hard to see how this situation could obtain unless moral properties just *are* naturalistic properties—properties that can be identified in the language of empirical science and whose existence can be determined by scientific methods.

Ethical naturalism is standardly put into this form, and as such it is a nonstarter for many philosophers. How could one come to know which naturalistic property is identical with a given moral property? It appears that the knowledge must be a priori. Otherwise, knowledge of the identity would presuppose that there is an independent empirical means of identifying the presence of the moral property, and that is precisely what is at issue. But how would this a priori knowledge be possible? Not through rational intuition surely. Perhaps through understanding how the moral property is defined. Any definition of a moral property faces a well-known dilemma. The definition will define the meaning of a moral term, such as "wrong". Either the definition is a report of what is ordinarily meant by this term, or the definition is a proposal for what we should or could mean by it. For a variety of reasons the first possibility has not met with wide acceptance. Critics have called this move "the definist fallacy" and have said that it is the source of the naturalistic fallacy. Some have argued that even if the definition were a faithful report of linguistic usage the upshot would not settle the issue.[19] If the definition is a proposal, the problems are deemed no less severe. Provided the definition doesn't simply change the subject or turn out to have no ascertainable practical implications, it will appear to constitute a substantive moral claim that needs justification and thus to raise again, but in an aggravated form, the very problem that ethical naturalism is supposed to solve.[20]

These comments are not meant to suggest that this form of ethical naturalism has been refuted to everyone's satisfaction. The worries that people have raised are serious enough, however, to warrant exploring another approach. The one that I wish to develop leaves open, but does not depend on, the possibility that there are moral properties and that they can be given a suitable naturalistic definition. Central to this approach is the fact that there is a connection between morals and motivation. A person for whom stealing is morally wrong normally can be expected to feel negatively toward stealing in a variety of distinctive ways (for example, to feel guilty when stealing or ashamed if family members steal), be intrinsically disposed to refrain from it, and want others to do so too. On the objectivist understanding of values the connection between the moral belief and the appropriate motivations is "external". Having the belief that stealing has the property of being morally wrong normally causes the person to have the right sort of motivation. On Wilson's emotivist view the connection is "internal". Having the appropriate feelings and dispositions is what constitutes having the moral belief. Expressions of moral belief, although they may purport to be about the existence of moral properties, are in reality an expression of the motivational structure that comprises the moral belief.

Given either conception of the motivational connection, we can ask whether the associated motivational structure can be justified. On the external conception the answer *appears* to depend entirely on whether the corresponding moral beliefs are true. The appearance probably results from the fact that we usually defend feelings and actions by citing our beliefs. Suppose I feel guiltly about something I did. Is that appropriate? Should I feel guilty? If I believe that what I did is not wrong, then the guilty feeling appears irrational, unjustified. But if I believe what I did is wrong, very wrong perhaps, well, yes, I should feel guilty. Or someone asks me, "Why on earth do you want to do that?" I answer, "Because it is the only right thing to do." If, on reflection, my interlocutor shares my belief, there is no room to come back: "Yes, I know that, but how do you *justify* wanting to do it?"

I want to suggest that the appearance is misleading. Suppose the objectivist is correct about what people are saying when they express their moral values. But suppose that there are no moral properties. It follows that the moral beliefs that people express are literally false. Or, more precisely, their positive moral beliefs, implying the existence of moral properties, are false. Now suppose further that there is a cogent philosophical argument (as there may be[21]) showing that both these suppositions are true. Then any claim that certain positive moral beliefs are true would not be justified. But can we go a step still further to conclude that the associated motivational structures are also not justified? I think not. All that we can legitimately conclude is that these motivational structures cannot be justified by appeal to the associated moral beliefs. It does not follow that no other kind of justification is possible.

The only contrary argument that I can imagine is the notion that what is demanded when we ask for justification of motivations associated with moral beliefs *is* justification of the corresponding moral beliefs. But why say that? Perhaps that sort of justification is usually what is demanded—but must this be so necessarily? The underlying assumption may be this: What we *mean* when we ask for a justification of the feelings and dispositions associated with moral beliefs is nothing but a justification of the beliefs themselves. But this assumption cannot be correct. We sometimes try to justify the feelings and dispositions associated with a moral belief by stating the moral belief itself. If the assumption were correct, the moral belief would have to be its own justification. Imagine that the reason that I give for my unwillingness to cooperate is my belief that what you are doing is wrong. On the assumption in question this justification for my unwillingness to cooperate—that is, my belief that what you are doing is wrong—would *ipso facto* be a justification of that belief.

At any rate I shall assume that it makes sense to consider the possibility of justifying moral motivations apart from determining the existence of moral properties. I shall adopt the view that whether or not moral properties exist, the basic moral motivations that are shared by most members of society form a system of social control that is institutionally enforced and transmitted culturally and biologically from generation to generation. There are obviously various ways in which this conception of moral motivation might be elaborated. Richard Brandt has argued that there are six special features that collectively distinguish a system of moral values from a legal code or other form of social control (1979, Chapter 9). These features include: intrinsic motivation to act or avoid acting in certain ways (such as to avoid injuring others) and to have others do likewise; a tendency to have autonomous guilt feelings when acting contrary to these motivations and to feel and express disapproval when others are; a belief that the actions involved are important enough that it is proper to use some degree of social pressure or coercion to induce the relevant behavior; a tendency to feel admiration toward those who have the right sort of motivation to an unusually high degree; a special terminology to express these motivations and feelings; and a belief that these motivations have some objective justification (such as that God wants us to act and be motivated in these ways).[22] Whether these features suitably distinguish systems of moral values from legal codes, norms of etiquette, and so on is perhaps debatable. I shall assume, however, that something close to this view is approximately correct for actual systems of moral motivation.

Can such a motivational system be appropriately justified in a manner that would fit into a scientific understanding of the world? It will be useful to consider Brandt's conception of justification in this regard. His conception contains two separable parts. The first I call "the Hypothetical Rational Choice model of *justification*" (the HRC model) and the second I call "The Reality Tested Motivation model of *rational choice*" (the RTM model). I want to argue that these models provide the structure for an ethical naturalism that could resolve the main problems canvassed earlier.

According to the HRC model, to justify a system of moral values (for a society) is to show that its members would choose this motivational system for a society in which they expected to live *if they were fully rational*. Thus stated, the model is vague at a number of critical points. Is the hypothetical choice by each member to be made on the assumption that the other members would be fully rational too, or on the assumption that they would be only as rational as they are now? The answer to this question is apt to make a large difference in any application of the model. Must all the members choose precisely the same moral system in order for it to be justified? How is the notion of choosing a motivational system to be explained? Most important, what constitutes a rational choice?

Brandt assents to the second possibility in answer to the first question[23] and gives qualified assent to unanimity of choice in answer to the second.[24] Choosing a motivational system is identified with having a stronger tendency to promote it than any of its alternatives, and the notion of strength of tendency is elaborated at length within the framework of behavioristic learning theory.[25] The notion of a rational choice is explained by the RTM model. A proper evaluation of the HRC model would require that all these matters be pursued in detail. For the arguments to follow, however, it is enough to focus on two features of this model that are particularly salient. First, the model presents a relatively non-question-begging normative principle linking the justification of moral values to rational choice. Second, this normative principle is completely in accord with a scientific world view. I shall comment briefly on these points before turning to the RTM model of rational choice.

As stated, the HRC model is compatible with diverse approaches to the problem of justification. Obviously a great deal depends on how the notion of rationally choosing a moral system is explained. A fully rational choice of a moral code for one's society could be interpreted as choosing the moral code that best fits that system of moral and nonmoral beliefs that constitutes a "reflective equilibrium" in Rawls's sense. On the HRC model—now coupled with what Harman would call an "autonomous" conception of rational choice[26]—we end up with a conception of justification for moral values that is miles apart from Brandt's. The difference could be more extreme. Reason might be conceived as having the power to discern the truth of synthetic a priori first principles that imply the existence of nonnatural moral properties. A fully rational choice of a moral system could be interpreted as a choice based on such principles. If HRC is compatible with this doctrine too, it cannot be said to be biased against the cognitivist or in favor of the naturalist.

The HRC model might beg some questions for some people. Imagine a person who believes that moral values are to be justified only by appeal to God's will and takes such an appeal to be a matter of faith rather than reason. The most that can be claimed for the HRC model is that it can be accepted by a wide range of reflective and informed persons without directly compromising *their* diverse moral convictions and meta-ethical views. Perhaps nothing more should be expected.

It is less easy to argue that the HRC model accords with a scientific world view. Or else all to easy, since I will not analyze the idea of a scientific world view. At least this much can be allowed perhaps. The enterprise of science does involve normative principles or criteria for rational choice because scientists appeal to these principles implicitly in trying to justify their preferences among competing scientific hypotheses and associated research projects. The HRC model therefore cannot be regarded as alien to this enterprise simply because it is normative or because it defines justification by rational choice. Nor can it be successfully maintained that rational choice in the HRC model presupposes a subject matter or aims that are alien to science. The subject of the choice is a motivational system in a society. There is nothing here that is not in principle amenable to scientific investigation. In particular, it is not assumed that there exist moral properties corresponding to our notions of "right" and "wrong". Moreover, the aims of the choice are left entirely unspecified in the model. The HRC model itself does not require, for example, that the aim of a rational choice among moral systems have the property of being morally good.

To provide a structure for ethical naturalism, the HRC model must be supplemented with a suitable account of rational choice. In Brandt's RTM model the rationality of an agent's choice is analyzed into two components: rationality of the tendency to make that choice, given the agent's desires and aversions, and the rationality of these desires and aversions. Very roughly, an action-tendency is rational when it is stronger than its competitors and the agent's expectations are as accurate as possible, within the limits of available information, regarding the likely effects of the various choices on the things that the agent desires to have or avoid. The desires and aversions themselves are rational when, again very roughly, they would survive vivid and repeated awareness of relevant information, especially as it pertains to how they were learned (1979, chapters 5 and 6). (Given Brandt's definitions and his learning theory, rational desires and aversions cannot have been learned through a conditioning process that has misrepresented reality. An aversion to all fish, for example, learned through an unrepresentative experience of tasting fish as a child would be an irrational aversion, since it would be extinguished, according to this learning theory, by a conditioning process involving more representative information.) A choice qualifies as fully rational when the action-tendency that results in this choice is rational, given the agent's desires and aversions, and these desires and aversions are themselves rational.

A fully rational choice, in sum, is a choice that is rationally motivated, and rational motivation is motivation that would pass certain tests. These tests appear to be such that there can be empirical evidence adequate to establish that certain motivation is rational. It appears, then, that Brandt has given a naturalistic definition of a fully rational choice. Does it follow that this definition of rational choice, when combined with the HRC model of justification, places ethics within a scientific conception of the world?

A standard move that may be made at this point is to question the status of the definition that has been offered.[27] Is Brandt trying to report ordinary usage of words like "rational"? He explicitly rejects this possibility. The definition contained in the RTM model is therefore to be viewed as a proposal for what we could or should mean. But here he faces a dilemma. He cannot just stipulate what "rational choice" means, on pain of begging the question of what is to count as a justified system of moral values. His is after all only one of many possible proposals. If, on the other hand, he defends his proposal by taking a moral stand on the issue of what is to count as a justified system of moral value, then he cannot be relying merely on a scientific conception of the world.

Although this style of objection is often extremely effective (it is essentially an extension of Moore's open-question argument), it misses the mark in this instance. We should not accuse Brandt of begging the question unless we can assume that he has no reason for accepting the RTM model other than its having certain moral implications. This is the assumption behind the second horn of the dilemma. In fact, it is not clear, independently of considerable empirical investigation, just what the implications of the model really are. The most that a critic can say a priori is that *for all we know now* the models may lead to the justification of such and such moral values. That by itself doesn't show that these models beg any moral questions.

Even if relevant empirical studies were to show that the models yield surprising conclusions about what moral values are justified, that fact alone would not make the models question-begging. There is no reason why a philosophical theory of justification, in this case a naturalistic one, should not yield surprising, perhaps uncomfortable, conclusions. The point of such a theory is not to reinforce our preexisting moral biases.

A good naturalistic account of rational motivation must obviously be more than non-question-begging. It should illuminate the nature of rational motiviation. A sure way to do that is to be itself a part of a successful scientific theory of human motivation. By incorporating concepts from learning theory, Brandt has made some progress in this direction. Unfortunately there are difficulties, since the RTM model is not itself a part of that theory, and the theory is at best moderately successful in explaining human behavior. Here objections to the RTM model are on much firmer ground, but notice that the objections of this kind are essentially from *within* a scientific conception of the world. The question whether some model of rational motivation can be scientifically illuminating is a *scientific* problem.[28] In this respect the success of the present approach to ethical naturalism depends fundamentally on scientific developments in the study of reasoned motivation.[29]

There can be no doubt that within the context of the HRC model any account of rational motivation will have a normative aspect. But this is no objection. In fact, empirical studies can illuminate the *normative* character of rational motivation by making its attractiveness as a norm for behavior more intelligible. Since sociobiological studies provide a case in point, it is worth making clear how this is possible.

3. THE RELEVANCE OF BIOLOGY
FOR RATIONAL MOTIVATION

It is widely accepted that a rationally motivated agent would choose the most efficient means to achieving her ends.[30] In a variant terminology, a rationally motivated agent seeks to maximize her expected utility. This conception of rationality is sometimes called *rational egoism*.[31] For the sake of familiarity I shall retain this terminology, although it is misleading. The agent's ends may be extremely unselfish; there is no restriction on their content. A person can deliberately sacrifice her own interest, narrowly construed, and do so through an exercise of rational egoism.

It is well known that there are conceptual puzzles surrounding the standard of rational egoism. These reflect on Brandt's RTM model, since rational egoism is a component of his conception of a "fully rational" choice. Full rationality is roughly rational egoism with the qualification that the agent's ends are themselves rational. Although we have noted how full rationality, when completely unpacked, is defined according to various empirical tests, this standard of rationality is also intended as a normative ideal to be used in justifying choices and indeed moral values. To the extent that egoistic rationality is not defensible as a *norm*, the RTM model will not be either.

A central problem for rational egoism is its application to a choice situation in which the expectations and possible outcomes for the agents form the structure of a Prisoner's Dilemma (PD).[32] The problem is that rational egoists will do worse for themselves in the context of a single PD or even a finite series of PDs than they would have if they both acted contrary to rational egoism. How can rational egoists defeat their own ends when they are in full possession of the facts and are acting in accord with rational egoism? A partial answer is that the agents must, as the problem is defined, assume that their actions are probabilistically independent.[33] Once we bear firmly in mind the independence stipulation, we see that rational egoists cannot, consistent with this restriction, count on each other's cooperation in reaching a mutually superior outcome; they must choose not to cooperate. But this line of reasoning merely restates the problem. It is possible to know why rational egoists must defeat their own ends in a PD yet to remain puzzled. A source of puzzlement may be the sense that somehow the norm of rational action has been misconceived. A satisfactory norm, it seems, should not be self-defeating in this way.

It is unclear, however, whether a better norm of rationality is possible. Presumably what is felt to be inadequate about rational egoism in this instance is its self-defeating character. Yet in making that criticism one would seem to be assuming the *same* standard of rationality that one is criticizing, since one would be arguing that decisions would be more "rational" if individual agents were more likely to achieve their ends. The ideal of maximizing expected individual utility *is* the norm that produces the problem in the first place.

Another aspect of the puzzle is contained in an analogy that philosophers have drawn between cooperative action in a PD and instances of moral action that require restraint in the pursuit of individual ends.[34] The analogy is that morality like cooperation is advantageous just because it requires restraint. Agents in a PD will achieve more of their ends acting cooperatively than acting noncooperatively, just as agents in a society will achieve more through a system of moral restraints than they would without them. Nevertheless, both cooperation and moral action demand restraint. Given that others are acting cooperatively or morally in society, there are instances in which an agent stands to achieve even more through acting noncooperatively or immorally. It follows from this analogy that moral action diverges in certain cases from action that meets the standard of rational egoism. If rational egoism is the most nearly acceptable standard that we have for rational action, there would appear to be no way that moral action can be rationally justified in the divergent cases. This conclusion is disconcerting, for we would like to believe that a person who is rational could be motivated in these cases to act morally.

Can biology be relevant to normative issues of this kind? There is a striking similarity in structure between these puzzles and problems that biologists have had in explaining the evolution of altruistic animal behavior through natural selection. An animal's behavior is said to be biologically altruistic if it increases the biological fitness of another organism at a net cost to its own fitness. This definition of altruistic behavior makes its existence puzzling. Although instances of altruistic behavior are evident throughout nature, how could it have evolved if natural selection favors the most fit individuals? From the definition of biological altruism, one would expect the most fit individuals to be the *least* altruistic. To put the problem another way, we can say that one behavior will be selected over another if it can be expected to add more to an individual's fitness; yet altruistic behavior is selected over nonaltruistic behavior even though the former can be expected to add less to an individual's fitness. Now consider the analogue for egoistic rationality. To state that problem we need only take the sentence before the last and substitute "more rational than" for "selected over", "utility" for "fitness", and "cooperative" (or "moral") for "altruistic". Given the structural similarity of the problems, a solution to one may suggest a solution to the other.

One solution that biologists have offered to explain the biological altruism is kin-selection (Hamilton, 1964). This theory is used to explain the altruism of one organism toward another genetically similar organism. Although the fitness of the individual making the sacrifice is lowered by an altruistic act, the fitness of the benefited individuals, who are likely to have the same genes and hence genes *for altruism*, is increased— and thus altruism toward genetically related individuals tends to be favored in natural selection. This mechanism of course does not explain why genetically unrelated individuals, such as individuals from different species, should ever behave altruistically toward each other. Keeping in mind the possible relevance of biology for rational egoism, suppose that two genetically unrelated individuals are in a PD situation. That is, the causal mechanisms governing their interaction are such that their individual choices between two forms of behavior are probabilistically independent and the possible payoffs in levels of fitness that will be the outcome of their choices have the characteristic PD structure. Biologists have in fact identified numerous cases of cooperative behavior that fit these constraints, sometimes where the individuals are of different species.

This kind of mutual cooperation has been called reciprocal altruism (Trivers, 1971). Since mutual cooperation is biologically better than mutual noncooperation, according to the payoffs in individual fitness, it is tempting to infer that cooperative behavior must be selected for in these instances. But that inference appears to contradict orthodox Darwinian theory, which implies that the selection pressure is primarily on the *individual* organism. In a PD situation an individual will benefit more in fitness from noncooperation than from cooperation, no matter which choice the other organism takes. Hence, mutual noncooperation should be selected, although in actuality the reverse is true.

Since there is some uncertainty in the biological literature on this point,[35] it is worth emphasizing that cooperative behavior in a PD situation fits the biological definition of altruism. If organism *A* behaves cooperatively, organism *B* will have a *higher* level of fitness and *A* will have a *lower* level of fitness (than if *A* had behaved noncooperatively) no matter which choice *B* makes. In other words, *A*'s cooperation produces a net gain in fitness for *B* and a net loss for *A*. The explanation of mutual cooperation in such cases is a genuine challenge to the orthodox understanding of natural selection.

This challenge is indeed virtually identical to the difficulty of explaining how mutual cooperation in a PD is individually rational—rational according rational egoism—given payoffs measured in units of individual utility. Natural selection favors the behavior with the higher expected individual fitness; rational egoism favors the behavior with the higher expected individual utility. The reciprocal altruism of mutual cooperation has neither higher expected individual fitness nor higher expected individual utility. To ask how reciprocal altruism is possible in nature on the assumption that nature has evolved through natural selection is only superficially different from asking how reciprocal altruism is rationally possible on the assumption that rationality is rational egoism.

Biologists like game theorists have found it useful to think of PDs in the context of a series of PD choices involving sometimes the same and sometimes different individuals. From this perspective it is possible to consider decision strategies governing all the choices in the series, and the central question becomes: Which overall strategy has the greatest expected individual fitness or utility? If the same two individuals are matched in a predetermined number of PD games, it is easily shown that a strategy of pure noncooperation—that is, never cooperating, has the highest expected individual score (in fitness or utility.).[36] Cooperation in such a case would be no less paradoxical than before. The assumption of a predetermined number of interactions between the same individuals, however, is not congenial to mathematical models used to analyze the forces of natural selection. In these models, interactions between the same individuals is viewed as having a fixed probability rather than being certain. When this characteristically biological approach is taken, it can be seen that pure noncooperation is no longer the overall best strategy, either from the standpoint of natural selection or rational egoism.

In a sophisticated treatment of the evolution of cooperation along these lines, Robert Axelrod and William Hamilton have argued (1981, and Axelrod, 1984) that a strategy of limited cooperation, known to game theorists as Tit for Tat (TFT), has the biological virtues of *stability, robustness,* and *viability* and has a surprisingly wide range of applications, including behavioral interactions at the microbial level. TFT is the strategy: Cooperate in the initial interaction with any given individual and thereafter do whatever that individual did in your previous interaction. For a strategy to qualify as evolutionarily stable, it must be shown that a population using this strategy cannot be "invaded" by a rare mutant adopting a different strategy. Axelrod and Hamilton provide a proof of the evolutionary stability of TFT assuming that the probability of interaction between the same individuals is greater than a certain value that is a precise function of the possible payoff values.[37] Pure noncooperation, however, is also an evolutionarily stable strategy. To show the superiority of TFT, the authors argue for its robustness on the basis of computer simulations. These show that in a variegated environment composed of individuals using a wide variety of more or less sophisticated strategies, including the simple strategy of pure noncooperation, individuals using TFT would eventually displace all other individuals in the population. In a more elaborate mathematical model mechanisms are included, based on kin-selection and "clustering", to explain how the TFT strategy might get started in an initially noncooperative environment. It turns out that these mechanisms for establishing the initial viability of TFT cannot be applied in the reverse situation to demonstrate the initial viability of pure noncooperation in an environment composed of TFTers. As Axelrod and Hamilton put it, "the gear wheels of social evolution include a ratchet."

The mathematical model that dissolves the paradox of biological altruism in PD interactions simultaneously demonstrates how continued mutual cooperation in such interactions is consistent with rational egoism. Given a series of PDs with a sufficient probability of the same persons interacting, the TFT strategy produces more expected individual utility than any of a wide variety of competing strategies, and it does better than any other possible strategy when most interactants are TFTers. It follows that rational egoism favors TFTing above other strategies if the probability of "rematches" is great enough. *In such cases mutual cooperation between TFTers is rational cooperation according to rational egoism.* The norm of rational egoism, applied in contexts that are realistic regarding severity of competition and density of social interaction, is thus vindicated in face of the two challenges noted earlier. It is not self-defeating in a context of realistic PD interactions, and it is consistent with cooperative restraint in the pursuit of individual ends—a restraint that is commonly thought to be paradigmatic of moral action. Since the vindication of rational egoism in these respects arises directly from the biological explanation of how cooperation has evolved, the example shows how a biological explanation can vindicate a norm for rationality.

It is theoretically possible for the tie between biological explanation and rational explanation to be tighter than I have suggested. Suppose that people's goals are to have things that in fact happen to be to their biological advantage.[38] Let us imagine, that is, that individual utility correlates extremely well with biological fitness. (Perhaps at some point in the past a good correlation of this kind existed; but imagine that it exists now.) Further suppose that people find themselves in PD interactions of the sort contemplated above. Assume finally that natural selection is a true account of the evolution of behavior. (Specifically assume that the Axelrod-Hamilton model holds true.) Then it follows that TFTing will be selected for and also that rational egoism will be selected for, since TFTing maximizes expected individual utility. In sum, the biological explanation of mutual cooperation in PDs would be identical in fact with the rational explanation of this behavior. If rational egoism is a norm that justifies behavior, then the biological explanation of this behavior would be its rational justification.

Although it is not generally believed that the evolution of human behavior is entirely biological, the theoretical possibility just described shows that it is at least in principle possible for the justification of behavior to be the correct explanation of its existence. Essentially the same point could be made if we assume that behavior is culturally transmitted over time according to some measure of cultural fitness M. If conscious goals correlate well with M, then the same mathematical model applied to the same PD choice structures will again select for TFTing and rational egoism. The general lesson is that if the norm of rationality is rational egoism, and if there is *some* mechanism of selective transmission of behavior over time, an evolutionary explanation of behavior *can* be its justification. If the HRC model of moral justification is acceptable, it is possible then that an evolutionary explanation of behavior can be its *moral* justification.

Some reasons have been considered for not identifying rational motivation with rational egoism. In this section I have addressed the question whether rational egoism is coherent, and I have outlined a biological answer. But there is another worry. One may feel that no standard of rationality can be an acceptable criterion for moral justification in the context of the HRC model unless that standard contains some element of altruistic motivation. Since rational egoism places no restriction on the content of an agent's ends, one might argue that it does not contain any element of altruistic motivation and hence cannot be acceptable for the purpose of moral justification. But doesn't rational egoism lead to cooperation? The TFT strategy, it may be answered, is still only an efficient means of maximizing *individual* utility. A rational egoist's TFTing therefore is not real altruism.

In reply to this objection I am tempted to argue as follows. I behave altruistically if my behavior yields a net gain to another at a net cost to myself. Choosing cooperation over noncooperation in a PD provides a net gain for the other party and a net loss for me, no matter whether or not the other party cooperates. Thus in cooperating I behave altruistically. Since rational egoism favors the TFT strategy, which in turn implies frequent cooperation, it is false that rational egoism contains no element of genuine altruism.

This argument is flawed because it implies that the relevant choice is between cooperation and noncooperation in a given PD interaction. Instead, the relevant choice is among TFT and various competing strategies. If TFT maximizes expected individual utility, how can the choice of that strategy entail any *sacrifice* of utility for the benefit of another? If it can't, then how can it be altruistic? Imagine a series of PD interactions between the *same* TFTers. Here there is no advantage to noncooperation and a great advantage to cooperation, more so the greater the number of repetitions. (A first act of noncooperation provides the best outcome on that occasion, but it provokes noncooperation by the other party on the next occasion with the second worst outcome and similarly thereafter, until the initial noncooperator resumes cooperation by paying the price of accepting the worst outcome.) In effect, nothing is sacrificed and hence no altruism exists in the continued cooperation of TFTers who expect to meet again.

Nevertheless, the rational egoist's use of TFT in a population of individuals with various competing strategies does constitute altruism toward many *other* individuals. In interactions with pure cooperators, for example, the fact that the rational egoist has chosen TFT over pure noncooperation yields a net gain to the pure cooperator at a net cost to the rational egoist. Even the pure noncooperator is treated with some degree of altruism, since the pure noncooperator does better than if the opposing strategy were also one of pure noncooperation. Similarly, another TFTer who is encountered just once does better than if the opposing strategy were one of pure noncooperation. Therefore, it is false that rational egoism contains no element of altruism. Rational egoism like some moral standards entails a limited altruism, but altruism nonetheless.

Discussion has focused on behavior rather than on any conscious goals that may lie behind it. Must the rational egoist's conscious goals be altruistic? The question is tricky. The payoff structure in the PD is supposed to reflect all the agent's interests in the possible outcomes, and the content of these interests has been left open. The question, however, can be usefully interpreted as a question about the agent's attitude toward conflict. In a PD the preferences of the agents, even when each agent has altruistic goals, are partly in conflict. What kind of attitude can a consistent TFTer be expected to have in such cases? Should we expect a steadfast TFTer to respect the preferences of others, even opposing ones, and to strive for mutual cooperation?

It would appear so. Consider the temptation to defect. To cooperate is to run the risk of getting the sucker payoff, knowing that the other party's choice is probabilistically independent and that you may not meet again. There will be times when a TFTer will receive several sucker payoffs in a row from different noncooperators. Some TFTers will be known not to have survived. (The robustness of TFTing does not guarantee that all TFTers will prosper.) Obviously the temptation to defect on a first encounter will be at times severe if the rational egoist is conscious and psychologically like us. It would be difficult to explain her steadfast policy of cooperating first unless we ascribe to her a strong measure of good will and respect for the preferences of others. The rationality appropriate to the justification of moral codes may not require a greater regard for others.

4. ARE THE MAIN PROBLEMS RESOLVED?

Five objections to Wilson's program were presented in the first section of this essay. By implication, these objections have been answered in the course of the last two sections.

(1) In the previous section I argued that it is theoretically possible for a biological explanation of the evolution of behavior to justify the behavior both rationally and morally. This argument meets the charge that a "genetic fallacy" would have to be committed in passing from evolutionary explanation to justification.

(2) The standard of rationality (rational egoism) and the understanding of moral justification (the HRC model) are consistent with the possibility that it could be morally defensible in dire circumstances that everyone refrain from sexual reproduction. There is no assumption that survival must be morally good regardless of the cost, and thus the second objection is answered as well.

(3) The third problem—how to pass from a statement of biological fact to a moral conclusion without commiting the alleged "naturalistic

fallacy"—is resolved on three different levels. Sometimes the naturalistic fallacy is taken to be the alleged mistake of identifying a moral property with a naturalistic property. Whether or not that would be a mistake, the understanding of moral justification developed in the second section does not presuppose the existence of moral properties. Hence, that alleged mistake cannot be made. At other times the alleged fallacy is taken to be the deduction of a normative conclusion from nonnormative premises or else the deduction of a moral conclusion from nonmoral premises. In the above understanding of moral justification, the connection between biology and morals is mediated by the HRC model of moral justification. This model presents a normative principle. (The principle is roughly that a system of moral motivations would be justified for a society if its members would be rationally motivated to want it in force in their society.) Hence, there is no suggestion that a moral conclusion is to be deduced from purely nonnormative premises. But should the principle also be classified as a moral principle? I see no reason why not—if one wants to maintain that it is logically impossible to deduce a moral conclusion from nonmoral premises. I have argued that the HRC model begs no interesting moral questions and can be accepted within a scientific world view. The moral status of this model would be no obstacle to the possibility of ethical naturalism.

(4) Since no moral properties are presupposed on this understanding of moral justification, the problem of Wilson's emotivism is met. Moral justification—the justification of a system of moral values for a society— is possible without the assumption that there exist moral properties. It may be wondered whether there might be second-order moral properties, like such-and-such moral values being *justified* for a society. There might be, but nothing in the HRC model requires that statements about the justification of moral values describe second-order moral properties.[39]

(5) The preceding arguments do not imply genetic determinism. I have assumed that there may be true explanations of the evolution of behavior through natural selection. Such explanations imply that genes are causally related to behavior, but only as INUS conditions.[40] Genes do not 'determine' animal behavior in the sense of making it occur independently of all other factors. Nor are the consequences of animal behavior created in a vacuum. Mathematical models of natural selection (and cultural selection too) apply only within a context of assumptions about environmental conditions. For example, in discussing the implications of TFTing, I assumed that the interactions were such that there was a fair probability that the same individuals would interact a second time and that the interactions were PDs. The point of such models is to show the consequences of various strategies as they affect each other under a set of environmental constraints.

Beyond the five familiar objections that I have tried to answer are other, perhaps deeper worries. In conclusion, I shall briefly address three of them.

Justified Genocide Is Not Logically Possible. Moral values concern not only the way members of a society should treat each other but also how they should treat individuals outside that society. It is logically possible that most or all members of a society could rationally choose a system of moral values that permitted or even demanded that another group of humans be destroyed. Ethical naturalism as conceived here is logically compatible with, for example, justified genocide. If nothing else constitutes a *reductio ad absurdum* of the proposal under consideration, this does.

This objection gets to the heart of one significant source of resistance to naturalism in ethics. The presupposition is that any adequate theory of justification for moral values should cover a wide range of logically possible situations. If something that is morally repugnant *could* be justified in some logically possible set of circumstances, then the theory of justification that has this implication should be rejected. But I do not accept this methodological principle. The principle provides a means of refuting any form of ethical naturalism, yet why accept this principle? I can see no reason for accepting it that would not be question-begging.

Suppose someone asks: "Would you still endorse the theory of moral justification if it turned out to justify genocide? This is not merely a logical possibility—*for all we know now about how rational motivation cashes out in some empirical theory of mind, people could rationally endorse genocide.*"[41] My answer is that I would not endorse the theory if it had that implication. I find the idea of genocide abhorrent, and since this reaction is deeply rooted in my moral values, I believe that the repugnance I feel is justified. Moral values, as Brandt has noted, generally come with the belief that they are justified. Notice, however, that it does not follow that I am committed to rejecting the theory of justification in question. I am committed to rejecting it only if it *does* have the unacceptable implication, not merely if "for all we know now" it does.

So Rawls's Reflective Equilibruim Is the Ultimate Test? It may seem so, on my view, since I won't accept a theory that justifies genocide and would not expect any right-thinking person to accept such a theory. But, no, the significance of this fact is that persons cannot jump out of their moral skins. People have moral values, and moral values, being what they are, cannot be changed as easily as philosophical theories. It doesn't follow that the kind of theory of justification proposed *itself* implies that moral values are justified when they can be held in "reflective equilibrium" with other things that are accepted. Nor does it follow that any acceptable theory of moral justification would imply that. The content of an acceptable theory of justification and the causal conditions governing its acceptance by a given person need not be the same. (Recall the genetic fallacy charged to Wilson.) What follows is that any theory of justification acceptable to a person x will not be known by x to imply that x's deepest moral values are unjustified. This conclusion is not startling.

Does This Conservatism Not Trivialize the Quest for Justification? Or, in other words, why should we worry about whether ethical naturalism is possible, since it won't really make much practical difference whichever way it turns out? One of the main points of finding an *objective* basis for moral values is to learn which of one's basic moral values are justified, with the understanding that some might not be. A related purpose is to have a means of resolving conflicts between opposing systems of moral value. If objectifying moral values is only a sophisticated form of self-congratulation, both points are lost.

This objection can be met by distinguishing sharply between two questions that are easily conflated: Which moral system, if any, would we choose to support (among certain alternatives) if we were fully rational? And which moral system, if any, would we choose to support (among those alternatives) if we knew the answer to the first question? Brandt makes this distinction and argues that the answers to these questions should tend to coincide for most people.[42] Brandt believes that most people have a certain degree of intrinsic interest in what they would choose if they were rational. Just knowing that one would choose a certain code if one were rational is, in Brandt's view, enough to make one want to choose that code to some significant degree. In response to the last objection, I denied that this was so. If I know that the code that I would choose if I were rational is in direct opposition to fundamental values that I now have, I may well lose interest in how I would choose if I were rational. In fact, I do have considerable interest in making rational choices as such, but not enough to override other, more basic values. This attitude is surely not uncommon. Rationality as such is a value for some, but for very few is it apt to be the most fundamental value that can be used to bring the rest into line. So how can the charge of conservatism be answered?

Let us not forget that the two questions that Brandt has distinguished really are distinct. There is still the matter of what people would choose *if they were rational.* Given a full-fledged empirical account of rational choice on which predictions can be made—and that is the possibility being entertained—it will be possible to predict that certain people will tend to adopt and support (choose) a different system of values as their motivations become more rational. There is nothing conservative in the implications on this side of the coin. If individuals come to have more rational motivations in empirical, specifiable respects, their basic moral values may be changed. The change may not depend in the least on valuing rationality as such.

The principal task of this essay has been to explain how ethical naturalism is possible. Sociobiologists have not succeeded in explaining this possibility. An approach is needed that does not assume that explaining the existence of moral values necessarily justifies them; that does not ignore the logical status of moral judgments *vis à vis* factual ones; and that does not foster the false impression that biology can justify moral values by removing the possibility of choice. Brandt's model of moral justification (HRC) provides a way to avoid these difficulties and others, but it needs to be supplemented with a conception of rational motivation that can be supported within a scientific conception of the world. My argument has been that sociobiology can have a significant role to play in this project.[43]

NOTES

1. Ethical naturalism is usually interpreted more narrowly to mean that moral judgments can be logically deduced from purely factual judgments or that moral properties are natural properties. The reason for the difference will be discussed. The clause modifying "purely factual premises" is not idle. Some understanding of "purely factual premises" is needed other than "premises that do not entail a moral judgment" or else ethical naturalism in the narrow sense becomes trivially false; the modifying clause explains roughly the sense intended.

2. See, for example, Ruse (1979), p. 200, Mattern (1978), p. 468, and Singer (1981), pp. 74–81.

3. Such as Sociobiology Study Group of Science for the People; see Caplan (1978), pp. 280–290. For perceptive comments, see Williams (1980), p. 281.

4. Similar points have been made by many authors, such as Mattern (1978), Group Reports in Stent (1980), and Singer (1981, chap. 3).

5. The theories of kin-selection and reciprocal altruism were originally published in Hamilton (1964) and Trivers (1971). For a speculative account of the origin of morality based on these theories, see Desmond (1979, chap. 11).

6. This example is taken from Ruse (1979), p. 203.

7. See Moore (1903) and Ruse (1979), pp. 204–7.

8. When Wilson writes about interpreting the activity of the emotive centers of the brain in order to decipher the meaning of the canons of morality (1975a, p. 563), he may be suggesting an emotivist analysis of moral discourse. But he is presumably not implying that such discourse is literally about the functioning of the human brain. He seems not to be implying, therefore, that moral statements are equivalent in linguistic meaning to statements of biological fact. In one place Wilson explicitly denies that he is guilty of the "naturalistic fallacy" (1975b), but he interprets this fallacy unconventionally to be the claim that whatever is ought to be.

9. See Singer (1973), Mackie (1977, chap. 1), Brandt (1979, chap. 1), and Putnam (1981, chap. 6).

10. Wilson's emotivism, since it is not specifically a view about the emotive meaning of moral discourse, differs from the emotivism of Ayer (1946) and Stevenson (1944).

11. This is roughly what I mean by "genetic determinism", which is not the same as the metaphysical thesis that every event in the universe has a complete causal explanation. For this reason the various positions on the traditional free-will–determinism issue are

usually not pertinent. An exception is Wilson's discussion of determinism (1978), pp. 73–76, where he defends a variation on "soft-determinism".

12. Wilson (1975b). For further comment on this and similar passages in Wilson, see Gould (1976) and Alper, Beckwith, and Miller (1978).

13. See Stent (1980), Block and Dworkin (1974), and Ruse (1979).

14. An event x is an INUS condition for an event y if x is insufficient for y but is a necessary part of a condition that is unnecessary but sufficient for y. See Mackie (1965).

15. Dawkins (1979), p. 3. See also Barash (1979), p. 12.

16. Wilson (1978), p. 122, on aggression and violence, and p. 173, on selfishness and moral development (with implications for issues surrounding equality and justice).

17. I shall use the term "moral value" ambiguously to cover two possible cases: motivational states, sometimes unconscious, that are normally associated with moral beliefs, such as a disposition not to steal; and moral beliefs. In the latter case "moral value" can refer to a person's mental state (believing that stealing is wrong) or to its content (that stealing is wrong). The philosophical question "What are moral values?" may be interpreted to be a puzzle about the proper analysis of the content of moral beliefs. The use of "moral value" adopted here does not presuppose any particular approach to this question.

18. For simplicity, the last qualification was omitted in the definition offered in the first sentence of this essay. It is necessary, since I am not assuming that the justification relation is one of logical entailment, yet I want at the same time to distinguish naturalism from intuitionism, such as in Moore (1903) and Ross (1939).

19. See note 9.

20. See Sturgeon (1982) for a critique of the reforming definition approach taken by Brandt in (1979). It might be thought that a reforming definition could be adequately defended by showing that it is part of a "reflective equilibrium" of beliefs in the sense explained in Rawls (1971). That approach runs counter to the qualification entered earlier in the definition of ethical naturalism: The justification of moral judgments has to fit a scientific conception of the world. The significance of this qualification is discussed below.

21. See Mackie (1977, chap. 1). Harman suggests an argument similar to Mackie's "argument from queerness" in his essay in this volume.

22. This sixth feature of a moral motivational system does not imply, of course, that Brandt has an objectivist conception of moral belief. See Brandt (1979), p. 170, on this point.

23. Some evidence for this conclusion is Brandt (1979), pp. 180 and 189. Part of the practical significance of construing rational choice this way is that it is easier to recommend a justified code to the members of the society for whom the code would be justified, given their present state of rationality, and easier to support it oneself.

24. Brandt (1979), p. 194; note qualifications on pp. 188, 200, 221, and 242.

25. Brandt (1979), pp. 188–193 and chap. 4.

26. Harman, this volume.

27. This is the main focus of criticism in Sturgeon (1982).

28. Alexander Rosenberg argues in (1980, chaps. 3–6), that terms such as "rational motivation" do not designate natural kinds, since they have a semantical connection with beliefs and desires and hence with *Homo sapiens*, which is not a natural kind; these terms therefore cannot occur in natural laws, and the social sciences, which use such terms, cannot explain human behavior. Sociobiology, he contends, does not have this problem, since properly understood it investigates the natural kinds studied in biological science, and there species are not natural kinds but discrete spatio-temporally bounded particulars. Although this view of species is not implausible, it is highly questionable whether the notions of belief and desire cannot be explained independently of *Homo sapiens*.

29. A behavioristic approach to human moral development is, on the other hand, not antithetical to sociobiology. It may be that sociobiology can, as Wilson has suggested (1975a, p. 562), incorporate the approach of learning theorists to understanding the cognitive mechanisms of moral development. Something like the RTM model might eventually be supported within this wider context and developed as an empirical and predictive account of what a choice would be like when its motivation is freed of cognitive error.

30. On this general point, see Gauthier (1975a).

31. As in Gauthier (1974a). The problem of coherency that Gauthier presents here is different from the one described below.

32. A Prisoner's Dilemma may be represented in the matrix below as a two-person game in which each player has two choices: to cooperate (C) or not to cooperate (NC). The payoffs for each player have the order: T (temptation not to C) $> R$ (reward for mutual C) $> P$ (punishment for mutual NC) $> S$ (the sucker payoff). The first letter in each cell represents the payoff to player A and the second letter is B's payoff.

Player B

		C	NC
Player A	C	R, R	S, T
	NC	T, S	P, P

33. Let $pr(p/q)$ represent the conditional probability of p on q, and AC represent A's cooperation, ANC represent A's noncooperation, etc. Then for A's choice to be probabilisitically independent of B's choice, $pr(BC/AC) = pr(BC/ANC)$ and $pr(BNC/AC) = pr(BNC/ANC)$. The Prisoner's Dilemma is often understood to involve only causal independence between the actions so that the PD becomes Newcomb's Problem; see Nozick (1969), p. 130. That interpretation deepens the paradox but does not affect the points to follow.

34. See, for example, Gauthier (1967) and Campbell (1979, chap. 3).

35. Robert Trivers has said, for example: "Models that attempt to explain altruistic behaviour in terms of natural selection are models designed to take the altruism out of altruism" (1971, p. 35). I return to this point toward the end of this section.

36. The argument is that noncooperation is best for both sides on the last repetition, and hence also on the penultimate repetition, and hence also on the one before that, and so on, all the way back to the initial game.

37. If the payoffs are represented as in the matrix in note 32 and the probability of meeting again is W, then both $W \geq T\text{-}R/T\text{-}P$ and $W \geq T\text{-}R/R\text{-}S$.

38. I have taken this suggestion from Gibbard (1982), who offers an evolutionary account of our sense of justice. It must be stressed that I am not assuming that human goal-seeking capacity is limited to its original functions when it was formed through natural selection. That would be hyperselectionism, a view often ascribed to sociobiologists by their critics. See Gould (1980), pp. 47–58.

39. Brandt himself advocates defining "is morally wrong" as "would be prohibited by any moral code which all fully rational persons would tend to support, in preference to all others or to none at all, for the society of the agent, if they expected to spend a lifetime in that society" (Brandt, 1979, p. 194). Since the latter expression appears to designate a natural property, so must the former on this definition. Moral properties would then exist. Notice, however, that although the HRC model permits this move, it does not require it.

40. See note 14.

41. The objection is similar in structure to Sturgeon's criticism of Brandt (1982, pp. 410–11): For all we know now, wife-beating would be acceptable to some persons who are guided by a rationally chosen moral code. Other than referring to selfishness and sex-stereotyping, Strugeon offers no account of the mechanisms through which motivations involved in wife-beating are learned or could be changed. It is an important empirical question whether such motivations are rational in Brandt's sense and whether they would be compatible with a rationally chosen moral code acceptable to those guided by a moral code justified by Brandt's method.

42. Brandt (1979, chaps. 8 and 17). In Chapter 17 Brandt focuses on the question whether a rational person would always act in accord with the system that such a person would choose for society, but the distinction between which system a rational person would support and which system a person would support, period, is implicit. Moreover,

in Chapter 8 the distinction is explicit between what one would choose if one were rational and what one would choose if one knew what one would rationally choose.

43. For helpful criticisms of this essay, I am indebted to Richard Brandt, David Braybrooke, Peter Danielson, Robert Martin, Alexander Rosenberg, Susan Sherwin, and the editors.

chapter thirteen

The Reconciliation Project

Gregory S. Kavka

Clarifying the nature of the relationship between ethical and self-interested conduct is one of the oldest problems of moral philosophy. As far back as Plato's *Republic,* philosophers have approached it with the aim of reconciling morality and self-interest by showing that moral behavior is required by, or at least is consistent with, rational prudence. Let us call this undertaking the Reconciliation Project. In modern times this project is generally viewed as doomed to failure.[1] It is believed that unless we make an outdated and implausible appeal to divine sanctions, we cannot expect to find agreement between moral and prudential requirements.

Can this negative verdict on the Reconciliation Project be avoided? Before we can deal with this question, we must distinguish among versions of the project along four dimensions. The *audience* dimension concerns to whom our arguments about coincidence of duty and interest are addressed. Sometimes it is supposed that a successful version of the Reconciliation Project must be capable of converting to virtue a hardened cynic or immoralist such as Thrasymacus. This is too much to ask. Immoralists are not likely to understand or appreciate the benefits of living morally, nor are they usually the sort of people who will listen to, or be swayed by, abstract rational arguments.[2] A more modest aim is to speak convincingly to the puzzled ordinary person, such as Glaucon, who fears that in following the path of morality he is being irrational and is harming himself, but who is willing to listen to and ponder arguments to the contrary. We shall here be concerned with versions of the Reconciliation Project having this more modest aim.

A second dimension concerns the sort of *agent* for whom morality and self-interest are supposed to coincide. Versions of the Reconciliation Project that are ambitious along this dimension might attempt to demonstrate such coincidence in the case of all actual human beings, or even all possible human beings. More restrained versions would concentrate on more limited classes, such as persons without severe emotional disturbances or persons capable of self-assessment and love for others. The audience and agent dimensions of the Reconciliation Project are related. If one's aim in pursuing the project is to create or strengthen moral motivation, one would normally choose an agent class that just encompasses one's audience, so as to convince one's listeners that it pays *them* (promotes their own interests) to be moral, while at the same time exposing one's argument to the fewest possible objections. But if one aims at promoting theoretical understanding, one's agent class may be broader or narrower than one's audience. One may, for example, seek to convince reflective persons of goodwill that it pays everyone to be moral. Agent and audience classes need not even overlap; one might argue to sophisticated theorists that morality pays for the unsophisticated, who could not be expected successfully to disguise their immoralities.

The third dimension of the Reconciliation Project is the *social* one. Whether morality pays is partly a function of others' responses to one's immoralities. Are morality and prudence supposed to coincide, then, in all imaginable social environments, all feasible ones, all (or most) actual ones, some feasible ones, or some imaginable ones? Different answers to this question yield importantly different versions of the Reconciliation Project.

Fourth and finally, if we say that morality and prudence coincide, does this mean that (i) each individual ethical act is prudent or (ii) that there are sufficient prudential reasons for adopting a moral way of life and acting in accordance with moral rules? This question concerns the nature of the objects or entities to be reconciled and calls attention to the *object* dimension of the Reconciliation Project. Reconciling all particular acts of duty with prudence is so unpromising a task as to have been largely shunned by the major philosophical exponents of the project. (Although, as we shall see below, much depends on whether prudential evaluations of acts are undertaken prospectively or retrospectively.) Thus Plato argues the prudential advantages of moral dispositions or ways of life, while Hobbes focuses on providing a prudential grounding for moral rules.

Taking note of the object dimension allows us to clarify the Reconciliation Project by answering a preliminary objection to it. According to this objection, the project must fail because supposedly moral actions are not really moral if they are motivated by prudential concerns. We may, however, accept this observation about motivation and moral action without damaging the Reconciliation Project properly construed. For that project is not committed to morality and prudence being identical, or to moral and prudential motives or reasons for action being the same.

Rather, prudence and morality are supposed to be reconcilable in two senses. They recommend the same courses of conduct (where conduct is described in some motive-neutral way). Further, it is consistent with the requirements of prudence to adopt and live a moral way of life, even though this involves developing a pattern of motivation in which nonprudential considerations play an important role.[3] Thus the Reconciliation Project survives the preliminary objection because it concerns, along its object dimension, acts or rules of action or ways of life, rather than motives or reasons for action.

Still, the Reconciliation Project is hopeless if we adopt very stringent interpretations of it along most or all of its four dimensions. We cannot expect to convince a clever immoralist that it pays everyone to act morally on every specific occasion in any sort of society. But why should we consider only such extreme versions of the project? Taking account of the dimensions of variation of the Reconciliation Project, I propose instead to discuss some less extreme versions (and modifications) of it to see to what extent they can be carried out and why they fail when they do. In the course of this investigation, I hope partly to vindicate the rationality of being moral and to clarify further the relationship between morality, prudence, and rationality.

I begin by sketching a Hobbesian verison of the Reconciliation Project that presupposes psychological egoism and relies exclusively on external sanctions (social rewards and punishments) to reconcile obligation and interest. This Hobbesian approach provides considerable illumination, but it suffers from serious defects. To correct some of these, I consider the significance of internal (self-imposed psychological) sanctions.[4] Next, I take up the two most intractable objections to all forms of the project. These concern the obligation to die for others, and those duties owed by members of strong groups to members of weak groups who are apparently not in a position to reciprocate benefits bestowed on them. Finally, I note how the recognition of nonegoistic motives transforms the Reconciliation Project. Throughout, my remarks are largely programmatic. I sketch alternatives, problems, and general strategies for solving problems and leave much detail to be filled in later. I hope nonetheless to say enough to show that the Reconciliation Project is still philosophically interesting and important.

I. THE HOBBESIAN STRATEGY[5]

As a starting point, let us consider Hobbes's version of the Reconciliation Project. In seeking to reconcile duty and interest, Hobbes is limited by two self-imposed restrictions: He rules out appeal to religious sanctions, and he leaves no place for internal sanctions (such as guilt feelings) in his account of human psychology. Hence, Hobbes is reduced to arguing his case solely in terms of external sanctions; that is, social rewards and punishments. He does, however, marshall these relatively meager resources to good advantage.

The core of Hobbes's view is that the general rules of conduct that a farsighted prudent man concerned with his own survival, security, and well-being would follow are essentially the rules of traditional morality. The function of these rules is to promote peace, cooperation, and mutual restraint for the benefit of all parties. The rules therefore forbid killing, assault, and robbery, and they require keeping one's agreements, settling disputes by arbitration, providing aid to others when the cost to one is small and the benefit to them is large,[6] and so on. The self-interested individual, if sufficiently rational and farsighted, will follow these rules because doing so is the best (and only reliable) way to ensure peaceful and cooperative relations with others. The person, for example, who wastes on luxuries what others need to survive is not likely to be helped by others if he later falls into want; nor will his person and property ever be safe from the desperate acts of the needy. The dangers of hostile reactions by others that confront the habitual assailant, thief, or contract-breaker are even more obvious. And while people may try to conceal their violations of moral rules, the long-run dangers of exposure and retaliation by others are great.[7] Thus, argues Hobbes, morality is superior to immorality as a general policy, from the viewpoint of rational prudence.

One may agree that normally morality is a more prudent general policy than immorality but raise doubts about its prudential rationality in two special circumstances: when one is confident that a violation would go undiscovered and unpunished, and when others are not willing to reciprocate restraint. In the first case, it appears that one would benefit by *offensively* violating moral rules; that is, by not complying with them when others are complying. In the second case, prudence seems to call for a *defensive* violation—for noncompliance motivated by the belief that others are not complying and the desire not to put oneself at a disadvantage. Hobbes recognizes and attempts to deal with both cases.

Hobbes's argument against offensive violations of moral rules is presented in his famous reply to the Fool (1651, 1958, pp.120–122). He acknowledges that such violations will in some cases turn out, *in retrospect*, to best serve the agent's interests. But because they risk serious external sanctions (such as the withdrawal of all future cooperation by others[8]), they are never *prospectively* rational. Since the consequences of failure are horrible and the chances of failure are not precisely calculable, it is not a rational gamble to offensively violate moral rules. Underlying this Hobbesian argument is an intuition about rational prudence that is reflected in the usual connotation of the word *prudence*. To be prudent is to play it safe and not take large, uncontrollable risks. It is not implausible to suppose that rational pursuit of one's own interests requires being prudent in this sense when one's vital interests are at stake.

To develop this point, let us follow decision theorists in drawing a distinction between choices under *risk* and under *uncertainty*. In the former cases, one has reliable knowledge of the probabilities that the various possible outcomes would follow the different available courses of action. In choices under uncertainty, one lacks such knowledge. Rawls contends that rationality requires that, when making vitally important choices under uncertainty, one follow a Maximin Strategy—choose the act with the best worst outcome (1971, pp. 152–158). I have argued elsewhere for using a Disaster Avoidance Strategy in such circumstances— choosing the alternative that maximizes one's chances of avoiding all unacceptable outcomes.[9] Both strategies favor playing it safe in the sense of aiming at avoidance (or minimization) of the risk of unacceptable outcomes.

Now suppose we view choices among actions in the real world as made under uncertainty. (This is plausible for the most part, given our limited understanding of the complex factors that determine the consequences of our actions.[10]) If, as Hobbes suggests, offensive violators risk the application of serious external sanctions, offensive violations would be irrational according to both the Maximin and Disaster Avoidance viewpoints. For the offensive violator accepts, under uncertainty, an unnecessary (or greater than necessary) risk of suffering disastrous consequences. So if either Rawls's analysis of rational prudential choice under uncertainty or my own is correct, Hobbes's argument against offensive violations under uncertainty is largely vindicated.

The considerations just presented attempt in effect to reconcile the requirements of morality and prudence as applied to (a certain class of) particular actions. They may serve, that is, as part of a Reconciliation Project focusing along the object dimension on *acts*. They function ever more effectively as part of an argument for the coincidence of *rules* of morality and prudence. We can imagine someone claiming that living by some rule such as the following would better serve one's interests than following moral rules: "Follow the moral rules except when you believe (or confidently believe) you can get away with violating them." But if one lives by this sort of rule, one is likely to undergo the risks inherent in offensive violations on a good number of occasions. And even if one is cautious in selecting the occasions, the risk of getting caught and suffering serious sanctions on one or more occasions will be substantial and much greater than the chance of getting caught on one particular occasion. Hence, insofar as rational prudence requires avoiding or minimizing risks of suffering serious sanctions, it would not recommend a policy of clever "compromise" between moral and immoral conduct as exemplified in this rule.

We have seen that Hobbes tries to reconcile duty and prudence in the case of offensive violations by denying that such violations are prudential. The opposite tack is adopted for defensive violations. These, Hobbes claims, are not contrary to moral duty. Agents are not obligated to follow the constraints of traditional morality unless others are reciprocating their restraint. To comply with moral rules unilaterally is to render oneself prey to others, and this, Hobbes urges, one is not required to do (1651, 1958, pp. 110, 130).

The governing principle of Hobbesian morality, then, is what I call the Copper Rule: "Do unto others as they *do* unto you." This principle enunciates a less glittering moral ideal than the familiar Golden Rule, which requires us to treat others well regardless of whether they treat us well in return. In thus opting for a reciprocal rather than unilateral interpretation of moral requirements, is Hobbes abandoning traditional morality?

To answer this question, we must distinguish between two aspects of morality—practice morality and ideal morality. Practice morality encompasses the standards of conduct actually expected of, and generally practiced by, persons living within a given moral tradition. It is roughly the part of morality concerned with *requirements,* those standards for which people are blamed, criticized, or punished for failing to live up to. Ideal morality refers to standards of moral excellence that a tradition sets up as models to aspire to and admire. Praise, honor, and respect are the rewards of those who live by its higher, more demanding standards. But, in general, people are not blamed for falling short of such ideals, or even for not aiming at them.

Now there surely are important strands of unilateralism in the ideal morality of the Western tradition. The Golden Rule, the admonition to love thine enemy, and the principle of turning the other cheek, all concern treating well even those who do not reciprocate. But if we turn to practice, and the standards of conduct that are actually treated as moral requirements, we find Copper Rule reciprocity to be a reasonable summary of much of what we observe. For practice morality allows us considerable leeway to engage in otherwise forbidden conduct toward those who violate moral constraints, especially when this is necessary for protection. Thus individuals may kill in self-defense, society may deprive criminals of their liberty, contracts may be broken when reciprocal fulfillment cannot be expected, and so forth.

We may then, without committing Hobbes to absurdity, attribute to him the claim that, in practice, traditional moral rules contain exception clauses allowing for defensive "violations" of the main clauses of the rule, if these are aimed at other violators.[11] In adopting this pruned-down conception of moral requirements, Hobbes has abandoned the ambitious dream of achieving a reconciliation between ideal morality and prudence. But he has avoided one telling objection to the Reconciliation Project: that morality requires us (as prudence does not) to sacrifice our interests to the immoral, who will be all too ready to take advantage of such a sacrifice. Note, however, that the companion objection that morality sometimes requires us to sacrifice our interests for others who are moral is not dealt with by the Copper Rule interpretation of morality. Forms of this objection will be considered later.[12]

As we have seen, Hobbes treats offensive and defensive violations of moral rules quite differently. In the former case, he reconciles prudence to morality by altering cynical interpretations of what prudence demands, while in the latter case he reconciles morality to prudence by offering a nonstandard interpretation of morality. Yet in each case he draws our attention to the oft-neglected social dimension of the Reconciliation Project. His discussion of defensive violations suggests that under certain conditions—anarchy or general noncompliance with traditional moral rules—moral and prudential requirements coincide, but only as a result of the effective loosening or disappearance of the former. Hence, *how* duty and interest are reconciled is a function of the social environment. In arguing for the imprudence of offensive violations of moral rules, Hobbes presupposes threats of external sanctions that are serious enough to make such violations a bad gamble. Therefore, his argument does not apply to imaginary situations in which society rewards immoral actions, or even certain real ones in which it ignores serious immoralities when they are committed by members of some privileged groups.

Suppose, then, that our aim is to reconcile prudence with traditional moral requirements (without the exception clauses); that is, do not kill or steal, aid the needy when the costs are small, and so on. Hobbes suggests that this reconciliation is possible only in a certain sort of social environment—one we may call *punitive*. In a punitive environment, serious violators of moral norms are sought out, apprehended, and given stiff punishments frequently enough to make immorality a bad prudential risk. As a result, there is general compliance with moral rules and little need for one to undertake defensive violations. In a punitive social environment, offensive violations of moral rules are irrational and defensive ones are unnecessary. If an actual social environment is punitive, the Reconciliation Project seems to have succeeded with respect to it. And if such an environment is feasible but nonactual, those who wish people to act morally but fear the distracting influence of self-interest will have some reason to create it.

Let us now briefly summarize the Hobbesian approach to the Reconciliation Project, which is based on external sanctions. It consists first of proposing specific interpretations of that project along two of the four dimensions. With respect to the object dimension, it focuses on rules or policies rather than on individual acts. (Although the reply to the Fool fits within an act version of the project as well.) And it presupposes a punitive social environment, avoiding the dubious claim that duty and interest coincide in any social context. Further, it provides a novel interpretation of moral requirements—the Copper Rule or reciprocal interpretation—and it rests on a "playing it safe" theory of rational prudential choice under uncertainty. All of these aspects of the Hobbesian strategy make contributions to the interpretation and development of the Reconciliation Project. None is without plausibility. However, there are two fatal objections that the Hobbesian Strategy cannot adequately answer.

The first concerns punitive social environments. These are beneficial in discouraging immoral conduct, but they have costs. To render immorality a bad risk solely via threats of punishments, such punishments must be made very heavy and/or very probable. In a society of significant size, doing the latter would normally require a massive policing establishment with large monetary costs (borne by the citizens), interferences with personal liberty and privacy (searches, eavesdropping, surveillance), and dangers of police power and influence over the political and economic institutions of society. Heavy penalties also have social costs—monetary costs of supporting prisons, lessened chances of reconciliation between offenders and society, dangers of gross injustice if the innocent might sometimes be punished, and so on. In short, we must accept trade-offs between various things that we value and the deterrence of serious immorality. And it may not always be possible for society, by use of external sanctions alone, to ensure that "crime does not pay" without sacrificing too much in the way of individual liberty, privacy, and protection from excessive state and police power.

Our second objection concedes that immorality generally does not pay, and even allows, that immorality is prudentially irrational under genuine uncertainty. However, *some* opportunities for immoral gain may present themselves under risk; that is, the probabilities of detection and punishment may be reliably known. In these situations, maximizing expected personal utility is arguably the most rational course, and this may imply engaging in an offensive violation. A slumlord, for example, may have relatively precise statistical data that allow him to estimate reliably the odds of his getting caught and punished if he hires a professional arsonist to burn one of his buildings so that he can collect the insurance. If the chances of arrest and conviction are low and the return is high, the crime may have positive expected value for him, and it will be prudentially rational for him to undertake it. The rules of a system of rational self-interest will be formulated to allow agents to take advantage of such situations.

These two objections reveal that while external sanctions alone can take us, via the Hobbesian Strategy, some considerable way toward reconciling duty and interest, they cannot take us far enough. We at least need some device other than a punitive social environment that can alter the calculations or dispositions of the slumlord and other potential criminals. The obvious candidates here are internal sanctions, psychic structures that punish immorality and reward virtue. Unlike external sanctions, these are relatively free of problems concerning evasion and detection, since one's conscience follows one everywhere,[13] and they do not threaten privacy and democracy as do secret police forces. In the next section, I will explore how their inclusion may extend and strengthen the Hobbesian arguments for the coincidence for morality and prudence.

II. INTERNAL SANCTIONS

Internal sanctions come in two varieties, negative and positive. The negative sanctions are guilt feelings and related forms of psychic distress that most of us are subject to feel when we believe we have done wrong. We develop the tendency to experience such feelings under such cir-cumstances as part of the socialization process we undergo in growing up. It is no mystery why society nurtures and encourages the development of this tendency; it benefits others to the extent that it inhibits or deters misconduct by the individual. And once one possesses the tendency, it imposes extra—and relatively certain[14]—costs on immorality, costs which may tip the prudential balance in favor of restraint. Arson may not be the most rational option for our slumlord, for example, if in addition to prison he risks, with high probability, significant guilt feelings over endangering the lives of tenants or over cheating his insurance company. With internal sanctions operating along with external sanctions in this way, the social environment need not be so punitive as to keep serious immorality within tolerable limits.

There is no entirely satisfactory label for the positive internal sanctions, the agreeable feelings that typically accompany moral action and the realization that one has acted rightly, justly, or benevolently. So let us opt for the vague term "the satisfactions of morality."[15] Moral people have long testified as to the strength and value of such satisfactions, often claiming that they are the most agreeable satisfactions we can attain. This last claim goes beyond what is necessary for our purposes.

All we need to assert is that there are special significant pleasures or satisfactions that accompany regular moral action and the practice of a moral way of life that are not available to (unreformed) immoralists and others of their ilk.[16] For if this is so, then the forgoing of these potential satisfactions must be charged as a significant opportunity cost of choosing an immoral way of life.

Can an individual have it both ways, enjoying the psychic benefits of morality while living an immoral life? He could, perhaps, if he lived immorally while sincerely believing he was not. Certain fanatics who selflessly devote themselves to false moral ideals, such as purifying the human race by eugenics or pleasing God by destroying nonbelievers, might fall in this category. Of more concern in the present context, however, is the individual who adopts morality as a provisional way of life or policy while planning to abandon it if a chance to gain much by immorality should arise later. This person, we would say, is not truly moral, and it is hard to believe that he would perceive himself to be, so long as his motives are purely prudential and his commitment to morality is only conditional. In any case, we would not expect him to experience the satisfactions of morality in the same way, or to the same degree, as the genuinely moral individual who is aware of the (relative) purity of his motives and the nature and depth of his commitment.

Note that if this is so we have arrived at a paradox of self-interest: *being* purely self-interested will not always best serve one's interests. For there may be certain substantial personal advantages that accrue only to those who are not purely self-interested, such as moral people. Thus it may be rational for you, as a purely self-interested person, to cease being one if you can, to transform yourself into a genuinely moral person.[17] And once you are such a person, you will not be disposed to act immorally, under risk, whenever so doing promises to maximize personal expected utility.

The lesson of this paradox, and the opportunity cost of being immoral, does not apply, though, to those (if any) who are no longer capable of learning to enjoy the satisfactions of living a moral life. Further, some people may still be capable of developing an appreciation of these satisfactions, but the transition costs of moving to this state from their present immoral condition may outweigh the advantages gained. For people such as these, especially those who are immune from guilt feelings, the prudential argument for being moral must essentially rest on external sanctions. And with respect to some individuals, such as hardened but cautious immoralists or clever psychopaths, the argument may fail.

Thus we must acknowledge a restriction of the Reconciliation Project along its agent dimension. It is too much to claim that it pays one to be moral, irrespective of one's psychological characteristics. Rather, the argument from internal sanctions supports the prudential rationality of living a moral life for the two classes of people constituting the vast majority of humankind: First, those who are already endowed with conscience and moral motivations, so that they experience the satisfactions of living morally and are liable to suffering guilt feelings when they do wrong. Second, those who are capable of developing into moral persons without excessive cost—immoralists who are not fully committed to that way of life, and children.

Should we be dismayed that the Reconciliation Project may not encompass, along its agent dimension, those incapable of enjoying the satisfactions of morality? This depends upon our aims in pursuing the project and the audience to whom its arguments are addressed. Insofar as our aim is to reassure the ordinary good man that he is not harming himself by being moral, or to encourage parents who want to do the best for their children to give them moral education, we need not worry. And if we seek theoretical illumination, we achieve more by recognizing the variation along the agent dimension than by denying it. Only if our aim were the hopeless one of convincing dedicated immoralists to be moral, by using rational arguments, would we be in difficulty. Am I confessing, then, that we are helpless in the face of the immoralist? No, we are not helpless in the practical sense, for we can use external sanctions to restrain immoralists. Nor should we perceive an immoralist's gloating that it does not pay him to be moral (because the satisfactions of morality are not for him) as a victory over us. It is more like the pathetic boast of a deaf person that he saves money because it does not pay him to buy opera records.

III. THE ULTIMATE SACRIFICE

We have seen how the recognition of internal sanctions allows us to deal with two objections that undermine the Hobbesian external-sanctions approach to the Reconciliation Project. Two difficult objections remain, however, even when internal sanctions are taken into account. The first is that morality sometimes requires the sacrifice of one's life, and this cannot be in one's interests. The second is that morality requires powerful groups to treat weak groups fairly and decently, while it better serves the interests of the powerful group's members not to do so.

The objection concerning death runs as follows. In certain circumstances, morality requires of us that we give up our lives to protect others. We are bound by obligations of fair play, gratitude, and perhaps consent to fight in just wars of national defense. Fulfilling these obligations costs many people their lives. Extreme situations can also arise in civilian life in which morality requires one to accept one's own death. If gangsters credibly threaten to kill me unless I kill an innocent person, I must refrain. If I am a loser in a fair and necessary lifeboat lottery, I am morally bound to abide by the outcome. If half of the expedition's necessary food supply is lost as a result of my recklessness, I must be the first to agree to go without food on the long return trip so that others may survive. And so on. In each of these cases, however, self-interest seems to counsel taking the opposite course. Where there is life there is hope, and even if the likely cost of saving my life is to suffer severe internal and external sanctions (such as imprisonment, depression, and guilt for the military deserter), that cost must be less than the premature loss of my life, since such loss would deprive me of all future enjoyments and frustrate all of my main plans and desires.

In response to this objection, let us first note that there are fates worse than death. And for some people, living with the knowledge that one has preserved one's life at the cost of the lives of others, the sacrifice of one's principles, or the desertion of a cause one loves may be such a fate. In addition, society is aware of the heavy value that people place on the continuation of their own lives and typically responds by using heavy external sanctions to encourage appropriate life-risking behavior in defense of society. Thus infantry officers may stand behind their own lines and shoot those who retreat, thereby rendering advance a safer course than retreat.[18] (Even if advance is virtually suicidal, death with honor at the hands of the enemy may be a lesser evil than death with dishonor at the hands of one's own officers.) On the positive side, those who risk or lose their lives in battle are often offered significant rewards by their fellow citizens—medals, honors, praise, and material compensation for themselves or their families.

The upshot of this is that in a substantial number of cases the sacrifice of one's life for moral ends may be consistent with the requirements of prudence because it constitutes the lesser of two extreme personal evils. It would, however, be disingenuous to suggest that this is so in most, much less all, cases. Officers cannot shoot all deserters or retreaters, nor are courts likely to sentence to death those who cheat in lifeboat lotteries.[19] And relatively few are so committed to morality that they could not eventually recover, at least partially, from the negative psychic effects of abandoning principle to preserve their lives. So we must concede that self-interest and morality will frequently, or usually, recommend divergent courses of action when there is a stark choice between immoral action and certain death.

Does this concession destroy the Reconciliation Project? Only if we have in mind a version of the project that focuses, along the object dimension, on acts. If instead we consider, as we have been, whether adopting the moral *way of life* is consistent with prudence, the answer may well be different. In adopting or pursuing a moral way of life, we are, it is true, running a *risk* of sacrificing our lives imprudently. For the requirements of morality may sometimes call for us to give up (or risk) our lives. And if we do develop the habits and dispositions appropriate to the moral life, we are likely (or at least more likely than otherwise) to live up to these requirements at the cost of our lives, if we find ourselves in appropriate circumstances. Notice, however, that in assessing this risk and weighing it against the advantages of the moral life, we must consider how likely we are to find ourselves in such circumstances.

Now this depends, in turn, on our view of what the substantive rules of morality require of us. If they demand that one right all wrongs and fight all injustices anywhere at any time with all the means one possesses and regardless of the personal cost, the likelihood that one would be morally obligated to lay down (or seriously risk) one's life at some time or another is obviously large. But surely on any reasonable conception they require much less than this. Perhaps you are obligated to give up your life (i) to protect your country in a just war; (ii) to protect those to whom you owe special duties of protection (your children, your passengers if you are a ship's captain); (iii) to protect those you owe immense debts of gratitude (your parents); (iv) to avoid seriously violating the rights of innocent others (as in the gangster threat situation); (v) to save others from dangers that your misconduct, recklessness, or negligence has created; (vi) to keep important agreements you have made (such as accepting employment as a bodyguard); or (vii) to save the lives of large numbers of innocent people when you are the only one who can do so. And perhaps there are other specific duties of sacrifice that I have left off this list. But as a whole, the duties are limited to special and quite unlikely circumstances. (Military service is the only seriously life-endangering-required activity that is at all likely to confront a significant segment of the population. Presumably such service is morally obligatory only if the war is just, which frequently is not the case. Further, in most wars the percentage of those serving who are killed is rather low.)

Now if the chances are small that you will ever confront a situation in which you are morally obligated to surrender your life, it may well pay you to adopt a moral way of life, even if doing so increases the likelihood that you would sacrifice your life in such a situation. For the relatively certain external and internal benefits of the moral life should far outweigh the very unlikely loss of one's life. Further, it is worth noting that many immoral lifestyles—crime, debauchery, deception of all those around you—may have much higher premature death rates than the moral life. Insofar as adoption of a moral way of life ensures that you will not lapse into one of these alternatives, it may even on balance increase your life expectancy.[20]

The argument, then, is that adopting a moral way of life carries at most a very small net risk to one's life. Since it provides significant benefits with high probability, it is a reasonable prudential choice.[21] It is useful in understanding this argument to compare adopting a moral way of life with two other activities that are not generally thought to be imprudent: joining the military and entering into a long-term love relationship, such as by marrying or having children. These undertakings are like becoming moral in the main respect relevant to our argument. They are likely to involve or produce changes in one's motivational structure that would render one more likely to risk or sacrifice one's life in certain circumstances, such as when your loved ones or comrades in arms are in danger. (In addition, military service carries a nonnegligible risk of finding yourself in precisely these circumstances.) But this feature of these undertakings is not usually thought to render them ineligible choices from a prudential perspective. Why, then, should the same feature render becoming moral a generally imprudent course of conduct? This activity, like entering a long-term love relationship, promises very large external and internal rewards while involving a relatively tiny risk of loss of life. The gamble is hardly more foolish in the case of virtue than in the case of love.

IV. GROUP IMMORALITY

Human beings, as has often been remarked, are social creatures. We need one another for a variety of practical and emotional reasons—for help in securing satisfaction of our material needs, for physical protection, for companionship, for love, and so on. The above arguments that duty and interest coincide all rest on this fact. Individuals need the help rather than the hostility of society to prosper, and in the process of social learning they internalize norms of conscience that further fuse their interests with those of the social group. However, one does not require the aid or cooperation of *all* others, only of a sufficient number of those with whom one is likely to come in contact. This fact generates the most telling objection to the Reconciliation Project: That it is not in the interests of powerful *groups* and their members to treat decently and to help, as morality demands, the members of weak groups, who are apparently not in a position to return good for good and evil for evil.[22]

It is clear that when we consider relations among groups, our earlier tools for reconciling interest and obligation cannot be used in the same way. External sanctions operate effectively, to the extent they do, because it is in the general interest of society and its members to restrain individuals from harming others. But if there is a split between groups in society, there may be no effective sanction against members of a dominant group harming members of a powerless group. For the others in the dominant group may condone, or even approve, such conduct, while the members of the powerless group are too weak to punish the offenders. And if the norms of the dominant group allow, or even encourage, mistreatment of the powerless group—as throughout history they often have—even well-socialized members of the dominant group may carry out such mistreatment without suffering substantial guilt feelings.

This objection shows that there cannot be a satisfactory solution to the Reconciliation Project if the project is strictly interpreted along the social and degree dimensions. That is, we cannot hope to show that in all historically actual (much less all conceivable) social circumstances it has been (or would be) in the interests of all groups and their members to act morally toward members of other groups.[23] Instead, particular cases of supposed divergence of group duty and interest must be considered on an ad hoc basis, and the most we can reasonably aspire to is the presentation of arguments that make it plausible that obligation and interest coincide in *actual* present circumstances. This will not ease the anxiety of moralists who seek a noncontingent guarantee that interest and duty will never diverge. But it could suffice to convince the attentive moral individual, or group leader, that he or she is not being foolish in acting morally, or in leading his or her group in a moral direction.

Before discussing the three most important specific instances of the objection before us, it should be pointed out that whether there is hope of reconciling group interest and duty depends on what we take the demands of duty to be. In the case of individuals, we saw that a unilateralist-idealistic interpretation of moral requirements might render the Reconciliation Project impossible. Similarly, if we interpret morality as requiring rich and powerful groups to share so much with the poor and weak as to create absolute equality, there is very little prospect that duty and interest can be reconciled. But it is far from obvious that morality demands this much. What morality does clearly require is that the rich and powerful refrain from actively harming the poor and weak, and that the former aid the latter when the costs of giving are small and the benefits of receiving are large. We shall see that with this modest interpretation of the obligations of the powerful, reconciling their obligations with their interests may be possible.

Let us turn to our examples, the first concerning justice within a society. Why should rich and powerful groups in a nation allow the poor opportunities for education, employment, and advancement and provide social-welfare programs that benefit the poor as morality requires? Why shouldn't they simply oppress and exploit the poor? There are several reasons why, in modern times, it is most probably in the long-term interest of the rich and powerful to treat the domestic poor well. First, some rich individuals, and more likely some of their children, may be poor at some time in the future and thus benefit from programs to help the poor. Second, offering opportunities to members of all groups widens the pool of talent available to fill socially useful jobs, which should provide long-run economic benefits to members of all groups.[24] Third, and most important, there is the reason that has impressed social theorists from Hobbes to Rawls: Decent treatment of all promotes social stability and cohesion and discourages revolution.[25] This reason is especially important in contemporary times, when ideals of human dignity, equality, and justice are known and espoused virtually everywhere, and when revolution is frequently proposed as a legitimate means of attaining such ideals.

Taken together, these reasons constitute a strong case, on prudential grounds, for decent treatment of the domestic poor by a nation's dominant groups. In fact, if we apply Disaster Avoidance reasoning, it turns out that the third reason alone shows that good treatment of the poor is prudentially rational. For if the poor find the status quo unacceptable and apply such reasoning, they will revolt. Thus Hobbes writes, "Needy men and hardy, not contented with their present condition, . . . are inclined to . . . stir up trouble and sedition; for there is no . . . such hope to mend an ill game as by causing a new shuffle" (1651, 1958, p. 87). The rich, being aware of this, will (if they follow a Disaster Avoidance strategy) seek to prevent the poor from falling into such unacceptable circumstances. For the rich thereby maximize their chances of obtaining an outcome acceptable to them: preservation of something resembling the status quo.

What about a wealthy and powerful nation aiding poor, weak nations? Is this in the long-run interest of the former as well as the latter? In a world of advanced technology, international markets, ideological conflicts among powerful nations, and nuclear weapons, it most probably is. In competition with other powerful nations, allies—even poor nations— are useful for political, economic, and military reasons. And economic development of poor nations should, in the long run, produce economic benefits for richer nations, such as by providing markets and reliable supplies of various raw and finished goods.[26] Most important, continued poverty in the Third World is likely to produce continued political turmoil, civil wars, and regional wars between nations. In a world armed to the teeth with nuclear weapons, and with more and more nations acquiring such weapons, the long-run danger of rich developed countries being drawn into a devastating military conflict started by a desperate poor nation, or some desperate group within such a nation, is far from negligible.

The above arguments about domestic and international justice suggest there is, after all, a form of reciprocity between powerful and weak groups because of interdependencies between the two in economic and security matters. The poor cannot return the aid of the rich in kind, but they can offer their talents, their purchasing power, and so on. If not treated well, they cannot directly punish the rich and powerful, but they can stir up serious trouble for them if they are willing to experience such trouble themselves. Thus they are able, and likely, to return good for good and evil for evil to the rich in the long run, and it will be rational for the rich to act accordingly.

Even this form of reciprocity is not available, however, to deal with our third and most puzzling example—the treatment of future generations.[27] Future generations (beyond the next few) are powerless to act upon us, since they will not exist until after we are dead. Yet we have substantial power to determine the quality of their lives by influencing their numbers and the nature of the social and natural environment into which they will be born. Given this absolute asymmetry in power to affect one another, how can it be in our interest to act morally toward future generations? Morality requires us, at a minimum, to leave our descendants with enough resources to allow future people to live decent lives. But this would necessitate having a lower material standard of living than we could obtain by depleting resources and contaminating the environment whenever it is convenient to do so. If future generations cannot punish us for ruthlessly exploiting the earth in this way, doesn't rational prudence require it of us?

The supporter of the Reconciliation Project can come some considerable way toward answering even this objection. He might point out first that misuse of resources and damage to the environment will often produce substantial negative effects within our own lifetimes. So, for the most part, it is in our own interests to follow conservation policies that will turn out to benefit future generations. This reply will take us only so far, however. For there are policies whose benefits are experienced now and most of whose costs will be borne generations later (such as building nuclear power plants without having solved the long-term waste storage problem). Also, optimal *rates* of use of scarce nonrenewable resources will vary greatly depending upon how long we care about the resource lasting. Hence, there is a far from perfect overlap between the resource and environmental policies likely to most benefit present people and those likely to ensure a decent life for future generations.

A more promising argument begins from the fact that most people care very deeply about the happiness of their own children and grand-children, and hence their own happiness would be diminished by contemplating the prospect of these descendants having to live in a resource-depleted world. Further, they realize that their children's and grand-children's happiness will in turn be affected by the prospects for happiness of *their* children and grandchildren, and so forth. Hence, the happiness of present people is linked, generation by generation, to the prospects for happiness of some likely members of distant future generations. This "chain-connection" argument has considerable force, but it falls short of constituting a full solution to the problem before us. This is because the perceived happiness of one's children and grandchildren is only one component of the well-being or happiness of the typical parent. And the perceived happiness of *their* children and grandchildren is, in turn, only one component of the happiness of one's children and grandchildren. So there is a multiplier effect over generations that quickly diminishes the influence on a present person's happiness of the prospects for happiness of his later descendants.[28] And we must seek some other device to link living peoples' interests firmly with those of distant future generations.

The most promising such device is an appeal to our need to give meaning to our lives and endeavors. I have suggested elsewhere that one strong reason we have for providing future people with the means to survive and prosper is that this is our best hope for the successful continuation of certain human enterprises that we value (and may have contributed to)—science, the arts and humanities, morality, religion, democratic government.[29] Similarly, Ernest Partridge has argued that human beings have a psychological need for "self-transcendence"; that is, a need to contribute to projects that are outside themselves and that will continue after their deaths (1981). Those without such goals are unlikely to find meaning in their lives, especially during the middle and later stages of life, when people typically reflect on their own mortality. Thus Partridge says, "We need the future, *now*" (1981, p. 217).

There is a great deal of truth in this argument, but there are some limits to what it can show. It cannot reconcile the interests and obligations to posterity of the narcissist who has no self-transcending goals and is incapable of developing them. However, this need not worry us anymore than did the corresponding remark made earlier about the person no longer capable of becoming moral. The self-transcending life may be the happier life for the vast majority who still can live it, and these people have good prudential reasons for doing so. The more important problem is that not all self-transcending concerns need be directed toward the distant future. They may involve goals that do not extend much beyond one's lifetime (such as the prosperity of one's children, or the eventual rise to power of one's favorite political movement). Such goals may give meaning to one's life without supplying reasons to provide for the welfare of distant generations. Perhaps, though, it is a psychological fact that enterprises that promise to continue into the indefinite future are better able to provide meaning in our lives, or to provide consolation for our mortality.[30] If so, there would be powerful prudential reasons for one's adopting self-transcending concerns of unlimited temporal scope, and for protecting the social and natural environments for future generations.

These are the best arguments I can think of for a coincidence of self-interest and our obligations to posterity. Many (including myself at times) will find them only partly convincing. Does this lack of complete conviction indicate that we should abandon the Reconciliation Project? No. Instead, we may broaden our interpretation of that project.

V. THE WIDER PROJECT

The general strategy I have followed in outlining a defense of the Reconciliation Project has been to restrain the project's ambitions where necessary. Thus the scope of the project has been narrowed in several ways. It applies to ways of life rather than particular actions and to practice morality rather than ideal morality. It succeeds with respect to most people and groups in actual social circumstances, but not with respect to all people and groups in all actual or possible circumstances. It may not convince the skeptical immoralist to change his ways, but it provides good reasons for moral people not to regret (or abandon) their way of life and for loving parents to raise their children to be moral.

However, to understand better the relationship between morality, rationality, and self-interest, we must briefly consider an important *widening* of the Reconciliation Project. For that project may be viewed as but a specific instance of a more general project: reconciling morality with the requirements of practical rationality. Given two special assumptions—the truth of Psychological Egoism and the interpretation of practical rationality as the efficient pursuit of the agent's ends (whatever they may be)[31]—this Wider Reconciliation Project would collapse into our original version concerning morality and self-interest. But the first of these assumptions is surely false; on any construal that does not render all motives self-interested by definition, people sometimes do have unselfish aims and possess and act upon non-self-interested motives. As a result, the question of whether moral requirements are consistent with the rational pursuit of the actual ends that people have is both distinct from and more important than the question of whether these requirements cohere with the demands of prudence.

Would shifting our focus to the Wider Reconciliation Project render irrelevant all we have said about the original project? If self-interested concerns played only an insignificant role in human motivation, it would. But clearly this is not the case. In fact, while Psychological Egoism is false, I would venture to propose that a milder doctrine, which I call Predominant Egoism, is probably true. Predominant Egoism says that human beings are, as a matter of fact, predominantly self-interested in the following sense. At least until they have achieved a satisfactory level of security and well-being, people's self-interested concerns tend to override their other-regarding, idealistic, and altruistic motives in determining their actions. Further, those nonselfish concerns that are sufficiently powerful to move people to acts that seriously conflict with self-interest tend to be limited in scope, such as to the well-being of family and friends and the advancement of specific favored projects or institutions.[32]

Now if it is true that people are predominantly self-interested, in this sense, many or most of their strongest motives and dearest ends are self-interested ones. And the above arguments about reconciling duty and interest will be highly relevant to the task of reconciling duty and the rational pursuit of people's actual ends. But in carrying out this Wider Reconciliation Project, there would be a new resource to appeal to—the altruistic and nonselfish ends that most everyone actually has to some degree. The presence of these ends may extend the range of cases in which the requirements of reason and morality coincide beyond those in which prudence and morality coincide.

Consider again our relationship to future generations. Most of us do have significant nonselfish concerns about the well-being of our children and grandchildren and the survival and prospering of the human species.[33] So we have reason to provide for these things *over and above* the contribution that our awareness of such provision makes to our own psychic well-being.[34] This further strengthens both the chain-connection and self-transcendence arguments for reconciling practical rationality with our duties to posterity. For it shows that in carrying out such duties we are fulfilling ends of ours not previously considered (that is, nonselfish ends) in addition to contributing to our own happiness.

The recognition of nonselfish ends also provides a fresh perspective on the sustenance of moral motivation over generations. We suggested earlier that parents seeking to promote their children's interests would have good reasons to raise their children to be moral. This suggestion would have little significance if we were operating upon an assumption of the truth of Psychological Egoism. (For then the only relevant question would be whether it is in a *parent's* interest to raise his or her children to be moral.) Since, however, concern for the well-being of one's children is among the strongest and most universal of non-self-interested human concerns, the suggestion is crucial to our understanding of how morality is rationally passed on from generation to generation. Typical parents who care strongly for the well-being of their children and care somewhat for the well-being of others have three significant reasons for raising those children to be moral: This will likely benefit the children (in accordance with our earlier arguments that being moral usually pays), it will likely benefit others who are affected by the children, and it will likely benefit the parents themselves (because their children will treat them better). And when children grow up as moral beings possessing consciences and the potential to experience the satisfactions of morality, it is, we have argued, most always in their interest to continue to live a moral life. Further, they, as parents, will have the same reasons for raising their children to be moral as their parents had for raising them in this manner. Thus morality can be seen to be potentially self-sustaining from generation to generation, without even taking into account socializing influences on the child from outside the family.[35]

In raising children to be moral, and in providing for future generations, some of the ends that we seek to achieve are non-self-interested ones. Given the content of moral rules and their connection with protecting the interests of others, many morally required actions will satisfy ends of this kind. As a result, the Wider Reconciliation Project should be successful in more cases than the original project. We may restate this crucial point: While it is normally prudent to be moral, it is sometimes rational to be moral even if it is not prudent.

NOTES

1. See, for example, Henry Sidgwick (1907); H. A. Prichard (1971); D. Z. Phillips (1968); and Jan Narveson (1967), pp. 263–265.

2. Cf. Robert Nozick, *Philosophical Explanations* (1981), pp. 406–411.

3. See the discussion of the paradox of self-interest in section II.

4. I borrow the internal/external sanction terminology from Sidgwick.

5. I further discuss some of the issues raised in this section in my "Right Reason and Natural Law in Hobbes's Ethics," (1983).

6. This aid principle is inferred from Hobbes's explanation of his fifth law of nature requiring mutual accommodation. See (1651, 1958), p. 125. On Hobbes's belief in the welfare state, see also p. 271.

7. See Silberman (1978), pp. 75–78, where it is argued that virtually all career criminals end up in prison at some time.

8. By treating the loss of the primary social reward of morality—the goodwill and cooperation of others—as the main punishment for immorality, Hobbes implicitly takes account of both the positive and the negative external sanctions of morality.

9. "Deterrence, Utility, and Rational Choice" (1980). A similar view is hinted at in Fishkin (1979), pp. 34 and 149 (fn. 17). To employ the Disaster Avoidance Strategy, ordinal knowledge of the relevant probabilities is required.

10. See, however, the second objection discussed at the end of this section.

11. For application of this idea, see my "When Two 'Wrongs' Make a Right: An Essay on Business Ethics," forthcoming.

12. See sections III and IV.

13. This claim may be qualified to take account of self-deception and related phenomena without greatly affecting my argument.

14. This is important because experts say that in achieving deterrence, the certainty of a sanction is generally more important than its severity. See, for example, Von Hirsch (1976), pp. 61–63.

15. There may be other satisfactions that are incompatible with the psychological structure of the immoralist's mind. For example, Richmond Campbell (1979) argues that immoral egoism is incompatible with self-respect and genuine love of oneself. If this is so, these satisfactions (or the chance to obtain them) may be included as "satisfactions of morality," and their loss may be regarded as an opportunity cost of living an immoral life.

16. Are there compensating special satisfactions of the immoral life that are not available to the moral individual? Without discussing cases of obvious psychopathology, we might consider the pleasures of, for example, being strong and independent or outsmarting others. It seems, however, that all of these pleasures are available within the context of various moral lives, since being moral does not rule out being strong and independent, outsmarting others, and so on.

17. Moralists should not be too comforted by this argument. For somewhat analogous arguments suggest that the abandonment of morality may be called for in certain imaginable circumstances. See my "Some Paradoxes of Deterrence" (1978).

18. See Geoffrey Brennan and Gordon Tullock (1981).

19. See the report on the United States *v.* Holmes lifeboat case of 1842, in Philip E. Davis (1966), pp. 102–118.

20. If it does not, then the decrease in life expectancy, together with the other costs of the moral life (such as lost opportunities to cheat), must be added together and compared to the benefits of the moral life. The decrease, if any, in life expectancy seems unlikely to be great enough to tip the prudential balance against the moral way of life.

21. This follows from the expected value principle if we treat the choice as one under risk. If we regard the choice as under uncertainty, we can obtain the same result by applying the Disaster Avoidance Principle. For rejecting, rather than adopting, the moral life is more likely to lead to an unacceptable outcome, such as imprisonment or ostracism.

Does prudence counsel selecting a particular nondangerous moral way of life, namely pacifism? No, for if one does not believe in pacifism, it may not be an eligible choice as a moral way of life. Further, its external costs may be large (such as imprisonment for conscientious objection), and it might even commit one to actions as dangerous as armed conflict (such as interposing oneself between aggressors and victims, or serving as a medic at the front).

22. See Bernard Boxill (1980).

23. In certain cases immoral conduct might conceivably be in the interest of an oppressed group; for example, if terrorism is the only way of ending the oppression. These cases raise special problems about the morality of revolutionary violence and will not be discussed here.

24. This argument is the liberal counterpart of the conservative "trickle-down" theory, which claims that direct benefits to the rich will indirectly benefit the poor.

25. John Rawls (1971), sec. 29. Hobbes (1651, 1958), p. 87, quoted in text, and p. 126. Psychological and statistical evidence supports this traditional view, with some qualifications (for example, *rapid* progress for poor groups can produce instability). See Ted Robert Gurr (1970).

26. This claim should be qualified by noting that worldwide development without environmental safeguards might be disastrous. See Donella Meadows et al. (1972).

27. As is pointed out in Brian Barry (1978).

28. We can illustrate this point using arbitrarily chosen and artificially precise numbers. Suppose that my happiness is half dependent upon my perception of my children's well-being and half dependent on other independent things, and that I assume the same will be true of them and their children, and so on. Then one-quarter of my happiness will be determined by the prospects of my grandchildren, one-eighth by the prospects of my great grandchildren, and so forth.

29. See section IV of my "The Futurity Problem" (1978a). I there discuss reasons for wanting the continuation of the species, but some of the same points apply to assuring future people decent lives.

30. The fact that most of us do care a good deal about the future survival and prosperity of humankind may constitute evidence that this is so.

31. This is a standard conception adopted by economists, social scientists, and philosophers such as Rawls (1971), pp. 142–146, and David A. J. Richards (1971), p. 28. One could follow Richard Brandt (1979) in rejecting some *ends* as irrational and still maintain the links described below between the original project and the Wider Reconciliation Project, given the plausible assumption that many of our self-interested ends (such as security and material well-being) are rational in the relevant sense. These links would be severed, however, and the Wider Reconciliation Project trivialized, if we adopted Thomas Nagel's view (1970) that practical reasons are by nature general and not agent-relative.

32. For historical antecedents of Predominant Egoism, see David Hume (1739, III, 2, ii), L. A. Selby-Bigge, ed. (1968), pp. 488–489, 494–495; and John Stuart Mill (1869), p. 225.

33. This is acknowledged even by Thomas Schwartz (1978, sec. 4), who argues that we have no obligations to distant future generations to promote their welfare.

34. I am here relying on a distinction, noted by critics of psychological hedonism, between desiring that X occur and experiencing pleasure at the thought that X will occur. To take an example, I purchase life insurance because I desire that my family be provided for after my death, not because I seek the peace of mind of now knowing that they will be provided for, although the latter is also a predictable and expected result of my action. This action contributes to the fulfillment of *two* of my ends: the safeguarding of my family's future after my demise and the attainment of peace of mind for me now. It is thus more likely to be rational for me (that is, worth the cost in terms of foregoing fulfillment of other ends I could use the insurance premium money to forward) than if peace of mind were the only of my ends achieved thereby.

35. These outside influences may be necessary, however, because many parents do not know how to raise their children to be moral, or they are unwilling to make the necessary sacrifices to do so, or they are unconvinced that being moral is in their children's interests.

Bibliography

Adams, Robert Merrihew (1981): "Divine Command Metaethics as Necessary A Posteriori," in Paul Helm, ed., *Divine Commands and Morality*, pp. 109–118. Oxford University Press, Oxford.

Alper, Joseph; Beckwith, Jon; and Miller, Lawrence (1978): "Sociobiology Is a Political Issue," in Arthur L. Caplan, ed., *The Sociobiology Debate: Readings on the Ethical and Scientific Issues Concerning Sociobiology*, pp. 476–488. Harper and Row, New York.

Anscombe, Elizabeth (1958): "Modern Moral Philosophy," *Philosophy* 33, pp. 1–19. (1968): in Judith Jarvis Thomson and Gerald Dworkin, eds., *Ethics*. Harper and Row, New York.

Aristotle. *Nicomachean Ethics*. (1954): translated by W. D. Ross. Oxford University Press, Oxford.

Arrow, Kenneth J. (1951): *Social Choice and Individual Values*. Second edition, 1963. Yale University Press, New Haven, Connecticut.

———. (1967): "Values and Collective Decision-Making," in Peter Laslett and W. G. Runciman, eds., *Philosophy, Politics and Society*, Third Series, pp. 215–232. Oxford University Press, Oxford.

Axelrod, Robert (1984): *The Evolution of Cooperation*. Basic Books, New York.

Axelrod, Robert, and Hamilton, William D. (1981): "The Evolution of Cooperation," *Science* 211 (March 27), pp. 1390–96.

Ayer, A. J. (1946): *Language, Truth and Logic*. Victor Gollantz, London.

Baier, Kurt (1958): *The Moral Point of View*. Cornell University Press, Ithaca, New York. (1965): Abridged edition, Random House, New York.

———. (1973): "Reason and Experience," *Nous* 7, pp. 56–67.

———. (1977): "Rationality and Morality," *Erkenntnis* 11, pp. 197–223.

———. (1978a): "Moral Reasons," in Peter A. French; Theodore E. Uehling, Jr.; and Howard Wettstein, eds., *Midwest Studies in Philosophy 3, Studies in Ethical Theory*, pp. 62–74. University of Minnesota, Morris.

———. (1978b): "Moral Reasons and Reasons to be Moral," in A. I. Goldman and J. Kim, *Values and Morals*, pp. 231–256. D. Reidel, Dordrecht, Holland.

———. (1978c): "The Social Source of Reason," *Proceedings and Addresses of the American Philosophical Association* 51, pp. 707–733.

———. (1981): "Defining Morality Without Prejudice," *The Monist* 64, pp. 325–341.

———. (1982): "The Conceptual Link Between Morality and Rationality," *Nous* 16, pp. 78–88.

Barash, David (1979): *The Whisperings Within: Evolution and the Origin of Human Nature*. Harper and Row, New York.

Barry, Brian (1978): "Circumstances of Justice and Future Generations," in Richard Sikora and Brian Barry, eds., *Obligations to Future Generations*, pp. 204–248. Temple University Press, Philadelphia.

Blackburn, Simon (1971): "Moral Realism," in J. Casey, ed., *Morality and Moral Reasoning*, pp. 101–124. Methuen, London.

Block, Ned (1978): "Troubles with Functionalism," in C. Wade Savage, ed., *Perception and Cognition: Issues in the Foundations of Psychology*. Minnesota Studies in the Philosophy of Science, vol. 9. University of Minnesota Press, Minneapolis. (1980): in N. Block, ed., *Readings in the Philosophy of Psychology*. Harvard University Press, Cambridge.

Block, N. J., and Dworkin, Gerald (1974): "I.Q. Heritability and Inequality, Part 2," *Philosophy and Public Affairs* 4, pp. 40–99.

Boorse, Christopher (1975): "On the Distinction between Disease and Illness," *Philosophy and Public Affairs* 5, pp. 49–68.

———. (1976): "Wright on Functions," *The Philosphical Review* 85, pp. 70–86.

Bowlby, J. (1969): *Attachment*. Basic Books, New York.

Boxill, Bernard (1980): "How Injustice Pays," *Philosophy and Public Affairs* 9, pp. 359–371.

Boyd, Richard (1982): "Scientific Realism and Naturalistic Epistemology," *PSA 1980. Proceedings of the 1980 Biennial Meeting of the Philosophy of Science Association*, vol. II. Philosophy of Science Association, East Lansing, Michigan.

———. (forthcoming a): "Materialism Without Reductionism: Non-Humean Causation and the Evidence for Physicalism," in *The Physical Basis of Mind*. Harvard University Press, Cambridge.

———. (forthcoming b): *Realism and Scientific Epistemology*. Cambridge University Press, Cambridge.

———. (forthcoming c): "How to be a Moral Realist," unpublished lecture delivered at the University of British Columbia, January 1984.

Brandt, Richard B. (1959): *Ethical Theory*. Prentice-Hall, Englewood Cliffs, New Jersey.

———. (1976): "The Psychology of Benevolence and Its Implications for Philosophy," *The Journal of Philosophy* 73, pp. 429–453.

———. (1979): *A Theory of the Good and the Right*. Clarendon Press of Oxford University Press, Oxford.

Brennan, Geoffrey, and Tullock, Gordon (1981): "An Economic Theory of Military Tactics: Methodological Individualism at War," Public Choice Center, Virginia Polytechnic Institute and State University.

Buchanan, James M. (1975): *The Limits of Liberty*. University of Chicago Press.

Campbell, Richmond (1979): *Self-Love and Self-Respect: A Philosophical Study of Egoism*. Canadian Library of Philosophy, Ottawa.

———. (1981): "Can Inconsistency be Reasonable?" *Canadian Journal of Philosophy* 11, pp. 245–270.

Caplan, Arthur L., ed., (1978): *The Sociobiology Debate: Readings on the Ethical and Scientific Issues Concerning Sociobiology*. Harper and Row, New York.

Cherniak, Christopher (1980): "Minimal Rationality," *Mind* 90, pp. 161–183.

———. (1981): "Feasible Inferences," *Philosophy of Science* 48, pp. 248–268.

Clarke, Samuel (1705): *On Natural Religion*. Boyle Lectures, first printed 1706. (1738): in *Collected Works*. (1897): in L. A. Selby-Bigge, ed., *The British Moralists*, vol. II. Oxford University Press, Oxford.

Cooper, David E. (1978). "Moral Relativism," in Peter A. French; Theodore E. Uehling, Jr.; and Howard Wettstein, eds., *Midwest Studies in Philosophy 3, Studies in Ethical Theory*, pp. 97–108. The University of Minnesota, Morris.

Copp, David (1982): "Harman on Internalism, Relativism and Logical Form," *Ethics* 92, pp. 227–242.

———. (forthcoming): *Morality and Society*.

Daniels, Norman (1979a): "Moral Theory and the Plasticity of Persons," *The Monist* 62, pp. 265–287.

———. (1979b): "Wide Reflective Equilibrium and Theory Acceptance in Ethics," *The Journal of Philosophy* 76, pp. 256–282.

———. (1980a): "Reflective Equilibrium and Archimedean Points," *Canadian Journal of Philosophy* 10, pp. 83–103.

———. (1980b): "Some Methods of Ethics and Linguistics," *Philosophical Studies* 37, pp. 21–36.

———. (1983): "Can Cognitive Psychotherapy Reconcile Reason and Desire?" *Ethics* 93, pp. 772–785.

Darwall, Stephen L. (1983): *Impartial Reason*. Cornell University Press, Ithaca, New York.

Davis, David Brion (1966): *The Problem of Slavery in Western Culture*. Cornell University Press, Ithaca, New York.

Davis, Philip E. (1966): *Moral Duty and Legal Responsibility*. Appleton-Century-Crofts, New York.

Dawkins, Richard (1976): *The Selfish Gene*. Oxford University Press, Oxford.

Dennett, Daniel (1981): "Three Kinds of Intentional Psychology," in R. Healy, ed., *Reduction, Time and Reality*, pp. 37–61. Cambridge University Press, Cambridge.

Desmond, Adrian (1979): *The Ape's Reflection*. Dial Press, J. Wade, New York.

De Sousa, Ronald (1982): Review of John Wallace, *Virtues and Vices*, *Nous* 16, pp. 161–165.

De Voto, Bernard (1942): *The Year of Decision: 1846*. Houghton Mifflin, Boston.

Dobzhansky, T. (1973): *Genetic Diversity and Human Equality*. Basic Books, New York.

Duhem, Pierre (1906): *The Aim and Structure of Physical Theory*. (1954): translated by Philip P. Wiener. Princeton University Press, Princeton, New Jersey.

Dummett, Michael (1978): *Truth and Other Enigmas*. Harvard University Press, Cambridge.

Donagan, Alan (1977): *The Theory of Morality*. Chicago University Press.

Dworkin, Ronald (1977): *Taking Rights Seriously*. Harvard University Press, Cambridge.

Falk, W. D. (1947–48): " 'Ought' and Motivation," *Proceedings of the Aristotelian Society* 48, pp. 111–138.

———. (1963a): "Action-Guiding Reasons," *The Journal of Philosophy* 60, pp. 702–718.

———. (1963b): "Morality, Self and Others," in H. Castaneda and G. Nakhnikian, eds., *Morality and the Language of Conduct*, pp. 25–68. Wayne State University, Detroit.

Festinger, Leon (1957): *A Theory of Cognitive Dissonance*. Stanford University Press, Palo Alto, California.

Feyerabend, Paul K. (1965). "Problems of Empiricism," in Robert G. Colodny, ed., *Beyond the Edge of Certainty: Essays in Contemporary Science and Philosophy*, pp. 145–260. Prentice-Hall, Englewood Cliffs, New Jersey.

Firth, Roderick (1952): "Ethical Absolutism and the Ideal Observer," *Philosophy and Phenomenological Research* 12, pp. 317–345.

Fishkin, James (1979): *Tyranny and Legitimacy*. Johns Hopkins University Press, Baltimore.

Fodor, Jerry (1974): "Special Sciences (or: The Disunity of Science as a Working Hypothesis)," *Synthese* 28, pp. 97–115.

Foot, Philippa (1967): *Moral Theories*. Oxford University Press, Oxford.

———. (1978a): *Moral Relativism*. The Lindley Lecture. University of Kansas, Lawrence.

———. (1978b): *Virtues and Vices*. University of California Press, Berkeley and Los Angeles.

———. (1983): "Moral Realism and Moral Dilemma," *The Journal of Philosophy* 80, pp. 379–398.

Frankena, William (1958): "Obligation and Motivation," in A. I. Melden, ed., *Essays in Moral Philosophy*. University of Washington Press, Seattle.

———. (1976): *Perspectives on Morality*, K. E. Goodpaster, ed. University of Notre Dame Press, Notre Dame, Indiana.

Frankfurt, Harry (1971): "Freedom of the Will and the Concept of a Person," *The Journal of Philosophy* 68, pp. 5–20.

Freud, Sigmund. *Standard Edition of the Complete Psychological Works*. The Hogarth Press, London, 1957–73.

Fried, Charles (1978): *Right and Wrong*. Harvard University Press, Cambridge.

Gauthier, David (1967): "Morality and Advantage," *The Philosophical Review* 76, pp. 460–475.

———. (1974a): "The Impossibility of Rational Egoism," *The Journal of Philosophy* 71, pp. 439–456.

———. (1974b): "Justice and Natural Endowment: Toward a Critique of Rawls' Ideological Framework," *Social Theory and Practice* 3, pp. 3–26.

———. (1974c): "Rational Cooperation," *Nous* 8, pp. 53–65.

———. (1975a): "Reason and Maximization," *Canadian Journal of Philosophy* 4, pp. 411–433.

———. (1975b): "Coordination," *Dialogue* 14, pp. 195–221.

_____ . (1978a): "Bargaining Our Way Into Morality: A Do-It-Yourself Primer," *Philosophic Exchange* 5, pp. 15–27.

_____ . (1978b): Critical Notice of *Essays on Ethics, Social Behaviour and Scientific Explanation*, by John C. Harsanyi, *Dialogue* 17, pp. 696–706.

_____ . (1978c): "Economic Rationality and Moral Constraints," in Peter A. French; Theodore E. Uehling, Jr.; and Howard Wettstein, eds., *Midwest Studies in Philosophy 3, Studies in Ethical Theory*, pp. 75–96. The University of Minnesota, Morris.

_____ . (1978d): "Social Choice and Distributive Justice," *Philosophia* 7, pp. 239–253.

_____ . (1978e): "The Social Contract: Individual Decision or Collective Bargain?" in C. A. Hooker; J. J. Leach; and E. F. McClennen, eds., *Foundations and Applictions of Decision Theory*, vol. II, pp. 47–67. D. Reidel, Dordrecht, Holland.

_____ . (1979): "Thomas Hobbes: Moral Theorist," *The Journal of Philosophy* 76, pp. 547–559.

_____ . (1980): "The Irrationality of Choosing Egoism," *Canadian Journal of Philosophy* 10, pp. 179–188.

Gert, Bernard (1966): *The Moral Rules*. Harper and Row, New York.

Gewirth, Alan (1960): "Positive 'Ethics' and Normative 'Science'," *The Philosophical Review* 69, pp. 311–330.

_____ . (1978): *Reason and Morality*. University of Chicago Press.

Gibbard, Allan (1982): "Human Evolution and the Sense of Justice," in Peter A. French; Theodore E. Uehling, Jr.; and Howard Wettstein, eds., *Midwest Studies in Philosophy 7, Social and Political Philosophy*, pp. 31–46. The University of Minnesota, Minneapolis.

Goodman, Nelson (1952): "Sense and Certainty," *The Philosophical Review* 61, pp. 160–167.

_____ . (1965): *Fact, Fiction and Forecast*. Second edition. Bobbs-Merrill, Indianapolis.

Goudge, T. A. (1967): *The Ascent of Life*. G. Allen and Unwin, London.

Gould, Stephen Jay (1976): "Biological Potential vs. Biological Determinism," *Natural History Magazine*, May (1978): reprinted in Arthur L. Caplan, ed., *The Sociobiology Debate: Readings on the Ethical and Scientific Issues Concerning Sociobiology*, pp. 343–351, Harper and Row, New York.

_____ . (1977): *Ever Since Darwin*. W. W. Norton, New York.

_____ . (1980): *The Panda's Thumb: More Reflections in Natural History*. Norton, New York.

Grice, Geoffrey Russell (1967): *The Grounds of Moral Judgment*. Cambridge University Press, Cambridge.

Gurr, Ted Robert (1970): *Why Men Rebel*. Princeton University Press, Princeton, New Jersey.

Hamilton, William D. (1964): "The Genetical Evolution of Social Behaviour," *The Journal of Theoretical Biology* 7. (1978): reprinted in Arthur L. Caplan, ed., *The Sociobiology Debate: Readings on the Ethical and Scientific Issues Concerning Sociobiology*, pp. 191–209. Harper and Row, New York.

Hardin, Russell (1983): "Unilateral Versus Mutual Disarmament," *Philosophy and Public Affairs* 12, pp. 236–254.

Hare, R. M. (1952): *The Language of Morals*. The Clarendon Press of Oxford University Press, Oxford.

_____ . (1976): "Some Questions about Subjectivity," in *Freedom and Morality: The Lindley Lectures*, pp. 191–208. University of Kansas Press, Lawrence.

_____ . (1981): *Moral Thinking: Its Levels, Method and Point*. The Clarendon Press of Oxford University Press, Oxford.

Harman, Gilbert (1973): *Thought*. Princeton University Press, Princeton, New Jersey.

_____ . (1975): "Moral Relativism Defended," *The Philosophical Review* 84, pp. 3–22.

_____ . (1977): *The Nature of Morality: An Introduction to Ethics*. Oxford University Press, New York.

_____ . (1978a): Relativistic Ethics: Morality as Politics," in Peter A. French; Theodore E. Uehling, Jr.; and Howard Wettstein, eds., *Midwest Studies in Philosophy 3, Studies in Ethical Theory*, pp. 109–121. The University of Minnesota, Morris.

———— . (1978b): "What is Moral Relativism?" in A. I. Goldman and J. Kim, eds., *Values and Morals*, pp. 143–161. D. Reidel, Dordrecht, Holland.

Harsanyi, John C. (1955): "Cardinal Welfare, Individualistic Ethics, and Interpersonal Comparisons of Utility," *Journal of Political Economy* 63, pp. 309–321.

———— . (1977): *Rational Behaviour and Bargaining Equilibrium in Games and Social Situations.* Cambridge University Press, Cambridge.

Harsanyi, Zsolt, and Hutton, Richard (1981): *Genetic Prophecy: Beyond the Double Helix.* Rawson, Wade Publishers, New York.

Hobbes, Thomas (1651): *Leviathan.* London. (1958): Bobbs-Merrill, Indianapolis.

Hoffman, Martin (1970): "Moral Development," in P. Mussen, ed., *Carmichael's Manual of Child Psychology,* vol. II, pp. 261–359. John Wiley and Sons, New York.

———— . (1981): "Developmental Synthesis of Affect and Cognition and Its Implications for Altruistic Motivation," *Developmental Psychology, Personality and Social Psychology* 40, pp. 121–137.

Hume, David (1739): *Treatise of Human Nature.* London. (1968): L. A. Selby-Bigge, ed. The Clarendon Press of Oxford University Press, Oxford.

Huxley, J., and Huxley, T. H. (1947): *Evolution and Ethics.* London. (1969): Kraus, New York.

Jouvet, M. (1978): "Does a Genetic Programming of the Brain Occur During Paradoxical Sleep?" in P. A. Buser and A. Routeulg, eds., *Cerebral Correlates of Conscious Experience,* INSERM Symposium Series, vol. VI. Elsevier, Paris.

Kalai, E., and Smorodinsky, M. (1975): "Other Solutions to Nash's Bargaining Problem," *Econometrica* 43, pp. 513–518.

Kant, Immanuel (1785): *Groundwork of the Metaphysics of Morals.* (1959): translated by Lewis White Beck. Bobbs-Merrill, Indianapolis. (1964): translated by H. J. Paton. Harper Torchbooks, New York.

Kavka, Gregory S. (1978a): "The Futurity Problem," in Richard Sikora and Brian Barry, eds., *Obligations to Future Generations,* pp. 186–203. Temple University Press, Philadelphia.

———— . (1978b): "Some Paradoxes of Deterrence," *The Journal of Philosophy* 75, pp. 285–302.

———— . (1980): "Deterrence, Utility and Rational Choice," *Theory and Decision* 12, pp. 41–60.

———— . (1983): "Right Reason and Natural Law in Hobbes's Ethics," *The Monist* 66, pp. 120–133.

———— . (forthcoming): "When Two 'Wrongs' Make a Right: An Essay on Business Ethics," *Journal of Business Ethics.*

Kim, Jaegwon (1978): "Supervenience and Nomological Incommensurables," *American Philosophical Quarterly* 15, pp. 149–156.

———— . (1979): "Causality, Identity and Supervenience in the Mind-Body Problem," in Peter A. French; Theodore E. Uehling, Jr.; and Howard K. Wettstein, eds., *Midwest Studies in Philosophy 4, Studies in Metaphysics,* pp. 31–49. University of Minnesota Press, Minneapolis.

King, L. (1954): "What is Disease?" *Philosophy of Science* 21, pp. 193–203.

Kohlberg, Lawrence (1973): "The Claim to Moral Adequacy of a Highest Stage of Moral Judgment," *The Journal of Philosophy* 70, pp. 630–646.

Kripke, Saul (1980): *Naming and Necessity.* Harvard University Press, Cambridge.

Kuhn, Thomas (1962): *The Structure of Scientific Revolutions.* Pheonix Books, Chicago.

Lackey, Douglas (1982): "Missiles and Morals: A Utilitarian Look at Nuclear Deterrence," *Philosophy and Public Affairs* 11, pp. 189–231.

Ladd, John (1957): *The Structure of a Moral Code.* Harvard University Press, Cambridge.

Lem, S. (1979): *A Perfect Vacuum: Perfect Reviews of Nonexistent Books.* Harcourt Brace Jovanovich, New York.

Levine, Andrew (1981): *Liberal Democracy: A Critique of Its Theory.* Columbia University Press, New York.

Lewontin, R. D. (1978): "Adaptation," *Scientific American* (September), pp. 212–230.

Lyons, David (1975): "Nature and Soundness of the Contract and Coherence Arguments," in Norman Daniels, ed., *Reading Rawls*, pp. 141–167. Basic Books, New York.

MacLean, P. (1969): "The Paranoid Streak in Man," in A. Koestler and J. R. Smythies, eds., *Beyond Reductionism: New Perspectives in the Life Sciences*, pp. 258–278. The Hutchinson Publishing Group, London.

Mackie, John L. (1965): "Causes and Conditions," *American Philosophical Quarterly* 2, pp. 245–264.

―――. (1977): *Ethics: Inventing Right and Wrong*. Penguin, Harmondsworth, England.

Mattern, Ruth (1978): "Altruism, Ethics, and Sociobiology," in Arthur L. Caplan, ed., *The Sociobiology Debate: Readings on the Ethical and Scientific Issues Concerning Sociobiology*, pp. 462–475. Harper and Row, New York.

McDowell, John (1978): "Are Moral Requirements Hypothetical Imperatives?" *Proceedings of the Aristotelian Society, Supplementary Volume* 52, pp. 13–29.

―――. (1979): "Virtue and Reason," *The Monist* 62, pp. 331–350.

―――. (1981): "Noncognitivism and Rule Following," in Steven H. Holtzman and Christopher M. Leich, eds., *Wittgenstein: To Follow a Rule*, pp. 141–162. Routledge and Kegan Paul, London.

Meadows, Donella; Meadows, Dennis L.; Randers, Jorgen; and Behrens, William W. (1972): *The Limits to Growth*. Universe Books, for Potomac Associates, New York.

Midgley, M. (1978): *Beast and Man: The Roots of Human Nature*. Cornell University Press, Ithaca, New York.

―――. (1979): "Gene Juggling," *Philosophy* 54, pp. 439–458.

Mill, John Stuart (1863): *Utilitarianism*. London. (1957): Bobbs-Merrill, Library of Liberal Arts, Indianapolis.

―――. (1869): "The Subjection of Women," in John Stuart Mill and Harriet Taylor Mill, *Essays on Sex Equality*, Alice S. Rossi, ed. University of Chicago Press, 1970.

―――. (1874): "On Human Nature," in *Nature, the Utility of Religion, Theism, Being Three Essays on Religion*. Longman, Green, Reader and Dyer, London.

Mill, John Stuart, and Mill, Harriet Taylor (1970): *Essays on Sex Equality*, Alice S. Rossi, ed. University of Chicago Press.

Moore, G. E. (1903): *Principia Ethica*. Cambridge University Press, Cambridge.

Munson, R., ed. (1971): *Man and Nature: Philosophical Issues in Biology*. Delta, New York.

Murdoch, I. (1970): *The Sovereignty of Good*. Cambridge University Press, London.

Nagel, Thomas (1970): *The Possibility of Altruism*. Oxford University Press, Oxford.

―――. (1979): "What Is It Like to Be a Bat?" in *Mortal Questions*, pp. 165–180. Cambridge University Press, Cambridge.

―――. (1980): "The Limits of Objectivity," in Sterling M. McMurrin, ed., *The Tanner Lectures on Human Values*, pp. 77–139. University of Utah Press, Salt Lake City; Cambridge University Press, Cambridge.

Narveson, Jan (1967): *Morality and Utility*. Johns Hopkins University Press, Baltimore.

―――. (1978): "Future People and Us," in Richard Sikora and Brian Barry, eds., *Obligations to Future Generations*, pp. 38–60. Temple University Press, Philadelphia.

―――. (1981): "Human Rights: Which, If Any, There Are," in James Roland Pennock and John W. Chapman, eds., *Human Rights. NOMOS XXIII*, pp. 175–197. New York University Press, New York.

Nielsen, Kai (1974): "Why Should I Be Moral?" in W. K. Frankena and J. T. Granrose, eds., *Introductory Readings in Ethics*, pp. 473–492. Prentice-Hall, Englewood Cliffs, New Jersey.

Nozick, Robert (1969): "Newcomb's Problem and Two Principles of Choice," in Nicholas Rescher, ed., *Essays in Honor of Carl G. Hempel*, pp. 114–146. D. Reidel, Dordrecht, Holland.

―――. (1974): *Anarchy, State and Utopia*. Basic Books, New York.

―――. (1981): *Philosophical Explanations*. Harvard University Press, Cambridge.

Parfit, Derek (1979): "Prudence, Morality and the Prisoner's Dilemma," *Proceedings of the British Academy*, pp. 539–564.

Partridge, Ernest (1981): "Why Care About the Future?" in Ernest Partridge, ed., *Responsibilities to Future Generations*, Prometheus Books, Buffalo, New York.

Peattit, Phillip (1981): "Evaluative 'Realism' and Interpretation," in Steven H. Holtzman and Christopher M. Leich, eds., *Wittgenstein: To Follow a Rule*, pp. 211–245. Routledge and Kegan Paul, London.

Phillips, D. Z. (1968): "Does it Pay to be Good?" in Judith Jarvis Thomson and Gerald Dworkin, eds., *Ethics*, pp. 261–278. Harper and Row, New York.

Plato. *Philebus.* (1937): translated by B. Jowett, in B. Jowett, ed., *The Dialogues of Plato*, pp. 343–403. Random House, New York.

――――. *Republic.* (1974): translated by G. M. A. Grube, Hackett Publishing Company, Indianapolis.

Platts, Mark (1981): "Moral Reality and the End of Desire," in M. Platts, ed., *Reference, Truth and Meaning*, pp. 69–82. Routledge and Kegan Paul, London.

Prichard, H. A. (1971): "Duty and Interest," in Joel Feinberg, ed., *Reason and Responsibility.* Second edition, pp. 478–486. Dickenson, Encino, California.

Putnam, Hilary (1967): "The Nature of Mental States," in W. H. Capitan and D. D. Merrill, eds., *Art, Mind and Religion*, pp. 37–48. University of Pittsburgh Press, Pittsburgh.

――――. (1975): "Language and Reality," in *Mind, Language and Reality. Philosophical Papers, Volume II.* Cambridge University Press, Cambridge. Includes:
—(1975a): "The Meaning of 'Meaning'," pp. 215–271.

――――. (1977): *Mathematics, Matter and Method. Philosophical Papers, Volume I.* Second edition. Cambridge University Press, Cambridge. Includes:
—(1977a): "The 'Corroboration' of Theories."
—(1977b): "On Properties."

――――. (1981): *Reason, Truth and History.* Cambridge University Press, Cambridge.

Quine, W. V. O. (1969): *Ontological Relativity and Other Essays.* Columbia University Press, New York. Includes:
—(1969a): "Epistemology Naturalized."
—(1969b): "Natural Kinds."

Quinn, Warren (1978): "Moral and Other Realisms," in A. I. Goldman and J. Kim, eds., *Values and Morals*, pp. 257–253. D. Reidel, Dordrecht, Holland.

Rapoport, Anatol, ed. (1974): *Game Theory as a Theory of Conflict Resolution.* D. Reidel, Dordrecht, Holland.

Rashdall, Hastings (1924): *The Theory of Good and Evil.* Second edition. Oxford University Press, Oxford.

Rawls, John (1971): *A Theory of Justice.* Belknap Press of Harvard University Press, Cambridge.

――――. (1980): "Kantian Constructivism in Moral Theory: The Dewey Lectures, 1980," *The Journal of Philosophy* 77, pp. 515–572.

――――. (1982): "Social Utility and Primary Goods," in Amartya Sen and Bernard Williams, eds., *Utilitarianism and Beyond*, pp. 159–185. Cambridge University Press, Cambridge.

Richards, David A. J. (1971): *A Theory of Reasons for Action.* Oxford University Press, Oxford.

Rorty, Richard (1965): "Mind-Body Identity, Privacy, and Categories," *Review of Metaphysics* 19, pp. 24–54.

Rosenberg, Alexander (1980): *Sociobiology and the Preemption of Social Science.* Johns Hopkins University Press, Baltimore.

Ross, Sir W. David (1930): *The Right and the Good.* Oxford University Press, Oxford.

――――. (1939): *Foundations of Ethics.* Oxford University Press, Oxford.

Roth, Alvin E. (1979): *Axiomatic Models of Bargaining.* Springer-Verlag, Berlin and New York.

Roth, Alvin E.; Malouf, Michael W. K.; and Murnighan, J. Keith (1981): "Sociological Versus Strategic Factors in Bargaining," *Journal of Economic Behavior and Organization* 2, pp. 153–177.

Rotkin, K. F. (1972): "The Phallacy of Our Sexual Norm," *RT: A Journal of Radical Therapy*, September.

Ruse, Michael (1979): *Sociobiology: Sense or Nonsense?* D. Reidel, Dordrecht, Holland.

Ryan, William (1976): *Blaming the Victim.* Second edition. Vintage, New York.

Sagan, Carl (1977): *The Dragons of Eden*. Ballantine Books, New York.
Scanlon, T. M. (1982): "Contractualism and Utilitarianism," in Amartya Sen and Bernard Williams, *Utilitarianism and Beyond*, pp. 103–128. Cambridge University Press, Cambridge.
Scheffler, Israel (1954): "Justification and Commitment," *The Journal of Philosophy* 51, pp. 180–190.
———. (1967): *Science and Subjectivity*. Bobbs-Merrill, Indianapolis.
Schelling, Thomas C. (1960): *The Strategy of Conflict*. Oxford University Press, Oxford.
Schopenhauer, Arthur (1897): *On Human Nature*. George Allen and Unwin, London. (1957): reprint.
Schwartz, Thomas (1978): "Obligations to Posterity," in Richard Sikora and Brian Barry, eds., *Obligations to Future Generations*, pp. 3–13. Temple University Press, Philadelphia.
Sen, Amartya (1970): *Collective Choice and Social Welfare*. Holden-Day, San Francisco.
Sen, Amartya, and Williams, Bernard, eds. (1982): *Utilitarianism and Beyond*. Cambridge University Press, Cambridge.
Shields, S. A. (1977): "Functionalism, Darwinism and the Psychology of Women," in R. Duncan and M. Weston-Smith, *The Encyclopaedia of Ignorance*. Pergamon, Toronto.
Sidgwick, Henry (1907): *The Methods of Ethics*. London. (1966): Dover, New York.
Silberman, Charles (1978): *Criminal Violence, Criminal Justice*. Random House, New York.
Simpson, G. G. (1967): *The Meaning of Evolution*. Yale University Press, New Haven, Connecticut.
Singer, Peter (1973): "The Triviality of the Debate over 'Is-Ought' and the Definition of 'Moral'," *American Philosophical Quarterly* 10, pp. 51–56.
———. (1981): *The Expanding Circle: Ethics and Sociobiology*. Farrar, Straus and Giroux, New York.
Skinner, B. F. (1974): *About Behaviorism*. Alfred A. Knopf, New York.
Stent, Gunther S. (1980): *Morality as a Biological Phenomenon: The Presuppositions of Sociobiological Research*. University of California Press, Berkeley and Los Angeles.
Stevenson, Charles L. (1944): *Ethics and Language*. Yale University Press, New Haven, Connecticut.
———. (1963): *Facts and Values*. Yale University Press, New Haven, Connecticut.
Stitch, Stephen P., and Nisbett, Richard E. (1980): "Justification and the Psychology of Human Reasoning," *Philosophy of Science* 47, pp. 188–202.
Sturgeon, Nicholas (1982): "Brandt's Moral Empiricism," *The Philosophical Review* 91, pp. 389–422.
Tannenbaum, Frank (1947): *Slave and Citizen*. Alfred A. Knopf, New York.
Taylor, Charles (1977): "What is Human Agency," in Theodore Mischel, ed., *The Self*, pp. 103–135. Basil Blackwell, Oxford.
Tiger, L. (1970): *Men in Groups*. Vintage, New York.
Trebilcott, Joyce (1978): "Sex Roles: The Argument from Nature," in Mary B. Mahowald, ed., *Philosophy of Woman, Classical to Current Concepts*, pp. 288–295. Hackett Publishing Company, Indianapolis.
Trivers, Robert L. (1971): "The Evolution of Reciprocal Altruism," *The Quarterly Review of Biology* 46. (1978): reprinted in part in Arthur L. Caplan, ed., *The Sociobiology Debate: Readings on the Ethical and Scientific Issues Concerning Sociobiology*, pp. 213–226. Harper and Row, New York.
Vandenberghe, Pl. (1980): "Incest and Exogamy—A Sociobiological Reconsideration," *Ethology and Sociobiology*, No. 2, pp. 151–161.
Von Hirsch, Andrew (1976): *Doing Justice: The Choice of Punishments*. Hill and Wang, New York.
Wallace, John (1978): *Virtues and Vices*. Cornell University Press, Ithaca, New York.
Warnock, G. J. (1967): *Contemporary Moral Philosophy*. Macmillan, St. Martin's Press, London.
Webb, W. B. (1977): "Sleep," in R. Duncan and M. Weston-Smith, *The Encyclopaedia of Ignorance*. Pergamon, Toronto.
Wiggins, David (1976): "Truth, Invention and the Meaning of Life," *Proceedings of the British Academy*, pp. 331–378.

Williams, Bernard A. O. (1973): *Problems of the Self.* Cambridge University Press, Cambridge. Includes:
—(1973a): "Ethical Consistency," pp. 166–186.
—(1973b): "Consistency and Realism," pp. 187–207.
———. (1980): "Conclusion," in Gunther S. Stent, *Morality as a Biological Phenomenon: The Presuppositions of Sociobiological Research,* pp. 275–285. University of California Press, Berkeley and Los Angeles.
———. (1981): *Moral Luck.* Cambridge University Press, Cambridge.
Williams, J. H., ed. (1979): *Psychology of Women, Selected Readings.* W. W. Norton, New York.
Wilson, Edward O. (1975a): *Sociobiology: The New Synthesis.* Harvard University Press, Cambridge.
———. (1975b): "Human Decency is Animal," *The New York Times Magazine,* October 12.
———. (1978): *On Human Nature.* Bantam Books, New York.
Woodfield, A. (1976): *Teleology.* Cambridge University Press, Cambridge.
Wright, Larry (1973): "Functions," *The Philosophical Review* 82, pp. 139–168.
Zimmerman, David (1980): "Meta-Ethics Naturalized," *Canadian Journal of Philosophy* 10, pp. 637–662.
———. (1983): "The Force of Hypothetical Commitment," *Ethics* 93, pp. 467–483.
———. (1984): Review of R. M. Hare, *Moral Thinking: Its Levels, Method and Point. The Philosophical Review* 93.

Notes on the Contributors

DAVID COPP   A member of the faculty at Simon Fraser University since 1974, David Copp is now Associate Professor of Philosophy at the University of Illinois at Chicago. He is an executive editor of *The Canadian Journal of Philosophy*, a co-editor of the anthology *Pornography and Censorship* (1983), and author of articles in ethics, political philosophy, the theory of action, and the history of philosophy. He is writing a book on the theory of moral justification. In 1984 he was president of the British Columbia Civil Liberties Association.

DAVID ZIMMERMAN   David Zimmerman is Associate Professor of philosophy at Simon Fraser University. He is the author of articles in ethics, political philosophy, the philosophy of mind and the philosophy of language. In 1982–83 he held an N.E.H. research fellowship at the Hastings Center. He is currently at work on a book on mental illness and moral responsibility.

KURT E. BAIER   Kurt Baier was born in Vienna, Austria, in 1917. He has held teaching positions at the University of Melbourne, The Australian National University, and is now Distinguished Service Professor of philosophy at the University of Pittsburgh. He was President of the Eastern Division of the APA and is currently Chairman of the National Board of Officers of the APA. He has published widely in philosophy of mind, in moral, legal, and practical philosophy. He is best known for his book, *The Moral Point of View*.

RICHARD BRANDT   Richard Brandt is currently Professor Emeritus of philosophy at the University of Michigan, where he taught from 1964 to 1980. Previously he taught at Swarthmore College for many years, and at Princeton University, Florida State University, the University of Maryland, and the Georgetown University Law Center. He has held Guggenheim and N.E.H. awards, and was John Locke Lecturer at Oxford University during the summer term, 1974. His previous books include *Hopi Ethics: A Theoretical Analysis* (1954), *Ethical Theory* (1959), and *A Theory of the Good and the Right* (1979).

RICHMOND CAMPBELL   Richmond Campbell is Professor of philosophy at Dalhousie University where he has taught since 1968. He is the author of *Self-Love and Self-Respect, A Philosophical Study of Egoism* (1979) and numerous journal articles in the areas of ethics, philosophy of science, epistemology, and philosophy of mind. Currently he is co-editing an anthology: *The Prisoner's Dilemma and Newcomb's Problem.*

NORMAN DANIELS   Norman Daniels is Professor of philosophy and Department Chairman at Tufts University. He has written *Thomas Reid's 'Inquiry' and the Geometry of Visibles* (1974), edited *Reading Rawls* (1975), co-edited *In Search of Equity* (1983), and completed *Just Health Care*, to be published by Cambridge University Press. He has written widely in philosophy of science and moral and political philosophy and is working on a book on moral epistemology.

RONALD DE SOUSA   Ronald de Sousa is Professor of philosophy at the University of Toronto. He is the author of articles on mind, language, psychology, epistemology, and ethics. He is currently working on a book on the rationality of emotions.

DAVID GAUTHIER   David Gauthier, a native of Toronto, and a member of the Department of Philosophy at the University of Toronto from 1958 to 1980, is now Professor of philosophy at the University of Pittsburgh, where he is also Chairman of the Department of Philosophy and a Senior Fellow in the Center for the Philosophy of Science. He was elected a Fellow of the Royal Society of Canada in 1979. He has written or edited three books, including a study of the moral and political thought of Thomas Hobbes, *The Logic of Leviathan.* His principal philosophical interest is in the development of moral theory within the context of the theory of rational choice, as exemplified in the essay in this volume, and in his forthcoming book, *Morals by Agreement.*

GILBERT HARMAN   Gilbert Harman, born on May 26, 1938, in E. Orange, New Jersey, is Professor of philosophy at Princeton University, where he has taught since 1963. His interests include the philosophy of behavioral science, artificial intelligence, cognitive science, linguistics, the theory of knowledge, the philosophy of mind, the philosophy of language, ethics, and aesthetics. He has been Visiting Professor at the University of California in Berkeley, at New York University, at Rockefeller University, and at The John Hopkins University. In 1971 he directed a six week Summer Institute in the Philosophy of Language at the University of California at Irvine and in 1982 he directed a two month NEH Summer Seminar for college teachers on reasoning. He is the author of *Thought* (1973) and *The Nature of Morality* (1977, German translation 1981), editor of *On Noam Chomsky* (1st edition 1974, Spanish translation 1981, 2nd edition 1982), and editor with Donald Davidson of *Semantics of Natural Language* (1970 and later editions) and *The Logic of Grammar* (1975). He has just completed a book discussing how reasoned reflection can lead people to revise their beliefs and plans.

GREGORY S. KAVKA   Gregory S. Kavka is Professor of philosophy at the University of California, Irvine, where he teaches political philosophy and ethics. He is currently writing a book on Hobbesian moral and political philosophy.

JAN NARVESON   Jan Narveson is Professor of philosophy at the University of Waterloo in Ontario, Canada. He has published a book, *Morality and Utility* (Johns Hopkins Press, 1967) and an anthology (*Moral Issues,* Oxford University Press, Toronto and New York, 1983) as well as numerous articles in philosophical journals and collections. His principal special interest outside philosophy is music. He is President of the Kitchener-Waterloo Chamber Music Society, and on the boards of several musical organizations.

KAI NIELSEN   Kai Nielsen, born in 1926, is Professor of philosophy at the University of Calgary. He has taught at Hamilton College, Amherst College, the State University of New York at Binghamton, Rhodes University, the University of Ottawa, the Graduate Center of the City University of New York, Brooklyn College and New York University. In 1981–82 he was Visiting Senior Scholar at the Hastings Center and in 1984 he was President of the Canadian Philosophical Association. He is an editor of *The Canadian Journal of Philosophy.* He has written *Reason and Practice* (1971), *Contemporary Critiques of Religion* (1971), *Ethics Without God* (1973), *Scepticism* (1973), *An Introduction to the Philosophy of Religion* (1982), *Equality and Liberty: A Defense of Radical Egalitarianism* (1984) and *In Defense of Atheism* (1985).

NICHOLAS STURGEON   Nicholas Sturgeon teaches philosophy at Cornell University. He has published articles on the history of ethics and on contemporary ethical theory, especially on issues related to ethical naturalism and ethical realism.